This volume is dedicated to Elisabeth Crowfoot.

TEXTILES IN NORTHERN ARCHAEOLOGY

NESAT III: TEXTILE SYMPOSIUM IN YORK
6 - 9 MAY 1987

NESAT

North European Symposium for Archaeological Textiles
Monograph 3

Edited by Penelope Walton and John-Peter Wild

IAP

ARCHETYPE   PUBLICATIONS

31-34 Gordon Square, London WC1

NESAT was founded in 1981 to promote the study and publication of textiles from archaeological sites in Northern Europe.

Cover design: Mic Claridge

Cover illustrations:
Front cover: detail of 8th-century embroidery techniques: gold couching and silk split stitch on the Maaseik embroideries (see p. 57-60) (photo: Brian Coxall)
Back cover: reverse of work on Maaseik reconstruction, showing economy of technique (photo: Brian Coxall)

Distributed and sold by: NESAT, Department of Archaeology, The University, Manchester M13 9PL
                                     and Textile Research, 12 Bootham Terrace, York YO3 7DH
                                     and Textilmuseum, Parkstrasse 17, D-2350 Neumünster

Printed by Galliard (Printers) Ltd, Great Yarmouth, Norfolk.
Cover printed by Wood Westworth & Co Ltd, St Helens, Merseyside.

Contents

Preface

Elisabeth Crowfoot through her research and publications has been the leading figure in archaeological textile studies in Britain for over thirty years. When NESAT members gathered in York for the third Symposium on archaeological textiles from northern Europe (the first to be held in Britain), it seemed wholly appropriate to dedicate to Elisabeth the volume of papers given at that Symposium. Her pre-eminence in textile studies owes much to her mother, Grace Crowfoot, the first scholar in Britain to demonstrate to archaeologists the value of recording their textile finds. Elisabeth, however, has taken her mother's techniques and applied them to a much greater volume of finds; her work ranges from Iron-Age England to Medieval Nubia, an unsurpassed breadth of experience in archaeological textiles. We dedicate our work to her in admiration and affection.

The third NESAT Symposium was held in the King's Manor, University of York, from 6-9 May 1987. On-the-spot support was given by the York Archaeological Trust and its Director, Peter Addyman, and we are greatly in their debt. Grants towards the cost of the meeting were made by the York Archaeological Trust, the Robert Kiln Charitable Trust, and the Pasold Research Fund; a British Academy subvention enabled an East European colleague to attend once more, and the Jorvik Viking Centre provided mementoes for the delegates. Important contributions to the cost of publishing these papers were made by the York Archaeological Trust, the Robert Kiln Charitable Trust, the Pasold Research Fund, Imperial Chemical Industries (Organics Division), the Dyers' Company and the Pilgrim Trust. The Marc Fitch Fund kindly offered us a guarantee, should there be a shortfall. To all these bodies we give our warmest thanks.

Last but not least we thank the staff of Archetype Publications for their efficient and sympathetic treatment of our manuscripts and artwork.

Participants in the York Symposium

1. Stone-Age textiles in North Europe

Lise Bender Jørgensen

Copenhagen

Until very recently, Stone-Age textiles have been virtually unknown in North Europe, although some dubious pieces kept popping up in the literature. An example which may be mentioned is the so-called cow-horn from Øksenbjerg, bound with flax and supposed to be Neolithic; Elisabeth Munksgaard, in a paper from 1979, showed this to be neither cow-horn, Neolithic nor flax, but instead a very recent piece.[1] Lately, however, some more reliable Stone-Age textiles have been found in Denmark, and they form the basis for this presentation.

In 1984 I received a letter from Søren H. Andersen, senior lecturer at the Department of Archaeology in the University of Århus. The letter contained a drawing of a piece of textile which had been found in the excavations of a submerged settlement of the Ertebølle culture at Tybrind Vig on the west coast of Funen.[2] From that moment a new chapter in the history of textiles was started: here were the first indisputable Stone-Age textiles from Denmark - and more than that: they were not even Neolithic, but Mesolithic. Previously the oldest Danish textiles were from the Early Bronze Age: now with a single leap we have been pushed 3,000 years backwards. The Tybrind Vig textiles are dated to the Dyrholmen II phase of the Ertebølle culture, or to *c.* 4,200 BC (calibrated), and they can boast the title of being the oldest textiles of Europe (fig.1.1).

Before the first textile fragment was found at Tybrind Vig, however, some indications had appeared that suggested what was to come, and under which conditions such finds could be expected. Here it will probably be a great advantage to take a look at a map of Denmark as it appeared around the end of the Mesolithic Period (fig. 1.2). Compared with a map of Denmark today it is clear that the land has changed much; the northern parts have risen, whereas the southern parts have sunk. In North Jutland the coastlines of the Stone Age are to be found inland, but in southern Denmark, particularly the archipelago south of Funen, Stone-Age settlements are often situated several metres below the surface of the sea. Archaeologists therefore have to put on divers' equipment when they want to excavate such sites. This has been done by several people, and a major result of this type of excavation has been the recovery of organic material like wood, bone, horn, basketry and now even textiles.

During the late 1970's the director of Langelands Museum, Jørgen Skaarup, excavated a number of Ertebølle settlements in the sea around the island of Ærø. One of these sites, off the small island of Dejrø, proved to contain large quantities of material, not only of flint tools but also of organic materials, and in 1979 a wooden float with a piece of fishing line still attached to it was recovered - the first trace of textile in an Ertebølle context.

In 1981 the next indication showed up, in the shape of a salmon spear with lashing, found off the north-west point of Ærø, Skjoldnæs. Like the fishing line from Dejrø the lashing was made of vegetable fibres.[3]

The Ertebølle settlement of Tybrind Vig is similarly a submarine site, and excavations have been performed with the help of sport divers. Here, however, the finds have not been restricted to string and

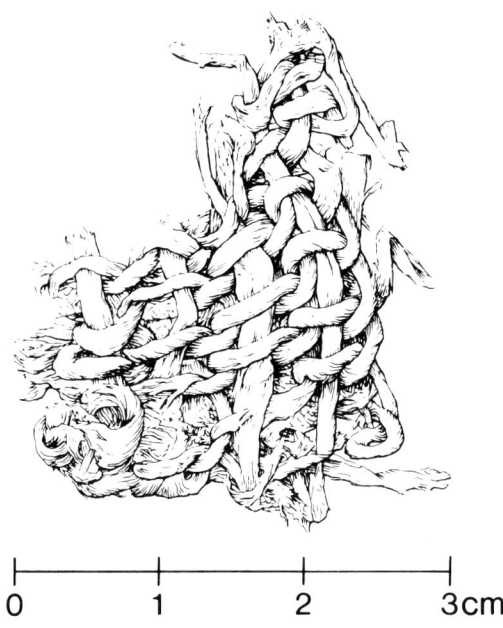

Fig. 1.1 Tybrind Vig, FHM 2033 LGV. Textile fragment of the late Ertebølle culture.

lines, but include pieces of cloth as well. According to the excavator, Søren Andersen, it was the development of a new digging technique, whisking the mud away instead of removing it mechanically, which led to the discovery of the first textiles. The textile remains are extremely fragile, and they easily dissolve completely if they are not handled wih extreme care - but after the discovery of the right method several pieces have been added to the first one, and now about a dozen fragments can be counted. They have proved to be made in a technique related to what has been termed knotless netting, although in a number of different variations and in several qualities.

The first piece has been analysed as couching buttonhole stitch according to Anne Butler's definition.[4] It must be interpreted as having been made with a needle. Other textile fragments from Tybrind Vig are slightly different, ie with an extra turn of the buttonhole stitch, or, as in a large piece of 8 x 5cm, with doubled couching (fig. 1.3,1.4). The quality of the pieces varies between something like coarse knitting and something similar to a shopping bag. The latter samples may very well be interpreted as the remains of carrier nets, whereas the finer pieces may quite well derive from clothing, or decoration on clothing. Apart from these textile fragments, the Tybrind Vig collection contains many examples of string and rope, some spun or plied, others plaited.

The fibres of the Tybrind Vig textiles are of vegetable origin - but although many fibre specialists have been consulted, for a long while it was not possible to identify them more precisely. After 6,000 years on the bottom of the sea the fibres are much decayed, although the specialists of the Pharmaceutical College of Copenhagen suggested that one of the samples might be willow. In June 1987, however, Professor Körber-Grohne of the University of Stuttgart-Hohenheim very kindly examined some of the samples of the Tybrind Vig textiles, and found not only definite examples of willow bast (*Salix*), but also grass (*Gramineae*) and bast of either willow or poplar (*Salix /Populus*).

The textile collection from Tybrind Vig is unique in Europe, and contains the only known true textiles from the Mesolithic Period. Fishing nets, however, have been found in a few finds from the Maglemose Period, or the Early Mesolithic. One such sample is the so-called Antrea net from the Karelian Cape in Finland, and a similar piece has been found at Friesach in the DDR.[5] They clearly belong to a different category of object, but nonetheless they suggest that the Tybrind Vig textiles may have older parallels - it is only a question of finding them. In archaeology, the first examples of a new find-group has often resulted in an avalanche of similar finds, either because the excavators have

Fig. 1.2 Denmark in the Late Mesolithic period. After J. Jensen, 'The Prehistory of Denmark

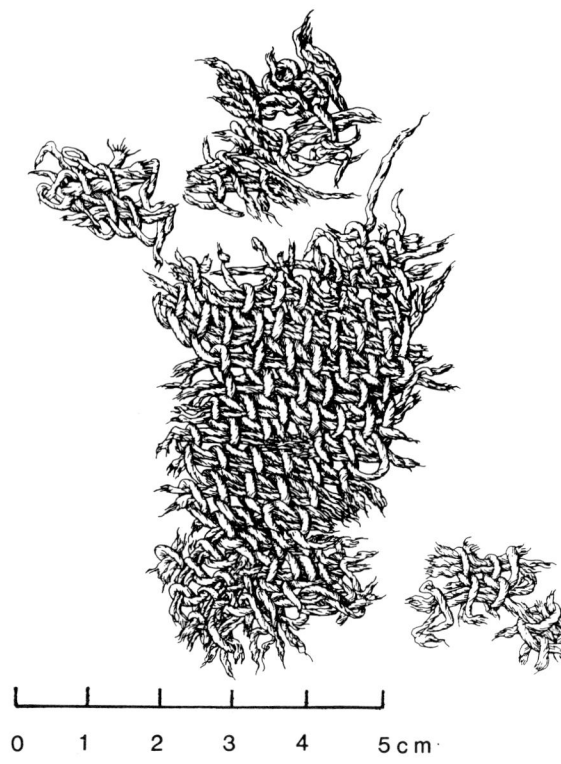

Fig. 1.3 *Tybrind Vig, FHM 2033 ODA. Textile fragments. Drawing, Orla Svedsen*

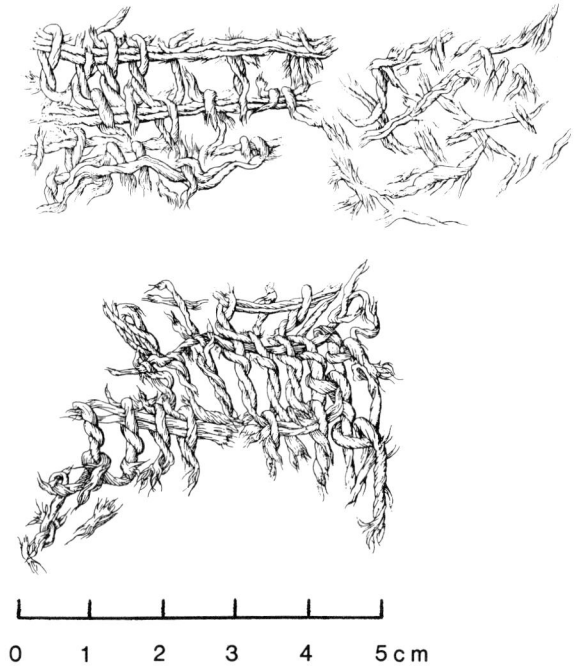

Fig. 1.4 *Tybrind Vig, FHM 2033. Textile fragments. Drawing, Orla Svendsen*

become aware of the possibility, or learned the proper technique; this may very well be true of Stone-Age textiles, too.

In fact the first parallel has already appeared: in 1985 Klaus Ebbesen of the Department of Archaeology at the University of Copenhagen asked me what I thought of some textile remains which had been kept in the stores of the National Museum of Copenhagen since 1946. They were found in connection with two skeletons found during peat digging at Bolkilde on the island of Als. The skeletons were those of two men, and the textiles were discovered directly on the body of one of them; he also had a piece of rope around his neck. As no datable material was found during the excavation, the skeletons had remained unheeded in the Museum of Sønderborg Slot in South Jutland, and the textiles, although briefly mentioned in Margrethe Hald's great book,[6] lay equally unheeded in the textile storeroom of the National Museum.

Klaus Ebbesen thought that the find-depth of the skeletons might indicate a Stone-Age date, and wanted to hear my opinion on the textiles; and as they showed a close resemblance to the pieces from Tybrind Vig my comment was that it was not unlikely. A Carbon-14 dating decided the matter: 3,400 BC (calibrated) or the phase C of the Early Neolithic. Then we had two Danish finds of textile dated around the transition between the Mesolithic and the Neolithic.[7]

The Bolkilde textiles consist of three fragments, each *c*. 8-10cm in diameter. Fig. 1.5 shows one of them after it had come under the care of Else Østergaard at the Textile Conservation Laboratory of the National Museum. Again we have a sample of knotless netting, or fancy buttonhole filling, but without the couching so characteristic of the Tybrind Vig fabrics. The fibres are similarly of vegetable origin; at first it proved impossible to identify them more closely - 5,500 years on the bottom of the

Fig. 1.5 Bolkilde, NM 540/46. Textile fragment. Photograph, N.E. Jehrbo

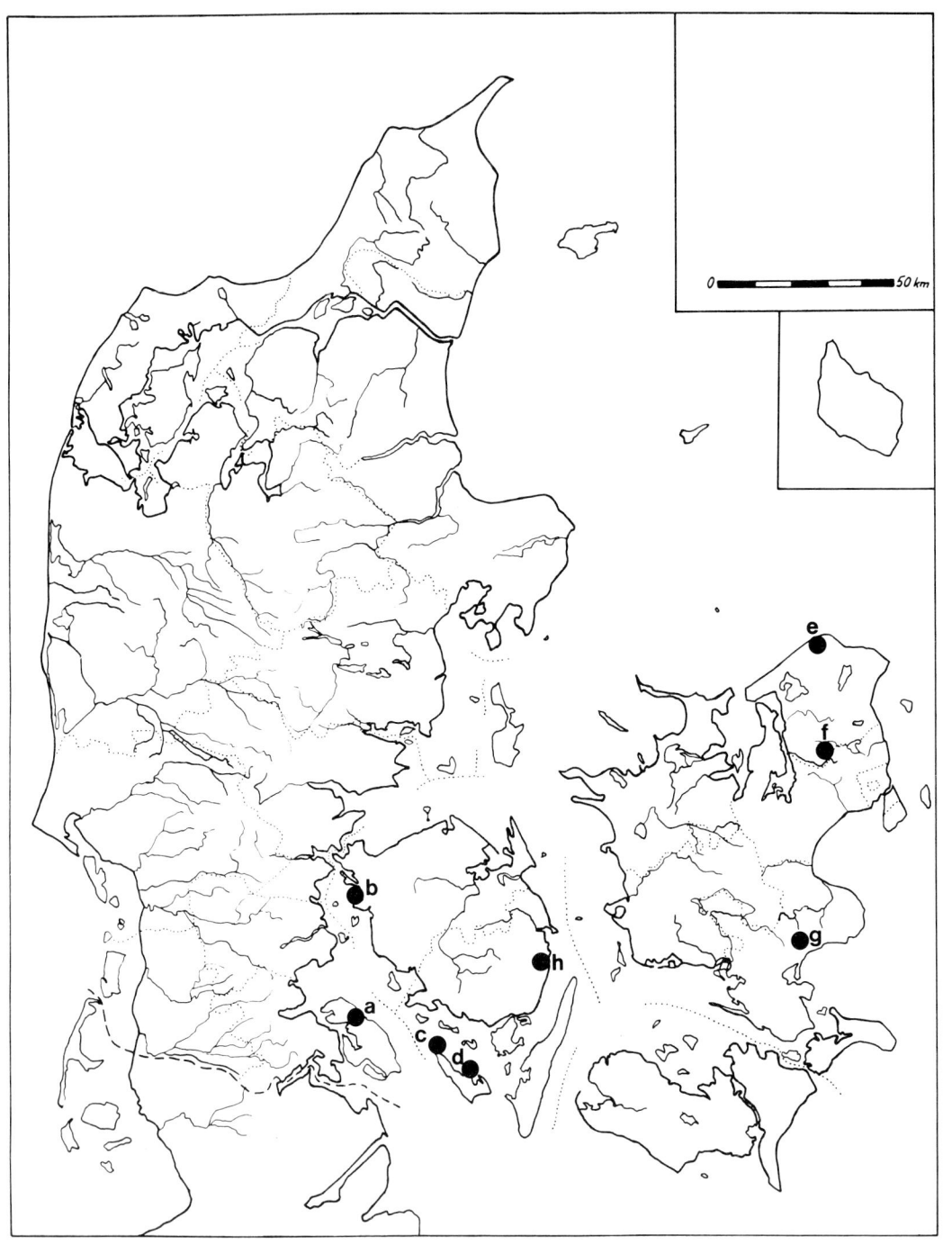

Fig. 1.6 Map of Stone-Age textile finds in Denmark: a) Bolkilde; b) Tybrind Vig; c) Skjoldnaes;
d) Møllegabet, Dejrø; e) Tulstrup Mose; f) Sigersdal Mose; g) Kongsted Lyng; h) Sludegaards Mose

bog, and perhaps particularly 40 years in the stores of the National Museum have made them too decayed - but when Professor Körber-Grohne got a sample under her microscope, she was able to establish that, although badly decayed, it was most probably lime bast (*Tilia*).

The size of the pieces - altogether *c*. 30 x 10cm - and the fact that they were found directly on one of the skeletons suggest that they may be the remains of the man's clothing, or the decoration of it; this is a case where I would dearly have liked to have been present during the excavation to see exactly how the textiles were placed. But then nobody dreamed of the possibility of a Stone-Age date for the find, and we must be content with the available information.

Apart from Tybrind Vig and Bolkilde another Early Neolithic find from Denmark may be mentioned: Tulstrup Mose on North Zealand.[8] The quality of this piece, however, is so coarse that basketry is a better term than textile; the technique is twined weave, and the fibres have been determined as lime bast. No samples of true weaving have been found in Denmark from this early stage.

The map, fig 1.6, shows Danish finds of textile or cords from the Late Mesolithic or Early Neolithic Period. Tybrind Vig, Bolkilde and Tulstrup Mose have more substantial pieces, whereas cords have been found at the two Ertebølle sites of Derjø and Skjoldnæs off Ærø, and three Early Neolithic sites, Sludegaards Mose on Funen, Kongsted Lyng on South Zealand, and Sigersdal Mose on North Zealand. The Sludegaards Mose cord has been determined as lime bast, so again bast made from trees is indicated; the remaining pieces are only determined as vegetable fibres.[9]

The oldest textile remains that I know of have been found in the Near East, and date to *c*. 7,000-6,000 BC. The find-sites are Çatal Hüyük in Anatolia, Hama in Syria, and the Nahal Hemar Cave in Israel. Here, samples of twined weave and knotless netting made of various bast fibres have been found, as in Denmark; but regular tabby-woven linen cloth was found too: the art of weaving had been invented.[10]

In Central Europe several Neolithic textile finds can be listed, first and foremost from the lake dwellings of Switzerland.[11] Here, twined weave and knotless netting in various bast fibres, such as lime and willow have been found; but the greater part of the material is linen tabby in two-plied yarn, often in fine qualities. Here, too, the art of weaving has been known. The DDR, the German Democratic Republic, has yielded three textile finds, like those of the Swiss lake dwellings belonging to the Trichterbecherkultur or Funnel-necked Beaker Culture. One find derives from Spitzes Hoch near the town of Halle; it is a tabby in two-plied yarn. A similar piece has been found nearby at Kreienkopp. They were once published by Karl Schlabow as wool cloth,[12] but the wool specialist M.L. Ryder examined them later and thought that they were flax.[13] At the moment they are being examined at the laboratories of the National Museum of Copenhagen, but no conclusive result has yet been obtained. A third East German textile find has been made at Gollwitz in Brandenburg; it has been described as *Leinengewebe*, ie probably flax. The quality of these pieces is between 10-20 threads/cm, ie rather fine.[14]

All this suggests that the Neolithic technology of North and Central Europe, that is including the Trichterbecherkultur, was based solely on vegetable fibres of various sorts, both basts like lime and willow, and flax; sheep's wool does not seem to have been employed yet.The sheep was domesticated in the Near East; according to my zoologist counsellors, this is supposed to have happened around 7,500 BC. The first domesticated sheep looked much like its wild ancestors, the Mouflon, and was primarily tamed to serve as a food reserve; it is worth noting that its pelts did not differ much from those of other animals, nothing indicating that this animal could be developed into a first-class supplier of fibres.[15]

Woolly sheep only appeared some millennia after the original domestication, and a small sheep figurine from Sarab in Iran has been interpreted as the first sign of this feature. It is dated *c.* 5,000 BC.[16] The earliest woollen textiles to my knowledge, from the cave of Nahal Mishmar in Israel, date to the Chalcolithic Period.[17]

In Europe no undisputed wool fabrics are known from the Trichterbecherkultur, as outlined above; and this tallies with the fact that sheep bones from the Trichterbecher settlements of Troldebjerg, Bundsø and Lindø in Denmark show that half of the animals were slaughtered before they reached the age of a shearling (18 months), when they can supply their first fleece. This pattern of slaughtering is typical for meat animals whereas sheep kept for wool would have been left to live longer.[18]

Some years ago, Andrew Sherratt introduced the concept of the secondary exploitation of animals, ie for milk, transport and wool. He suggests that sheep were introduced in Europe with the Corded Ware cultures, and mentions a recently found carbonised wool fabric from Switzerland, dated *c.* 2,900 BC.[19] H.-J. Hundt has recently published the textiles from the site in question, and they include only a single fibre of wool.[20]

To this can be added a find from Lützendorf near Weimar in Germany, published by W. von Stokar in 1938. It is described as a grave of the Corded Ware culture with a corded skirt made from a mixture of bast, flax and wool.[21] Regrettably, it has been lost during the war, and it is no longer possible to examine it and check the determination of v. Stokar. A third find, similarly published by v. Stokar, can however, not be disputed, either as regards the date or the fibre. It is a flint dagger of Lomborg's type I, found in 1935 at Wiepenkathen near Stade at the mouth of the Elbe, complete with a wooden handle and a leather sheath. Between the wooden handle and the flint some threads are to be seen, and they are without any doubt wool, of a type very similar to that of the Bronze-Age textiles of Denmark. Von Stokar described the piece as a tabby with wool yarn in one system, whereas the second system was almost vanished vegetable fibres. The latter are no longer visible, but five or six threads are still sticking out from under the wooden handle of the dagger.[22] This piece marks the first known example of wool in North Europe, and also the first woven fabric, dated to the beginning of the Late Neolithic Period, or about 2,400 BC.

The first Danish loomweights similarly show up in the Late Neolithic Period,[23] and indicate that the art of weaving only reached the North at this late stage, although it was known in Central Europe much earlier, during the Trichterbecherkultur. Whether the wool sheep and the loom reached Denmark at the same time is another question, but it is certainly a possibility; and here it is worth noting that the wool yarn from Wiepenkathen is S-spun, opposite to the Z-spun bast yarns from the Late Mesolithic and Early Neolithic, but similar to most Bronze-Age yarns. This detail may very well mark the appearance of a new technology, not only as regards raw material, but also tools for spinning and weaving.

The collection of North European textiles from the Stone Age is still very small, and the interpretations put forward here naturally must be seen with this in mind. Nonetheless a Late Mesolithic/Early Neolithic textile technology can be outlined, based on bast fibres and variations of knotless netting; its products may have served as carrier nets, lashings etc, but very well also as clothing. Furthermore the finds suggest that the wool sheep, and the art of weaving, first reached the North towards the end of the Stone Age, with the Corded Ware culture, or during the Late Neolithic, and that the new technology was the beginning of the wool fabrics known from the Danish Bronze Age. Here, the weaving is often quite clumsily done, whereas embroideries and other needlework are of a high standard. This latter feature most likely reflects a long tradition - an example is the embroideries on the 'jumper' of the Skrydstrup woman,[24] with direct parallels in the textile remains from Tybrind Vig and Bolkilde.

Acknowledgements

This paper is part of a research project on European textiles in prehistory, funded since 1985 by the Carlsberg Foundation. The Danish Research Council for the Humanities financed a trip to Germany to study the textiles from Kreienkopp, Spitzes Hoch and Wiepenkathen, and my participation in the NESAT meeting in York: I owe thanks to both these institutions for their support. Thanks are also due to Søren H. Andersen of the University of Århus, who entrusted me with the investigation of the Tybrind Vig textile remains, and Klaus Ebbesen of the University of Copenhagen, who invited me to join the team of researchers publishing the Bolkilde find.

Several specialists have helped with various aspects of the Stone-Age textiles: Tove Hatting of the Zoological Museum of Copenhagen helped me find my way in the subject of early sheep, Bente Lorentzen and Anne Marie Rørdam of the Pharmaceutical College of Copenhagen, Birgitte Krag Thomsen and David Robinson of the National Museum of Denmark have all examined the fibres of the Stone-Age textile remains, and after the NESAT symposium in York Professor Udelgard Körber-Grohne, Universität Stuttgart-Hohenheim, very kindly also looked at fibre samples from the Danish Stone Age and succeeded in identifying several pieces. Finally Heidemarie Farke of the Museum für Ur- und Frühgeschichte Thüringens in Weimar, DDR, chased up information on the lost find from Lützendorf. I am greatly indebted to them all for their generous help.

References

1. E. Munksgaard, 'Det såkaldte kohorn fra Øksenbjerg, omspundet med hør', *Aarbøger for Nordisk Oldkyndighed og Historie* 1979, 5-10

2. S.H. Andersen, 'Tybrind Vig. A preliminary report on a submerged Ertebølle settlement on the west coast of Fyn', *Journal of Danish Archaeology* 4, 1985, 52-69; S.H. Andersen, L. Bender Jørgensen, 'Gamle klude', *Skalk* 1985:1, 8-10; S.H. Andersen, L. Bender Jørgensen, 'Ältester europäischer Textilfund in Dänemark', *Deutsches Textilforum* 1986: 2

3. J. Skaarup, 'Submarine stenalderbopladser i det Sydfynske Øhav', *Antikvariske Studier* 6, 1983, 137-161

4. A. Butler, *The Batsford Encyclopedia of Embroidery Stitches*, London, 1979

5. S. Pälsi, 'Ein steinzeitlicher Moorfund', *Finska Fornminneföreningens Tidsskrift* 28/2, 1920, 1-19; B. Gramsch, 'Ausgrabungen auf dem mesolithischen Moorfundplatz bei Friesack, Bezirk Potsdam', *Veröffentlichungen des Museum für Ur- und Frühgeschichte Potsdam* 21, 1987, 89, Taf.25

6. M. Hald, *Olddanske Tekstiler, Nordiske Fortidsminder* 5, 1950, 66

7. P. Bennike, K. Ebbesen, L. Bender Jørgensen, 'Early Neolithic skeletons from Bolkilde bog, Denmark', *Antiquity* 60, 1986, 199-209; P. Bennike, K. Ebbesen. L. Bender Jørgensen, 'Menneskefundet i Bolkilde', *Nordslesvigske Museer* 13, 1986, 86-115

8. C.J. Becker, 'Mosefundne Lerkar fra yngre Stenalder', *Aarbøger for Nordisk Oldkyndighed og Historie* 1947, 10ff

9. E. Albrectsen, 'Et offerfund fra Sludegaards Mose', *Fynske Minder* 1954, 4-14; Becker (1947), 42; P. Bennike, K. Ebbesen, 'The bog find from Sigersdal. Human sacrifice in the early Neolithic', *Journal of Danish Archaeology* 5, 1986, 85-115; L. Bender Jørgensen in Bennike, Ebbesen (1986), 105-106

10. H. Burnham, 'Çatal Hüyük - the textiles and twined fabrics', *Anatolian Studies* 15, 1965, 169-174; T. Schick, 'Perishable remains from the Nahal Hemar Cave', *Mitekufat Haeven: Journal of the Israel Prehistoric Society*, New Series 19, 1986, 95-97

11. E. Vogt, *Geflechte und Gewebe der Steinzeit*, Basel, 1937; E. Rouff, 'Stein- und bronzezeitliche Textilfunde aus dem Kanton Zürich', *Helvetica Archaeologica* 12, 1981, 252-264

12. K. Schlabow, 'Beiträge zur Erforschung der jungsteinzeitlichen und bronzezeitlichen Gewebetechnik Mitteldeutschlands', *Jahresschrift für mitteldeutsche Vorgeschichte* 43, 1959, 101-120

13. A. Sherratt, 'The secondary exploitation of animals in the Old World', *World Archaeology* 15/1, 1983 90-104

14. E. Kirsch, 'Ein Neufund von "Rheinower Krügen" bei Gollwitz, Kr. Brandenburg', *Ausgrabungen und Funde* 23, 1978, 61-64

15. F.E. Zeuner, *A History of Domesticated Animals*, London, 1963, 170ff; J. Clutton-Brock, *Domesticated Animals from Early Times*, London 1981, 56

16. M. L. Ryder, 'The evolution of the fleece', *Scientific American* 256/1, 1987, 104

17. P. Bar-Adon, *The Cave of the Treasure. The Finds from the Caves in Nahal Mishmar, Judean Desert Studies*, Jerusalem, 1980

18. C.F.W. Higham, 'The economic basis of Danish Funnel-Necked Beaker (TRB) Culture', *Acta Archaeologica* 40, 1969, 206

19. Sherratt (1983)

20. H.-J. Hundt, 'Tissus et sparteries néolithiques' in P. Pétrequin (ed), *Les Sites Littoraux Néolithiques de Claivaux-Les-Lacs (Jura), 1: Problématique Générale. L'Exemple de la Station III*, Paris, 1986

21. W. von Stokar, *Spinnen und Weben bei den Germanen, Mannus-Bücherei* 59, Leipzig, 1938, 38ff

22. von Stokar (1938), 103

23. K. Davidsen, 'Bronze-Age houses at Jegstrup, near Skive, Central Jutland,' *Journal of Danish Archaeology* 1, 1982, 72; F.O. Nielsen, P.O. Nielsen, 'Middle and Late Neolithic houses at Limensgaard, Bornholm,' *Journal of Danish Archaeology* 4, 1985, 111

24. H.C. Broholm, M. Hald, *Costumes of the Bronze Age in Denmark*, Copenhagen, 1940, 91ff. The 'jumper 'is called a jacket here.

2. Textiles, fishing nets, wickerwork and rope from the Neolithic sites of Hornstaad and Wangen on Lake Constance (Bodensee): botanical investigations

Udelgard Körber-Grohne

Stuttgart

The sites of Hornstaad and Wangen are situated on the western shore of Lake Constance (Bodensee). Archaeological excavations have been carried out there every year since 1981 by the Institute of Archaeology, University of Freiburg. The sites belong to the earliest part of the late Neolithic Age, the Hornstaader and Pfyner cultures, between 4000 and 3500 BC (dendrochronological dates).

A large number of textile fragments have been unearthed, together with fishing nets, wickerwork and rope, some of which was charred, some uncharred. All these fabrics were first given to the laboratory of the Museum of Stuttgart for cleaning and documentation. Analyses of the types of structure were made by Mrs Feldtkeller, who is working at the Museum. Each year, Mrs Feldtkeller, the archaeologist and excavator of the Neolithic settlements, Dr H. Schlichtherle, and I select a number of representative samples from each kind of fabric for botanical identification of the raw material. For final publication it is planned that Mrs Feldtkeller will report on the manner of construction and I will try to determine the raw material on the basis of microscopic analysis. Some of these samples are described here.

Textiles and fishing nets

Both textiles and nets are made from two-plied yarn, the thinnest single thread being 0.5-0.6mm in diameter in its charred state (fig. 2.1). As it was not possible to determine the plant species from the fibres in their charred state, I treated some of the yarn with ammonium hydroxide (NH_4OH) to which I added one drop of hydrogen peroxide (H_2O_2). This results in the formation of a lot of very small bubbles of oxygen (O_2). These bubbles isolate those fibres which are not bound together in natural fibre bundles, and the oxygen also releases those fibres which have not been fully charred (fig. 2.2, right). After this treatment all the characteristics of flax (*Linum usitatissimum* L.) can be seen: 'nodes' (*Knoten*), transverse lines (*Verschiebungen*) and a narrow lumen. The diameter (6-12μm) remains nearly the same along a length of more than one millimetre. On this basis it has been shown that all the woven textiles and all the excavated fishing nets are made from flax. In addition to the fabrics themselves bundles of flax stems have been found, and also small heaps of highly fragmented stems (scutching debris,`shives', *Scheben*). By taking cross-sections and small pieces of the epidermis it could be stated from microscopy that the scutching debris of plant stems is also from flax (fig. 2.3).

Other possible sources of fibre to be taken into consideration are hemp (*Cannabis sativa* L.) and nettle (*Urtica dioica* L.). Hemp, however, was introduced into Central Europe, from the Scythians in the southern Soviet Union, no earlier than the Iron Age. Under the microscope, hemp's stomata and fibres look quite different from those of flax, as I have documented in connection with the Celtic burial of Hochdorf near Stuttgart.

For nettle I have studied modern fibres. Nettle has a broader lumen, a variable diameter along relatively short lengths of the fibres, and also the microstructure is different from hemp and flax, as can be shown best in polarized light. In Hornstaad and Wangen no products of nettle could be determined.

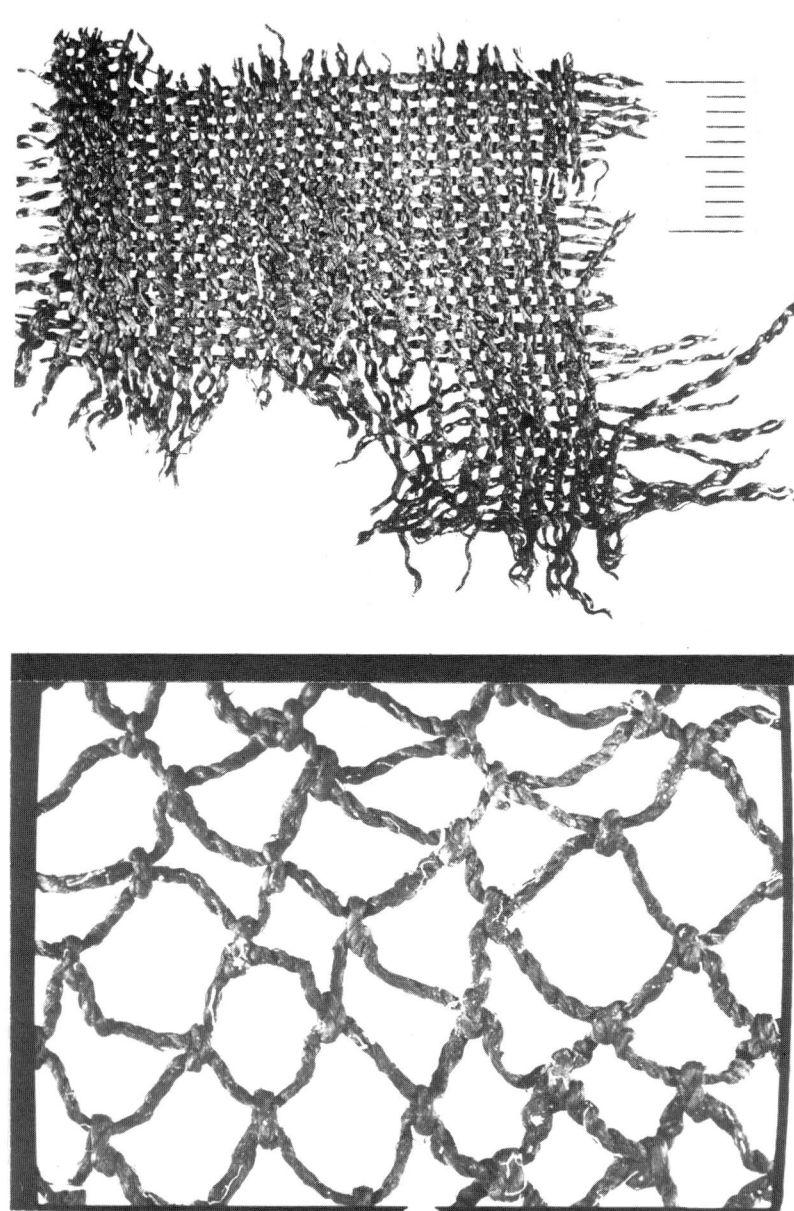

Fig. 2.1 Fabrics of flax, charred. Top: a piece of woven textile from Wangen. Bottom: fishing net from Hornstaad, x 2.5

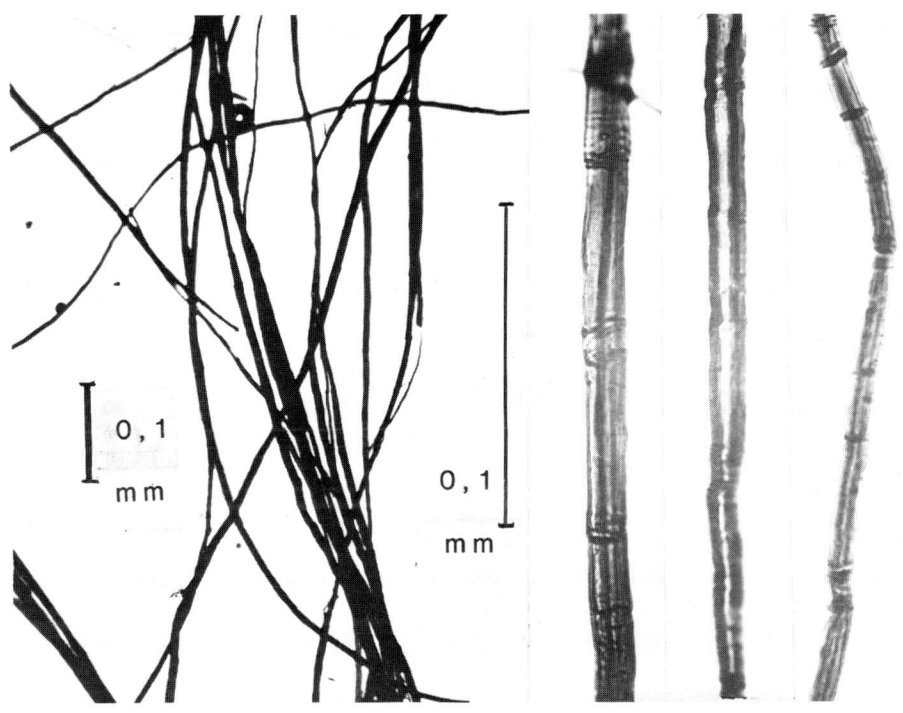

Fig. 2.2 Fibres of flax from the woven textile of fig. 2.1, after treatment with ammonium hydroxide and hydrogen peroxide. Left: the separated fibres. Right: three cleared fibres showing the characteristics of flax fibre.

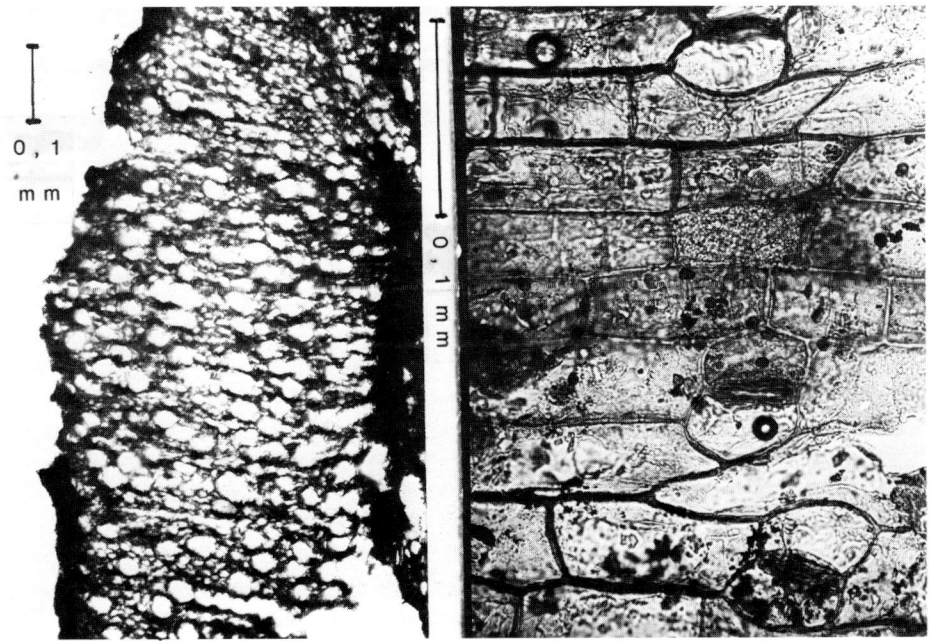

Fig. 2.3 Scutching debris (Scheben)from flax, uncharred, Wangen. Left: transverse section. Right: epidermis cells with stomata from Linum *usitatissimum*

Fig. 2.4 Wickerwork for matting from Hornstaad, made from single stems of lake rush (Schoenoplectus lacustris) *bound together by twisted strips of wood bast*

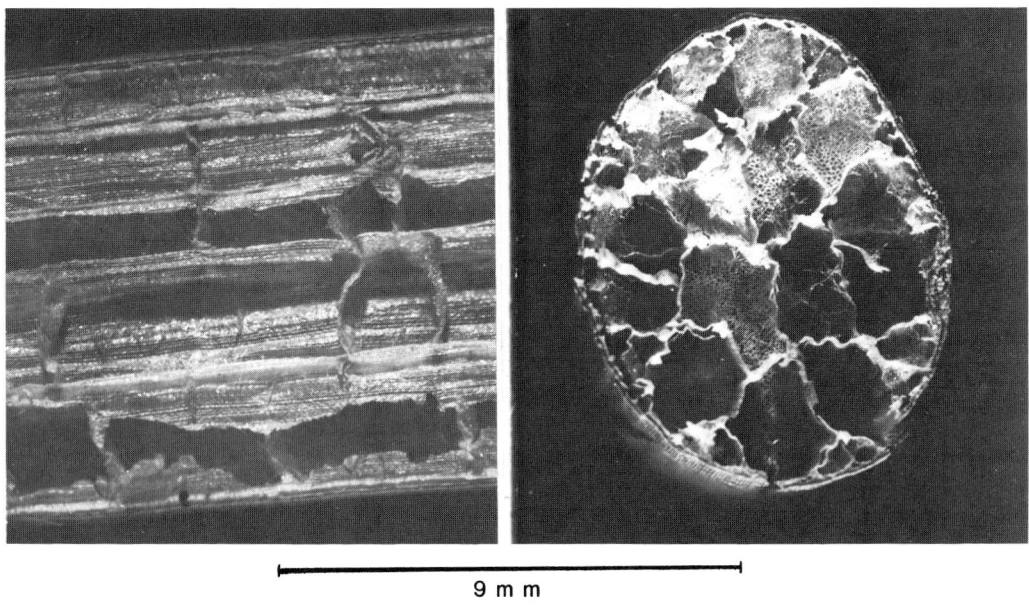

9 m m

Fig. 2.5 Modern, uncharred stems of lake rush (Schoenoplectus lacustris) *for comparison with fig. 2.4. Left: longitudinal section. Right: transverse section: both showing the characteristic ridges*

Fig. 2.6 Wickerwork for basket from Wangen, charred, made from stems of rushes (Juncus *cf.* glaucus), *bound with strips of lime bark*

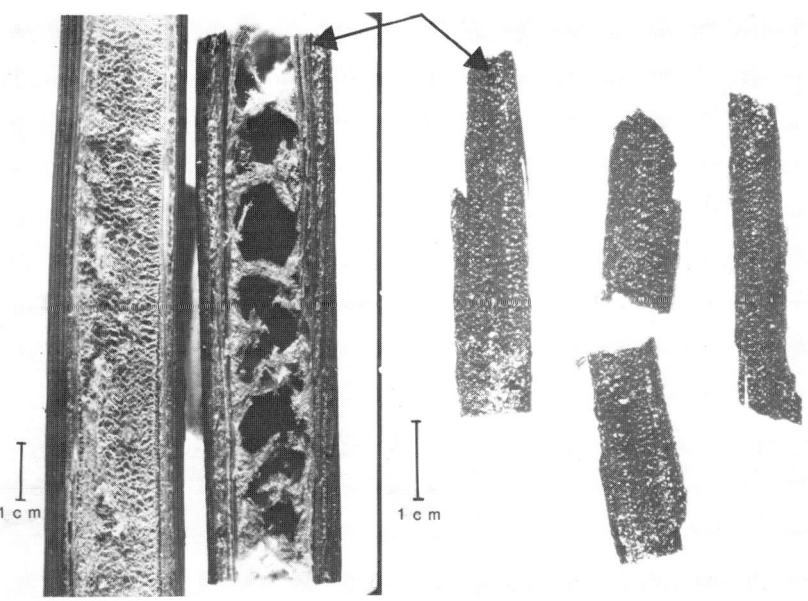

Fig. 2.7 Modern and fossil stems of rushes. Left: one stem of Juncus effusus *(far left) and one stem of* Juncus glaucus, *both in longitudinal section. Right: pieces of charred stems of rushes from the basket (fig. 2.6), but at larger magnification. The black lines show the layer of rectangular cells which correspond in the fossil and modern stems.*

15

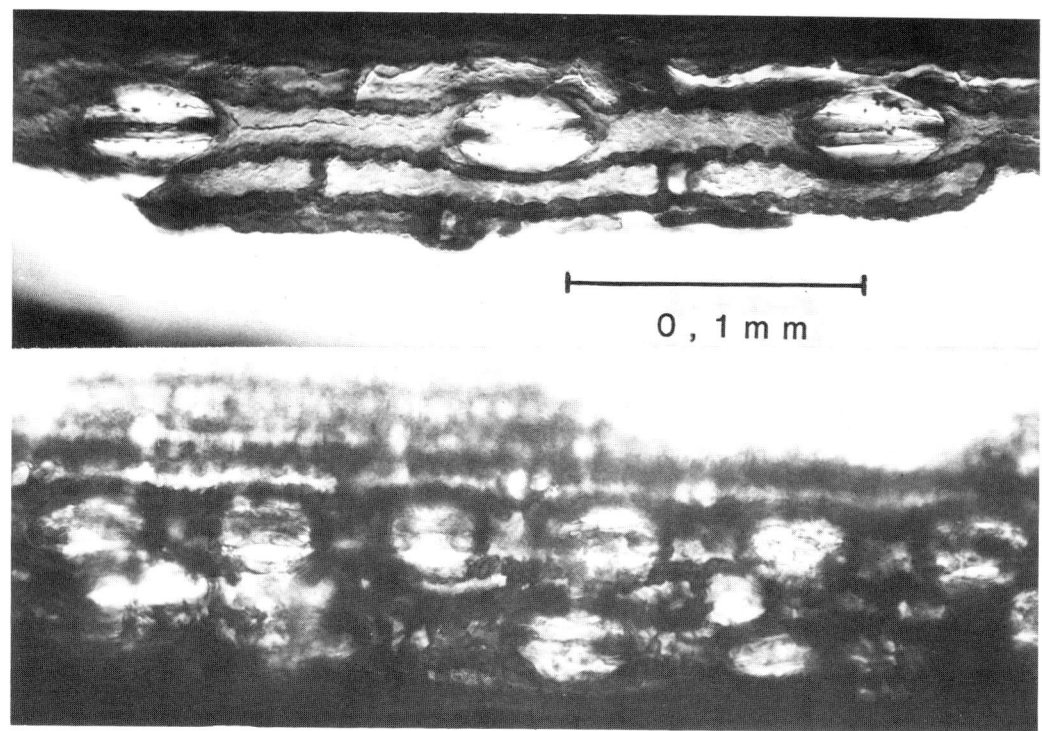

0 , 1 m m

Fig. 2.8 Epidermis cells of thin grass stems from another basket, x 400

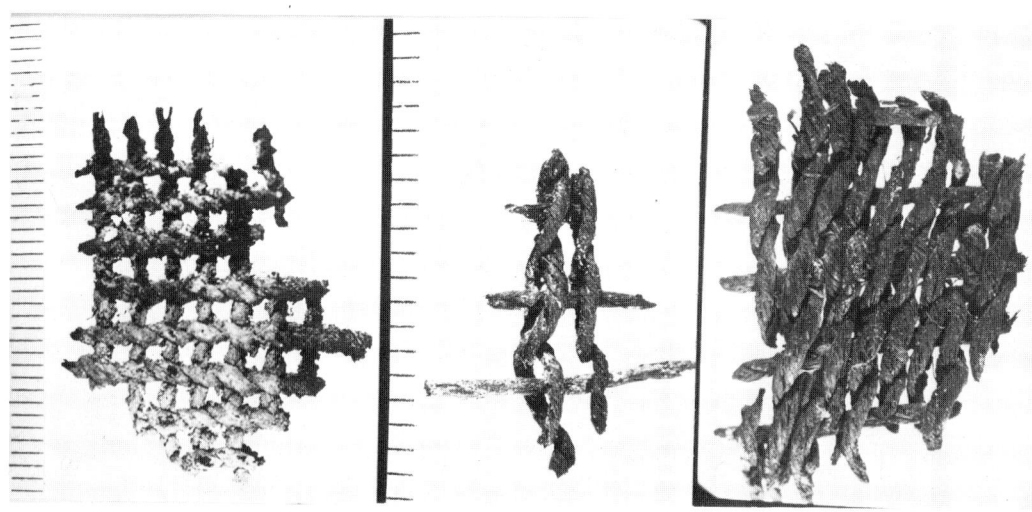

Fig. 2.9 Two kinds of charred wickerwork (twined, Zwirngeflecht). Left: a sieve for cereals. Middle and right: one of the finest pieces of wickerwork which has been found in Hornstaad. Material: wood bast, the one on the right lime

Wickerwork

(a) Wickerwork for matting was present in a charred state. One fragment is made from stems of lake rushes (*Schoenoplectus lacustris*), which grow in lakes. Individual stems have been continuously bound by twisted strips of wood bast. The identification was made by cross-sections and longitudinal sections. Under the stereo-microscope with incident light the same internal structures (or rather the remains of them) as in modern stems could be seen (fig. 2.4 and 2.5).

(b) The wickerwork used for baskets was partly charred, partly uncharred *(Wulstgeflecht für Körbe)*. The foundation bundle *(Wulst)* was made from stems of smaller rushes (*Juncus* cf. *glaucus*), sometimes together with narrow strips of wood bast, and one basket was made from grass stems. They were bound together with strips of bark from young branches mostly of lime (*Tilia* sp.) (fig. 2.6). The species of rush has been determined by the study of two modern species of rush (*Juncus glaucus* and *Juncus effusus* L.), both of which grow in meadows. The white pith has not survived, only the rectangular layer of cells from the stem. This layer is thicker in the case of *Juncus glaucus* (*Blaugrüne Binse*) than in *J. effusus* (*Flatter-Binse*) (fig. 2.7).   Another photomicrograph shows some epidermis cells with stomata from grass stems: these come from one of the baskets which was made entirely from thin grass stems (fig. 2.8).

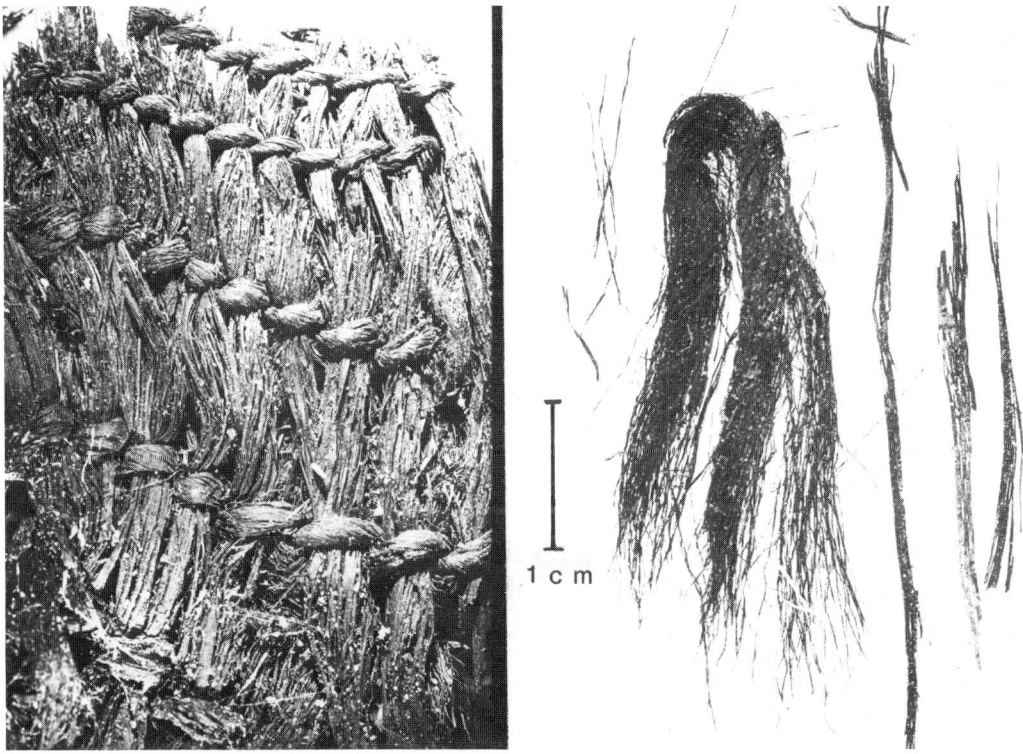

Fig. 2.10 Left: charred wickerwork (Vliesgeflecht) *from the inside. Right: a tuft (Schlinge) from the outer side, which is densely covered with these tufts, like loden. The material is lime* (Tilia) *bast*

17

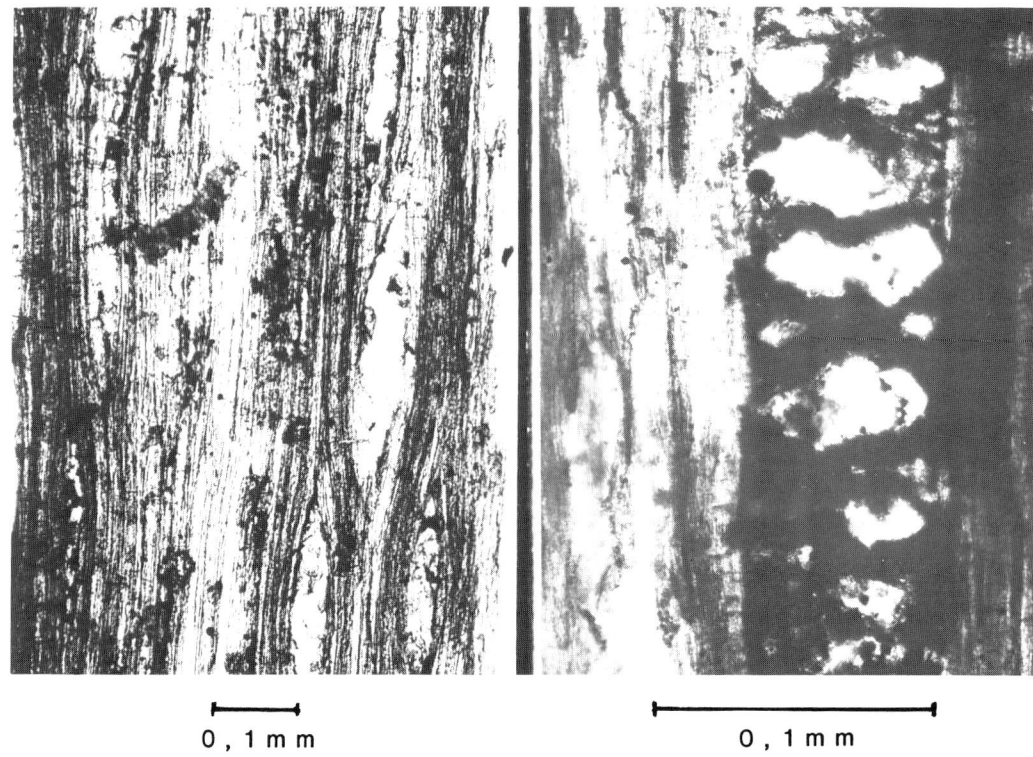

0 , 1 m m   0 , 1 m m

Fig. 2.11 Photomicrograph of lime (Tilia) *bast. Left: the inner (finer) part of the tree bark. Right: the outer (coarser) part of the tree bark.*

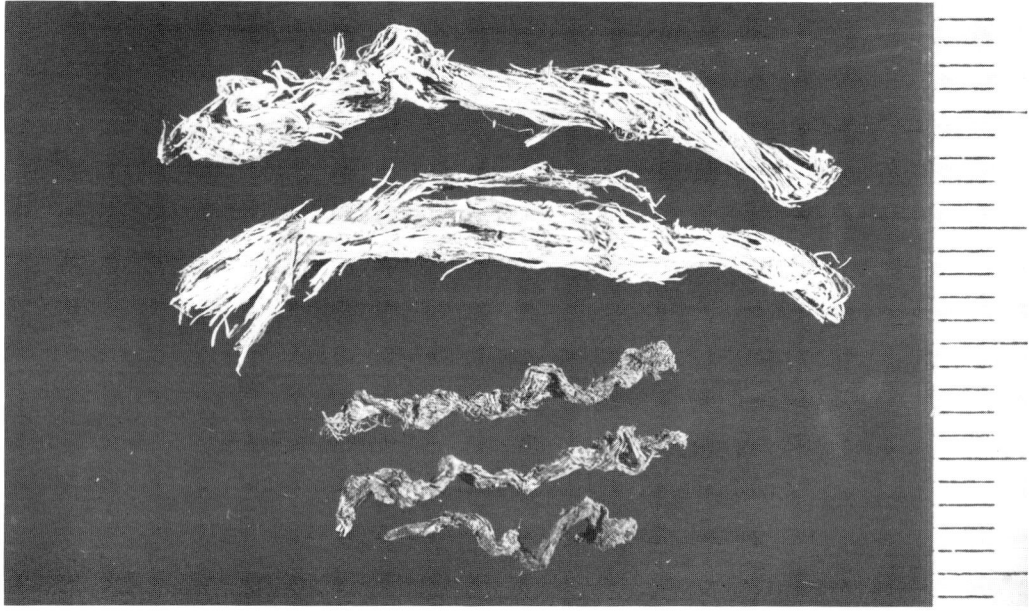

Fig. 2.12 Two species of raw material. Above: two strips of a coarse yellow-white tree bast (oak or elm). Beneath: three strips of a plait from a fine red-brown material from a herbaceous plant, probably a member of the Cyperaceae

18

(c) The wickerwork used for bags, sieves, perhaps clothing etc (in twined weave, *Geflechte in Zwirnbindung*) was partly charred, partly uncharred. Fig. 2.9 shows one part of a sieve for cereals: fig. 2.9, middle and right, one of the thinnest and finest pieces of wickerwork made from wood bast. In those cases where microscopic determination was possible, the raw material was lime bast (*Linde*). Fig. 2.10, left, shows one special kind of wickerwork (*Vliesgeflecht*) from the inside where it is smooth. In fig. 2.10 right, there is one tuft (*Schlinge*) and some narrow strips of lime bast, all in a charred state. The outer side of the *Vliesgeflecht* is densely covered with such tufts so that it looks like loden. Perhaps it was used as clothing for rainy weather. The microscopic identification as lime bast is to be seen from fig. 2.11.

Most of the wickerwork fabrics were made from lime bast. There are also examples of fabrics made from oak and elm. In a few cases two kinds of raw material were used. They look different in colour, as for example in fig. 2.12. Above, there are two strips of wood bast from oak or lime, yellowish white in colour. Below there are three thin strips of a red-brown material which under the microscope proved to be from a herbaceous plant, perhaps from the plant family Cyperaceae (*Sauergräser*).

Rope

A large number of pieces of rope have been excavated in both charred and uncharred states. In general they are twisted from two single threads. The thinnest two-plied ropes are only 2-3mm in diameter, the thickest 13-15mm. Some of the thicker ones, however, are twisted from three single threads. All have been made from wood bast. Where it could be determined it was mostly lime bast. Not all the raw materials of the fabrics could be identified, however. Often the state of preservation was so bad, especially in the uncharred state, that it could only be identified as a herbaceous plant.

In addition to the type of raw material it was also possible to learn something about the Neolithic techniques for preparing these materials. You can read about this in the planned final publication.

Zusammenfassung

Seit 1981 finden alljährlich archäologische Ausgrabungen in den beiden jungneolithischen Pfahlbausiedlungen Hornstaad und Wangen am westlichen Bodensee statt. Die Grabungen erfolgen durch das Institut für Ur- und Frühgeschichte an der Universität Freiburg. Beide Siedlungen gehören dem ältesten Teil des Jungneolithikums an (4000-3500 v. Chr., nach dendrochronologischer Datierung).

Die zahlreichen gewebten Textilien, Fischnetze, Geflechte und Schnüre werden von Frau Feldtkeller im Landesmuseum Stuttgart auf ihre Herstellungsweise bearbeitet. U. Körber-Grohne versucht, die Rohmaterialen zu ermitteln. Es wird hier über einige mikroskopische Bestimmungen berichtet. Die gewebten Textilien und Fischnetze sind alle aus Lein (Flachs *Linum usitatissimum* L.) hergestellt, mit Ausnahme der jeweiligen Schnur vom Netzanfang, die aus Gehölzbast besteht. Von den verschiedenen Geflechten ist eine Matte aus Seebinsen (*Schoenoplectus lacustris*) hergestellt worden. Bei den Wulstgeflechten für Körbe sind die Wülste meistens aus Binsen (*Juncus*) gemacht, manchmal unter Beifügung von schmalen Gehölzbaststreifen. Bei einem Korb haben die Neolithiker für die Wülste dünne Grashalme benutzt. Als Binder dienten Streifen von Gehölzrinde (meistens von Linde, *Tilia*). Zu den Geflechten in Zwirnbindung gehören Fragmente von Getreidesieben, Taschen und anderen Verwendungszwecken, darunter auch Vliesgeflechte. Diese sind auf der Innenseite glatt und auf der Außenseite von ausgefransten Schlingen besetzt. Nahezu alle Geflechte in Zwirnbindung bestehen aus Gehölzbast. Soweit dieser sich bestimmen ließ, war Linde das Hauptmaterial. Vereinzelt ist auch Bast von Eiche (*Quercus*) und Ulme (*Ulmus*) benutzt worden. Für das eine oder andere

Produkt haben die neolithischen Bewohner von Hornstaad und Wangen zwei verschiedene Arten von Rohmaterial verwendet. Das ist schon für das bloße Auge erkennbar an unterschiedlichen Farbnuancen, wie weiß-gelb und rot-braun sowie gröberer und feinerer Struktur. Auch zur Aufbereitung der Rohmaterialien konnten Beobachtungen gemacht werden. Hierüber und über die Gesamtbearbeitung soll in einer späteren Endpublikation berichtet werden.

3. *Nålebinding:* definition and description

Egon H. Hansen
Moesgaard

Under the inspiration of a couple of inquiring conservation technicians I have looked at the problem of the description of *nålebinding* methods.

Although textiles made in *nålebinding* are not very widespread during Antiquity proper, they appear in somewhat larger numbers during the Middle Ages. It is important, therefore, that both definition and descriptions of methods be looked into.

Without having had time for a more intensive examination of the literature at hand, I have been able to establish that in the Scandinavian languages, in German and in English *nålebinding* is described with more than 20 different names for more or less the same process. The only absolutely firm definition we have is in Margrethe Hald's schematic analysis of what she sums up as 'looped needle-netting'. The variations with which she works are characterised by a construction which always has two or more loops ready-formed, through which the needle is passed in a darning technique, in order to form the next loop. This technique is clearly distinguished from all forms of buttonhole stitch, with or without loops: it has no connection with sewing techniques where the thread wraps around the same stitch (or with coiled basketwork, where the thread passes around bunches of bast).

Unfortunately my knowledge of English is not extensive enough for me to judge whether the expression 'looped needle-netting' used by Hald fully covers the definition mentioned above, nor has it been possible to find an expression in German that directly covers it. I suggest therefore that in future research on this kind of textile we use the modern expression *nålebinding,* bearing in mind that Märta Brodén, who was the first to use this word, was also the first to make this almost forgotten technique known among needlework people of today.

Years ago, in *Primitive Scandinavian Textiles,* Odd Nordland proposed a new stitch-description, which was based on the idea that a thread-loop could be regarded as a circle, which meant that you only had to describe the course of the thread in one of the quadrants. This could have a certain validity if all stitch variations were symmetrical, which I am afraid they are not. The system Nordland presented also did not describe the course of the working thread nor the variety of ways of combining the new row of stitches with the preceding. His system was therefore soon rejected, even by people not acquainted with practical research work, or needlework in general.

Our definition of *nålebinding:*
A textile technique where the material is produced in a darning technique, with a needle, and where the thread of the new stitch is passed arbitrarily through at least two unfinished thread-loops of arbitrary size.

This means that the technique can be employed for thick materials by using small loops, as well as for more loose materials. Most of the preserved fragments seem to have had a finger used as a gauge for

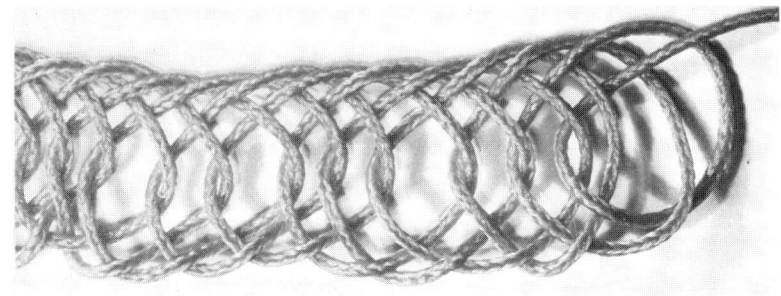

Fig. 3.1 Nålebinding UO O/U UOO

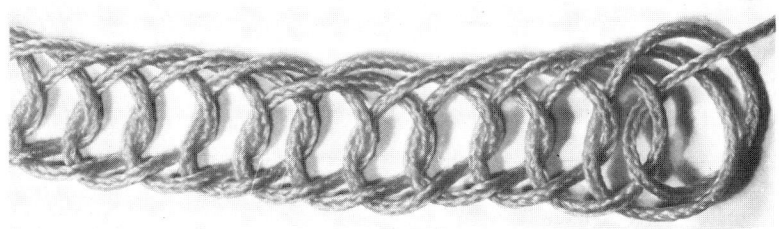

Fig. 3.2 Nålebinding UO/UOO

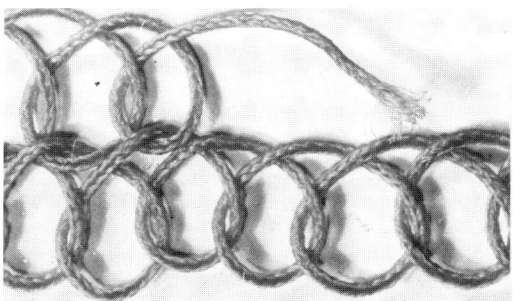

Fig. 3.3 Nålebinding O/UO F1

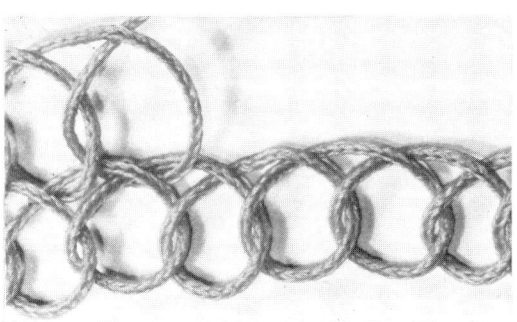

Fig. 3.4 Nålebinding U/OU F1

the size of the loops. The technique is best known from mittens, and appears to have been climate-dependent, as, apart from Northern Europe, it is also widely known in the mountain areas of Central Asia, where it is still just as common as knitting is here.

Stitch description

Fig. 3.1 shows a loose row of stitches with three unfinished loops to the right. This variation would be called Type 3 by Hald. A stitch with this ending could theoretically occur in 2048 variations (although half of these would be mirror versions of the others). The type definition, therefore, must be considered rather meaningless.

Instead we may describe the course of the needle and thread through the loops already made with a U when it crosses under, and with an O when it crosses over, and indicate passage through the innermost loop with a /.

In the stitch in fig. 3.1, the thread that forms the last loop has been passed under the outermost loop and over the preceding, before being passed down through the third loop from the right, which is now complete. It is then passed under the second loop from the right, and over both the outermost loop and the working thread, before being pulled in, so that it forms a new outer loop. In our system the description would look like this:

UO O/U UOO

The passage down through the inner loop is indicated with /. As we always have to pass the needle down through this loop one way or the other, the two letters at either side of the / will be dependent on each other: thus we have halved the number of possible variations. *Nålebinding* with three unfinished loops can therefore only be made in 1024 variations.

Fig. 3.2 shows a more simple row of stitches. The thread is passed under one, over one, completing the second loop from the right by passing under one and over two threads. This variation is called UO/UOO. Note the mistake in the middle of the row.

Figs. 3.3 and 3.4 show *nålebinding* techniques which terminate in only one loop, which means that Hald would call them Type 1. According to our definition they belong to the buttonhole variations, but they are shown here, as they are so closely related to *nålebinding* that the definition can be questionable. The two are not alike, as the thread in the first illustration (3.3) is passed from the top, down through the loop second from the right, while in the next (fig. 3.4) it is passed from the bottom up. If we use our suggested description system, fig. 3.3 will be O/UO and fig. 3.4 U/OU.

In *nålebinding* it is only at the beginning that we work with loose rows of stitches: later we have to combine these rows with the preceding rows to get an unbroken piece of material. The simplest way to do this is, as shown, to pass the thread from the front or back and through one of the border loops of the preceding row, before making the new stitch. This, too, can be done in more ways than one and each variant gives its own character to the structure of the final material.

The technique may also be varied by passing the working thread either from the front or from the back, and through one or more loops, thus making smaller or larger beads between the rows of stitches.

In most cases the description could be made using F= front/top and B= back/bottom, and adding a number for the number of loops that the needle has to be passed through before forming the next loop. There are, however, variations where you have to join up further down in the preceding row, and in these cases, such as with the Aaslev mitten, a more detailed description has to be added. Using our extended system of description, the examples in figs. 3.3 and 3.4 have to be defined as O/UO F1 and U/OU F1. From this we can see that even such simple stitches as these can be varied in many ways.

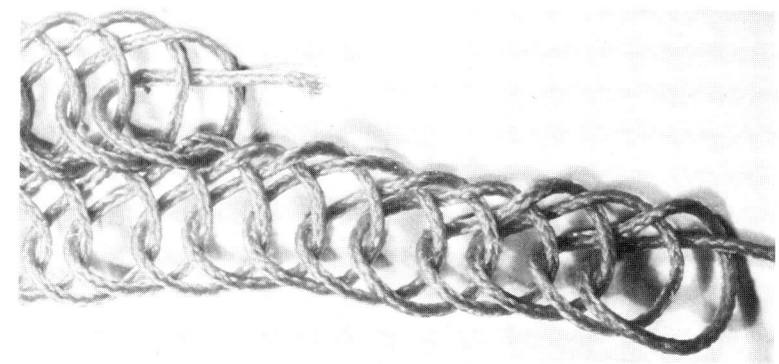

Fig. 3.5   Nålebinding   OO/UUO B1

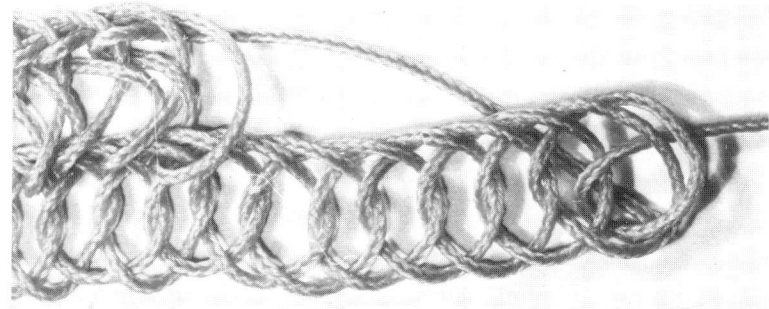

Fig. 3.6   Nålebinding   OU/ OUU F2

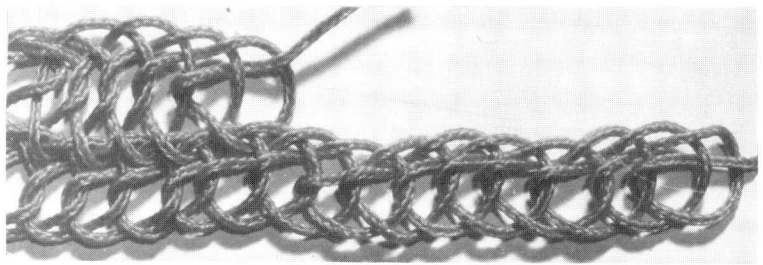

Fig. 3.7   Nålebinding   OU/OUO B2

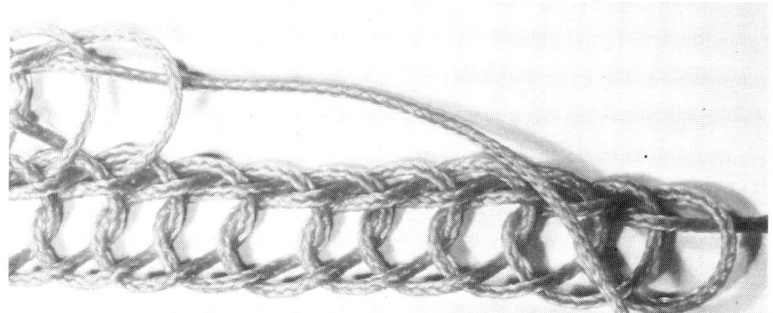

Fig. 3.8   Nålebinding   UO/UOU F2

In fig. 3.5 the working thread is passed over two threads, then passed under the same two and finally over the working thread. It is joined up to the preceding row by passing under the loop from the back. Description: OO/UUO B1.

In fig. 3.6 there is a distinct difference between the loose row of stitches to the right and the same row where it has been affected by the new row. The original even loops have been bent by the needle and the thread, and have been pushed into their final placing. At the same time the work has become tighter. The picture shows how necessary it is to make a sample with several rows before judging a variation, as it can be difficult from an analysis to get an idea of how the original row of stitches looked. Description: OU/OUU F2.

Figs. 3.7 and 3.8 show variations in the preceding stitches. Now the thread has been passed over and not under the working thread at the end of the stitch. A more pronounced feature is that in fig. 3.7 the thread is passed from the back through two loops in the preceding row, and in fig. 3.8 from the front through one. Description: Fig. 3.7: OU/OUO B2. Fig. 3.8: UO/UOU F1.

Fig. 3.9 shows another variation, which can be compared with fig. 3.1, as it also ends with three unfinished loops. The technique here gives a thin tabby-like material, where the fullness depends on the method chosen for joining up to the preceding row. Description: UOU/OUOU, which tells us at once that it is an inter-weaving similar to tabby.

The examples illustrated so far should give a basis for understanding the description system, and make it possible to produce *nålebinding* from the decription and to improve it if needed. For example, Margrethe Hald shows an anlysis of a Finnish mitten in a variation which can be described UUOOUUU/OOOUUOOO. Produced in wool of 9/4 quality and pulled over one finger, it results in a row of stitches approximately 30mm broad, when it has been joined up to the preceding row with F1. The quality is surprisingly thick and soft.

The Aaslev mitten is one of the best known examples of *nålebinding* from the past. It is produced in a relatively thin thread and because of the structure of the stitch has both thickness and softness. A related variation has been used for a milk-strainer from Dalarne.

Fig. 3.10 shows the construction of the last-mentioned stitch, when it has been pulled together firmly. Here the thread has been passed under the outermost loop, after which it has completed the inner loop by passing down through it from top to bottom. The thread is next brought back and passed through the outer loop from top to bottom, before it is passed over the running thread.

A variation is achieved by passing under the outermost loop and completing the next-to-last loop in the usual manner: the loop on the needle is then pulled forward and the stitch is finished by first passing down through the outermost loop and then over the running thread. A description according to the system discussed above would be U O/U O/U O, but as we see, this description is not clear and we can improve on it as follows:

> The first U in the description is only used temporarily and therefore we place it in brackets: (U)
>
> The first O/U in the description covers the finishing of the preceding stitch and can be used as it stands.
>
> The last O/U covers the outer threadloop, where we first passed (U), but as we have decided to indicate the passing through the inner loop with a / we cannot use a (/) here, and therefore we replace it with a (:) = O:U in this case.

Thus we have established the following rule:

A temporary treatment of a loop is indicated by () brackets, and the later pick-up of this loop is indicated by O:U or U:O. The final indication will then be: (U) O/U O:U O.

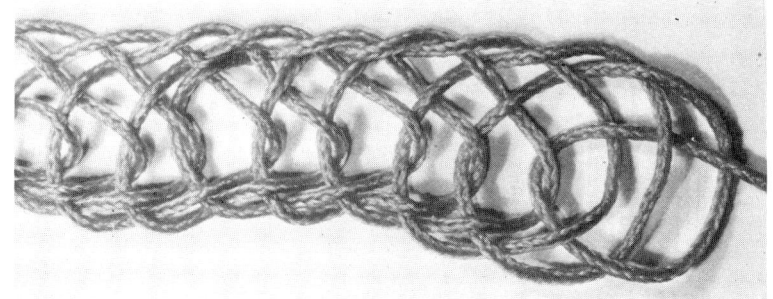

Fig. 3.9 Nålebinding   UOU/OUOU

Fig. 3.10 Nålebinding (U) O/U O:U O

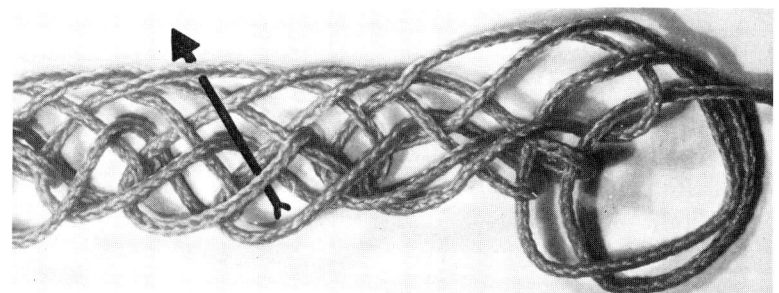

Fig. 3.11 Nålebinding U (U) O/U O:U OO

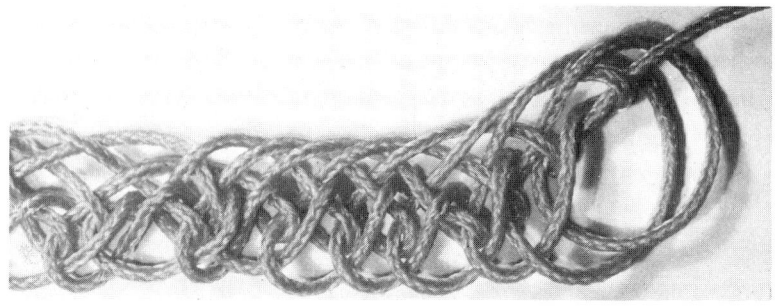

Fig. 3.12 Nålebinding   O (U) O/U O:U OO

26

A similar variation can be made with several loops. Fig. 3.11 shows the construction of the stitches of the Aaslev mitten. Here the description will be: U (U) O/U O:U OO. The arrow points to the pick-up for the next row of stitches and the description for this will be F1+1; as, however, there are more possibilities for picking up, an arrow must always be drawn to indicate where. Because of the pick-up the stitches will overlap each other, thereby making it possible to produce thick materials with a thin thread.

Finally, fig. 3.12 shows a starting row which is a mirror-image of the Aaslev stitch, but which is quicker to produce. The decription of this is: O (U) O/U O:U OO.

It can be very difficult to analyse materials produced in *nålebinding,* particularly as they are so often very felted. This felting may have resulted from use, and is not necessarily made during production. We have also seen mistakes made during the analysis, which suggest it is necessary to sew through the preceding stitch several times before forming a new stitch. These mistakes are mostly seen in analyses that have been made from the wrong side of the work. It must be assumed that most stitches, if not all, are made by sewing through the preceding stitch once before making a new loop, and it can be an advantage to make trial pieces for comparison while working. For this it is best to use a needle, no longer than 7cm, made from wood or bone and with a blunt point. Longer needles are slow to work with and long needles with the eye in the middle are more or less impossible to work with.

It is my hope that these few pages will make it easier to describe the various forms of *nålebinding.* It is also important for us to agree an unequivocal definition of the term. If anyone wishes to take up this work, or suggest alterations to the system, or if anyone wishes to receive information about the easiest *nålebinding* methods, he or she is welcome to write to me. It would be pleasing to see younger people continue this work.

We are sorry to inform readers that, since completing this article, Egon Hansen has died - edd.

4. Weaving systems in South-West Europe: prehistoric to Roman

Carmen Alfaro

Valencia

The main problem I faced some months ago, when Dr Wild kindly invited me to participate in this third NESAT Symposium, was to choose a subject that, being well-known to me, could at the same time be interesting to those working with early textile materials in other areas of Europe. To analyse in some detail a recent Iberian find did not seem to me a very appropriate task for this occasion. Instead, I think it more suitable to make a synthesis of some of the most important weaving systems used during Antiquity in South-West Europe, starting with the basketry and textile finds I have studied. In what follows, I will attempt to summarize the differences as well as the similarities between these two textile systems of North and South-West Europe.

The circumstances that surround the survival of materials as delicate as textiles, baskets, leather etc have been difficult in many cases. Until recently not very much interest has been taken in Spain in finding or preserving these types of object, perhaps because of the great amount of other more beautiful and desirable objects in our museums. Also, the characteristics of a climate with extreme temperatures and drought are a serious drawback to the preservation of organic materials.

For long periods of time the rite of incineration has alternated on many occasions with that of inhumation burial. Graves are the places where textiles have appeared in many cases, almost always little fragments, sometimes half-burned, sometimes stuck to weapons, coins, mirrors, even pottery. We have thus nothing to compare with the well preserved pieces of grave furniture, nor fragments of any importance because of their size. Only basketry is comparable because it is well preserved and there are plenty of examples that have been found in numerous caves, some dating to Prehistoric times, but most to the Roman period in South Spain.

That having been said, it would be convenient to remind oneself that circumstances of preservation may be more favourable to some fibres than to others. The superiority of linen and esparto over wool is a well-known fact, among other things because linen resists fire better than wool. It does not mean that wool was less commonly employed than other fibres; rather the opposite can be deduced after the systematic analysis of written sources[1] and faunal remains.[2]

The clothes illustrated by Iberian statuary, as well as those represented upon ceramic vessels, confirm what may have been a reality: the use of wool in the making of clothes was necessary in the cold highlands and tablelands of the interior. Undoubtedly all these facts could explain the lack of variety in weave types in the Iberian Peninsula. Linen has hardly any variants. It was a necessary element in the making of small and big pieces of household furnishings, and for underwear or even outer clothes for both sexes. Many of these pieces were decorated with borders or 'clavas', usually superimposed, sometimes of wool. I want to say that the virtual non-survival of woollens has surely deprived us of weave-structures as varied as those so well preserved in North Europe or Scandinavia.

Wool, because of its special quality as a fibre and because of the fact that it was employed for outer clothes, requires a very complicated manufacture. The same could be said of silk, of which unfortunately nothing has been preserved in the Peninsula.

Fig. 4.1 Plain weave with folds from Carmon, Sevilla (6 x 3cm)

Fig. 4.2 Tabby and half-basket weave from Puerto Lumbreras, Murcia (4.5 x 2.5cm) (Bronze Age)

The linen textile remains that we know include a great amount of tabby or plain weave 1/1. That requires the employment of a simple warp, as much on the warp-weighted loom as on different horizontal looms. Areas of North and South Europe do not coincide in this point. We found that 88% of 142 Iberian textiles were of the tabby type, whereas Dr Wild found it only to be 60% in the northern Roman Provinces. It is convenient to point out, though, that this apparent technical monotony is alleviated by the great variety of thickness and transparency; there was delicate linen in the Bronze Age (14/16, 16/19, 18/20), Iron Age (16/32, 18/22, 20/24, 22/30) and Roman period (26/30, 26/32), besides coarser linen (Bronze Age 4/7, 6/10; Iron Age 6/12, 8/10; Roman 8/12). There are also pieces with delicate vertical folds (very well preserved due to incomplete combustion) that remind us of Egyptian clothes (fig. 4.1).

Fig. 4.3 Diagram of tabby and half-basket weave from Puerto Lumbreras

Fig. 4.4 Diagram of basket weave from El Albir, Altea, Alicante (4th century BC)

Fig. 4.5 2/2 twill on Iron-Age pottery from Azaila, La Bovida and Castillejo de la Romana in Teruel

Fig. 4.6 Tablet-weaving from El Cigarrelejo, Murcia

Fig. 4.7 Carbonised linen net from Albufereta, Alicante (4th century BC)

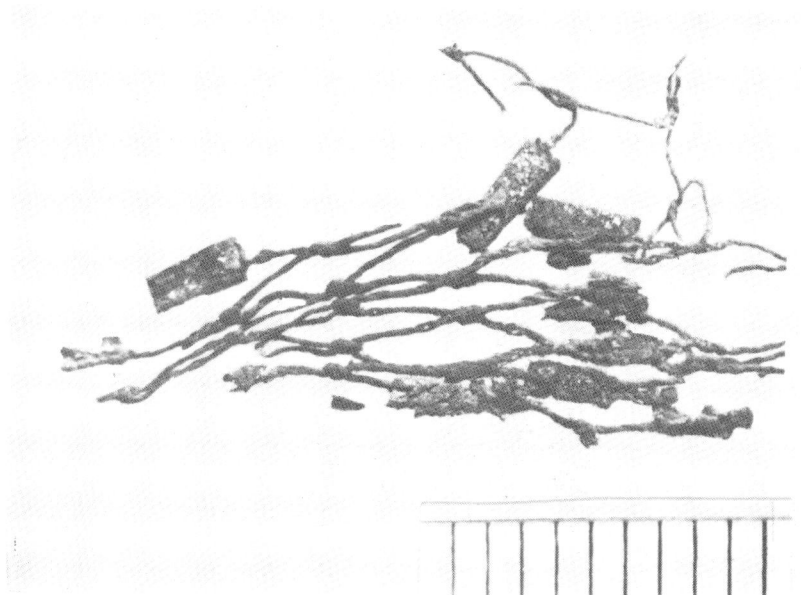

Fig. 4.8 Roman net adorned with gold from Medinasidonia, Cádiz

We found only one fragment of half-basket weave. This fragment is a starting border from the Cerro de la Cruz, a Bronze-Age site in Puerto Lumbreras, Murcia (figs. 4.2, 4.3).

Four fragments of basket weave come from a little moneybag of the 4th century B.C. The bag was found near its owner's skull in an inhumation burial (El Albir, Altea, Alicante) (fig. 4.4).

Twill is represented in its well-balanced variant (2/2 twill) by five small pieces. These pieces were probably part of the clothes worn by an individual buried in the Iberian necropolis of Albufereta (Alicante) in the 4th century BC. More examples of this twill in certain cases appear on pottery found in the Iron-Age oppidum of Azaila, La Bovina and Castillejo de la Romana in Teruel. Perhaps it had a woody fibre structure, because of the thickness of its threads (about 1mm) (fig. 4.5).

The most complex type of weave we have among our textile fragments is tablet-weaving (fig. 4.6). There are only two small fragments from the Iberian necropolis of El Cigarralejo (Mula, Murcia).[3] Four square tablets, partly preserved, were employed to make them. The differing thicknesses ofboth of these fragments shows that they were parts of the different garments of a man and a woman buried with rich household furniture. Was it the practice to incinerate with the deceased the weaving instruments with which the funerary clothes were made?

Other interesting structures, not made on looms but with simple needles, are three linen, half-burned nets (fig. 4.7). Two are from the above-mentioned Iberian site of Albufereta (Alicante), and the third, thinner and richly adorned with gold, was found in Cádiz, in an Iberian-type *larnax,* ballot box (1st century BC). It covered the ashes and was put there to protect them (fig. 4.8).

Basketry offers a much more varied spectrum of weaving systems. Most of them are represented in the material coming from 'La Cueva de los Murciélagos' (Albuñol, Granada). The complex is ancient (*c.* 3450 BC on Carbon-14 evidence) and well known due to having been published and quoted by many authors.[4] But let us start by mentioning the most basic system: two series of threads 1/1 at right angles, as in weaving, for which we have nothing but the imprint of a Bronze-Age mat from Mallorca. Plaited basketry, sewn, is a slight variant of the same. We have good examples of it in baskets, miners' bonnets, mats etc.

Of the so-called simple twined basketry (fig. 4.9), there are many examples belonging to the La Cueva de los Murciélagos collection (fig. 4.10), with its variants in twill (fig. 4.11).

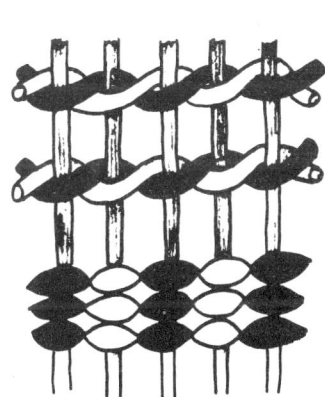

Fig. 4.9 (above) Simple twined basketry from La Cueva de los Murciélagos (c. 3450 BC)

Fig. 4.10 (right) Twined basketry from Albuñol, Granada (height 8.7cm)

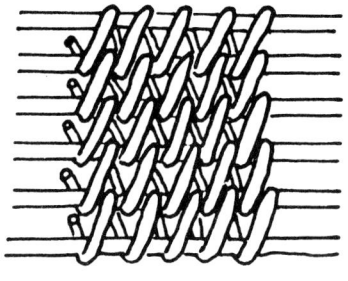

Fig. 4.11 (left) Twill variant of twined
basketry from Albuñol, Granada

Fig. 4.12 (above) Coiled basketry type

Fig. 4.13 Roman coiled basketry from the Cartagena area (height 28cm)

Coiled basketry in its variants of strip-piercing-coil type I and strip-piercing-preceding-stitch or
type II, are often used, too (fig. 4.12). Most of the mineral baskets used by the Romans in the Iberian
Peninsula were made with this system (fig. 4.13). Similar to this is the technique of sprang, with only
five fine examples from El Cigarralejo (fig. 4.14).

One of the most rich and beautiful methods of building basketry is the so-called 'pseudo-braid' (*Zopfbindung*) (fig. 4.15). We have some very interesting examples of it (fig. 4.16).

And to end this short glimpse, there is the reproduction of a piece of braid basketry, a small and badly preserved fragment (fig. 4.17), as well as some specimens of various slipper soles from Albuñol, too.

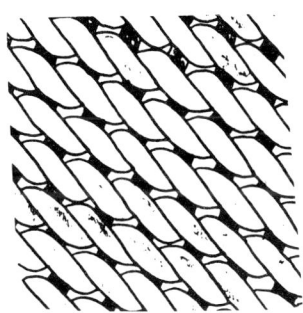

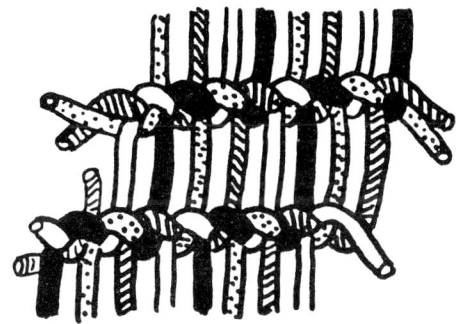

Fig. 4.14 Sprang from El Cigarrelejo   *Fig. 4.15 'Pseudo-braided' basketry*

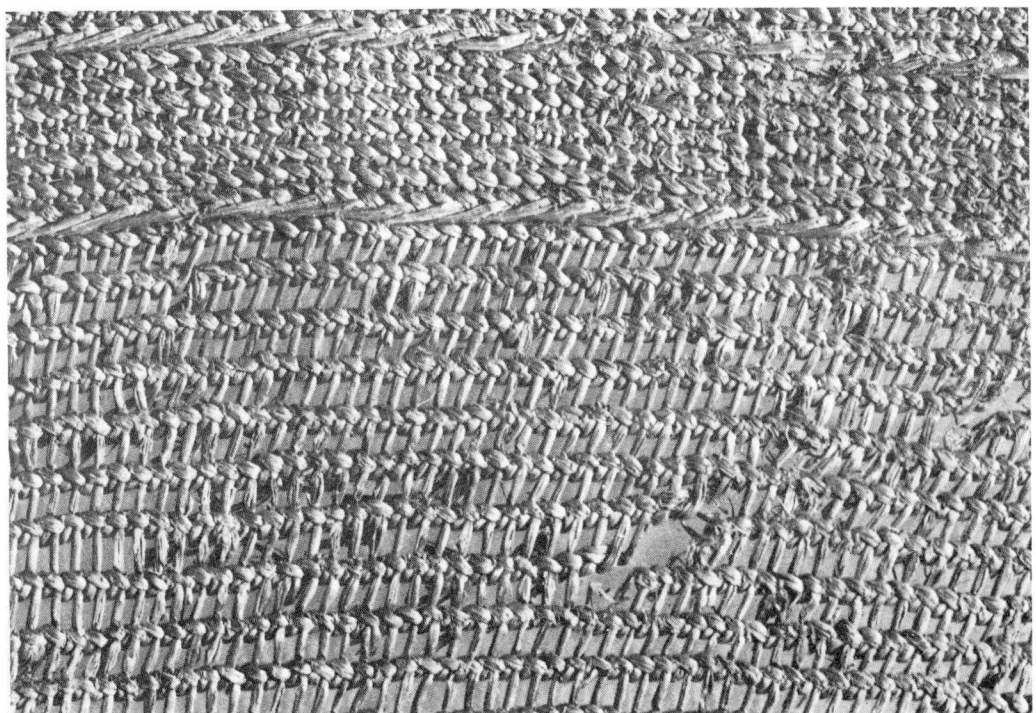

Fig. 4.16 'Pseudo-braided' basketry from Albuñol, Granada (31 x 24cm)

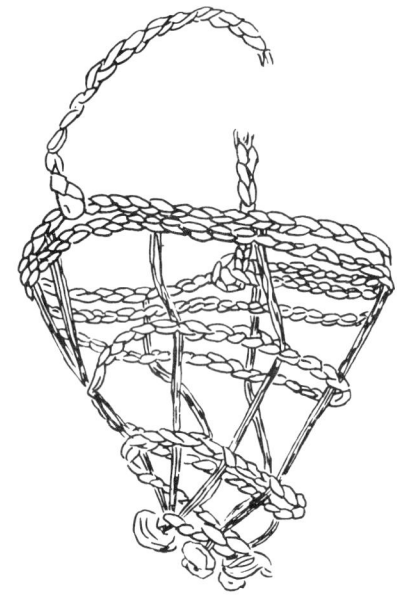

Fig. 4.17 Braid basketry fragment

References

1. The classical authors often speak about the diverse types of wool cloth originating in different areas of the Peninsula (Diodorus V, 33, 2; Martial I, 96, 8; Pliny, *NH* VIII, 191; Nonius Marcellus p. 549) showing us that these products were sometimes used as a tribute of war (Livy XXIX, 3,5; Diodorus XXXIII, 16, 1)

2. The greater abundance of adult sheep bones relative to those of younger animals has led us to believe in the greater use of adult sheep's wool.

3. H.-J. Hundt, 'Die verkohlten Reste von Geweben, Geflechten, Seilen, Schnüren und Holzgeräten aus Grab 200 von El Cigarrelejo', *Madrider Mitteilungen* 9, 1968, 187-205

4. C. Alfaro, 'Estudio de los materiales de cestería procedentes de la Cueva de los Murciélagos (Albuñol, Granada)', *Trabajos de Prehistoria* 37, 1980, 109-162

5. Reds and purples: from the classical world to pre-conquest Britain

George W. Taylor

Harrogate

> The Turks indulge in all combinations of costume. The meanest merchant in the Bazaar looks like a Sultan in an eastern fairy tale. This is mainly to be ascribed to the marvellous brilliancy of their dyes, which is one of the most remarkable circumstances in their social life, and which has been explained to me. A common pair of slippers that you purchase in the street is tinged of a vermilion or a lake so extraordinary, that I can compare their colour to nothing but the warmest beam of a southern sunset.

Thus the young Disraeli in Constantinople in 1830.[1] Reds and purples have always been exotic colours, from the Tyrian purple of the Roman emperors to the scarlet of the Roman Catholic cardinals. Reds and purples based on natural dyes appeal to the analyst working on old textiles not only because of the glamour of these rich colours, but also because of the variety of (reasonably easily distinguishable) colorants that could have been, and are now known actually to have been, used to produce these tints.

This paper is mainly concerned with recent research to determine to what extent reds and purples were used in Britain, from Roman times to the Norman conquest; we start, however, with a review of the situation in the Classical World.

Reds and purples in the classical world

It is well known that the dyes known in classical times were capable of producing strong, bright shades of the primary colours red, blue and yellow (and hence any other colour by the mixing of dyes).

Several reds were available to the old dyers. The most commonly used was madder (*Rubia tinctorum* L). Pliny said that it was grown near Rome, and it was also the basis of the Turkey red process. Madder was also used to produce a much-prized violet, a speciality of the Hellenistic cities of western Turkey.[2] The most prestigious red was kermes (from the insect *Kermococcus vermilio* Planch, not *Kermes ilicis*, a different insect which produces no pigment).[3] The colorant is kermesic acid. The best known insect red today, cochineal, was unknown in the Old World before the 16th century; its colorant is carminic acid. Very like this was the prized Armenian cochineal,[4] from the insect *Porphyrophora hameli* Brandt; the colorant is again carminic acid,[5] and, analytically, it is not as yet possible to distinguish between cochineal and Armenian cochineal; this could pose problems for textile conservators trying to decide between an original Armenian cochineal dyeing and a relatively modern repair dyed with cochineal itself. Yet another insect red is Polish cochineal (from the insect *Porphyrophora polonica* L.), widely found in eastern Europe; the colorant is a mixture of carminic and kermesic acids with the former much predominating.[5] This dye was reported to be found on textiles from classical Palmyra,[6] while Armenian cochineal may have been found on certain Egyptian, Hebrew and Nubian textiles dating from around 2000 years ago;[7] the colorant was carminic acid and no kermesic acid was detected. All these red dyes are mordant dyes, and the question of suitable mordants is considered later.

Coming to purples, purple dyeings could of course be made by mixing red and blue, and this approach was widely used in classical times. For example, such purples occur on textiles from Egypt recently studied.[8] The blue component was always indigotin, probably from woad but perhaps, in an Egyptian context, indigo, too. For the red component, the Romans in Egypt tended to favour madder (apparently following an Egyptian tradition: the same purple was found on 18th dynasty textiles from Tel el-'Amarna (see appendix), whereas kermes was more common in Islamic times.

There were, however, dyes which were purple in their own right. We have mentioned Tyrian purple, from shellfish of the murex type, principally *Phyllonotus (murex) trunculus*.[9] The colorant is a vat dye like indigotin, and indeed it is a close relative, dibromoindigotin.

Much more widely used in classical times was what we now call archil or orchil, a purple dye produced from lichens.[10] It was made by treating the lichens with a dilute form of ammonia and oxygen (stale urine and air respectively). In the Mediterranean area the principal lichen was *Roccella tinctoria* D.C. The detailed structure of the colorant is not completely understood, although known in outline (fig. 5.1).[11]

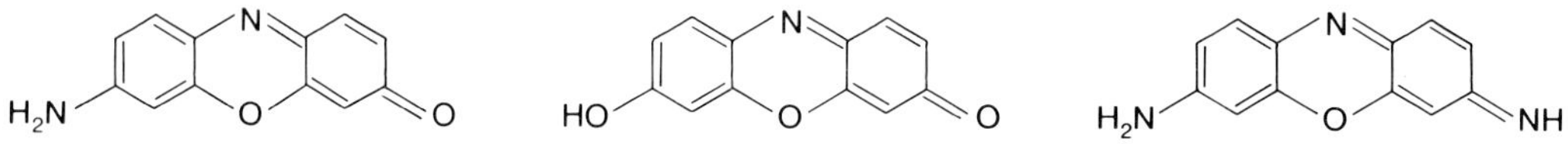

Fig. 5.1 Structures of the colorants in orchil (drawing A. Thomas, York Archaeological Trust)

Reds and purples in Britain

The main red and purple dyes known in classical times were madder, kermes, Polish cochineal, Tyrian purple, lichen purple and indigotin as the blue component of a red/blue mixture. Which of these were available in pre-Norman Britain ? We shall probably never know the complete answer. We *can* say that kermes, Polish cochineal and Tyrian purple were probably *not* known. But by Medieval times madder[12] and woad[13] were cultivated in Britain, and would have been known earlier. Tyrian purple itself is not thought to be an exportable dye (the dyeing was done close to where the living shellfish were taken) and would not have been available in Britain. The same colorant, however, is produced by a common local shellfish, *Purpura lapillus* L. Work in York has shown that, apart from the usual main purple colorant, dibromoindigotin, there is also a red component which is probably not an indirubin derivative. Certainly the glory of shellfish purple was known in Britain at an early date: for example, Bede[14] refers in glowing terms to such a purple, particularly in Ireland. There is indeed evidence for shellfish purple dyeing activities around the Irish coast in Bede's time, probably earlier and certainly later, using *Purpura lapillus*. Henry[15] describes a coastal site in County Mayo, probably 7th-century, which she concludes was a dye-manufacturing site. She mentions other extensive shellfish middens, particularly in Donegal, which might also be the sites of dye 'works'. In a footnote (p.174), she states: "Professor Gerard Murphy tells me that the Irish word for purple, *corcar*, derived from the Latin *purpura*, can only be a borrowing anterior to the 5th century; this seems to point to an introduction of the process of fabrication [of purple dye] in Ireland before the collapse of the Roman empire". Henry goes on to suggest that the dye production seemed to be on too small a scale for use in dyeing yarn for textiles and suggests rather that the dye was used in staining the 'purple pages' in early illuminated Irish manuscripts - although the chemical evidence for the latter statement seems to be lacking.[16]

There is some evidence for this purple being used in textile dyeing in Ireland at a later date, a lead which was followed up in the late 17th century in England; this story is entertainingly told by Bancroft.[17] Indeed, purple dyeings have been produced from *Purpura lapillus* by Mrs Grierson[18] in our own time, although the tediousness of the process is graphically described by her (in a letter to the author) as follows: "... I do wonder how many friends you have who would sit on a Scottish beach in mid March in a force 9 sleet storm splatting whelks for you ? Indeed I wonder that the monks were ever so inclined...they probably gave it out as a penance...'and in atonement for thy sins of today my son thou shalt goeth to the beach and splat 200 whelks.'" Clearly the production of shellfish purple must have been expensive and consequently rare. It is, perhaps, not surprising that shellfish purple has not (yet) been found on any old British (or Irish) textile sample.

We have seen that in the classical world, a good purple dye was produced from lichens. Very similar purples can be produced from lichens native to Britain[19] and the preparation and properties of a number of these purples have been recently described.[20] This is part of the Scottish and Scandinavian tradition of the preparation and use of lichen dyes, and leads us directly to the question of whether dyes from local plants could give similar results to those of the (as it were) 'commercial' dyes of the Mediterranean world.

Taking red dyes first, the bedstraws and in particular lady's bedstraw (*Galium verum* L.) are sources of a red mordant dye chemically very similar to (though distinguishable from) the colorant in madder. Now, although madder was cultivated in England in Medieval times, the plant is not native to Britain and does not grow in the wild (although its cousin, wild madder, *Rubia peregrina* L. still has a foothold in South-West England and Ireland; its colorant is distinguishable from that of madder itself, however). Hence, it is possible that bedstraw was used as a local source of red dye.

There are other possibilties too, for example, mushrooms, for which there is some tradition of use in Scandinavia.[21] For example, the colorant in the genus *Boletus* is boletol, which is a close chemical relative of both kermesic acid (in kermes) and purpurin (a colorant in madder), as is dermorubin, the pigment in several mushrooms of the genus *Cortinarius*.[22]

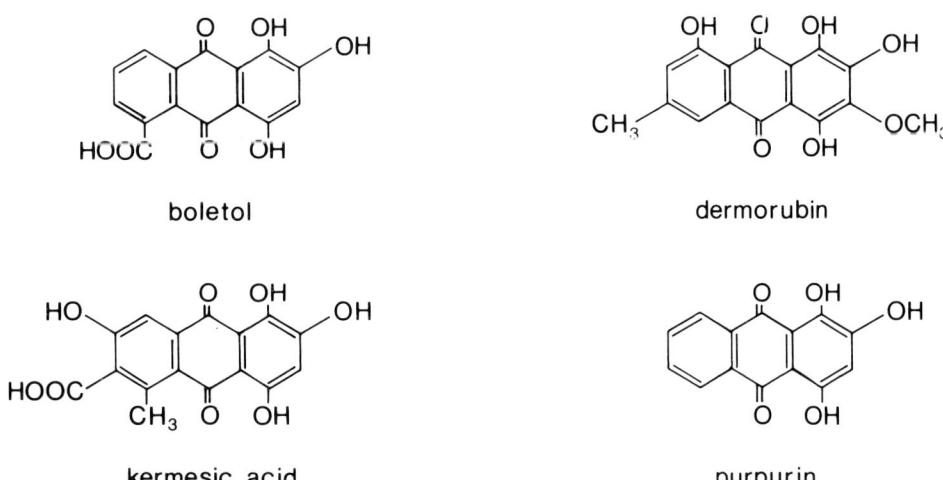

boletol

dermorubin

kermesic acid

purpurin

Fig. 5.2 Some of the colorants in mushrooms. Note, the carboxyl group in boletol may be para *to the position shown (drawing A. Thomas, York Archaeological Trust)*

In fig. 5.2 the right-hand sides of the formulae (which largely determine the colour of the dyeings) are much the same and hence one would expect boletol and dermorubin to give good reds with the appropriate mordant.

There is even a purple alternative to lichens and shellfish; the mushroom *Paxillus atromentosus* gives a purple colour with alum mordant, the colorant being atromentin (fig. 5.3).[23]

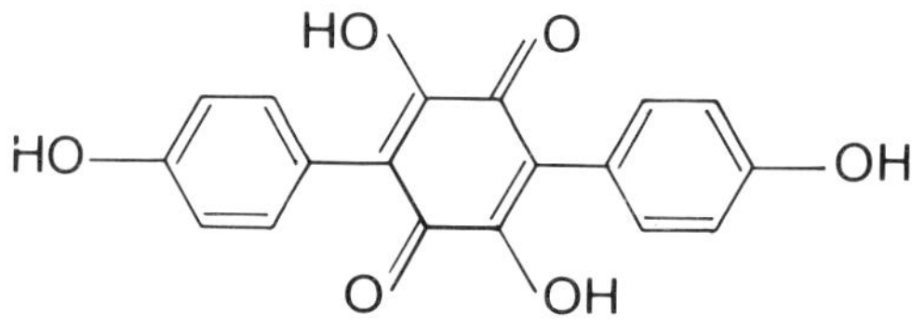

Fig. 5.3 The structure of atromentin (drawing A. Thomas, York Archaeological Trust)

Mordants

Many of the widely used natural dyes were of the mordant type. The colour of the dyeing depended on the nature of both dye and mordant. Mordants generally involve common metals such as aluminium and iron. While it is practicable to identify such metals on unstained textiles, textiles recovered from archaeological excavations have usually been contaminated by dirt which contains just such metals. Therefore, in most analytical investigations of dyes on textiles of archaeological origin, the mordant itself has not been identified. While for the Mediterranean world in the period under consideration here, it is likely that the mordant for bright shades contained aluminium (for example as natural alum), different, generally darker, colours might be obtained using iron.

The problem for Britain is what mordant could have been used for bright shades. The sources of alum in Britain yield material which requires chemical processing which was not practised until the late 16th century.[24] For a cottage dyeing industry, crude native alum-type mordants are said to be had from wood ash, human urine, sheep manure, oak galls, the sediment of certain pools and filtered smoke.[25] Perhaps. In many parts of Ireland up to recent times, chips of the oak or alder tree were used as mordants, and this was called 'barking the yarn'.[26]

A number of plants are biological accumulators of aluminium, for example, the clubmosses, and in particular, *Lycopodium clavatum* L., *Diphasium alpinum* L., and *Diphasium complanatum* (L.) Rothm.[27] The former two are native to Britain while the latter is found in Scandinavia. The percentage aluminium contents (based on dry plant weight) are reported to be as follows:

D. alpinum	0.80
D. complanatum	1.04
L. clavatum	0.27

The first two are particularly rich in aluminium and potentially suitable for use as mordants. Deposits of *D. complanatum* were found along with the residues of other dye plants in Anglo-Scandinavian contexts in York.[28] Tests have shown that this clubmoss is indeed an excellent mordant for madder (giving a rather more crimson hue than alum), while Mrs Grierson, in joint work with Paisley College of Technology, has shown that wool does take up a useful amount of aluminium.[29]

Scottish traditions of the use of clubmosses as mordants have recently been reviewed,[30] and the remains of the two Scottish clubmosses, *L. clavatum* and *D. alpinum*, have been found in Medieval contexts in Perth.[31] So it seems reasonable to suppose that mordants were to hand to produce bright shades with dyestuffs such as madder without relying on imports of alum (although, of course, such imports might well have been taking place).

Results of dye analyses on British textiles

The results of the main dye analytical work on textiles found in archaeological investigations in Britain, dating from Roman times to the Norman Conquest, are now briefly considered.

Dyes on the Vindolanda textiles

A large number of 1st-century textile fragments were found at Vindolanda, Northumberland, and have been described.[32] All the textiles were of sheep's wool, and were thought to have been produced in Britain from British wool, perhaps as part of a Roman army contract. Many of the textiles were of unpigmented wool (and hence suitable for dyeing), but all were heavily stained from burial. About 100 fragments, from over 50 separate textiles, have been analysed for dyes.[33] Evidence for dye was found on nine textiles. In eight cases, the dye was madder or a close relative. In three of the eight, the dye was indeed madder, but in the other four, not all the tinctorial components which fingerprint madder dyes had survived. So in two cases, only alizarin was present, in another, only purpurin, and so forth; but it seems likely that all the dyeings were indeed madder, with only selective survival of certain tinctorial components due to the passage of many centuries underground.

The ninth textile was most interesting as it appeared to have been dyed with a lichen purple, surviving only sporadically. The dye was identified by comparison of its absorption spectrum in the presence of acid and base with those of orchil (from a 19th-century Spanish carpet) and a modern sample of purple dye prepared commercially in the last 20 years or so. The identification of the Roman dye was based on the general resemblance of its spectra and pH sensitivity to those of the recent lichen purples; the Roman dyeing, however, would have had a more bluish tint than that of a modern orchil dyeing - unless the difference was due to the ageing processes taking place with the Roman dye during the centuries of burial. It is presumed that both the lichen purple and the madder had been imported, along with the alum mordant probably used.

It is interesting that the earliest British textiles so far analysed for dye appear to have been coloured red and purple. One textile, on excavation, appeared to have a purple stripe, arousing the exciting prospect of an Imperial visit (or perhaps an early Irishman ?), but analysis showed that the dye was of the madder type. Perhaps the red colour had been modified by lime in the dyebath ? Meanwhile all those pictures which we see of the Roman soldier clothed in madder red could well be correct !

Dyes on early Anglo-Saxon textiles

These textiles came from burials of the 6th and 7th centuries, as follows:

Chessell Down braid	second half of 6th century
Sutton Hoo	early 7th century
Taplow	early 7th century
Kempston embroidery	mid 7th century
'Warrior' grave, Broomfield	mid 7th century

The Sutton Hoo and Broomfield textiles were investigated by Whiting;[34] Broomfield and Taplow samples were studied by Walton,[35] while fragments from Chessell Down, Taplow and Kempston were examined by the author.

Whiting reports that on the Sutton Hoo and Broomfield samples, survival of the dye was sporadic and in general only tentative conclusions could be drawn. Several of the textiles may have been dyed with madder, and in one (SH9), indigotin was also found, though it is not clear whether this finding represents a purple or whether the blue and red are on separate parts of the textile.

Walton examined Broomfield samples B1 to B6. Her results and Whiting's are summarised in the following table:

Sample	Whiting	Walton
B1	trace madder	no dye detected
B2	trace madder	trace madder
B3 dark thread	-	natural pigment
orange thread	-	trace orange dye, possibly tannin
B4	-	? trace lichen purple
B5	-	? trace lichen purple
B6	-	natural pigment, no dye detected

Again, red and purple dyes are prominent.

The material from the Taplow and Chessell Down textiles examined by the author was merely the abraded residues from the boxes storing the textiles, as the textiles themselves are too valuable to be depleted by sampling. Apart from what appeared to be non-dye stain, no colorant was identified on these residues. Walton, however, was more fortunate with the Taplow samples she examined (TB4, TB6 and TB7), finding madder (rich in alizarin) in the wool pattern weft of TB4 and traces of madder in two tabbies of TB7.

Samples from the Kempston embroidery were supplied by Elisabeth Crowfoot and the British Museum; these were also abraded residue from the container, but there was an indication of lichen purple being present. The fragments supplied by Crowfoot *could* be construed (with the eye of faith) as 'blue', 'red' and 'yellow'. The 'blue' and 'red' samples were tested, and indeed, the blue contained indigotin, and the red, lichen purple (which, of course, can have a red tone). The 'yellow' fragments await the development of more sensitive tests for yellow dyes than are available at present.

Summarising, we find indications of reds and purples on these early Anglo-Saxon textiles, the purples perhaps using both the lichen purple and the red plus blue approach.

Dyes on Late Saxon textiles from London

These wool textiles date from the 9th to 11th centuries and have been described.[36] Of the 27 fragments, 11 yielded identifiable dye, the dyes being madder, indigotin and lichen purple. On one textile, a purple was produced by overdyeing blue with madder. On another, a four-shed twill, every third weft had been dyed with madder, while the rest of the cloth used yarn dyed with indigotin; this interesting pattern was revealed by the careful analytical work of Penelope Walton.

Once again a predilection for reds and purples is revealed in Saxon London.

Dyes on Viking textiles from Dublin

The results will be reported by Pritchard,[37] who again collaborated with Walton on the analytical side. Dyes found were madder, indigotin, lichen purple, and some evidence for yellow or orange. So red and purple again appear in Viking Dublin.

Dyes on Anglo-Scandinavian textiles from York

These textiles, which are described by Walton,[38] date mainly from the 9th to 11th centuries, and were found in excavations at York. Most were of wool with a few of silk. The first phase of the dye investigation has been reported;[39] further work has shown the presence of lichen purple on a number of fragments. In general, evidence of dye was found on over half of the textiles, suggesting that dyeing was a normal practice. The main dyes were madder, indigotin and lichen purple, and there was evidence for kermes on one or two high quality textiles that may have been imported.

After this work was completed, a number of dye plant residues were found in contexts associated with the textiles:[40] woad (the probable source of the indigotin), madder root, dyer's greenweed (*Genista tinctoria* L.) which is a source of yellow mordant dye but also has other uses, and the clubmoss already referred to. The madder root was still capable of producing attractive dyeings in the expert hands of Mrs Grierson.

General conclusions

The results of the examination of Middle Eastern and British textiles from the first millennium AD seem to suggest a preference for reds and purples. This may be true; but it must be mentioned that yellow dyes are less robust than reds, blues and purples, at least from the point of view of surviving to be detected. Moreover, surviving traces are more difficult to characterise reliably than is the case with the other colours.

While exotic dyes such as kermes and (perhaps) Armenian cochineal appear on Middle Eastern textiles from classical times, nevertheless madder seems to have been very generally used, and most likely to give red shades. On British textiles (or rather, those found in British archaeological investigations), the only other red dye found is kermes and, as expected, this appears only on textiles that were probably imported.

Though Tyrian purple has been found on Byzantine textiles from as late as the 12th century,[41] examples of such dyeings from classical times are very rare, and no example of a shellfish-purple dyeing has been found in Britain.

Purples are commonly made by mixing red and blue, the identity of the red component (and perhaps the choice between woad and indigo) depending on the time and place to some degree. Lichen purples of the orchil type also enjoy widespread use. In Britain the finding of this type of purple throughout the period supports the view advanced by Kok,[42] that in North-West Europe it would be surprising if a dye based on lichens went out of use in the Dark Ages, and refutes a common view that the dye was reintroduced into Europe only at the beginning of the 14th century;[43] perhaps that conclusion may apply in the case of true Mediterranean orchil, however. The predilection for purple, already expressed so far as the Saxons are concerned seems to hold for Britain throughout the first millennium.[44]

Acknowledgements

The author is indebted to Penelope Walton for expert guidance on textile history, to Su Grierson for supplying dyed samples, occasionally at much personal inconvenience, to Gillian Vogelsang-Eastwood and Elisabeth Crowfoot in particular for supplying many textile fragments for analysis and to the York Archaeological Trust for making available laboratory facilities.

Appendix: Egyptian textiles analysed at York

The textiles came from digs sponsored in part by the Egypt Exploration Society and were mainly supplied by Gillian Vogelsang-Eastwood and Elisabeth Crowfoot. The Karanis textiles were supplied by Angela Thomas of the Bolton Metropolitan Museum.

Gillian Vogelsang-Eastwood was also involved in some of the dye analytical work. She also summarised the sources.[45] Her table 1 is as follows:

Site	Date
Tel el-'Amarna (rubbish dumps)	*c.*1370 BC
Qasr Ibrim (occupation layers)	4th century BC-18th century AD
Karanis (occupation layers)	3rd century BC-5th century AD
Quseir al-Qadim (A) (occupation layers)	1st-2nd century AD
Gebel Adda (occupation layers)	3rd-18th century AD
Armant (cemetery)	4th-5th century AD
Quseir al-Qadim (B) (occupation layers)	13th-16th century AD

References

1. Benjamin Disraeli's letter quoted in Blake, *Disraeli's Grand Tour*, London, 1982

2. D. Magie, *Roman Rule in Asia Minor* 1, Princeton, 1950, 48

3. H. Schweppe, 'Identification of Dyes in Historic Textile Materials', in (edd) H.L. Needles and S.H. Zeronian, *Historic Textile and Paper Materials* (*Advances in Chemistry Series* 212), Washington, 1986, 153-174

4. H. Kurdian, 'Kirmiz', *Journal of the American Oriental Society* 61, 1941, 105-107; R.A. Donkin, 'The Insect Dyes of Western and West-Central Asia', *Anthropos: Internationale Zeitschrift für Völker und Sprachkunde* 72, 1977, 847-880

5. G.W. Taylor, 'New Light on the Insect Red Dyes of the Ancient Middle East', *Textile History* 18 (2), 1987, 143-146

6. R. Pfister, 'Matériaux pour servir au Classement des Textiles égyptiens postérieurs à la Conquête Arabe', *Revue des Arts Asiatiques* 10, 1936, nos. 1-2, pp.1-15, 73-85

7. L. Masschelein-Kleiner, L.R.T. Maes, 'Ancient Dyeing Techniques in Eastern Mediterranean Regions', *ICOM Committee for Conservation, 5th Triennial Meeting Zagreb*, 1978, 78/9/3

8. See Appendix

9. I.I. Ziderman, 'Purple Dyes made from Shellfish in Antiquity', *Review of Progress in Coloration* 16, 1986, 46-52

10. A. Kok, 'A Short History of the Orchil Dyes', *The Lichenologist* 3, 1966, 248-272

11. H. Musso, H. Bucken, E.M. Gottschalk, U.V. Gizycki, H. Kramer, D. Maasen, H.G. Matthi, C. Rathgen, U.I. Zahorsky, 'Orcein und Lackmus', *Angewandte Chemie* 73 (20), 1961, 665-685

12. P. Walton, 'The Textile Industry' in J. Blair, N. Ramsay (edd), *English Industries of the Middle Ages*, 1989

13. P. Walton, 'Textiles, Cordage and Raw Fibre from 16-22 Coppergate', *The Archaeology of York* 17/5, York, 1989

14. Bede, *Ecclesiastical History* I, 1 ed. J.A. Giles, 1843

15. F. Henry, 'A Wooden Hut on Inishkea North, County Mayo', *Journal of the Royal Society of Antiquaries of Ireland* 76, 1952, 163-178

16. H. Roosen-Runge, A.E.A. Werner in T.D. Kendrick *et al*, *Evangeliorum Quartuor, Codex Lindisfarnensis* II, v, London, 1960, 261-277 discount Henry's reference source, A.P. Laurie.

17. E. Bancroft, *The Philosophy of Permanent Colours* I, 2nd ed. London, 1813, 133ff.

18. S. Grierson, *The Colour Cauldron*, Perth, 1986

19. Kok (1966)

20. Grierson (1986)

21. *Garnfarvning med Sopp* (*Ottar* No 152, 1), Tromsø, 1985

22. R.H. Thomson, *Naturally-Occuring Quinones,* 1st ed. London, 1957, 186

23. R.H. Thomson (1957), 29

24. A. Clow, N.L. Clow *The Chemical Revolution*, London, 1952, 235

25. B. Mahon, 'Traditional Dyestuffs in Ireland' in A. Gailey, D. O'Hogain (edd), *Gold under the Furze*, Dublin, 1981, 115-128

26. *Ibid*

27. G.E. Hutchinson, A. Wollack, 'Biological Accumulators of Aluminium', *Transactions of the Connecticut Academy of Arts and Sciences* 35, 1943, 73-127

28. R.A. Hall, A.R. Hall, G.W. Taylor, P. Tomlinson, P. Walton, 'Dyeplants from Viking York', *Antiquity* 58, 1984, 57-60; P. Tomlinson, 'Use of Vegetative Remains in the Identification of Dyeplants from Waterlogged 9th-10th century AD Deposits at York', *Journal of Archaeological Science* 12, 1985, 269-283

29. Grierson (1986)

30. *Ibid*

31. D. Robinson, 'Clubmosses from Medieval Perth', *Antiquity* 60, 1986, 49-50

32. J.P. Wild (with M.L. Ryder), *Vindolanda III: The Textiles*, Bardon Mill, 1977

33. G.W. Taylor, 'Detection and Identification of Dyes on pre-Hadrianic Textiles from Vindolanda', *Textile History* 14 (2), 1983, 115-124

34. E. Crowfoot, 'The Textiles' in R.L.S. Bruce-Mitford, *The Sutton Hoo Ship Burial* III, 1, London, 1983, 404-479 (dye analyses described by Mark Whiting)

35. P. Walton, unpublished work

36. F.A. Pritchard, 'Late Saxon Textiles from the City of London', *Medieval Archaeology* 28, 1984, 47-76

37. F.A. Pritchard, in preparation

38. P. Walton, 1989, see note 13; P. Walton in A. MacGregor, 'Anglo-Scandinavian Finds from Lloyds Bank, Pavement and Other Sites', *The Archaeology of York* 17/3, 1982; P. Walton in D. Tweddle, 'Finds from Parliament Street and Other Sites in the City Centre', *The Archaeology of York* 17/4, 1986

39. G.W. Taylor, 'Detection and Identification of Dyes on Anglo-Scandinavian Textiles', *Studies in Conservation* 28, 1983, 153-160

40. See note 25

41. B. Schmedding, *Mittelalterliche Textilien in Kirchen und Klöstern der Schweiz*, Bern, 1978

42. F. Brunello, *Art of Dyeing*, English edition, Vicenza, 1973, 133

43. *Ibid* for example

44. F.A. Pritchard, 'Self-patterned Twills from Late Saxon London', *Weavers' Journal* 130, 1984, 11-14

45. G.M. Eastwood, 'Egyptian Dyes and Colours', *Dyes on Historical and Archaeological Textiles, Third Meeting, York, 1984*, Edinburgh, 1984, 9-19

6. Textile fragments from 'relic-boxes' in Anglo-Saxon graves

Elisabeth Crowfoot
Geldeston

The notes on these textiles were prepared in the early 1970's, to be used as an appendix to a paper on 'So-called workboxes' by David Brown (Ashmolean Museum, Oxford). Before this was published, he learnt that Audrey Meaney's proposed study of 'Amulets and Curing Stones' covered the same ground, and since their conclusions agreed, his paper did not appear.[1] Though Meaney made some use of my notes the technical details of the textiles were not included and are therefore published here.

The small copper-alloy boxes found in Anglo-Saxon women's graves of the 6th to 7th centuries are almost all of the same type (fig. 6.1.1-3), cylinders between 4.5 and 6.5cm high, some with punched dot decoration, others with incised lines. All are well made with close-fitting lids, sometimes hinged, suspended by chains from the waist with the 'keys' and other symbols of female authority. Unlike the herbal and aromatic remains in the more varied boxes and amuletic capsules of Frankish burials, in England the contents, where preserved, seem always to have included threads or fragments of cloth.[2] This gave rise to the name 'thread-boxes' or 'work-boxes' used to describe them by early archaeologists.[3] Contrary to their descriptions, no recognisable needles have been found in the boxes, though a few include a splinter of wood or metal. Where they have suffered damage, probable textile matter can be indicated by dark organic remains;[4] but in the better-preserved examples the close fit of the lid has saved the contents from the contamination of other grave-goods, soil, coffin-wood and the body itself. Instead of the usual brown staining and fibre deterioration, and the even more common mineralisation of the fibres, textiles, often of high grade, have been preserved. In some of them colour is still visible, and these include two of particular interest, the earliest piece so far of Anglo-Saxon wool embroidery (Catalogue A, Kempston) and the earliest silk threads found in an Anglo-Saxon burial (Catalogue G, Updown).

When produced for examination by me the textile fragments had been separated from the metal goods, and the name 'work-boxes' was taken to indicate larger practical containers. The suggestion that the contents of the beautifully decorated little cylinder from Polhill (fig. 6.1.3) could indeed be fragments left from a woman's needlework is clearly untenable.[5] In this box flax had deteriorated into a fibrous lump, with a few recognisable threads and ?moss fibres round a wooden splinter, but fragments from six other cemeteries are clearly recognisable (Catalogue 5 A-E, G below). All are too small to have been kept for any useful purpose; for most are only one or two centimetres in length. Many seem to have had cut edges, though unravelled threads are often preserved with them; most are of good quality, particularly the wool remains, and include either hems or decorative details such as tablet-weave bands and embroidery.

The largest collection of textiles is that from Kempston (Catalogue A). They may come from two boxes, larger and less well-made than the Polhill box, but described by the excavator as having traces of gilding.[6] Though the boxes are very similar, the graves are regarded as being of different dates: Grave 46 is of the 6th century, Grave 71 possibly mid-to-late 7th century. D.J. Kennett

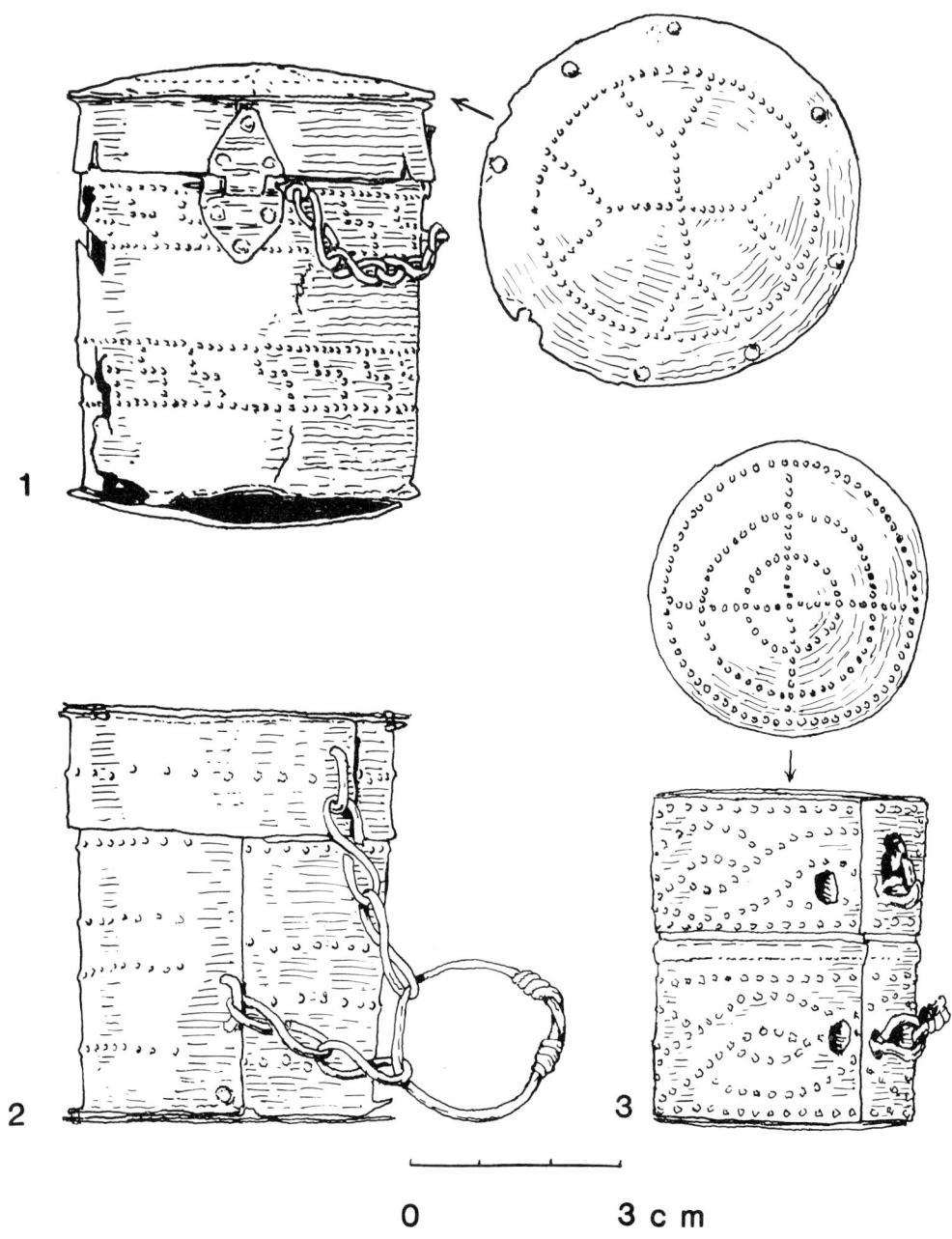

Fig. 6.1 Boxes from Anglo-Saxon women's graves (natural size);
1. Sibertswold Down, Kent. Grave 60
2. Updown, Kent. Grave 34
3.. Polhill, West Kent. Grave 43

considered that most of the pieces probably came from the box in Grave 71, described as containing a fragment of 'worsted fabric' and 'linen manufacture of three distinct qualities'.[7] These flax weaves include tabbies, one scrap with remains of a hem, and several cut pieces of a regular well-woven four-shed twill (fig. 6.2.1). Its broken diamond is of the usual Anglo-Saxon pattern, as in flax examples from other sites, but here the diamonds are widely spaced.[8] The worsted textile (fig. 6.3), originally purple, is shown by its reversing diagonals to have also been a broken diamond twill, though the surface is too concealed by embroidery for the weave pattern to be clear. The decoration, in fine plied thread, shows part of a scroll border in double lines of stem-stitch, yellow or white in the main curve, blue or green in the ?leaves and ?bud, all outlined with single reddish lines (fig. 6.2). Traces on other tiny pieces are difficult to distinguish from the faded ground-weave. There are so far no contemporary wool examples of this style of embroidery, but it is strikingly reminiscent of some parts of the 10th-century embroidery, perhaps on a cloak, from the chieftain's grave at Bjerringhøj, Mammen, Denmark.[9] The stitching is bolder and coarser, but in the same technique, and shows an acanthus scroll with lines of stem-stitch edged in a different colour, in this case visibly lighter, though all has now faded to shades of brown. Margrethe Hald indeed suggested possible Anglian influence on this embroidery.[10] But the acanthus scroll, a popular classical form of decoration, is very widely distributed, and Munksgaard, in a recent study, when discussing fully the diverse elements in other areas of the work, concludes that they incorporate so many features of the Borre and Jelling styles that she has no doubt of the embroidery being of purely local manufacture.[11]

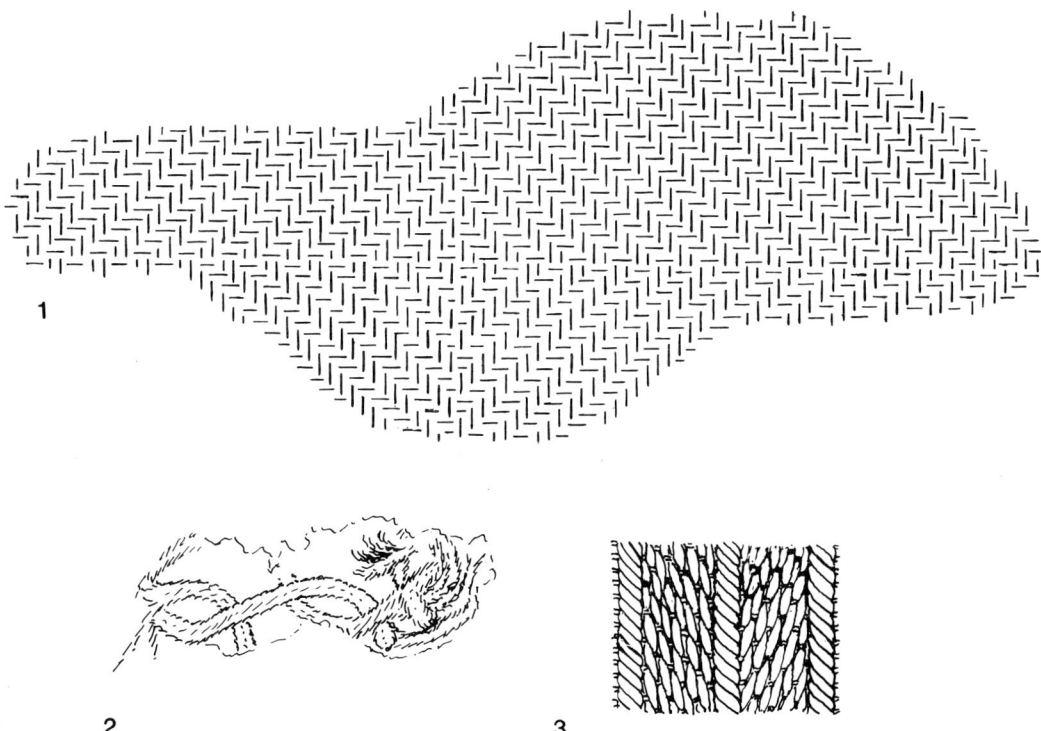

1

2   3

Fig. 6.2 1. Weave diagram, broken diamond twill, flax (Kempston)
2. Embroidery, stem-stitch (Kempston)
3. Tablet-braid (Sibertswold Down)

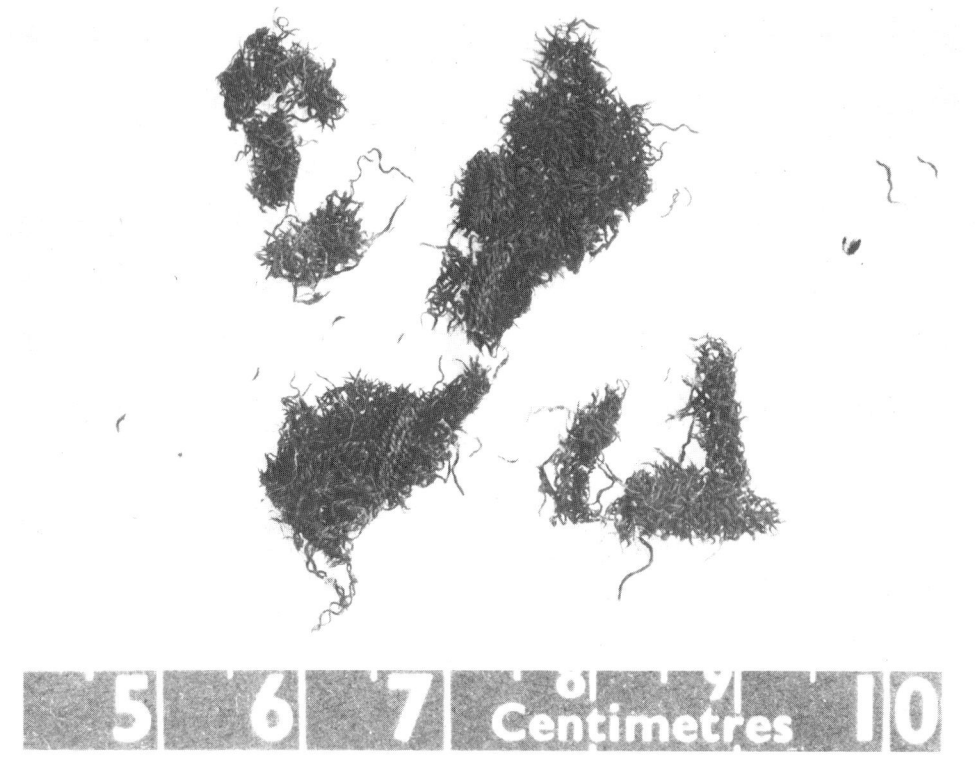

Fig. 6.3   Wool embroidery from the Kempston work-box

The wool in the Kempston fragments is very good quality worsted, a characteristic also of that from two other boxes, Uncleby (Catalogue B) and Sibertswold Down (Catalogue C), where the high shine on the fine threads deceived the excavators into describing them as silk.[12] In both these boxes colours are still visible, and red, blue and yellow dyes have been identified. In contrast, both at Kempston and at Uncleby, coarse threads of black naturally pigmented wool have also been preserved.

Probable fragments of tablet-weave, a popular technique in Anglo-Saxon weaving for braids and borders, were found in three boxes. At Sibertswold Down fragments of a fine band show diagonal pattern in a technique using threads in only two holes of the tablet, originally identified by Hans Dedekam in a narrow mid-6th century braid from Snartemo, Norway, and found in England at Wakerley, Northants.[13] In the Sibertswold braid the edges have a thick 4-thread cord, probably red, and the pattern is further embellished with a similar cord in the middle of the band (fig. 6.2.3); fragments of loose 4-ply threads, again red, of very similar appearance might come from the braid, but slight marks suggest that they were sewn, perhaps as a cord to decorate an edge. In the Uncleby box tiny mineralised fragments appear to come from a tablet-weave, and loose threads here, 3-plied in tight spirals, look very like warp-ends left from tablets. This, however, would imply the use of 3-hole tablets, which, though well known from Roman sites, have not so far been identified in an Anglo-Saxon context.[14]   At Barton-on-Humber (Catalogue D) mineralised traces on an iron pin and detached fragments, probably again tablet-weave, are possibly of vegetable fibre; the Wakerley braid mentioned above was of flax, and other examples suggest it was often used for patterned braids.[15]

Hems on linen tabby weaves are again present at Marina Drive, Dunstable (Catalogue E), and Updown, Kent.[16] The contents of the latter box at once dispose of the suggestion that these might hold relics of the woman's weaving skill or housewifely status. This box is in the grave of a small child (fig. 6.1.2), and contains only a tiny fragment of fine undyed flax tabby, a folded edge, perhaps from its plied warps from a selvedge, across which one white silk thread has been woven or darned, and a small bunch of unravelled threads, mixed flax and white silk (Catalogue G).

Audrey Meaney's description of saintly relics ("the kind of thing that would have been sold in the Medieval equivalent of a souvenir shop as a genuine piece of the saint's robe; or something which a pilgrim had placed on a shrine for a while in order to imbue it with the saint's merits") seems to cover the contents of these boxes most convincingly - the tablet-weaves and embroidery from vestments or the robes of royal saints, the flax fragments from the shifts and veils of holy women, even the coarse black threads from the habits of monks or hermits.[17] Vegetable remains, present only in two boxes, unidentifiable seeds, pierced as if to be strung as beads, from Sibertswold, and seeds of caper spurge at Barton-on-Humber, could come from some famous monastery garden, rather than suggest the woman's skill as the family doctor.

But the conclusion that these boxes are to be regarded specifically as Christian reliquaries perhaps needs a little qualification. The burials in which they are found, of the 6th to 7th centuries, come from a period of transition, when Christianity was officially embraced, but perhaps not wholeheartedly accepted below the upper levels of society. Christian practice has never suggested the burial of relics; they are prestige possessions to be displayed and venerated - witness the vast collection of such items donated by Athelstan to his monastic foundation at Exeter.[18] They are a visible aid to devotion, not to be treated as insurance for an individual soul. If as seems possible, these fragments were indeed treasured as relics, their burial perhaps demonstrates a last mingling of pagan with Christian beliefs, safeguarding the woman in death as with the old amulets, but making doubly sure by including a plausible relic from the new religion.

Catalogue of textiles from boxes

A. Kempston, Bedfordshire[19]
Graves 46 (6th century) and 71 (7th century):

1. Two fragments, *c*.2.0 x 5.0, 2.2 x 2.4cm. Flax, undyed, Z/Z, spin irregular, close tabby weave, thread counts 26/22, 22/21 per cm. On the smaller piece, hem edge folded under, stitch-holes along fold, remains running stitch in coarse Z flax thread.

2. One fragment, flax, undyed, Z/Z, tabby weave, count estimated *c*.25/16 (12-13/8 on 5mm); more uneven spin and weave than (1), heavily stained bronze.

3. Four fragments, 2.4 x 4.5, 1.5 x 0.8, 1.0 x 1.5, 1.5 x 1.5cm. Flax, undyed, ?warp slightly finer, weave four-shed twill with widely spaced broken diamond (fig. 6.2.1), thread count 26/24 per cm. Three pieces show diamonds.

4. Two fragments, adjoining, 1.3 x 2.0, 1.5 x 1.3cm, and five tiny scraps (figs. 6.2, 6.3). Wool, worsted, now brown with blue tinge, originally purple, spinning Z/S, weave four-shed broken diamond twill, obscured by embroidery, thread count c. 28/22 per cm. Embroidery, stem-stitch, fine wool, Z,S ply, red, ?yellow and blue (?green), pattern scroll and leaves, outline a single red line, filling two lines stem-

stitch, yellow and blue. On two small scraps, traces yellow and red stem, and other red lines.

5.   Unravelled, Z,Sply threads, from embroidery, most red, a few still looped as in stem-stitch.

5b. Tangled with (5), fragments coarse wool, S-spun, black.

6.   Fragment 1.5 x 1.0cm, flax, undyed, Z/Z, tabby weave, thread count 11/11 per cm.

Fibres: Dr M.L. Ryder, Animal Breeding Research Organisation, Roslin.

(1,3) Both yarns flax.

(4,5) Five yarns, three no pigment or dye. All have fine and medium fibres, like previous Saxon examples, and appear to be a fine variety of this generalised medium wool (29/4/69, 13/5/69).

Dyes: K. Starkie, Dyestuffs Division, Imperial Chemical Industries Ltd:

Extraction with 40% pyridine shows faint red and blue; the blue is possibly indigo (or woad); the red does not appear to be madder, lac or kermes; one of the natural wood dyes is a possibility.

G.W. Taylor, Dye Consultant (14/5/85):

Blue, indigotin; ground weave (4) lichen purple. No mordant dyes.

B.   Uncleby, Yorkshire[20]

Grave 29 (6th century):

Contents well preserved, all mixed together.

1.   Ball of thread, vegetable fibre ?flax, greyish loosely spun, yarn up to 0.75mm diameter; a few loose Sply threads of same.

2.   Mass of threads, Z, S3ply, some dark blue ?green, some lighter, longest thread detached *c.* 12.0cm. Wool springy and brittle, shiny, ply a tight spiral, *c*.1.5mm circumference.

3.   Small roll very fine Z, Sply wool thread, red.

4.   Rather coarser threads, wool, dark golden yellow mixed with (2) and loose threads of (1).

5.   Fragments coarse black wool threads, Z, Sply, spin and ply both loose (caught in (3)).

6.   Three tiny fragments, nearly completely mineralised, 0.8 x 0.5, 1.4 x 0.25, 1.0 x 0.35cm, the largest deteriorated, the others Z-spun one system, Z,Sply the other (weft?). Surface where clear ?tabby, but broken edges suggest tablet-weave.

7.   Fragments of hide, largest 0.8 x 0.8cm, folded, with loose threads, light, from (2) or (4) caught on one side, and inside traces of (6), ie perhaps leather tag from braid. (7) may account for resinous traces on (1) and (2).

Fibres: Dr M.L. Ryder, Animal Breeding Research Organisation, Roslin:

(1) Vegetable ?flax.

(2) Light, fine wool fibres among debris; dark, fine to medium wool.

(3) Red threads, very fine wool.

(5) Black thread, heavily pigmented fine to medium wool.

Dyes: C.L.Haddock, Organics Division, Imperial Chemical Industries, Ltd.:

(2) 3ply threads, green or gold. Indigo present

3ply threads, blue or green. Indigo present, rather more.

(3) 2ply threads, red. ?madder present.

(4) 2ply threads, gold. ?weld present.

Tests on (3,4) were complicated because of the amount of copper present; on (2) the indigo was present in spots rather than evenly distributed throughout the wool fibres, the difference in colouring being due to the more scattered distribution in the lighter threads. The unevenness is perhaps due to the use of the fermentation method of preparing the dye, from the leaves of woad, *Isatis tinctoria* L. , which at this period is likely to have been in use.[21]

C. Sibertswold Down, Kent[22]

Grave 60 (7th century):

1. Two fragments, 1.4 x 0.7, 1.3 x 0.7cm, from tablet-woven band, diagonal pattern on ten 2-hole cards, with one 4-hole at each edge, and one in the centre (fig. 6.2.3), red edges,green; warp Z, weft Z pairs, 4 on 2.5mm. Two other scraps coated with preservative.

2. A mass of wool fibres, unspun, mixed with Z,Sply threads, ?unravelled tablet-twists from (1), red, dark and light green?; also unplied threads, ?warp ends from (1), and a knot or brown (red) yarn, 8 threads tied together.

3. Fragments of thick threads, four Z,Sply threads plied together S, red, loosely rolled up, no weft holes clear, but marks suggest these may have been sewn to another fabric.

4. One fragment similar red thread, Z,Sply, rolled up.

5. Plant ?seeds, pierced as if to be strung, unidentifiable but something like 'Marvel of Peru'.

Fibres: Dr M.L. Ryder, Animal Breeding Research Association, Roslin:

All fine fibred wool, some threads naturally pigmented brown.

Dyes: Penelope Walton, Textile Consultant:

   (2,3) red, madder from *Rubia tinctorum* L. Both samples showed the presence of alizarin and purpurin. The presence of a strong alizarin component indicates that the dye is almost certainly derived from dyers' madder, *R. tinctorum* and not wild madder or bedstraw.[23]

   (2) Dark green, pale yellow green, no dye detected. The green threads derived their colour not from dyes, but from copper salts, corrosion products from the copper-alloy box.

D. Barton-on-Humber, Lincs[24]

Grave 1 or 2:

1. Adhering to Fe ?pin, deteriorated Z,S ply threads, wound round one end and lying side by side lower down; ?decayed tablet warp.

2. Two threads, Z,S ply along length of pin, mineralised, confused traces crossing, ?weft of (1).

3. Detached, fragment 2.5 x 2.5mm, impregnated rust, Z/Z, tabby weave, thread count 5/4, ie *c.* 20/16 threads per cm.

4. Scraps of coarse Z-spun threads ?from (3).

5. Deteriorated fragments, fine Z-spun threads; twists visible at edge, estimate *c.*18 per cm, if tablet weave; some coarser may be from weft.

6. Loose spun fibres Z from (1) and (2).

7. Seeds of caper spurge, *Euphorbia lathyris*.

Fibres: H.M. Appleyard FTI:

(5) Vegetable origin, but fibres not clear.

E. Marina Drive, Dunstable, Bedfordshire[25]

Grave E 1/2 (late 6th century to early 7th century):

1. Loose fibres, stained bronze, longest 2cm, flax, Z, tight spin, several threads 2ply, and one ?4ply, but this may be two threads.

2. Fibres in small bunches, one large bunch from round Fe bar or pin, flax, fairly fine, some thicker fibres, loose Z-spin, stained Fe.

3. Four fragments, 2.8 x 1.5, 3.2 x 1.6, 0.8 x 2.2, 2.1 x 1.7cm, flax, Z/Z, slight twist, tabby weave, count 22/24-26 threads per cm. Three first fragments have narrow (2.5-3mm) hem one side, hemmed flax thread slightly coarser than that of the fabric.

4. Five small fragments, largest 2.0 x 1.2cm, wool, fibres almost completely mineralised (Fe), Z/Z, tabby weave, thread count 10-14/10-14 per cm (18/16 where mineralised).

Grave B 3/4:

A few threads of wool.

Fibres : Dr A.B. Wildman, Wool Industries Research Association:

(1,2,3) All linen. (4) Wool.

Dr A.B.D. Cassie, Director of Research, Wool Industries Research Association:

(4) The wool fibres are fairly coarse, scale pattern similar to coarse fibres from present day mountain breeds.

F. Polhill, West Kent[26]

Grave 43 (late 7th century):

Lump of deteriorated fibres round splinter of wood, some threads Z-spun, some plied fragments. A few tiny fragments of moss caught in them.

Fibres: Dr M.L. Ryder: Too degraded for identification, but the appearance suggests flax.

G. Updown, Kent

Grave 34 (7th century):

1. Tiny scrap, folded, 0.7 x 0.3cm , flax, undyed, warp Z,Sply, weft Z, tabby weave, count 6/7 threads, ie *c.*9-10/23 per cm; one white silk thread lies in the same shed as a flax weft. The plied warps suggest this may be from a selvedge, perhaps tubular, but the loops are missing.

2. Small bunch of mixed undyed Z-spun flax and white S-spun silk threads.

Fibres: H.M. Appleyard FTI:

Z-spun threads, warp and weft, clearly vegetable, flax characteristics. S-spun threads; both fine silk (from weave, and loose), very light in colour, but some fibres badly degraded.

Acknowledgements

I am most grateful to Dr S. Chadwick Hawkes for permission to include the Updown box (fig. 6.1.2) and describe its contents, prior to publication; to the Department of Medieval and Later Antiquities, the British Museum, for Kempston; to the Luton Museum, for permission to use their notes on textiles from Marina Drive, Dunstable; to Mrs Elizabeth Hartley, Keeper of Archaeology, Yorkshire Museum, for the Uncleby Textiles; and to the Liverpool Museum, for arranging re-examination and dye-testing on those from Sibertswold Down.

References

1. A.S. Meaney, *Amulets and Curing-stones* (*British Archaeological Reports* 96), 1981, 184-186

2. David Brown notes two Scandinavian boxes containing threads in C.J. Becker, *Acta Archaeologica* 24, 1953, 135f and 145f; M. Ørsnes Christensen, *Acta Archaeologica* 26, 1955, 69

3. G. Baldwin Brown, *The Arts in Early England* IV, London, 1915, 412

4. B. Faussett, ed. C. Roach Smith, *Inventorium Sepulchrale*, London, 1856, 57-58

5. E. Crowfoot, 'Textile Fragments from Polhill' in B.J. Philp, *Excavations in West Kent 1960-1970*, Dover, 1973, 202-203

6. E. Fitch, 'Discovery of Anglo-Saxon Remains at Kempston', *Bedfordshire Architectural Society* VII, Part II, 1894, 289-293

7. *Ibid*, 291

8. E. Crowfoot, 'The Textiles' in R. Bruce-Mitford, *The Sutton Hoo Ship Burial* 3, I, London, 1983, 422 SH12; 466, Mound 4; Mucking, Essex, Graves 553.2, 998.2 (in preparation)

9. M. Hald, *Ancient Danish Textiles from Bogs and Burials*, Copenhagen, 1980, fig.294

10. Hald (1980), 104

11. E. Munksgaard, 'The Embroideries from Bjerringhøj, Mammen' in *Festskrift til Thorleif Sjøvold, på 10-Årsdagen (Universitetets Oldsaksamlings Skrifter* Ny rekke 5), Oslo, 1984, 168-169

12. Faussett, ed. Roach Smith (1856), 112

13. H. Dedekam, 'To Tekstilfunde fra folkevandringstiden', *Bergens Museums Aarbok* 1924-1925, 3-57 figs. 21,22; E. Crowfoot, Textiles: Wakerley, Northants, *A.M. Laboratory Report* 44/88, Grave 78

14. J.P.Wild, *Textile Manufacture in the Northern Roman Provinces*, Cambridge, 1970, Table 0, 140-141

15. G.M. Crowfoot, 'Textiles of the Saxon Period in the Museum of Archaeology and Ethnology', *Proceedings of the Cambridge Antiquarian Society* 44, 1951, 28-30

16. C.L. Matthew, 'The Anglo-Saxon Cemetery at Marina Drive, Dunstable', *Bedfordshire Archaeological Journal* 1/2, 1962, 25-47

17. Meaney (1981), 186

18. *Ibid*

19. E. Fitch, 'Discovery of Saxon Remains at Kempston', *Bedfordshire Architectural Society* VII Part II, 1894, 289-293

20. R.A. Smith, 'The excavation by Canon Greenwell, F.S.A., in 1908, of an Anglo-Saxon cemetery at Uncleby, East Riding of Yorkshire', *Proceedings of the Society of Antiquaries* 24, 1911-12, 146-158

21. R.J. Forbes, *Studies in Ancient Technology* IV, Leiden, 1956,151

22. Faussett, ed. Roach Smith (1856), 112

23. G.W. Taylor, 'Detection and Identification of dyes on Anglo-Scandinavian Textiles', *Studies in Conservation* 28, 1983, 153-160

24. T. Sheppard, *Saxon Relics from Barton, Lincs and Elloughton, Yorks (Hull Museum Publications* 208), 1940

25. Matthew (1962)

26. Crowfoot (1973)

7. Maaseik reconstructed: a practical investigation and interpretation of 8th-century embroidery techniques

Helen M. Stevens
Bury St Edmunds

Readers may like to refer to the cover illustrations of this book which show, respectively, the front and reverse of the work in detail.

The task of stepping into another's shoes with a view to recreating their work is one which is rarely sought by any artist. Yet only by doing so has it been possible to reach any conclusions as to the practices and techniques employed in an embroidery workshop of the 8th century - conclusions which the writer has formed by following in the footsteps of her unknown predecessor and meticulously reconstructing her methods of working.

Research into the early Medieval textiles at Maaseik, Belgium, has centred on a jigsaw of fragments which includes the earliest extant group of Anglo-Saxon embroideries.[1] Pre-dating the St. Cuthbert relics by at least a century, their design is vigorous and entertaining, their execution finely detailed and highly professional. Of the four strips surviving, the most complete was chosen for reconstruction. Measuring 63 x 10cm it incorporates gold thread, surface couched in various designs, set in a mosaic ground of silk worked in split and stem stitch. The embroidery is worked upon a dense linen of even weave (c. 20-26 threads per cm in both systems).

Before commencing the reconstruction it was necessary to draw a 1:1 line drawing of the original to eliminate distortions of shrinkage and warping. The pattern was then transferred to the correct gauge of linen.

The writer is a professional hand-embroiderer specialising in silk and gold work. The description which follows is the result of 18 months' experimentation and each statement has been verified by practical application. Working from detailed photographs and the bare technical facts mentioned above it has been possible to construct the following description of how the piece was worked.

A simple frame was necessary to support the linen at the correct tension. This must have been free standing to allow the use of both hands. Considerably more linen than needed for the embroidery itself was mounted, again to maintain the correct tension, and whilst much of the design was worked freehand, the 'architecture' of the pattern was probably picked out on the fabric and immediately outlined to provide a framework for the detailed motifs. This outline was worked in red silk stem or split stitch, depending on the curvature of the line, and formed a series of nine arcades.

The repeat design fell into three sections, an arcade, a pier and spandrel bordered by a ribbon of chevrons forming one 'set' of approximately 10 x 7cm, and ultimately taking about 30 hours to complete (fig. 7.1). The order of working was paramount: if an incorrect sequence was followed, the linen was pulled out of shape. Inner arcade, outer arch, pier, spandrel and border chevrons were worked respectively in a cruciform directional pattern, with chevrons worked left to right. Within each field the designs were laid out sequentially as follows: outline, mosaic infill, gold motif. Colours other than red were applied in diminishing amounts, ie green, dark blue, yellow, light blue and beige. Remaining

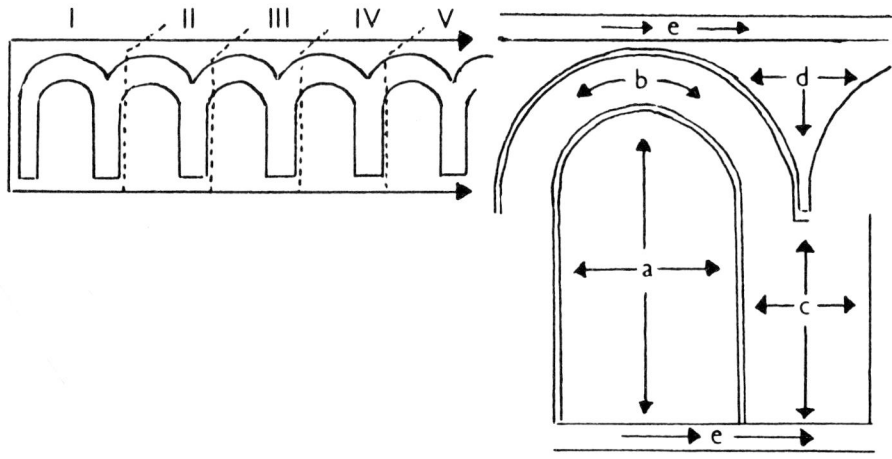

Fig. 7.1 Composition of each 'set' (left); sequential and directional working technique (right): a. arcade; b. outer arch; c. pier; d. spandrel; e. chevron strips

sections were infilled with red, the predominant colour, to complete the mosaic effect.

Strict adherence to the sequence not only ensured uniform tension, but also allowed immense efficiency of materials. Split stitch is a technique which minimises the amount of silk visible (and therefore wasted) on the reverse of the work. By applying the coloured silks in a pre-determined order and in pre-set lengths waste was further reduced. In practice this worked as follows: in each arcade the artist decided to use a specific amount of each colour, in order to balance the design of the preceding arcades. If, having achieved that balance, there was a small amount of any shade remaining this was included in the outer arch (or equivalent section) of that set and the appropriate fraction deducted from its allocation of such colour, resulting in the impression of uniformity whilst keeping an exact track of materials used with no wastage. The principle is applied repeatedly for each colour in each set. Whether the choice of colours reflects personal taste or economic stricture is a matter for debate.

This rigid discipline was also applied to the application of the gold thread, but in no way lessened the spontaneity of design, emphasizing the professionalism and experience of the artist, which resulted in an ability to judge with precision the amount of thread required to complete a specific motif. Take, for example a certain spandrel which was to contain a zoomorphic motif. Working freehand the artist fashioned the beast, surface couching the gold thread in a decreasing coil from the red outline inwards to the core of the motif. In doing so she used almost exactly one measure of gold thread. (For an interpretation of measurements see statistical analysis below.) Should there be a slight excess this was incorporated into the nearest ribbon of chevrons, accounting for the variation of sizes within these sections.

The use of specific, uniform lengths of thread, both silk and gold, and the 'using up' of excesses in the peripheral areas of the overall design occurs far too often to be relegated to the status of coincidence. It points to commercially sound business practice whilst allowing the expression of the artist's own distinctive, style. In her use of interlace, animal and foliate motifs she variously diverges from and adheres to the principles of symmetry; some arcades are subdivided, some form larger fields, but in every case a broadly similar overall effect is achieved.

In describing her 8th-century counterpart as feminine the writer has followed her own instinct. Confident, however, that a single hand undertook this piece of embroidery, she is supported by evidence and experimentation. The uniformity of tension, style and execution clearly points to an individual worker from inception to completion. The texture of the finished embroidery is rigid and inflexible and suggests a static decorative use for the piece (fig. 7.2).

The Maaseik embroideries, whilst unique within today's corpus of Anglo-Saxon work, in their day reflected a long tradition of such pieces. The materials employed were costly and techniques had evolved to reduce waste to the bare minimum, whilst allowing a fairly fast rate of progress. It was (and still is) possible to complete a set of motifs in one working week, allowing 4.5 to 5 hours close embroidery per day - the maximum possible to maintain high standards of execution.

Finally, readers might like to know that the acquisitive tastes of the buying public have altered little in twelve centuries. Since completing and exhibiting the Maaseik reconstruction the writer has effected the sale of a number of pieces in the same style, technique and materials to contemporary collectors. How's that for an Anglo-Saxon attitude?[2]

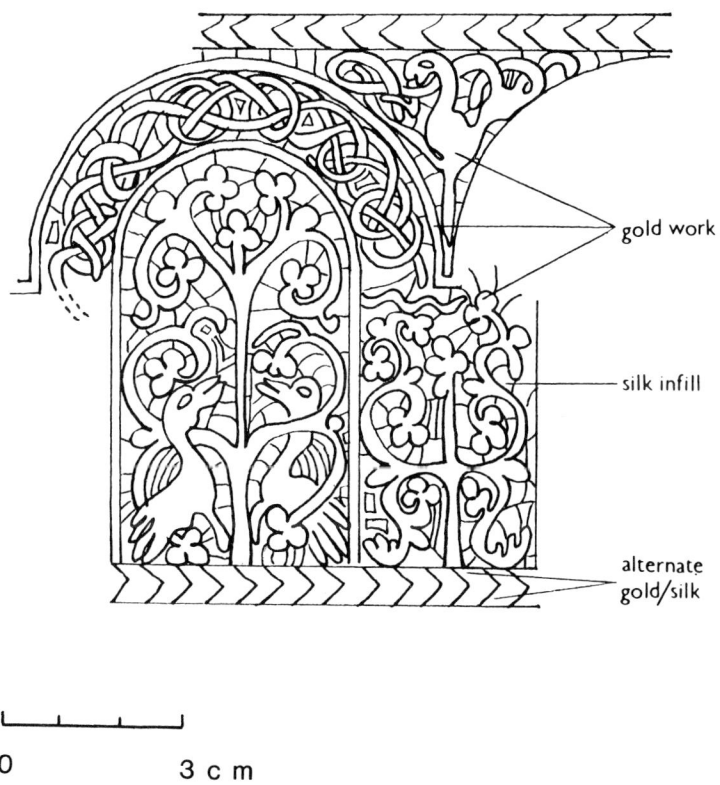

Fig. 7.2 Set VI incorporating each type of motif: animal, foliate and interlace together with typical mosaic infill

References

1. Mildred Budny, Dominic Tweddle, 'The Early Medieval Textiles at Maaseik, Belgium', *The Antiquaries Journal* 65, 1985, 353-389
2. The White King in Lewis Carroll, *Alice through the Looking Glass*, Chapter VII

Appendix: statistical analyses

Each set comprises arcade, pier, spandrel and chevrons as descibed in the text.

1. Use of Materials

The most commonly used length of thread can be roughly equated to one 'half yard'. Experimentation proves this to be approximately half the traditional handworkers' measurement of a 'yard', being 'nose to fingertip', ie 'elbow to fingertip'. Figures below represent 'yards' approximated in this way.

	Red Outline	Red Infill	Green	Blue Dark	Yellow	Blue Light	Beige	Total Silk	Gold Thread
SET I	12.00	7.25	2.25	2.50	2.50	1.50	0.75	28.75	12.75
SET II	9.00	7.25	3.00	1.50	1.75	1.25	-	23.75	11.50
SET III	10.25	6.25	3.00	1.25	1.50	1.75	0.25	24.25	12.00
SET IV	13.00	5.75	4.50	2.00	2.25	1.50	-	29.00	9.00
SET V	8.25	7.00	4.00	0.75	2.25	1.50	0.75	24.50	10.00
SET VI	9.25	6.75	3.00	2.00	1.25	1.50	1.25	25.00	9.50
SET VII	6.50	6.25	3.50	1.50	1.25	1.00	1.25	21.25	9.50
SET VIII	8.75	5.75	2.50	2.00	2.00	2.00	0.75	23.75	10.50
SET IX	7.00	8.75	3.00	2.00	1.75	1.00	-	23.50	9.75
TOTAL PER SET	84.00	61.00	28.75	15.50	16.50	13.00	5.00	223.75	94.50

2. Hours

These figures have been calculated to the nearest 15 minutes. Fluctuations of less than this period have been ignored.

SET	Hours
I	34.75
II	29.75
III	27.50
IV	27.75
V	29.00
VI	26.50
VII	26.25
VIII	32.25
IX	23.25
TOTAL HOURS	257.00

8. Textile production at Coppergate, York: Anglo-Saxon or Viking?

Penelope Walton
York

In the 7th and 8th centuries York was a small ecclesiastical, administrative and commercial centre, serving the Anglian kingdom of Northumbria. The town stood at the junction of a road from the west coast with a major north - south land-route. Being situated on the River Ouse, which at this date was easily navigable, York also had direct access to the North Sea. The main overseas contact of the Anglian period seems to have been with the Frisian region, through trade[1] and through the activities of the Church.[2]

In AD 793 Viking raiders began their attacks on the Northumbrian coast and by 866 York itself had been captured by a combined 'Great Army' of Scandinavians. A period of settlement followed, during which York became a commercial centre for the Danelaw, the Scandinavian-controlled north of England.[3] Despite many political upsets in the 10th-11th centuries, trade flourished and the town, with its mixed population of Anglo-Saxons and Scandinavians, expanded.

Since 1972, the York Archaeological Trust has been carrying out excavations in the heart of the Anglo-Scandinavian town. The sites at Pavement and Numbers 5 and 16-22 Coppergate used to lie in a main thoroughfare which ran north-eastwards from the river crossing. At the largest site, 16-22 Coppergate (fig. 8.1), the Trust has uncovered the remains of four tenement buildings, with gable-ends facing the road and back yards running down to the River Foss, a tributary of the Ouse.[4]

The buildings proved to have been used both as living quarters and workshops, in which several crafts, such as leather-working, wood-turning and jewellery-making, were practised. The excavators also found extensive remains of textile working, including raw wool and flax, dye plants, spinning and weaving equipment, together with many fragments of textiles. Full details of all these finds are to be published in the series *The Archaeology of York*. The present paper, however, addresses the problem of how far the influence of the Scandinavian element in the population can be detected in the textile and textile-related finds.

Textile tools

The implements used in textile production include one iron woolcomb, four wooden spindles, 214 spindle whorls of bone, stone, lead and antler (whole and fragmentary), fragments of 33 baked clay loomweights and three glass linen-smoothers. The forms of most of these artefacts are similar to those found throughout north-west Europe at this time and give little indication of any particular cultural or ethnic origin. It is, however, significant that almost all of the 150 stone spindle whorls are made from types of rock (predominantly chalk and limestone) which can be found in the hills of North Yorkshire.[5]

In shape the whorls range from hemispherical, a form which predominates in the 9th-10th centuries, through cylindrical, which is most common from the late 10th to 11th centuries, to spherical or globular, which occurs only in the period after the Norman Conquest. There are no examples of the conical whorls which have been found at Scandinavian sites such as Trabjerg,[6] Århus[7] or Lund.[8]

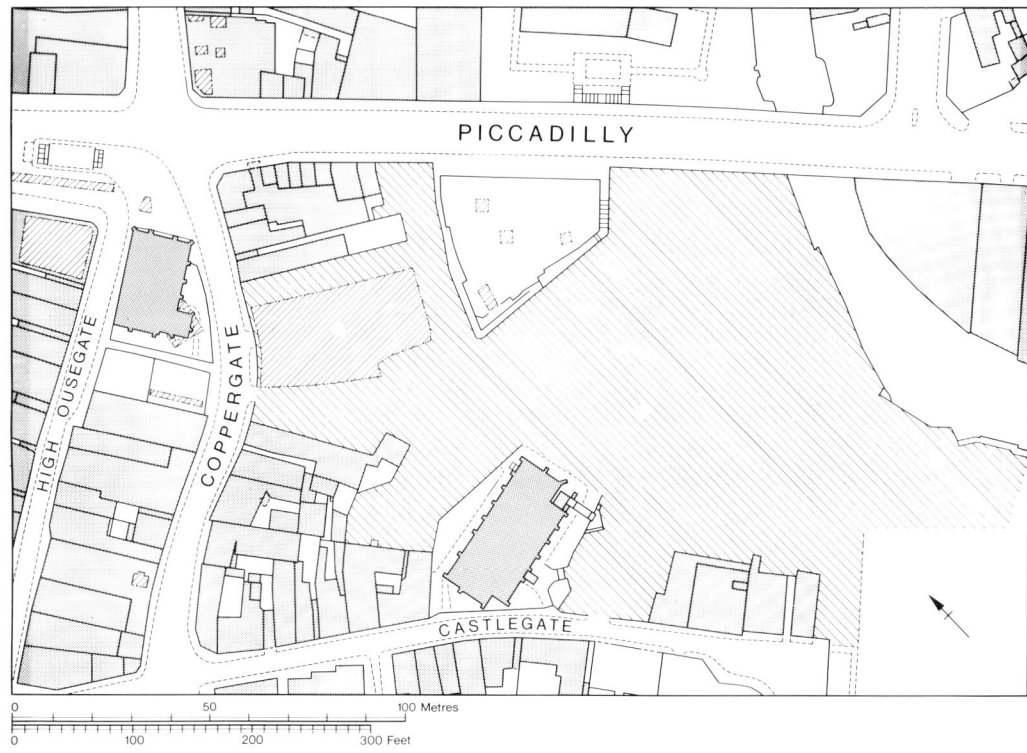

Fig. 8.1 The excavation at 16-22 Coppergate (T. Finnemore, York Archaeological Trust)

Raw materials

Stems and seeds of the flax plant (*Linum usitatissimum* L.)[9] and several examples of raw wool were recovered from the site. The wool varied considerably in quality, but most commonly (48%) it was of a very hairy type, comparable with the shaggy fleeces found nowadays on British mountain breeds such as the Scottish Blackface and the Swaledale. Not just the raw wool, but many of the yarns in the wool textiles were made from fleeces of this type. This hairy wool is noticeably rare in textiles from before the Viking invasions[10] and has only been found in 6% of the late Saxon textiles from London.[11] Whether the Vikings brought with them a new breed of sheep is a matter for archaeo-zoologists to discuss, but the evidence of the textiles suggests that the arrival of the Vikings coincided with a considerable change in the wool being used for textile production.

Botanists at York University's Environmental Archaeology Unit have also found extensive remains of dye plants in soil samples from 16-22 Coppergate. Dr A.R. Hall and P. Tomlinson have identified vegetative remains of madder, *Rubia tinctorum* L., woad, *Isatis tinctoria* L., dyers' greenweed, *Genista tinctoria* L., and a clubmoss, *Diphasium complanatum* L. Rothm. (fig. 8.2), along with seeds of weld, *Reseda luteola* L.[12] Madder and woad were probably both cultivated in England at this time, while weld and greenweed would have been relatively common wild plants. The *Diphasium* clubmoss, however, is a plant of the heathlands of Scandinavia and North Germany. It is therefore almost certainly an import. Dr Hall's research suggests that clubmoss may have been used as a mordant, as an alternative to alum,[13] which would have been difficult to obtain in Viking-Age Europe.

Textiles

There are 121 woven items from the 16-22 Coppergate site, with one needle-worked object. Of these finds 107 come from the Anglo-Scandinavian period: 33 are of wool, 23 of silk and 48 of flax - or probable flax - with three of indeterminate fibre. The number of linens is unusual: many of them appear to owe their preservation to the fact that they were charred (fig. 8.3), probably in a house-fire, before being discarded and eventually buried in the backyard area of the tenements.

The Anglo-Scandinavian wool textiles consist of thirteen 1/1 tabbies, six 2/2 twills, seven 2/2 chevron twills and six 2/2 diamond twills. Almost all have a Z-spun warp and S-spun weft, and are coarse to medium in quality: thread counts range from 3Z x 3S to 22Z x 11S and 18Z x 16S per cm. There are none of the fine ZZ diamond twills of the type found at Birka and other Viking-Age sites in Scandinavia.[14]

Such finds as these fit easily into the general picture of Anglo-Saxon textiles. Apart from the predominant use of hairy wool, there is little to distinguish them from the textiles of early Anglo-Saxon cemeteries or from those of late Saxon London - or indeed from the textiles of North Germany and Holland, with which the English finds show a close affinity.

Local products

For most of the finds from 16 - 22 Coppergate, we can only suggest that they are local products on the rather tenuous grounds that they are of such unremarkable quality that they are unlikely to have been traded. There is, however, one textile which provides more evidence for being locally made. This is

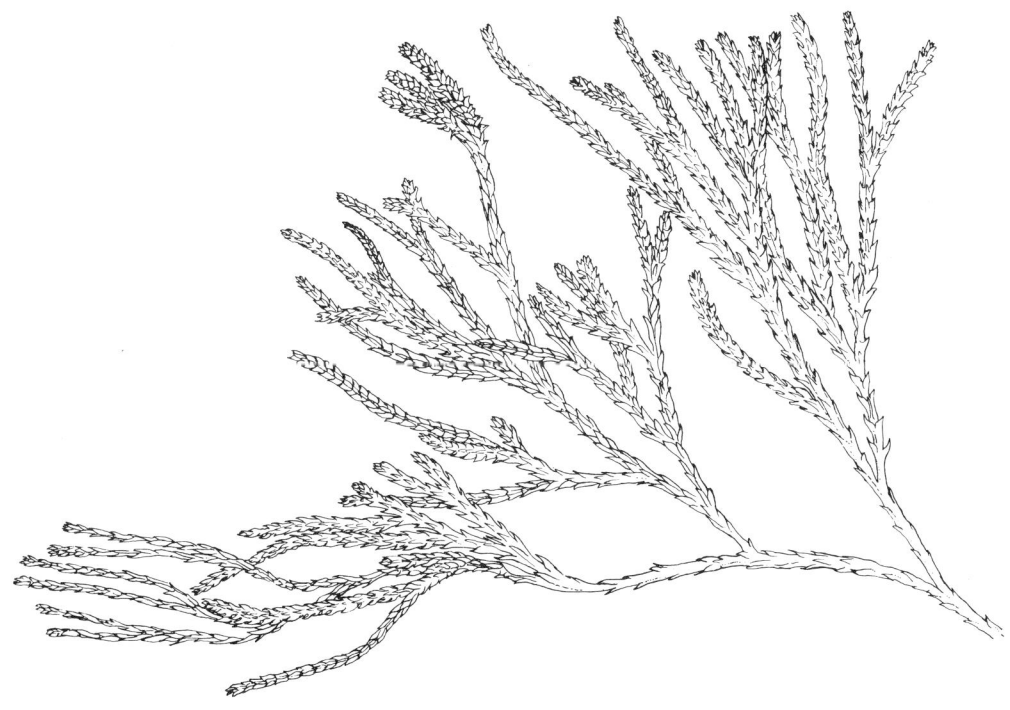

Fig. 8.2 The clubmoss, Diphasium complanatum *(L.) Rothm. (A. Robertson, Environmental Archaeology Unit, University of York)*

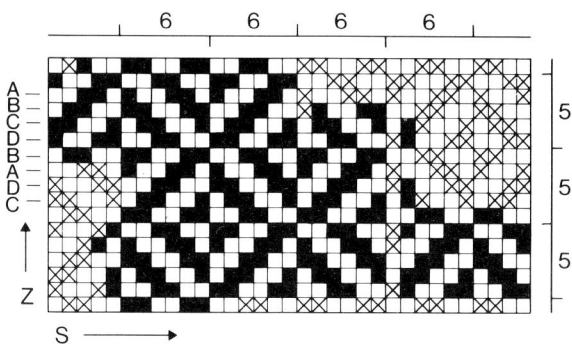

Fig. 8.3 (left) A charred piece of linen tabby, no. 1390, possibly the remains of a child's shirt sleeve (K.M. Buck, YAT)

Fig. 8.4 (above) 2/2 diamond twill, no. 1308, with small pattern repeat (D. Patrick, YAT)

a 2/2 diamond twill with a small pattern repeat, 12Z x 10S threads per diamond (6Z x 5S between reverses).

Fragments of this weave have been found at 16-22 Coppergate, no. 1308 (fig. 8.4),[15] at Lloyds Bank, Pavement,[16] and at Parliament Street.[17] All three have counts of 15 x 12 per cm, and are Z-spun in one direction and S-spun in the other. There are no examples of the same pattern repeat among the 184 diamond twills from Elisenhof[18] nor has it been found on any other published site. To the three examples of the weave from York, a fourth may now be added, from a 5th-6th century Anglian cemetery at West Heslerton in North Yorkshire, some 20 miles north-east of York.[19] The West Heslerton piece has a count of 14Z x 10S and was found in a woman's grave, adhering to both faces of a square-headed brooch. A working hypothesis would be that these textiles with small repeating patterns were produced in Yorkshire to a traditional Anglian pattern.

There is another group of textiles which have some claim to being local products. These are the four piled fabrics which have been found, two at Pavement[20] and two at 16-22 Coppergate (nos. 1295, 1460). Although piled fabrics are known from several sites of NW Europe, dating from the 7th century to the 12th century,[21] in all cases in which the technique of construction has been identified, it has proved to be by working in the pile while weaving was in progress. Not so the four York examples, which have had the pile stitched in after weaving was completed: the threads of the pile pass through the cloth at varying angles to warp and weft and in places pierce the threads of the weave, indicating that a needle has been used. Perhaps the York weavers did not know the technique of pile-weaving, and were trying to imitate it by sewing the pile on to cloth which was already woven.

Foreign goods

Two examples of chevron twill, 18Z x 16S and 16Z x 12S per cm, nos. 1305 (fig. 8.5) and 1306, are comparable with the kind of cloth which Lise Bender Jørgensen has suggested is the famous *pallium fresonicum*, cloth traded or made by Frisians.[22] Other similar examples of chevron twill are known from late Saxon London.[23] Significantly, one of the York examples and possibly three of the London pieces are dyed with lichen purple, a dye which has not been found in any of the contemporary wool textiles from York or London (and indeed, the lichens from which the dye is produced do not grow in southern or eastern England). On balance, it would seem that these goods are foreign to York, perhaps from Frisia, which was known for its range of dyes. Similar chevron twills have been found at Elisenhof, in the Frisian region of North Germany. Several of them have proved to be from narrow bands, probably used as puttee-like leg bindings.[24]

There is reason to suspect that one group of linen finds may not be locally made. Most of the linens from the site are in tabby weave, but one curious mid 10th-century group of fragments consists of fourteen different weaves patchworked together. The weaves include tabby, in several different qualities (nos 1317, 1319-21, 1324-5, 1328), 2/1 twill (1331), 2/2 twill (1332), 2/1 chevron twill (1333), 2/2 chevron twill (1334), a honeycomb weave *Wabengewebe* (1336) and a plaited diamond mesh (1327).

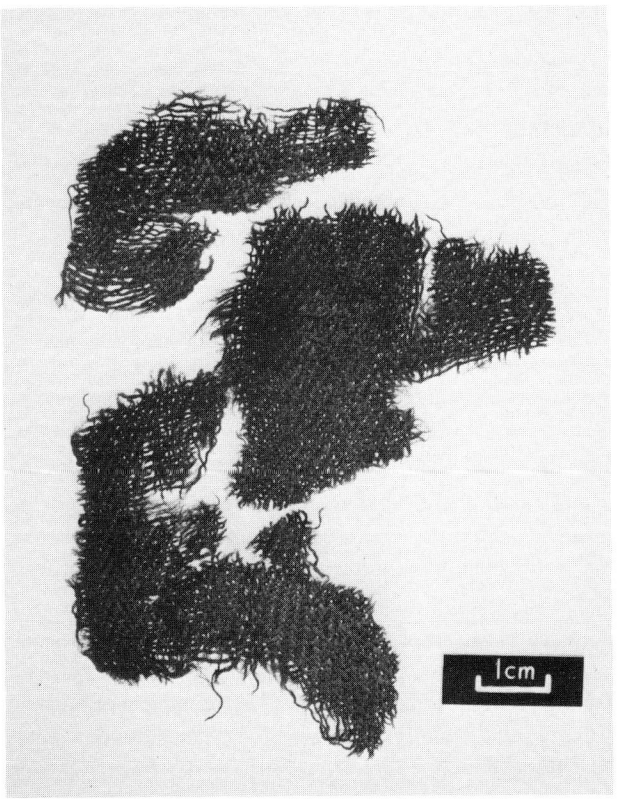

Fig. 8.5 2/2 chevron twill no. 1305 (K.M. Buck, YAT)

Fig. 8.6 Honeycomb weave (Wabengewebe) *no. 1336, a) weave diagram, b) overall effect (D. Patrick, YAT)*

The most important of the textiles in this group is the honeycomb weave (fig. 8.6). Other examples of the weave have been found at Valsgärde and Vendel in Sweden,[25] at Sievern[26] and Alladorf[27] in North Germany and Lise Bender Jørgensen has more recently found another at Osmarsleben, near Magdeburg in East Germany.[28] It seems likely that this weave belongs with the other patterned linens which are to be found in the German *Reihengräber* cemeteries,[29] such as ribbed twill (*Rippenköper*), rosette twill (*Rosettenköper*) and the tabby weaves with pattern of floating threads. Their prevalence on German sites may suggest that region as a place of origin, although France and southern Europe must also be possibilities (we have too few finds from these areas from which to judge).

Scandinavian influence

What of the Vikings, who were playing such an important role in the life of the town? Only two textile finds indicate a definite Scandinavian presence. They were found together in a mid 10th-century deposit, along with one of the piled textiles, some raw wool, a clump of horse hair and a collection of cords and yarns.

The first is a wool sock, no. 1309, worked in *nålebinding* technique (fig. 8.7). Dr Taylor has identified madder in the dark band around the ankle, but the rest of the sock may have been undyed. There appears to have been a repair patch originally around the ball of the foot, although only the outline, in stitching, has survived. The *nålebinding* stitch of the ankle region is very simple (fig. 8.8), although it is possible that a more complicated stitch was in use in the foot part. Unfortunately this area is rather matted on the inside and difficult to decipher.

This is the very first find of *nålebinding* anywhere in England, although in Scandinavia it is relatively common. Examples of this technique date back to the 3rd or 4th century in Sweden and there are several Viking-Age and Medieval examples, including another sock from Medieval Uppsala.[30]

The second piece to suggest a Scandinavian connection is a 2/2 chevron (herringbone twill), no. 1303 (fig. 8.9). This is one of the most common weaves from 16-22 Coppergate, but the fragment under discussion is heavily matted and has a smooth, dark, naturally pigmented warp and a soft, pale weft. These features are not found in English textiles, but are typical of Scandinavian, especially from the 10th century onwards. There is, for example, a similar piece in non-reversed twill, from Hedeby, identified as a fragment of hose.[31]

Of course it is not possible to know whether these two finds were brought in from Scandinavia, or whether they were made in York by resident Scandinavians - or indeed by Anglians copying Scandinavian goods. There can be little doubt, however, that the sock and the matted twill together indicate a Scandinavian presence in the population.

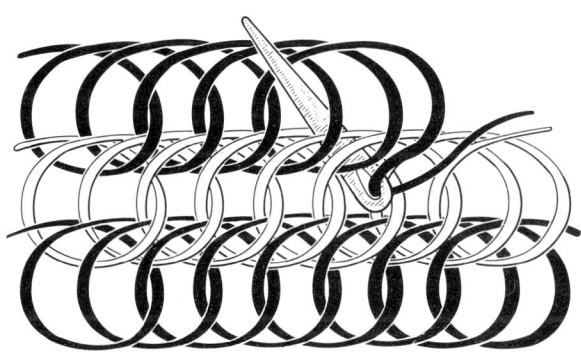

Fig. 8.7 (above) Sock in nålebinding *no. 1309 (M.S. Duffy, YAT)*

Fig. 8.8 (left) The nålebinding *stitch of the ankle region of sock no. 1309. In Hansen's terminology (supra), the technique is uu/ooo F2 (D. Patrick, YAT)*

Fig. 8.9 (below) Heavily felted 2/2 chevron twill no. 1303, with dark warp and pale weft (K.M. Buck, YAT)

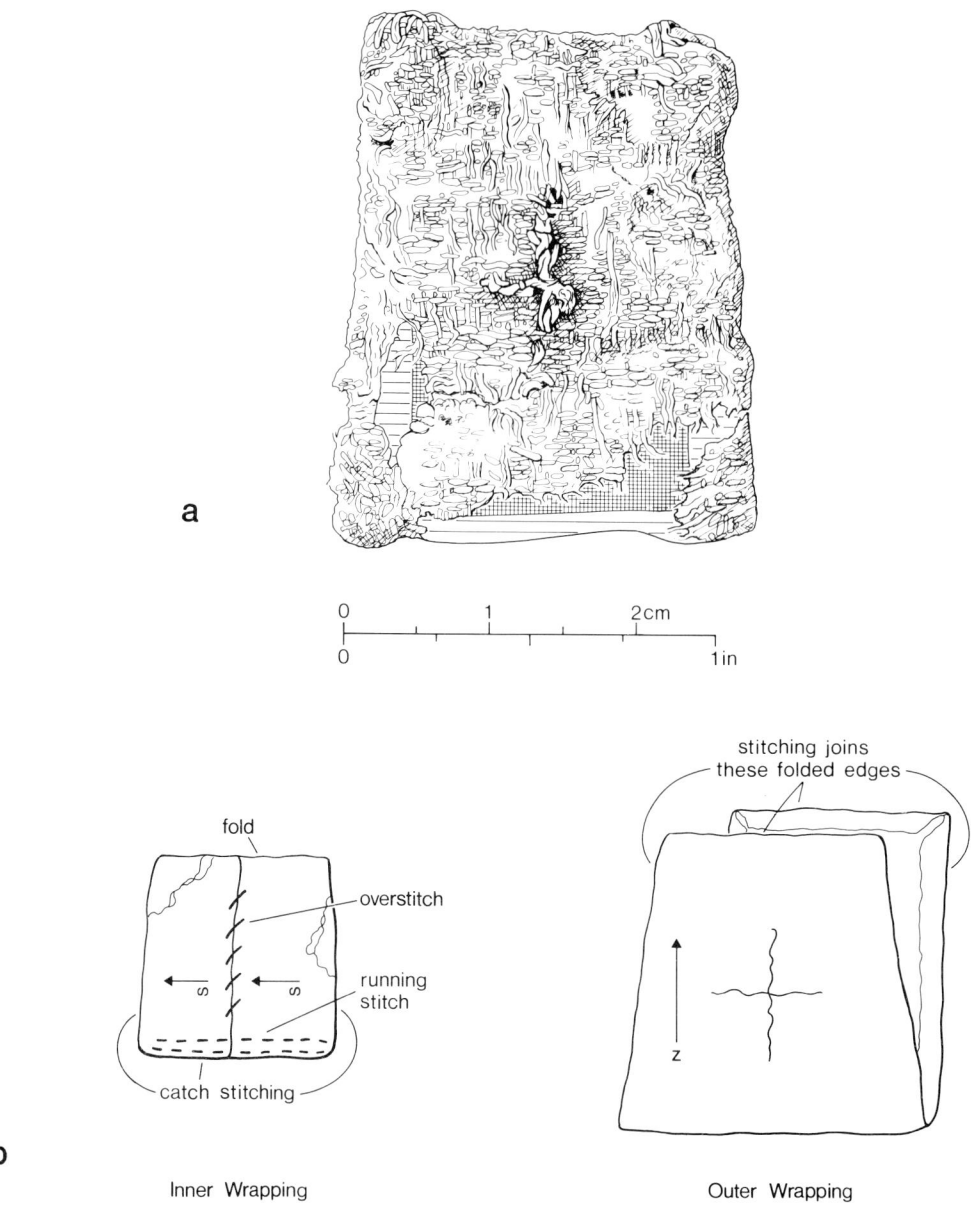

a

0   1   2cm

0   1in

fold

overstitch

running stitch

catch stitching

s   s

b

Inner Wrapping

stitching joins these folded edges

z

Outer Wrapping

Fig. 8.10   Silk reliquary pouch no. 1408, showing a) the pouch, b) the construction of the outer and inner pouches (D. Patrick, YAT)

Silks

It is perhaps in the trade links of Viking-Age York that the influence of the Scandinavians is most evident. A certain number of exotic finds from the Near and Middle East have been recovered from the 16-22 Coppergate excavation, including a 10th-century coin from Samarkand and a cowrie shell from the Red Sea or the Gulf of Aden.[32] Silks are also present in surprising numbers, representing 22% of the Anglo-Scandinavian textiles.

The silks include a compound twill, used for a small relic pouch, no. 1408 (fig. 8.10). This twill would have come from some Byzantine or Islamic weaving centre, before being made up, perhaps in this country, into a holder for holy relics. There are also four pieces of silk ribbon, one dyed with the Mediterranean insect dye, kermes (nos. 1353 - 5, 1407). The ribbons appear to have been used as a decorative edging for garments, perhaps at the cuff or tunic-opening.

Silk tabbies, variously dyed, had also been made up into head-dresses in a simple cap style (figs. 8.11, 8.12). These head-dresses have no parallels in contemporary Anglo-Saxon art, but are not unusual from Viking sites in the British Isles. One example comes from nearby 5 Coppergate,[33] one from Lincoln[34] and others from Dublin (Heckett, *infra* pp 85-89). It is possible that this is a peculiarly Scandinavian or Anglo-Scandinavian fashion.

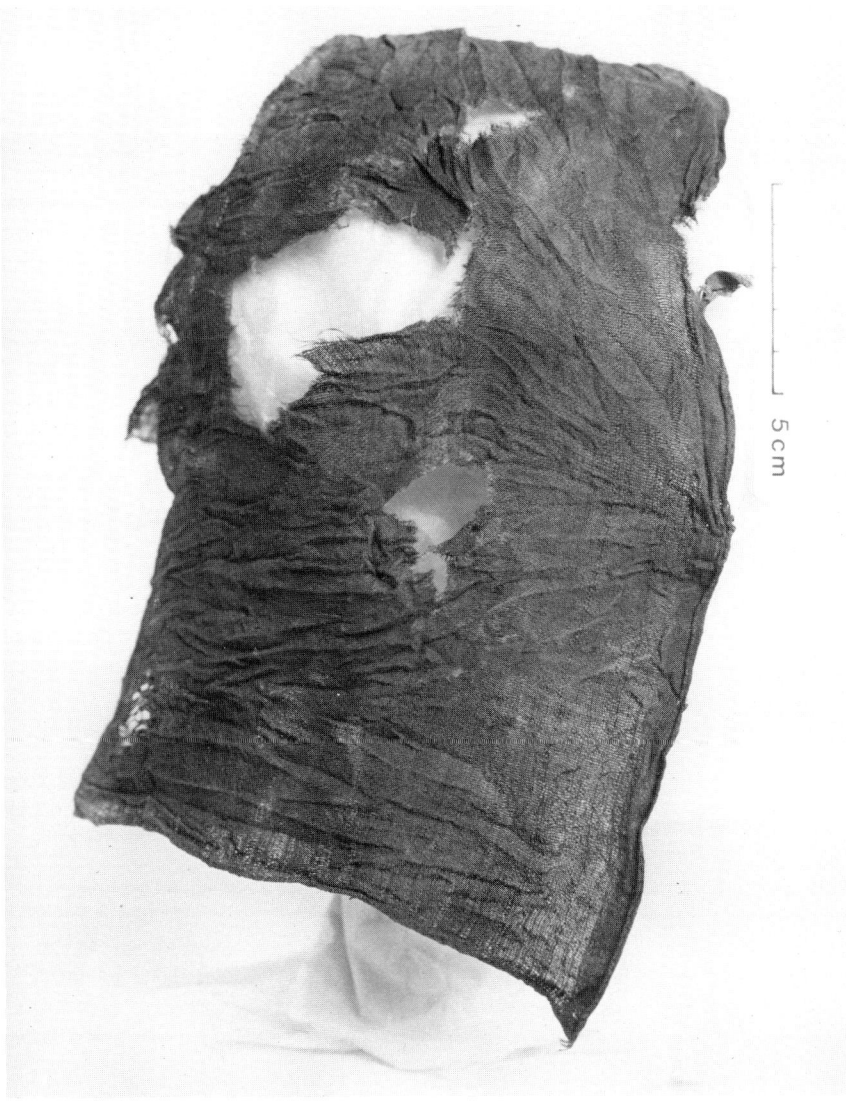

5 cm

Fig. 8.11   Silk head-dress no. 1332 (M.S. Duffy, YAT)

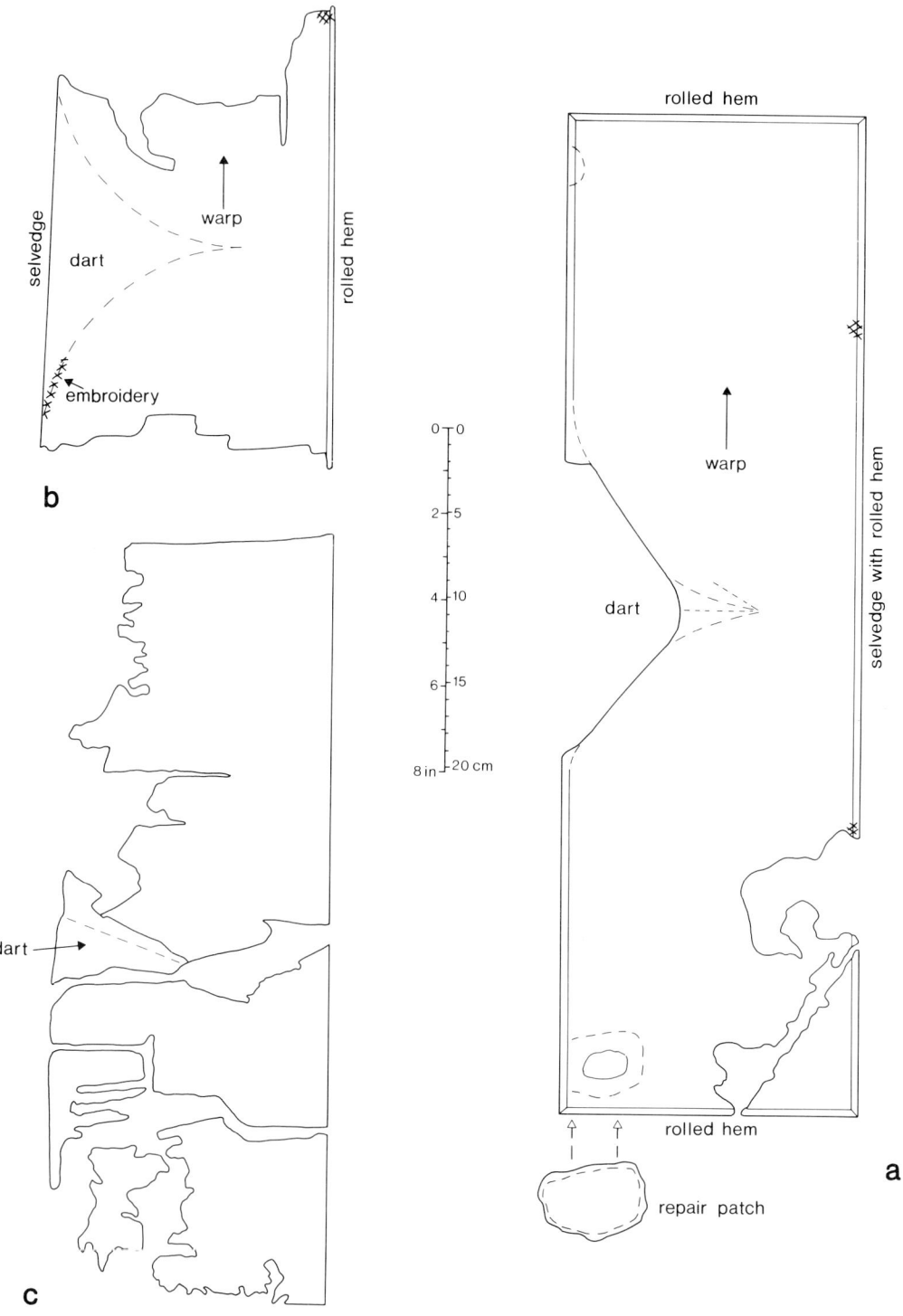

Fig. 8.12   Construction of silk head-dresses from a) 16-22 Coppergate number 1332, b) 5-7 Coppergate no. 651,
c) Saltergate, Lincoln (D. Patrick, YAT)

70

Conclusion

In summary, only two finds, the sock and its associated piece of twill, indicate a Viking presence. Most of the remaining textiles are little different from those of the Yorkshire Anglians before the Viking invasions or the Saxons in the South of England. Some of the finds also suggest a continuation of the pre-Viking trade with Frisia and the Rhineland.

It is, of course, possible that Scandinavian merchants were now in charge of the Frisian traffic. The silks, from Arab or Byzantine workshops, are even more likely to have passed along Scandinavian-controlled trade routes. For example, Scandinavian merchants are known to have travelled from the Baltic via the Russian rivers and into the heart of the Arab world. The amount of silk from the site, almost a quarter of the woven finds, must surely owe much to the enterprise of these merchants and to the wealth which was generated by their trading activities.

References

1. A. MacGregor, 'Industry and Commerce in Anglo-Scandinavian York' in R.A. Hall (ed), *Viking Age York and the North* (*CBA Research Report 27*), 1978, 37

2. W. Levison, *England and the Continent in the 8th century,* Oxford, 1946, 49-59

3. R.A. Hall, 'Markets of the Danelaw' in E. Roesdahl, J. Graham-Campbell, P. Connor, K. Pearson (edd), *The Vikings in England,* London, 1981, 95-140

4. R.A. Hall, *The Viking Dig*, London, 1984; R.A. Hall, *The Archaeology of York* 8 (series ed. P. V. Addyman), in prep.

5. G.D. Gaunt, 'Geological report on the lithic spindle whorls from 16-22 Coppergate', in P. Walton (ed), *The Archaeology of York* 17/-, in prep.

6. L. Bender Jørgensen, T. Skov, 'Trabjerg', *Acta Archaeologica* 50, 1979, 133

7. H. Hellmuth Andersen, P.J. Crabb, H.J. Madsen, *Århus Søndervold*, Århus, 1971, 225-8

8. R. Blomqvist, A.W. Martensson, 'Thulegrävningen 1961', *Archaeologica Lundensia* II, Lund, 1963, 173

9. A.R. Hall in *AY* 14/-, in prep.

10. M.L. Ryder, 'Fleece changes in sheep', in M. Jones, G. Dimbleby, '*The Environment of Man: the Iron Age to the Anglo-Saxon Period*, (*BAR International Series 87*), 1981, 225

11. F. Pritchard, 'Late Saxon Textiles from the City of London', *Medieval Archaeology* 28, 1984, 72-3

12. A.R. Hall, R.A. Hall, G.W. Taylor, P. Tomlinson, P. Walton, 'Dyeplants from Viking York', *Antiquity* 58, 58-60; P. Tomlinson, 'Use of vegetative remains in the identification of dyeplants from waterlogged 9th - 10th century AD deposits at York', *Journal of Archaeological Science* 1985, 269-283

13. A.R. Hall, personal communication

14. One diamond twill (number 1382) has Z-spun yarn in both systems, but it lacks the high warp-count of the Scandinavian examples and has a pattern repeat which is typical of Bender Jørgensen's Frisian cloth

15. P. Walton, 'Textiles, cordage and raw fibre from 16-22 Coppergate', *The Archaeology of York* 17/5, 1989

16. P. Walton in A. MacGregor, 'Anglo-Scandinavian finds from Lloyds Bank, Pavement and other sites', *AY* 17/3, 1982, number 664

17. P. Walton in D. Tweddle, 'Finds from Parliament Street and other sites in the city centre', *AY* 17/4, 1986, number 956

18. H.-J. Hundt, *Die Textil- und Schnurreste aus der frühgeschichtlichen Wurt Elisenhof, Elisenhof* 4, Frankfurt am Main, 1981, 24-32

19. West Heslerton grave HP 2BA 606: P. Walton in D. Powlesland in prep.

20. J. Hedges in A. MacGregor (1982), numbers 579, 581

21. E. Guðjónsson, 'Forn Röggvarvefnadur', *Arbok hins Islenzka Fornleifafelags*, 1962, 12-71

22. L. Bender Jørgensen, *'Prehistoric Scandinavian Textiles'*, Copenhagen, 1986, 361-2

23. F. Pritchard, (1984), 53, 55, 69

24. H.-J. Hundt, (1981), 47-9

25. G. Arwidsson, *Valsgärde* 6, Uppsala, 1954, 101-3

26. H. -J. Hundt, 'Textilereste' in P. Paulsen, H. Schach-Dörges, 'Das alamanische Gräberfeld von Giengen an der Brenz', *Forschungen und Berichte zur Vor- und Frühgeschichte in Baden-Württemberg* 10, 1980, 153-5, 160

27. *Ibid*

28. L. Bender Jørgensen (1986), 365 n.84

29. Summarised from the work of H.-J. Hundt by L. Bender Jørgensen (1986), 356

30. A.M. Franzen, 'En medeltida socka i nålning', *Årsboken Uppland*, 1963, 38-47

31. I. Hagg, 'Die Textilfunde aus dem Hafen von Haithabu', *Ausgrabungen in Haithabu* 20, 1984, 20-24

32. R.A. Hall, *The Viking Dig*, London 1984

33. A. Muthesius in A. MacGregor (1982), 132-6

34. *Ibid*

9. Spinning implements of the Viking Age from Elisenhof in the light of ethnological studies

Gertrud Grenander Nyberg
Stockholm

The Viking-Age village, now called Elisenhof, was excavated at the end of the 1950's and during the 1960's. The excavation and finds have been described in a series of publications. The first volume is written by Albert Bantelmann, who was the leader of the excavations.[1] Textiles are dealt with in the fourth volume by H.-J. Hundt; the fifth volume, on wooden finds, is written by M. Szabó, Janken Myrdal and the author of this paper (her work on the leather finds is also included there.)

Elisenhof, near Tönning, formerly named Olversum, was situated on the northern bank of the River Eider, which formed a part of the important trade route from the North Sea to Hedeby (now Haithabu) and the Baltic. It was a typical farming village, at least as it appears in the excavation, which was unable to take in the whole village area. It was probably inhabited by Frisians.[2]

The buildings were placed on the high river bank beside a marshy piece of land, which was flooded annually. The main long-houses consisted of a living area and a section for cattle. There are also smaller buildings with peat walls, some of these being so-called 'pit houses'. The long-houses had walls made of wattle and daub.

Loomweights have been found in both types of house. The weights are usually made of clay and are disc-shaped, with a hole in the middle and impressed marks. (Like the other finds from Elisenhof the loomweights are in the Landesmuseum für Vor- und Frühgeschichte, Schloss Gottorp, Schleswig.) They have been found in so many places that one may suppose that weaving was common and carried out on warp-weighted looms. This is also clear from Hundt's description of the textiles.[3] In Elisenhof only woven textiles of wool are preserved, but there was also flax cultivation as well as linen weaving. Hundt finds the weights rather heavy, which indicates that the weaves are comparatively coarse.[4]

The village was probably abandoned in the 12th century, but objects of wood, leather, clay and bone have been preserved in the ground, where the composition was partly of dung.[5] On the other hand the iron objects found are few (and like the ceramics not yet published). The wooden objects, like the other organic materials are considered to date mostly from the 8th and 9th centuries.

Hundt asserts that bands, too, were made in Elisenhof, and some implements connected with band weaving have been found. There are also some objects that have been used for preparing fibre materials. In this article I am concentrating on spinning. In order to find out how the objects were used I have sought parallels from later times, partly from recent ethnological material. Principally three different types of spindle and spinning will be described here.

Spinning equipment from Elisenhof

In Elisenhof some objects have been found which might have been used for spinning. There are no objects, however, that can without doubt be described as distaffs for holding the fibre material. They might be very simple sticks, the use of which is difficult to determine from their shape alone.

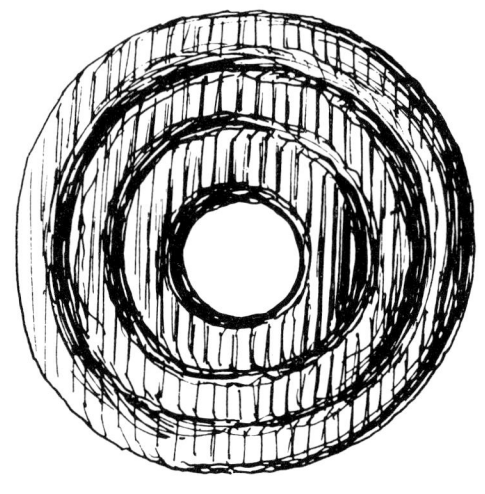

Fig. 9.1 Small whorl of oak from Haus 26, Elisenhof.
Diameter 5.0 - 5.4cm. Inv. no. 265

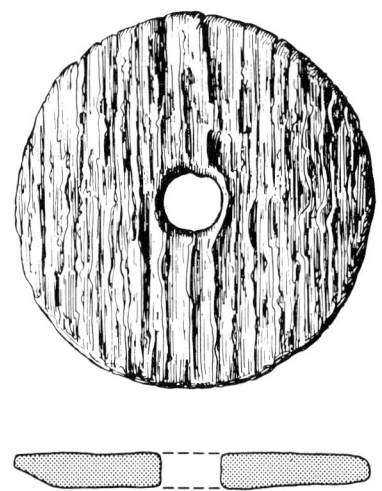

Fig. 9.2 Big whorl of oak from Elisenhof (no. 80).
Diameter 10.5cm

Spindle whorls of many different sorts have been found. There are whorls made of clay, bone, stone (sandstone) and wood. The forms vary: some are disc-shaped, sometimes convex on the upper side, others are conical or double conical. One small wooden whorl (fig. 9.1) has a special shape.[6] This shows that spinning methods have varied, depending principally on the quality of the spinning material and the thread required.

Sticks for holding the whorls also have different forms. A great many spool-shaped and double-pointed pins have been found. Not all of them can be classified as used for spinning. This is especially true of the short ones that cannot hold much yarn. Such pins could at this period have been used as a sort of hook on a fishing-line, an implement found in many countries, for example, in NW Europe and Finland.[7] The inhabitants of Elisenhof had, of course, much opportunity for fishing. Other pins can possibly be considered as instruments used for closing leather bags and suchlike.[8]

The Finnish ethnologist V. Vallinheimo describes in her thesis different types of spindles.[9] The shortest spindle stick she shows is 20cm long. Pins in Elisenhof which are shorter than 15cm are difficult to classify as spinning implements as these must be long enough to allow space for winding up the yarn. As many of them are broken, it is impossible to determine the original length.

Some sticks can be defined as tools for spinning (fig. 9.3). They have a hook or notch to fasten the strand during the spinning process. One double-pointed wooden stick with a smooth surface is 15.5cm long and decorated on the middle part like one of the same shape but of bone.[10] As the bone one has a notch for fastening the strand, both must be spinning sticks. Some sticks have a swelling, others are of uniform thickness. A few have a swelling near the top. It is supposed that a loop was made

74

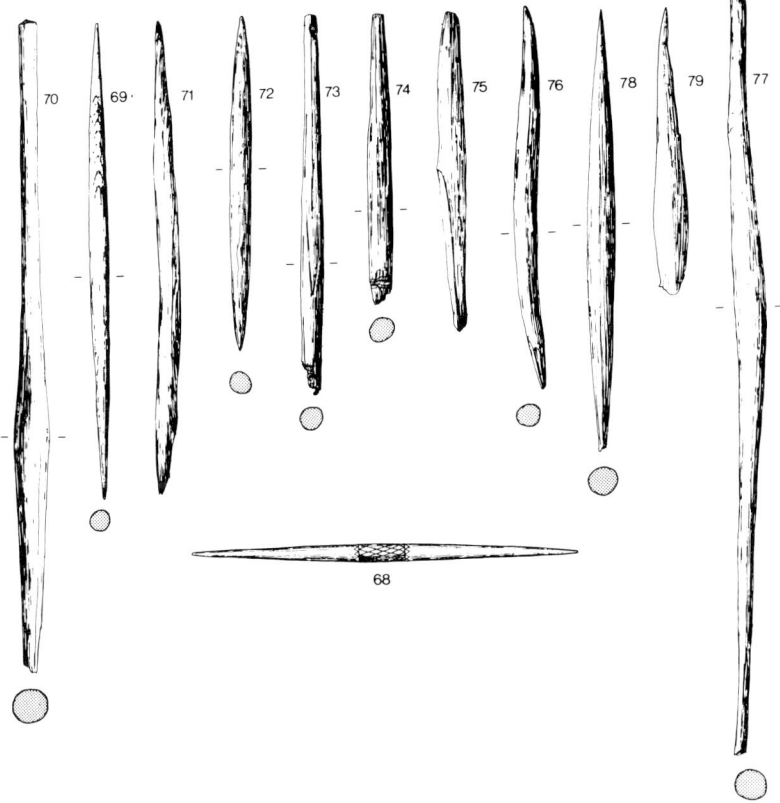

Fig. 9.3 Pointed sticks of wood from Elisenhof. Some could have been used as spindle sticks. One stick of bone with the same shape and decoration as no. 68 (15.5cm) has a scoring for fastening a fibre strand.

around the top of the stick, if there was no hook or notch,[11]something especially necessary when the spinner let the spindle drop down during spinning.

Some of the spinning sticks have been analysed with regard to material. Many are made of yew, eg the decorated one mentioned above; others are made from the spindle tree, but maple has also been used. Spinners have often apparently chosen hard wood.

Spinning with a spindle fitted with a whorl

The question now is how these sticks might have been used. The two principal types of hand-spindle are the bottom-weighted, where the whorl is placed on the lower part of the stick, and the top-weighted one, where the whorl is placed on to the upper part of the stick. Unfortunately the whorls are seldom preserved on the sticks, and there is no example at Elisenhof. A bottom-weighted spindle from Juellinge (Lolland in Denmark) from the 1st century AD, and a top-weighted one from the Norwegian Oseberg find from the Viking Age, both found with a whorl on the stick, can be taken as examples of the two types (figs. 9.4, 9.5).[12] At the Novgorod excavations of AD 900 onwards three sticks with whorls were found. They are bottom-weighted.[13]

One of the principal methods for spinning with a hand-spindle is the one in which the spindle goes round freely without support after having been set in rotation by hand. The whorl prolongs the movement and the fibre-strand is stretched out by gravity until the spindle is near the floor, when the thread must be wound up on the stick. Naturally the easiest way is to rotate the spindle clockwise, and so a Z-spun thread is produced.[14] The freely rotating spindle is often bottom-weighted.

Another method is to give the spindle a support, at least at the beginning of the spinning, by rolling the spindle against the thigh (fig. 9.6). The rolling is usually done towards the knee, and this is the easiest and most natural way. Thus the spindle can be under eye control while it is freely rotating during the last moments of the spinning procedure. Spinning according to this method is best done with a top-weighted spindle.[15] When plying two or more threads the twist is made in the opposite direction.

A free spindle demands a strong and long-fibred material, because gravity acting on the hanging weight of the spindle stretches the strand. The Z-spun thread is also used as warp, which is especially strained in the warp-weighted loom. The method with the top-weighted spindle, with support during the first part of the spinning, does not strain the fibres and is suitable for short-fibred wool and flax as well as for cotton. Such a thread has been preferred as weft in woollen weaves. This combination of

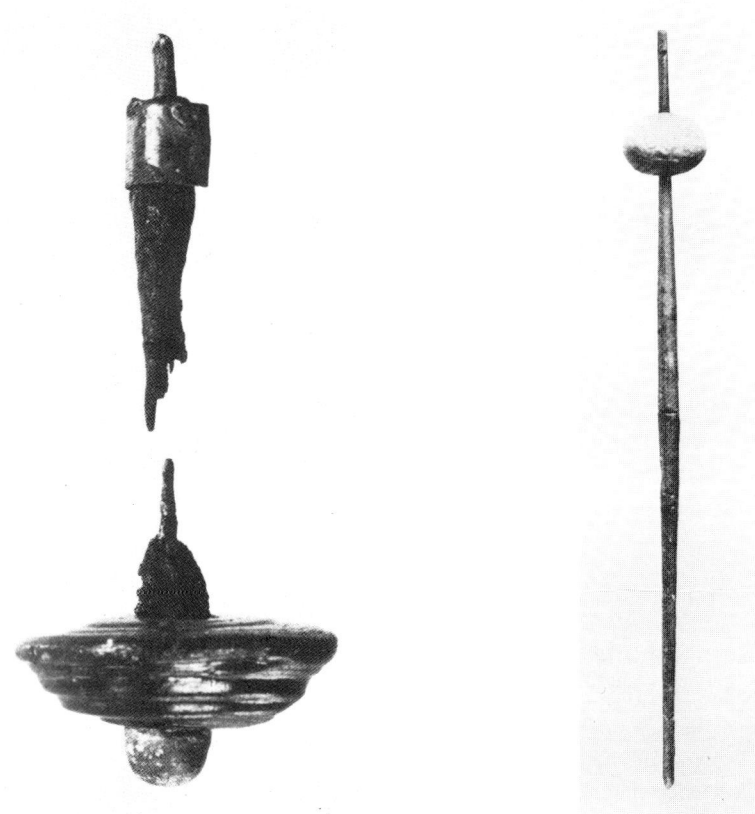

Fig. 9.4 Wooden spindle with a glass whorl from Juellinge, Denmark, 1st century AD. After Munksgaard

Fig. 9.5 Wooden spindle with a stone whorl from the Norwegian Oseberg find. 9th century AD. 29.3cm. After Grieg

Fig. 9.6 Spinning with the spindle first rolling along the thigh, then free rotating. Photographs from the first part of the 20th century in the province of Värmland, Sweden. After Jirlow

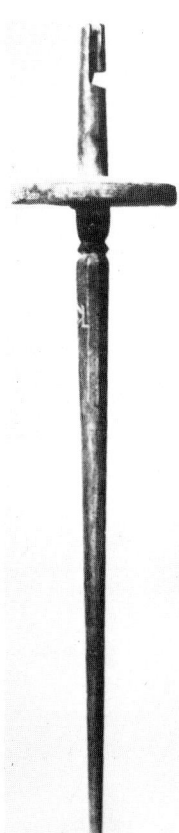

Fig. 9.7(left) Big spindle from the province of Dalarna, Sweden. For plying. After Levander

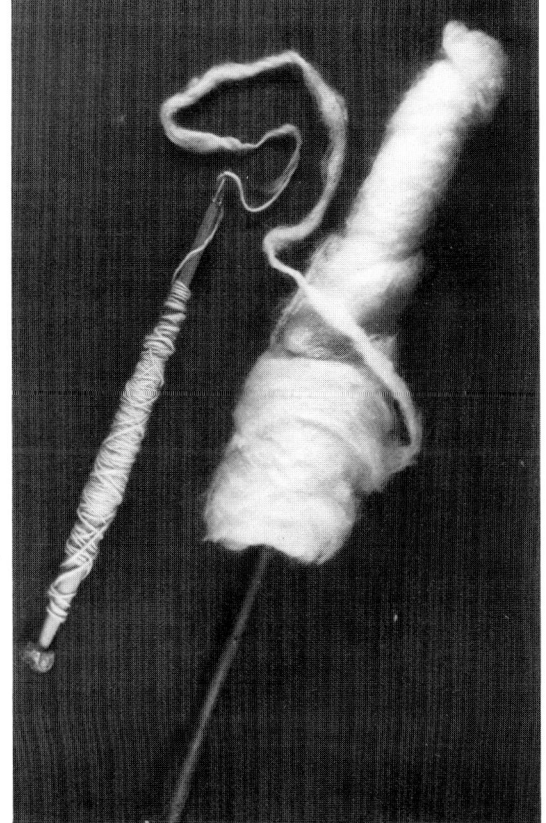

Fig. 9.8(right) Spindle and distaff from Crete. Used 1979, later photographed by Kjellgren

Z-spun warp and S-spun weft dominates in the wool cloth from Elisenhof.[16] It is especially important for making cloth tight and suitable for felting. The warp in a horizontal band weave is not so strained and an S-spun yarn can be used. There are other examples, too, of the importance of the different strains on a spindle.

M. Hald has stated that no whorls have been found before the end of the Bronze Age in Denmark and E. Munksgaard thinks that it is probable that wooden whorls, which have decayed in the ground, were used earlier on, and this is, of course, quite possible.[17] Hald writes that you could also spin without a whorl.[18]

To make very thick yarn and cord people have used big top-weighted spindles, entirely of wood, for example in Dalarna, Sweden (fig. 9.7).[19] Accordingly I have interpreted two round discs from Elisenhof, each with a hole in the middle, as whorls from big spindles (fig. 9.2). They are made of oak. In Hundt's investigation of the textiles it appears that most of the wool cords, and there are more than 200 of them, are S-spun and Z-twined.[20] Thus they have probably been spun with a top-weighted spindle.[21]

Spinning with a spindle without a whorl

There is a spinning method where no whorl is needed to prolong the rotating movement, which can be observed in the south of Europe, for example in Greece (figs. 9.8, 9.9). By this method of spinning the hand never leaves the top of the stick, but rotates all the time, while the arm stretches further and further out with the twisted strand and the thread grows ever longer. When the arm is stretched out to the full length, the thread must be wound on the stick, which may carry some sort of small lump,

Fig. 9.9 Crete: after spinning, the thread is wound up on the spindle stick. Photograph 1979, GGN

78

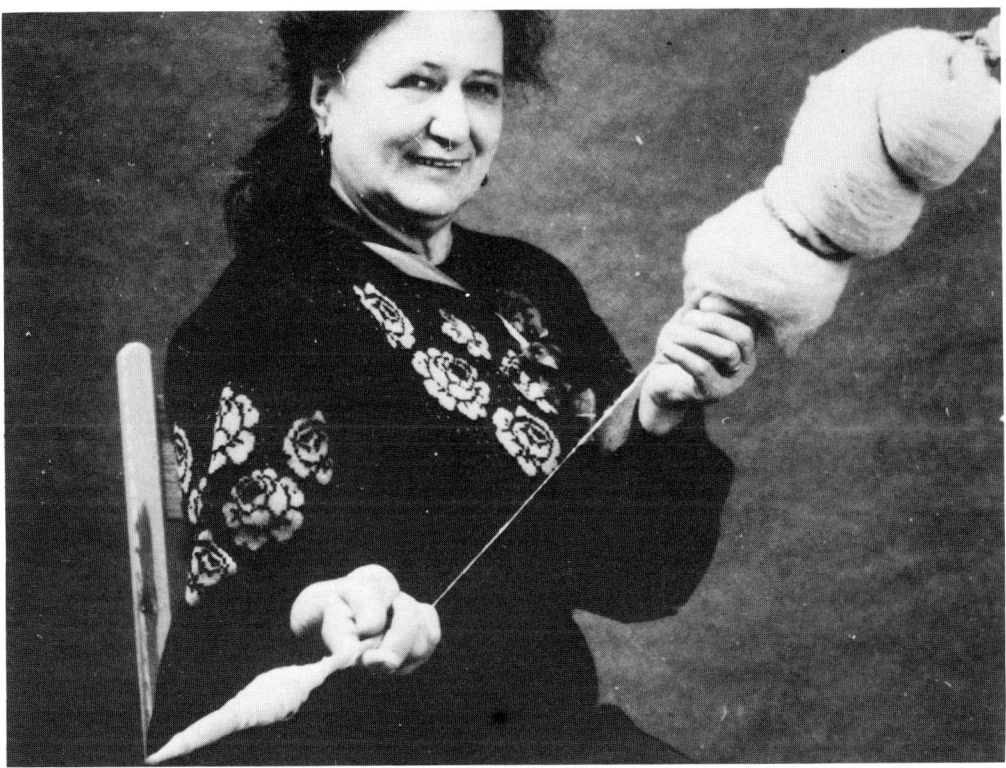

*Fig. 9.10 Spinning with a nearly horizontal stick without whorl, demonstrated by
a Yugoslav woman in Nora, Sweden, 1987. Photograph Källstig*

eg a piece of dried fruit, to hold the yarn (as I have observed on Crete). Some spinners hold the strand against the top of the stick without making a loop or fastening it to any hook or notch. (This method was demonstrated for me by a Yugoslav immigrant in 1987 in Nora, Sweden (fig. 9.10).)

Among the finds in the Hjortspring boat (*c.* 200 BC) there is a stick with a swelling, that might have acted as a stabiliser during the rotation of the stick when spinning a thread. There are also later examples of this form.[22] In her book of 1956 V. Vallinheimo shows spinning sticks without any special whorls on them (fig 9.11).[23] These are from Finland and from Rumania, and greatly resemble some of the sticks from Elisenhof, which have a slight thickening and seem to be longer than the others. Vallinheimo writes that she has found such sticks not only in eastern Europe, but also in Medieval pictures in western Europe. C. Östling, who has studied Medieval wall- and glass-paintings in Swedish churches, has found spindles with whorls as well as without (fig. 9.12).[24] She interprets the missing whorls, however, as artistic neglect.

With spindle sticks without whorls one can spin both fine and thick yarn, both Z- and S-spun. For Z-spinning the spindle stick is rotated by hand all the time, as is described above. For S-spinning the spindle stick lies in the hand nearly horizontally and it rotates there, principally turned by the thumb, as was demonstrated by the Yugoslav immigrant (fig. 9.10). This method without whorl demands of course more work than the one with whorl, since it prolongs the hand movement. When spinning with a free spindle, one must also stop the spinning quite often to wind up the thread, since the length of the arm is shorter than the distance from the hand down to the floor when spinning wih a free spindle. In

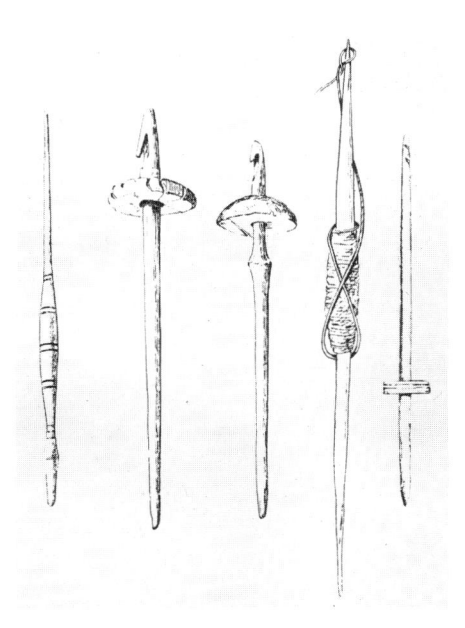

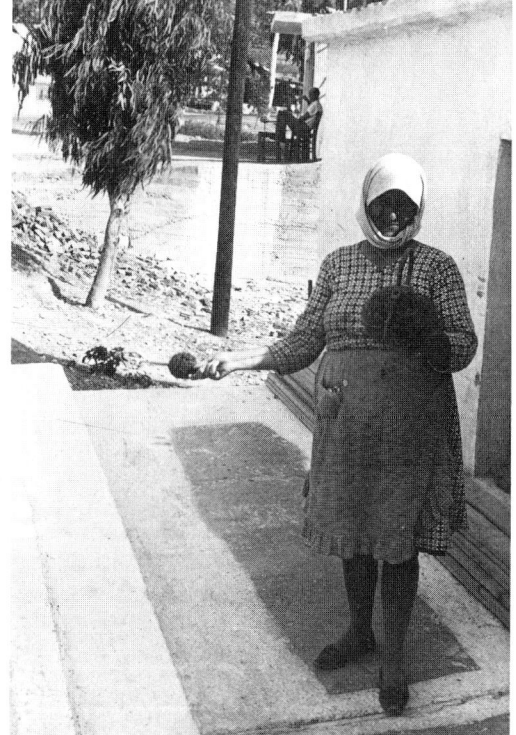

Fig. 9.11 (above, left) Spindles from Finland. Two of them have no whorl. After Vallinheimo

Fig. 9.12 (above, right) Adam digs and Eve spins. The spindle has no whorl. Glass painting from Hejde old church on Gotland. Photograph ATA, Riksantikvarieämbetet, Stockholm

Fig. 9.13 (left) Spinning short fibres from a ball on a distaff. At Mycenae, Greece, 1966. Photograph GGN

both cases the spinner can be standing or walking (fig 9.13).

Preparatory spinning

The horizontal stick is suitable for loosely spun yarn and for preparatory spinning, where a continuous strand is made ready for the actual spinning to take place. The first part of the spinning against the leg may also be described as preparatory spinning. The question is whether it is this sort of pre-spun yarn that is placed on the short distaff pictured in the well-known vase painting from Orvieto (490-480 BC) (fig. 9.14).[25] The woman in the picture is apparently spinning flax fibres, as she is wetting the yarn with saliva from her lips. This might explain the shape of the short distaffs from the Rhineland that J.P. Wild shows in his book on textile manufacture in the Roman provinces. Some of them especially look very much like spindles (fig. 9.15).[26] Spinning implements of almost the same shape have also been found in the Oseberg find (fig. 9.16) [27] - M. Hoffmann has proposed that they were used as distaffs.[28] They may have been used both as spindles for pre-spinning and as distaffs. When carding of wool started during the Middle Ages pre-spinning of short wool was not needed any longer. Spinning of flax with a short distaff of this type is shown in a 20th century picture from the north of Dalarna in Sweden (fig. 9.17).[29] Swedish ethnologists at the beginning of this century took this as an example of long-lived cultural traditions stemming from classical antiquity.[30]

Fig. 9.14 Spinning scene on a Greek vase from Orvieto, Italy. 5th century BC.

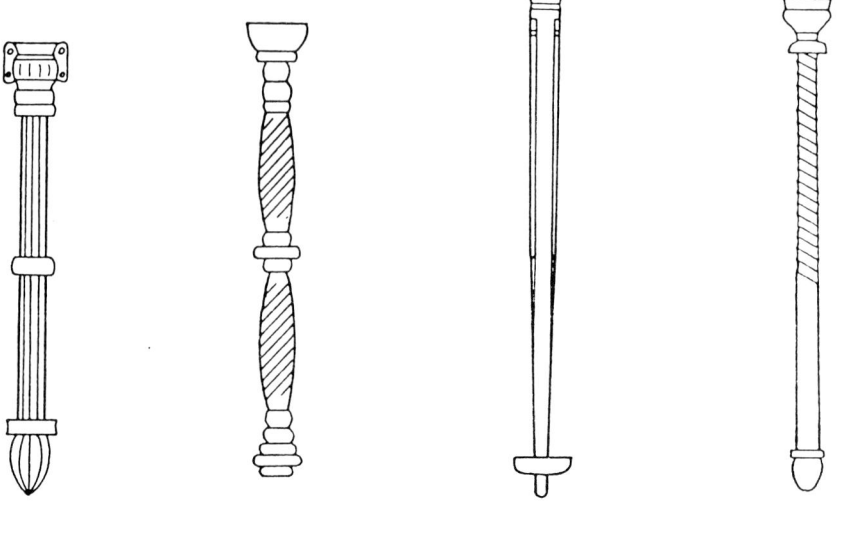

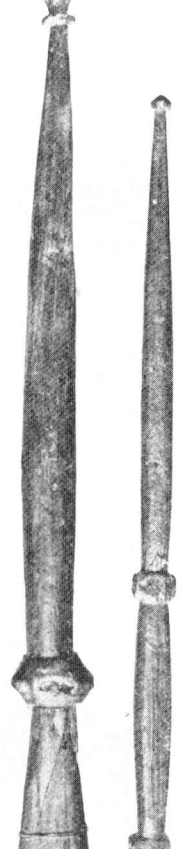

Fig. 9.15 (above) Distaffs or spindles from the Rhineland. After Wild

Fig. 9.16 (left) Distaffs (38.5 and 34.2cm) from the Oseberg finds. After Grieg

Fig. 9.17 Spinning with a short distaff in Dalarna, Sweden, at the beginning of the 20th century. After Jirlow

References

1. A. Bantelmann, *Die frühgeschichtliche Marschensiedlung beim Elisenhof in Eiderstedt: Landschaftsgeschichte und Baufunde, Elisenhof* I, 1975

2. *Ibid*, 188

3. H.-J. Hundt, *Die Textil- und Schnurreste aus der frühgeschichtlichen Wurt Elisenhof, Elisenhof* 4, 1981, 69

4. K. E. Behre, *Die Pflanzenreste aus der frühgeschichtlichen Wurt Elisenhof, Elisenhof* 2, 1976, 18; Hundt (1981), 87

5. J. Myrdal, 'Elisenhof och järnålderns boskapsskötsel i Nordvästeuropa', *Fornvännen* 1984, 73-92

6. O. Rydbeck, *Den medeltida borgen i Skanör, Kungl. Humanistiska Vetenskapssamfundet i Lund* 20, 1935, 13

7. K. Eldjárn, R. Norberg, K. Vilkuna, 'Fiskeredskap', *Kulturhistoriskt Lexikon för Nordisk Medeltid* 4, Malmö, 1959; U.T. Sirelius, *Suomen Kansanomaista Kulttuuria* I, Helsinki, 1919,70

8. M. Szabó, G. Grenander Nyberg, J. Myrdal, *Die Holzfunde aus der frühgeschichtlichen Wurt Elisenhof, Elisenhof* 5, 1985,154

9. V. Vallinheimo, *Das Spinnen in Finnland, Kansatieteellinen Arkisto* 11, 1956, 131

10. M. Tiessen, *Die Tierknochenfunde von Haithabu und Elisenhof* (unpublished dissertation), 1970

11. J.P. Wild, *Textile Manufacture in the Northern Roman Provinces*, Cambridge, 1970, 157; Vallinheimo (1956), 131

12. E Munksgaard, *Oldtidsdragter*, Copenhagen, 1974, 27; S. Grieg, *Kongsgaarden, Osebergfundet* 2, Oslo, 1928, 181

13. B.A. Kolchin, *Novgorodskie Drevnosti, Derevjannye Izdelija*, Archeologija SSSR, 1968, 161

14. G. Grenander Nyberg, 'Über die Z- und die S-Drehung von Garnen,' in I. Hägg, *Die Textilfunde aus dem Hafen von Haithabu, Ausgrabungen in Haithabu* 20, 1984, 287-88

15. L. Warburg, *Spindebog*, Copenhagen, 1974, 86

16. M. Hald, *Olddanske Tekstiler, Nordiske Fortidsminder* 5, 1950, 131; Hundt (1981), 10-33

17. Hald (1950), 133; Munksgaard (1974), 27

18. See Crowfoot, *Methods of Hand Spinning in Egypt and the Sudan*, Halifax, 1931, 9

19. L. Levander, *Övre Dalarnas Bondekultur, 3 Hem och Hemarbete, Kungl. Gustav Adolf Akad. för Folklivsforskning* 11, 3, 1947, 180

20. Hundt (1981), 82

21. See R. Jirlow, 'Sländspinning i Sverige', in S. Erixon, S. Wallin (edd), *Svenska Kulturbilder*, Band 5, Part 9, Stockholm, 1931

22. H.C. Broholm, M. Hald, *Costumes of the Bronze Age in Denmark*, Copenhagen, 1940, 108; G. Rosenberg, *Hjortspringfundet, Nordiske Fortidsminder* 3, 1937, 68

23. Vallinheimo (1956), 131, 136

24. Chr. Östling, *När Adam grävde och Eva spann* (manuscript, Acad, paper), Stockholm, 1984

25. R.J. Forbes, *Studies in Ancient Technology* 4, Leiden, 1964, 166

26. Wild (1970), 155

27. Grieg (1928), 109-110

28. M. Hoffmann, 'Spinning', *Kulturhistoriskt Lexikon för Nordisk Medeltid* 16, Mälmo, 1971

29. Jirlow (1931), 117

30. M. Collin, 'Om primitiva spinnmetoder', *Rig* 1921, 75-80; N. Lithberg, 'Den korta herkuln eller handrocken', *Fataburen* 1930, 151-169

10. Some silk and wool head-coverings from Viking Dublin: uses and origins - an enquiry

Elizabeth Heckett

Cork

This paper presents an opportunity to describe very briefly and generally aspects of some of the textile material from 10th- and 11th- century levels of the Viking-Age town of Dublin. These are but a tiny part of the textile finds from the National Museum of Ireland's excavations of 1975-81 in Fishamble Street/St. John's Lane directed by Dr Patrick Wallace. The majority of the textile finds, which amounted to over 2000 pieces, are being analysed by Frances Pritchard of the Museum of London. There were, however, a group of 65 textiles which were kindly made available to the present writer for study, some of which seemed to represent caps, scarves or kerchiefs and bands of both wool and silk.[1]

Of this total thirteen pieces seemed to be caps or remnants of caps. Nine textiles may well have been used as headbands and fourteen rectangular items may be described as scarves or kerchiefs. Examples of these exist in both wool and silk. There is one silk piece measuring 870mm x 240mm which is larger than the rest and may also have been used as a head-covering. All the cloth, both wool and silk, was made in tabby weave. The wool pieces and one type of silk cloth were woven from Z-twisted yarn. A second type of silk used Z-twisted warp yarn and a weft yarn without a twist; a third was made from a silk thread which lacks twist in either system.

The caps

The caps were made from a rectangle of material measuring roughly 480mm x 170mm, doubled over and sewn at one side to form the back. Whether the piece is made from silk or wool there is a clearly defined pattern to which the cap conforms. From the nine examples of which large parts have survived, an average or type can be formulated (fig. 10.1). The front edges of the rectangle of fabric were rolled and hemmed, or a decorative cord edging was whipstitched on to a selvedge. The bottom edges were turned under twice and hemmed, the turn-up being about 5mm. The back of the cap was made by turning to the inside the selvedge (or the cut edges if the cap was cut from a wider piece of cloth). The stitches joining the back edges together are on the outside of the material on some examples. Towards the top of the back of the cap a curve was stitched in with a running stitch following the line of the head and leaving a peak of material on the exterior. This stitched curve appears again and again on the caps. Ties were attached to the two front bottom edges: this can be seen from the way the cloth has pulled downwards and forwards from the strain of the ties, although no actual braids or ribbons are preserved in place. There were variations in the details of sewing of individual caps. Specific information on technical aspects of these pieces is given in the table.

It is not possible, of course, to determine just how these head-coverings were worn or what other articles of dress were worn with them. At this point it would seem productive to ask some questions. To start the enquiry one may ask whether these caps were worn by men, women or children? For example it is possible that one cap (E172: 14370, fig. 10.2) may have had a secondary use by a child. A torn piece of the selvedge was re-used as a tie, being placed high on the side of the cap in a way that does not leave enough depth for an adult's head if secured under the chin. This is not the original braid or ribbon tie that fastened the cap, but a piece taken from the fabric and carefully sewn into a strip. Does this suggest the passing on of a treasured silk piece to a child? Or could the cap have been worn by an adult by having the ties brought to the back of the head and secured there? Another cap (E172: 10540, fig. 10.3) with a tear on one side has been patched from the inside, leaving the rough edges of the torn area exposed on the exterior. Generally speaking most people would mend a garment by placing the patch on the outside of the fabric, so as to hide the torn part from view. Does this mean it did not matter that the tear was not covered, because the cap was worn under another head-covering? Could it also be that the cap was not torn until it was discarded and that the patch had already been put on at some earlier time for another purpose, perhaps to provide extra warmth and protection? Or was

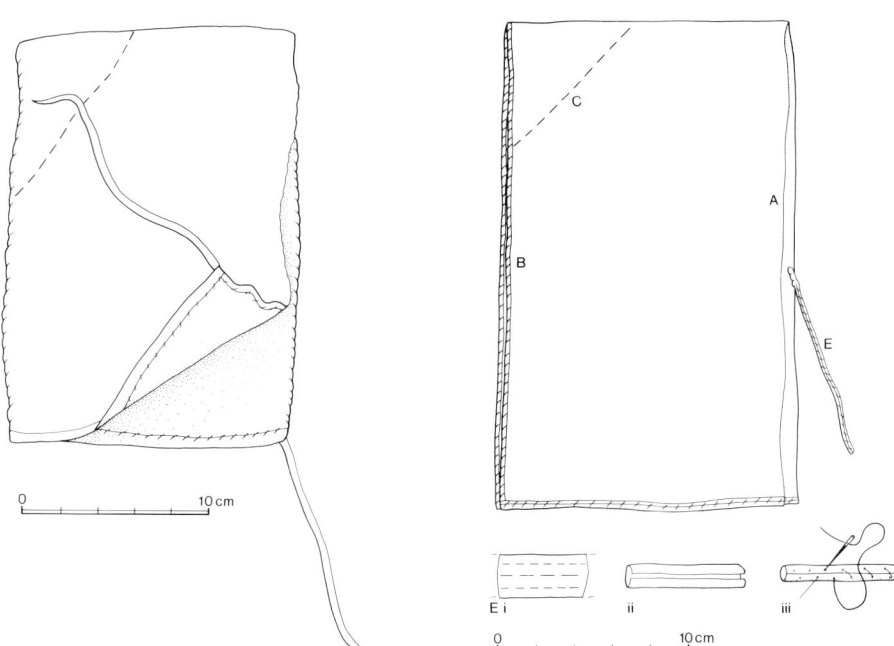

Fig. 10.1 (left) Basic mode of construction of the caps: a rectangular piece of cloth, with an average size of 45cm x 16cm, is folded double and stitched along the back.

Fig. 10.2 (right) Silk cap E172:14370. A selvedge, A, forms the front edge. The opposite raw edge has been given a rolled and whipped hem, B. The back edges do not appear to have been joined, but a line of wool hem-stitching, worked from the outside, forms a curve at the crown, C. The lower edges, D, have hems 2mm deep, where the cloth has been rolled, folded double and stitched. At the front edge a strip of cap fabric 8mm wide has been stitched, knotted and tied on to the cap, E. The construction of the tie is shown at E(i), (ii), (iii).

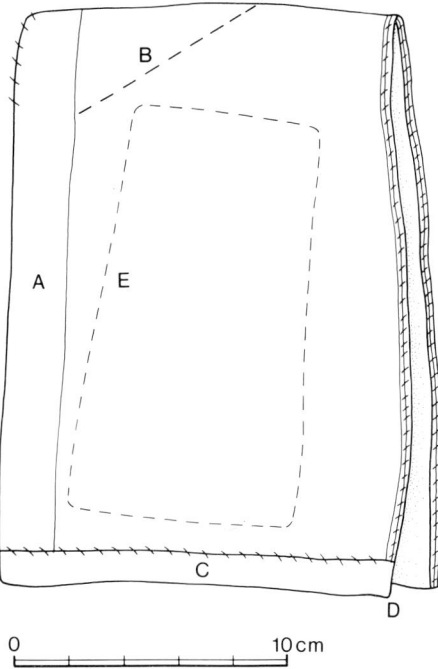

Fig. 10.3 Wool cap E172:10540. A selvedge, turned inside to a depth of 25mm, forms the back edge, A; a line of stitching forms the crown of the cap, B. At the lower edge the fabric has been turned under twice to form a hem 10mm deep, C. The front corner, D, has been pulled forward as if from a former tie. A patch, E, has been stitched to the inner side of the fabric. The sewing yarn is 2-ply, self-coloured for the lower hem and reddish brown for the back seam and patch.

the patched cap eventually used as a night cap, and so it did not matter how it was patched? It would therefore seem an open question who wore the caps, and whether they were worn on their own or with other kinds of head-coverings.

Other questions present themselves: were these caps a widely used mode of dress in Viking Dublin? Were they worn only by the incoming Scandinavian townsfolk or did Irish people in other parts of the country wear such headgear? One way to attempt an estimate of how common a fashion this may have been is to consider the fact that the caps were recovered from 11 house sites that were lived in by succeeding generations for about 200 years. The excavation yielded up between 9 and 13 examples from what must be, of course, the random abandonment of items of clothing. It is impossible to quantify what these discarded rags represent out of an original total, but it would seem legitimate to say that such caps were not uncommon in Dublin.

The second question is concerned with whether the caps may have been generally worn in Ireland or whether they were specific to the Dublin townspeople. There is little concrete evidence about the dress of the Irish at this time. No similar archaeological textiles have been recovered from other Irish sites, although it must be noted that nothing like the abundant finds from Dublin have been seen in such excavations. The evidence from stone carvings such as the Irish High Crosses does not seem to show such headgear. There do appear, however, to be strong Irish influences in the Viking-Age town. In particular the director of the excavation, Dr Patrick Wallace, believes that the building and carpentry techniques of the Dublin houses were greatly influenced by local Irish traditions.[2]

He points also to the absorption of the Norse community into the political structures of the country; to the payment of levies to Irish Kings; and the conversion of the incomers to Christianity by the 11th century. Dr Wallace would consider that certainly by the mid-11th century the inhabitants of Dublin should be considered as Hiberno-Norse, with considerable emphasis on the Hibernian element. Would this mean that local forms of dress were adopted? Here again there is a difficulty; for although Irish dress is reputed to have had distinctive features, it is not yet possible to establish firmly the types of dress in vogue in Ireland in the 10th and 11th centuries.

It would seem, therefore, that the incomers in Dublin were in some ways assimilated into the Irish framework, but that one cannot assess whether they had adopted local styles. It is perhaps likely that women in Dublin were no longer wearing the traditional dress of the Scandinavian homeland, since no oval brooches associated with this fashion were found in the Dublin excavations[3] (although such brooches were found in a 9th-century Scandinavian cemetery site at Kilmainham, Dublin, dating from the first occupation of Dublin by the Norse).[4] Is it possible that the women were wearing the types of sleeved gown and undergarment suggested by Dr Gale Owen-Crocker[5] as being worn by Anglo-Saxon women in the 10th and 11th centuries? It is known that the Norse who were thrown out of Ireland by a successful coalition of Irish kings in 902 became involved in the politics and warfare of English Mercia.[6] Did this 15- or 20-year stay in England influence their mode of dress? The Dublin Norse were also, of course, closely linked with York, with the same royal house providing kings for both towns during the first half of the 10th century.[7] At present there are very few hard facts to support any particular theory, but perhaps the results of research into textiles and other artefacts from Dublin will suggest some firmer possibilities.

There is, however, one clear piece of evidence. Similar caps to the Dublin pieces have been found in excavations of Viking-Age sites in York[8] and Lincoln.[9] One cap from York and another from Lincoln have been analysed by Dr Anna Muthesius and a second cap from York by Penelope Walton. It would seem from the examination of the caps, their pattern, and the silk material from which they were made, that there are strong similarities between all these pieces. In particular two Dublin caps were made from the same type of silk cloth in which the warp yarn is Z-twisted and the weft left untwisted, with similar densities of threads to the centimetre, and also golden brown in colour. The York and Lincoln caps have the same stitched curve below the crown of the cap and are each made from a length of cloth which retains one selvedge and has the other edge sewn. One of these silk caps from Dublin is also made from cloth with one selvedge and one sewn edge. The dimensions of all five caps are much the same. It would seem, therefore, that there was access to similar types of silk, and familiarity with a particular style of cap pattern in these three areas of Scandinavian influence. In addition, the incidence in Dublin of the same cap pattern made up both in other types of silk and in wool would seem to suggest a general style rather than a one-off article of dress in an idiosyncratic mode.

Here must be raised the question of the interpretation of this geographic distribution of the caps. Is their occurrence in places of Scandinavian influence a matter of chance? Were they worn in Ireland and England generally and happen to have survived in York, Lincoln and Dublin by good luck? Or are we looking at a specifically Scandinavian fashion with its ancestry in the Viking homelands? These are questions which I cannot answer, but about which I would very much like to have more information.

Assuming for a moment that the caps were worn by women, another aspect of the discussion might be to consider whether at this time the type of headdress worn may have differed, not only with the geographic area, but also with social class. Did wealthy or high status women such as those largely portrayed in Anglo-Saxon illuminated manuscripts wear the same type of head-coverings as working women and traders? The pictorial evidence from manuscripts is biased towards the upper social levels since many donors and patrons were portrayed. Even the few saintly women who were depicted were seen as being of high status. Alternatively the representation of clothes worn by holy women may have been taken from other cultural or biblical traditions[10] and so may bear little resemblance to the actual dress of the epoch. Another question, therefore, arises: may one speculate that the caps, undoubtedly worn in Dublin by townspeople, represent part of the dress of women who were scarcely ever portrayed in manuscripts or on sculptures?

Origins

We are led, therefore, to the question of origins. Is there any relevant evidence from earlier periods either in the British Isles or in the North-West of Europe? There are, of course, the Danish Bronze-Age sprang caps from Borum Eshøj and Skrydstrup[11] and the Iron-Age sprang cap from Arden Mose,[12] so the use of a fitted cap was not a new idea in Scandinavia by the 10th century. Neither was it in Britain where there are fragmentary remains of a netting cap from a Bronze-Age inhumation burial at Garton

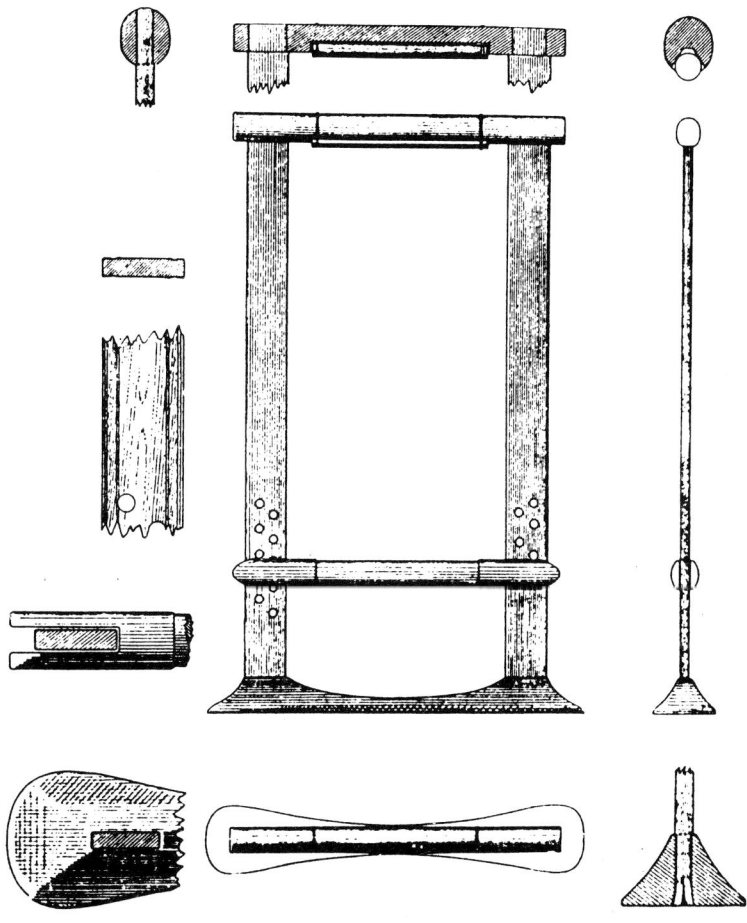

Fig. 10.4 The loom from the Oseberg ship burial (after Oseberg II *in Hoffmann (1974))*

Fig. 10.5 A Byzantine handloom, miniature from an Octateuch, 11th century, Biblioteca Apostolica Vaticana (Conway Library, Courtauld Institute of Art)

90

Slack, Yorkshire.[13] Indeed, a fitted cap firmly secured under the chin is a good solution to the problem of carrying out physical tasks in a cold climate. Perhaps one may postulate that rectangular loom-pieces of appropriate size were for centuries shaped into caps to be worn alone or under other head-coverings. In more general terms a small rectangular loom-piece would surely have been worn as a scarf or head-covering by many people. This basic rectangle of woven cloth needs only elementary stitching and shaping to become a cap in the Dublin style. Nothing need be added or cut away; all that is necessary is for the cloth to be folded, the ends neatened, the back edges stitched together, a running stitch sewn in to mark the head curve and ties sewn on. It is a straightforward pattern that seems close to homely ways of life, where a woman would weave a piece of cloth to the size required for the particular article of dress needed and then make it up for herself.

Margrethe Hald[14] has drawn attention to the antiquity of the use of loom-pieces as complete articles of dress. Although it cannot be ascertained whether the wool cloth of the Dublin caps represents single loom-pieces (the sewn hems make this impossible to find out), the existence of both selvedges in many pieces giving a width of circa 170mm, would suggest comparatively small pieces of cloth. An upright loom similar to that found in the Oseberg ship burial[15] (fig. 10.4) with overall dimensions of 119cm x 75cm, a small thin rod 33cm long to hold the warp threads and a moveable beam to regulate the length of the piece might be of appropriate size. Perhaps a type of small vertical loom was well distributed through north-western Europe and used for the production of small lengths of cloth? It would seem that small looms were in use in Byzantine workrooms (fig. 10.5).

In the case of the Dublin caps there is a further interesting point to be noted. As mentioned above in several wool pieces the width from selvedge to selvedge measures about 170mm. Where silk cloth has been made into caps the material seems to have been cut to conform with this width. The three silk examples from England are also approximately 170mm wide. Other types of cloth in the sample, however, which were not used for cap-making can be as much as 240mm wide, so it is clear that wider material was available. It would appear, therefore, that the people sewing the caps were making a definite choice in wanting them to conform to this specific narrow width. Does this denote a strong tradition for making the caps in this particular way? From the dimensions of the caps given in Table 1 it can be seen that the width of the cap is quite narrow and would have probably only just covered the ear. It might be felt that a wider cloth would offer more protection to the head. So why was this a popular choice? Does tradition play a role here?

Are there any other caps relating to the same general period? There is some relevant material from Birka, from the female burials. For example, there was a silk fragment found in association with a silver band (Grave 946)[16] which was described by Dr Geijer as a *rundes Käppchen* or small cap on the back of the head. Dr Geijer also proposed that the cloth used as head-coverings in the female burials may have been some kind of cap rather than an unshaped headscarf, since traces of stitching were found on one or two of the fragments.[17]

There are some interesting remains of head coverings from the female burials at Humikkala, Masku, in Finland.[18] Here pieces of wool cloth in a broken twill weave of heavier weight but of roughly similar dimensions to the Dublin head-coverings were reconstructed as being worn as a stiffened cap secured at the back of the head with decorative fringing falling behind. Do these head-coverings have some kind of relationship to either the Dublin caps or the scarf/kerchiefs also excavated in the town?

Here I must rest the question of the caps hoping that some answers will be forthcoming on all the points I have raised. More space has been devoted to discussing the caps than other items in the sample, but it seems pertinent to describe briefly the scarves and bands studied and to consider the source of the materials used.

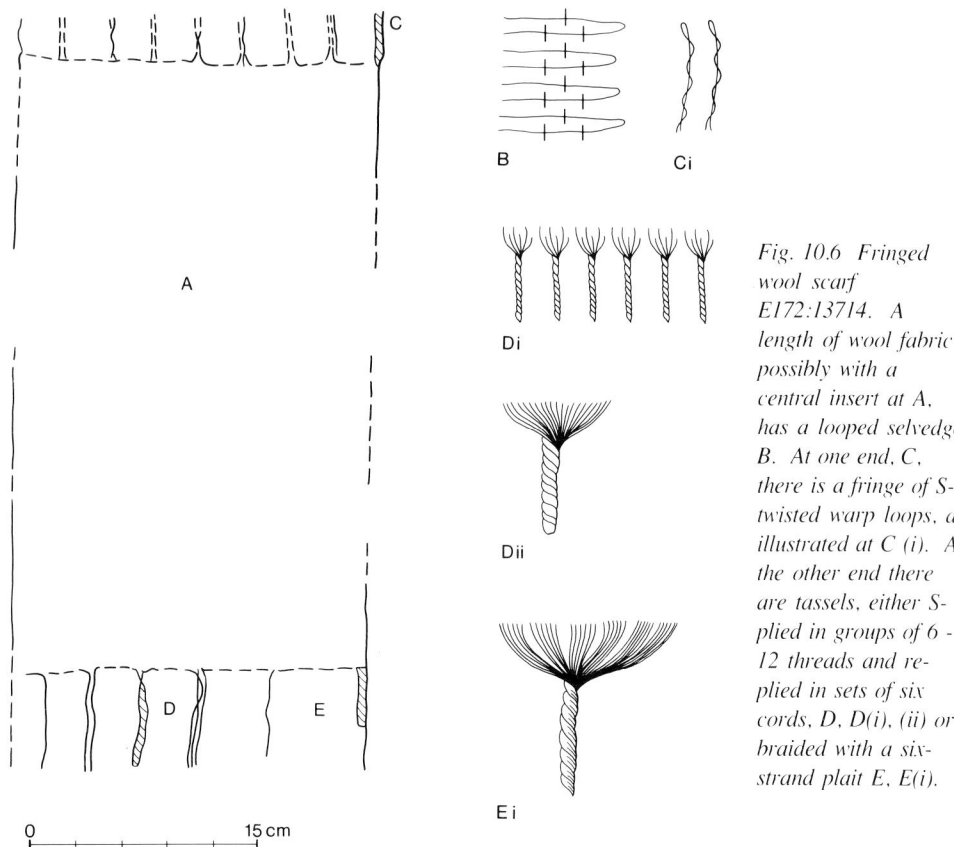

Fig. 10.6 Fringed wool scarf E172:13714. A length of wool fabric, possibly with a central insert at A, has a looped selvedge, B. At one end, C, there is a fringe of S-twisted warp loops, as illustrated at C (i). At the other end there are tassels, either S-plied in groups of 6 - 12 threads and re-plied in sets of six cords, D, D(i), (ii) or braided with a six-strand plait E, E(i).

Scarves and bands

In the sample there were also rectangular pieces of cloth, fringed and tasselled at both ends; some were as long as 600mm and 700mm and between 150mm and 240mm wide. They were made from both silk and wool. Their dimensions were larger than those of the caps and they could perhaps have been worn on the head or around the shoulders. Since they were more ample than the caps these pieces could be draped around the head and knotted under the chin or at the back of the head. Indeed one silk piece (E172: 15348) has the ends still knotted together, perhaps after some such use. The fringes at the ends of the scarf/kerchiefs have been finished in different ways, with groups of threads twisted and plied together to create varying decorative effects (fig. 10.6).

As well as being worn on their own, it seems likely that the scarves may have been worn in conjunction with other head-gear. If set squarely on the head, the silk or wool rectangles would fall on either side to the ear or to the shoulder (fig. 10.7). They could have been kept in place by a band tied round the head, or by a metal fillet. In relation to this suggestion of cloth bands there are narrow bands of silk or wool from Dublin that might serve this purpose, or be worn on their own. There is one

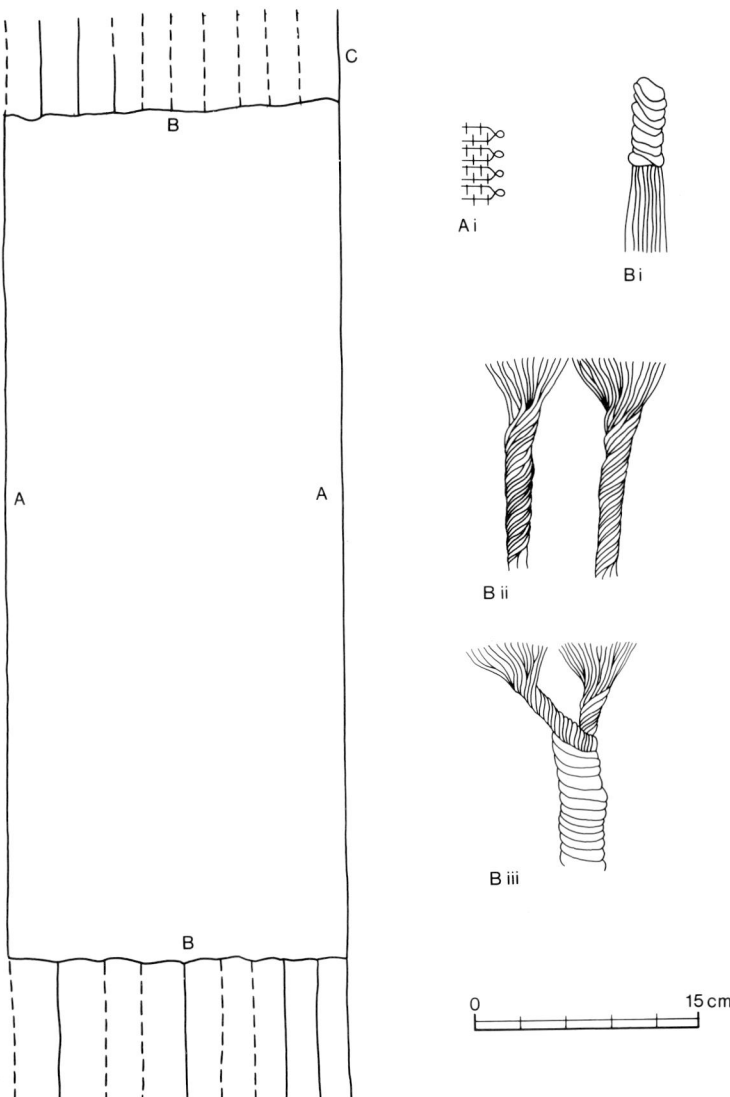

Fig. 10.7 Silk scarf E172:14407. A length of silk fabric has selvedges at either side with loops 2-4mm long and a double warp cord, A, A(i). At either end, B B, there is a fringe of tassels, some (C) still with intact warp loops. The tassels are constructed as illustrated B(i), (ii), (iii).

long silk band (E172: 15235, fig. 10.8), broken in the middle, but still knotted at the ends. It seems likely that the original length between the knots is approximately 380mm, which is about right for spanning the head. There are also short bands, originally hemmed at the ends which, with the addition of ribbons or braids, could be tied around the head. It is possible that the bands may not only have been worn with other head-dresses but also were used on their own. Perhaps they were used by men as well as women. It is interesting to visualize the fierce Viking of popular imagination wearing, not a helmet, but a silken headband. In Njal's Saga[19] we are told that Skarp-Hedin rode to the Icelandic Althing and 'his hair was combed well back and held in place by a silk headband. He looked every inch a warrior'. Did the men in Dublin also affect this fashion?

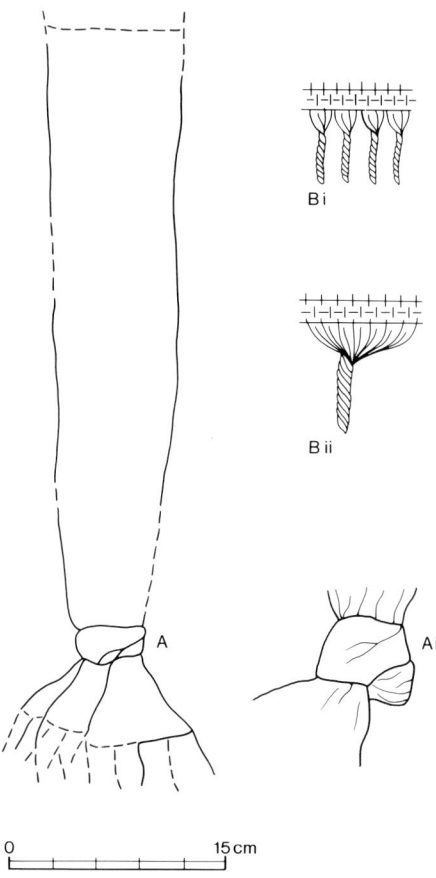

Fig. 10.8 Silk band E172:15235. A length of silk with a selvedge on one side and another possible selvedge on the other is tied together with a fragment of the same, A A(i). The fringed ends are constructed as shown in B(i), (ii), S-plied from 14 threads.

B i

B ii

A

A i

0   15 cm

Origins of the cloth used

The last and perhaps the widest question in relation to the wool and silk tabbies is that of their origin. The source of the light tabby silks may very well be Byzantium. The trade routes up through present-day Russia are well documented and there were undoubtedly other routes continuing on to Dublin from the trading centres of Scandinavia. Other points of origin perhaps in the Middle East are possible, but it would seem that Byzantium would be most likely. As to the wool pieces it is an open question whether they would have been imported, or woven in Dublin. Weaving equipment has been found in the houses of the town, and good levels of skill were seen in other crafts such as wood-carving and comb-making. The very fine, regularly woven wool yarn would suggest a high degree of proficiency among the spinners. Good reserves from which suitable fibres for fine spinning could be selected would have been needed. At present it is difficult to estimate whether these would have been available in the Dublin hinterland among the farms serving the needs of the town. Comparable material for the wool pieces is scarce, so again there is a question-mark: are these light-weight pieces the product of Dublin or must one look for the place of manufacture further afield? Perhaps here also there will be some answers from other studies.

In conclusion, after so many questions there is one thing that is certain. The excavations at Dublin produced a wealth of finds, both organic and artefactual which show quite clearly the comfortable and confident lifestyle of the townspeople. Whether they were more Norse than Irish, or more Irish than Norse, the trading and voyaging of those early Dubliners provided the town with a wide range of goods including the silk material that seems to have been freely enough available to have been widely used.

Perhaps I may end with one last query and a quotation. Here is a report on the Vikings in Ireland by the Spanish Muslim geographer Al-Udhri writing in the 11th century: [20] 'The Vikings have no capital save this island in all the world. Its circumference is one thousand miles. Its people have the dresses and customs of the Vikings. They wear valuable hooded mantles, one of which is worth a hundred dinars. Their nobles wear mantles adorned with pearls'. Should we believe in this kind of picture or should we envisage a much more cosmopolitan community taking fashions from the rest of Ireland, from Britain and from other parts of Europe? The questions are all still to be answered.

References

1. The study took the form of an M.A. thesis, *'A group of Hiberno-Norse silk and wool head-coverings from Fishamble Street/St. John's Lane, Dublin'*, vol I Text, vol. II Catalogue and Photographs, University College Cork, unpublished 1986. Frances Pritchard suggested that the present writer should undertake a separate study of this group of textiles since they seemed to be linked by similarity of weave and were perhaps used for similar purposes. Frances Pritchard's constant encouragement and skilled advice on the thesis were greatly appreciated and contributed largely to its completion. Other aspects of this group of textiles have been discussed in E. Heckett, 'Some Hiberno-Norse head-coverings from Fishamble Street and St. John's Lane, Dublin', *Textile History* 18 (2), 1987, 159-74.

2. P.F. Wallace, 'The Archaeology of Viking Dublin' in H.B. Clarke, A. Simms (edd), *The Comparative History of Urban Origins in Non-Roman Europe*, British Archaeological Reports International Series 255, 1985, 128-129

3. P.F. Wallace, personal communication

4. G. Coffey, E.C.R. Armstrong, 'Scandinavian Objects found at Islandbridge and Kilmainham', *Proc. Roy. Irish Acad.* 28, 1910, 107, 119

5. G.R. Owen-Crocker, *Dress in Anglo-Saxon England*, Manchester, 1986, 138-141

6. P.F. Wallace (1985), 108

7. D. 'O Corráin, *Ireland before the Normans*, Dublin, 1980, 102-104

8. A. Muthesius, 'The Silk Fragment from 5 Coppergate', in A. MacGregor (ed), 'Anglo-Scandinavian finds from Lloyd's Bank, Pavement and other sites', *Archaeology of York* 17/3, 1982, 132-133

9. P. Walton, 'A silk cap from Coppergate', *Interim* 7 (2), 1980, 3 5

10. G.R. Owen-Crocker (1986), 1, 132

11. M. Hald, *Ancient Danish Textiles from Bogs and Burials*, Copenhagen, 1980, 251

12. *Ibid*, 29-30

13. A. Henshall, 'Textiles and Weaving Appliances in Prehistoric Britain', *Proc. Prehist. Soc.* 16, 1950, 131

14. M. Hald (1980), 376

15. M. Hoffmann, *The Warp-Weighted Loom*, Oslo, 1974, 391

16. A. Geijer, *Birka III. Die Textilfunde aus den Gräbern*, Uppsala, 1938, 146

17. *Ibid*, 156

18. P.-L. Lehtosalo-Hilander, *Ancient Finnish Costumes*, Helsinki, 1984, fig. 30

19. M. Magnusson, H. Palsson, *Njal's Saga*, Harmondsworth, 1982, 248

20. D. James, 'Two Medieval Arabic Accounts of Ireland', *Journ. Roy. Soc. Antiq. Ireland* 108, 1978, 5-9

Museum Registration No.	Fibre	Dimensions (estimated original -mm)	Yarn twist direction warp/weft	Degree of twist warp/weft	Diameter of yarn (mm) warp	weft	No. of threads per cm warp	weft	Selvedges	Colour* hue value chroma	Verbal description
E172:											
10241	wool	440 x 180	Z/Z	M L	0.24 - 0.25	0.18 - 0.21	14 - 16	15 -17	1	5YR 2.5/2	Dk reddish brown
10300	wool	380 x 160	Z/Z	L L	0.19 - 0.21	0.21 - 0.23	14 - 20	15 -16	2	5YR 2.5/2	Dk reddish brown
10540	wool	460 x 180	Z/Z	L L	0.22 - 0.25	0.17 - 0.21	19 - 22	9 - 13	2	5YR 2.5/2	Dk reddish brown
11066	wool	120 x 130	Z/Z	L L	0.26 - 0.29	0.24 - 0.26	14 - 18	8 - 9	1	5YR 2.5/2	Dk reddish brown
11205	wool	490 x 185	Z/Z	L L	0.25 - 0.34	0.26 - 0.29	12 - 15	9 - 11	2	10YR 2.5/2	Very dark brown
13241	wool	100 x 48	Z/Z	ML ML	0.31 - 0.34	0.20 - 0.26	14 - 16	11 - 14	1	5YR 2/2	Dk reddish brown
14499	wool	380 x 140	Z/Z	ML L	0.23 - 0.25	0.19 - 0.23	16 - 17	10 - 12	1	5YR 2.5/1	Black
E190:											
7431	wool	460 x 165	Z/Z	L M	0.18 - 0.19	0.19 - 0.23	16 - 21	10 - 13	2	10YR 2.5/1	Very dark brown
E173:											
4253	wool	480 x 150	Z/Z	L M	0.20 - 0.23	0.18 - 0.24	18 - 24	18 - 23	2	5YR 3/4	Dk reddish brown
E172:											
10959	silk	390 x 170	Z/ -	L -	0.12 - 0.17	0.30 - 0.32	19 - 21	22 - 27	1	2.5Y 5/4	Light olive brown
12831 a)b)c)d)	silk	210 x 150	Z/ -	LM -	0.36 - 0.39	0.22 - 0.24	32 - 36	21 - 24	-	2.5Y 4/4	Olive brown
13590	silk	480 x 168	Z/ -	L -	0.10 - 0.18	0.38 - 0.50	19 - 23	19 - 27	-	10YR 3/4	Dk yellowish brown
14370	silk	540 x 160	Z/Z	L L	0.13 - 0.16	0.14 - 0.15	30 - 34	19 - 25	1	5YR 2.5/2	Dk reddish grey

Table : Caps and possible caps of wool and silk (tabby weave)

L   Loose
ML   Medium to Loose
M   Medium

*Textiles colour-coded by the Munsell Color Chart

11. The costumes depicted on gold-sheet figures (*guldgubbar*)

Elisabeth Munksgaard

Copenhagen

In 1791 a Swedish vicar wrote the history of his parish, Ravlunda, *Topographia parochie Raflunda* - and in this work he mentioned that the local population called tiny gold-sheet figures *guldgubbar* (*gubbe*: a very old man). This name is still in use in Scandinavian archaeological terminology.

The learned vicar of Ravlunda parish was not, however, the first person to decribe these minute, brittle figures. In 1700 Otto von Sperling (who administered the Royal Curio Cabinet, the 'Kunstkam- mer') described a collection of gold-sheet figures (the provenance of which did not, unfortunately, interest him), which may be of Norwegian origin. In 1725, Jacob von Melle, who was a vicar in Lübeck, described a find of gold-sheet figures from Rønne, Bornholm. The find then consisted of 20 specimens, and today, believe it or not, 14 intact ones and two fragments are left. In 1791 the famous Danish numismatist, Count Hielmstierne, decribed the gold-sheet figures in his *Description of the Danish Coins and Medals in the Royal Collection.* So these tiny gold figures have a more venerable tradition of study than many other antiquities.

I shall not go into details by enumerating how many gold-sheet figures have been found in Scandinavia and where they have been found. I shall concentrate upon the various types, how to date them, and the costumes depicted.

The distribution of gold-sheet figures centres on Denmark, owing to the fact that during the past two years more than 1000 specimens have come to light at the dwelling site of Sorte Muld ('Black Soil') on the island of Bornholm. Apart from a few Danish gold hoards, all the Scandinavian gold-figures are found at dwelling sites such as Helgö in Mälaren, Eketorp on Öland, Hauge in South-West Norway, Møre church in Nordtrøndelag (in house ruins underneath the oldest church), and Borg on Lofoten. These finds also give the spread of the type, from Bornholm to Öland, from Jutland over to Uppland - where a gold figure from the second half of the 6th century was found in Vendel grave 14 - and right up to northern Norway.

The various types are:

1) Men's figures cut out of gold foil, with or without incised details, such as a belt: this may indicate that the man wears breeches and that the upper part of his body is naked.

2) Pressed figures of men or women. The women wear a skirt, a patterned shawl and a hairstyle which we also know from bracteates dated to the 5th to the 6th centuries AD. The men almost always wear a kaftan (fig. 11.1), that is, an obliquely closed coat, very different from the ordinary man's shirt which we know from the Migration period. The kaftan had been known ever since the Scythian nomads appeared in eastern Europe in the 6th century BC, and also appears in helmet decorations of the 7th and 8th centuries from Sutton Hoo in England and Vendel and Valsgärde in Sweden.

The odd thing about this apparently beloved kaftan is that we have no trace of it in actual textile finds, neither from bogs nor from burials. I can, however, quite easily see the difficulties: when we

Fig. 11.1 Man dressed in kaftan bordered with patterned braids (actual size 1 x 2cm). Drawn by Eva Koch. From Sorte Muld, Bornholm

Fig. 11.2 Three women dressed in patterned cloaks or shawls; their skirts are bordered with braids (approx. 2:1). From Bornholm

work with costume pictures we never know whether they depict the local style of dress or if they were imported with the models. As, however, gold-sheet figures are exclusively a Scandinavian feature, I think that they also depict Scandinavian styles of clothing.

The women are, like the men, always shown in profile (fig. 11.2) - although there is no rule without exception and at Eketorp on Öland there were 15 sheet figures struck with three different dies, of which 6 are women shown *en face*, except for the feet (which must have been most uncomfortable). Their dress does not differ from that of the women in profile: strings of beads, a patterned shawl, and a skirt with a patterned trimming. The men wear a short shirt or cloak and tight-fitting trousers or naked legs. The Eketorp figures date from the earlier habitation of the site, ie 5th-8th centuries and they were found together with payment gold (*betalingsguld*) from the 5th - 6th centuries.

Double figures depicting a man and a woman face to face (figs. 11.3, 4) are extremely rare in Denmark (two specimens), but they are a common type in Norway and Sweden: an example is the find from Hauge in southern Norway. The men wear a long cloak fastened on the right shoulder and the women a long shawl. Their hair is now set in the Irish ribbon knot which was introduced into Nordic art during the 7th century. The same knot is seen on a gold figure from Gudme on the island of Fyn; the woman wears a large button-bow fibula (*rygknap-fibula*) which was in use in Scandinavia from the 7th to the 8th century. The same fibula appears on one of 26 gold-sheet figures from Helgö in Mälaren, Sweden.

The dating of the gold-sheet figures has been given throughout as early Germanic Iron Age up to the 7th or 8th century. Groups of finds are scarce, as the figures mainly derive from settlement sites. At Sorte Muld, however, where there were approximately 1000 specimens, we have traces of habitation from the pre-Roman Iron Age and onwards to the 9th century.

I am not certain that the figures also existed in the Viking Age, as is often asserted. The characteristic female garment of that period, a skirt or gown with a long train, which we know from the tiny Swedish silver figures and from the Oseberg tapestry, is not seen on the gold-sheet figures. The man's cloak, however, is found on several picture-stones from Gotland, although a man's cloak is naturally always fastened on the right shoulder, so that this detail cannot be given any chronological value.

The gold-sheet figures can, therefore, be dated from the 5th century to the 8th century. But where do they come from? They do not appear in finds from the late Roman Iron Age. From the end of this period, the 4th century, however, we have a gold hoard from Brangstrup, Funen, a find which heralds the gold riches of the Germanic Iron Age. This hoard has a strong affinity with the Gothic cultural areas in Hungary and two little gold-sheet figures may give an inkling of whence the inspiration derived.

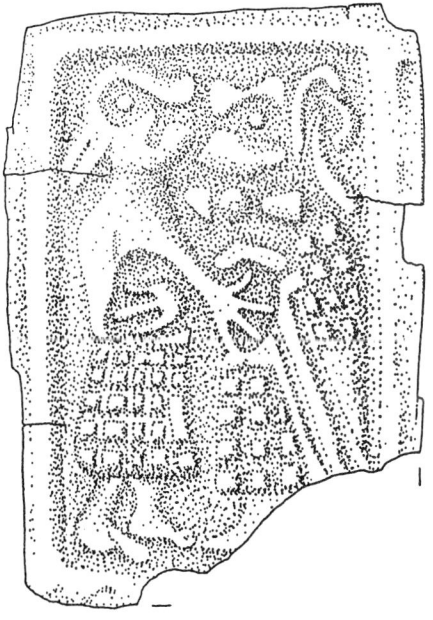 

Fig. 11.3 (left) Man (left) and woman embracing each other. The woman's hair is arranged in an entrelac knot (7th century); she wears a brooch across her throat, her shawl and skirt are chequered, as is the lower part of the man's shirt (actual size 0.7 x 1cm). Drawn by Eva Koch. From Sorte Muld, Bornholm
Fig. 11.4 (right) Silhouette of embracing couple in fig. 11.3

Finally, what was their use? That is impossible to state because we cannot - however much we want to - excavate beliefs, thoughts or religion. We can only say that the persons depicted are of the higher orders of society. Women wearing finely decorated clothes, with strings of beads and large fibulae, must certainly belong to the 'nobility' or 'peerage'. And it seems to me that the kaftan is eminently suited for riding (the Scythians were after all mounted nomads) and to own a horse was not within poor men's means. Are they identical with pagan Nordic gods and goddesses (Freja in her feather cloak); do the double prints depict the love meeting between Frøj and Gerd? If only we knew.

12. Women's dress in the Viking period in Denmark, based on the tortoise brooches and textile remains

Anne Hedeager Madsen

Moesgaard

Women's dress in the Viking period is generally considered to have followed an identical pattern throughout Scandinavia. The classic interpretation is that the dress consisted of a linen shift or chemise without sleeves, though perhaps worn with the full width hanging beyond the shoulders and thereby forming a sleeve. Over this linen shift women wore either one or two outer dresses, each consisting of a length of material passing around the body and held up in front and back by shoulder-straps sewn in place. To these were attached two identical tortoise brooches. To this dress was added a cape, normally of fine-woven wool.

While earlier researchers into costume were of the opinion that the same type of dress was in use over the whole of Scandinavia and in all social strata, more recent researchers have drawn attention to geographical and social differences in the appearance of the costume.

The source material for our knowledge of women's dress in Viking-period Denmark is very scanty. There are some few written records and a very small number of illustrations, both seriously lacking in detail and capable of several possible interpretations. The largest body of source material is archaeological, consisting of burials, where the dress-ornaments are of special importance, and where small fragments of textile can in fortunate circumstances be preserved. Of this material we shall consider here the tortoise brooches, placing them in a chronological framework and at the same time viewing their distribution in Denmark, in order to trace possible geographic variation in their use.

Tortoise brooches are the most common dress adornments of the Viking period, first appearing in the Later Germanic Iron Age, although the majority belong to the Viking period. They have a northern and easterly distribution, a far greater number being known from Sweden and Norway than from Denmark.[1] Through a registration and survey of the Danish tortoise brooches and textile remains it is my object to find out whether the women's dress of the Viking period agrees with the previously assumed classic model.

The distribution of tortoise brooches in Denmark

According to my register 232 tortoise brooches of the Viking period are known in Denmark. This is only a fifth of the number known from either Sweden of Norway. In general they show an easterly distribution, by far the greater number being found on the islands and in East Jutland. In addition, the majority of finds with tortoise brooches are from the 9th century, 70 discoveries belonging to this period, while only 32 are known from the 10th century, in both cases excepting Bornholm. In other words there are twice as many finds with tortoise brooches from the 9th century as from the 10th. In general, also, there is a greater geographical spread of tortoise brooches in the 9th century, whereas in the 10th they are more centralized. There is, for example, a concentration of discoveries of the later period at Århus and the same is true of Trelleborg, which may reflect the importance of the towns and ring-forts in the 10th century. A similar difference is seen on Bornholm, where 33 discoveries with tortoise brooches are registered from the 9th century, while only seven are known from the 10th century. In other words, on Bornholm there are five times as many discoveries of tortoise brooches from the 9th century as from the 10th century.

In the distribution maps (figs. 12.1, 12.2) more specific differences in the spread of the tortoise brooches can be perceived. On the map showing 9th-century brooches, four areas are indicated which show a concentration of brooches, whereas the same areas are almost empty in the 10th century. These four groupings of 9th-century tortoise brooches all lie in the south-west of Denmark. A line can be drawn across the country, to the north-east of which graves are found with tortoise brooches of the 10th century, whereas to the south-west there are graves without tortoise brooches, with one or two exceptions. There are thus 'broochless' areas in Denmark in the 10th century. This cannot be accidental, but must mirror a change in the fashion of dress.

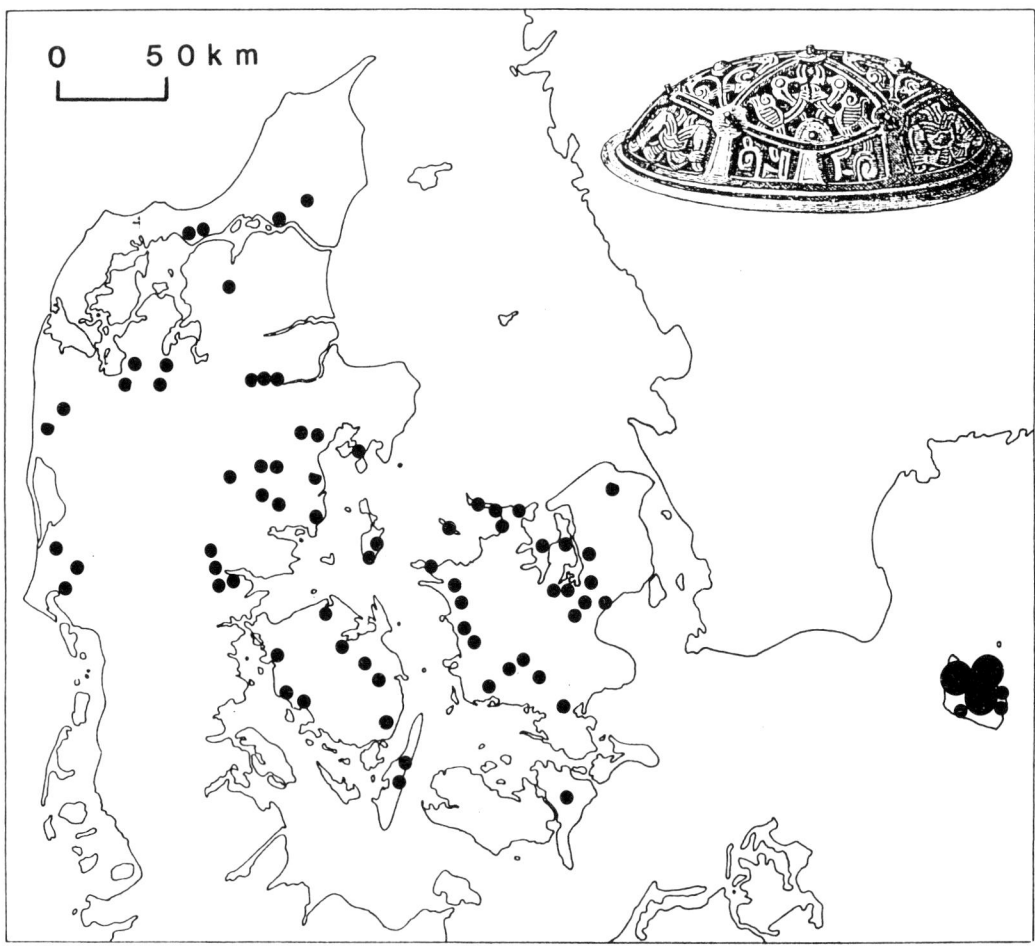

Fig. 12.1 9th-century tortoise brooches in Denmark

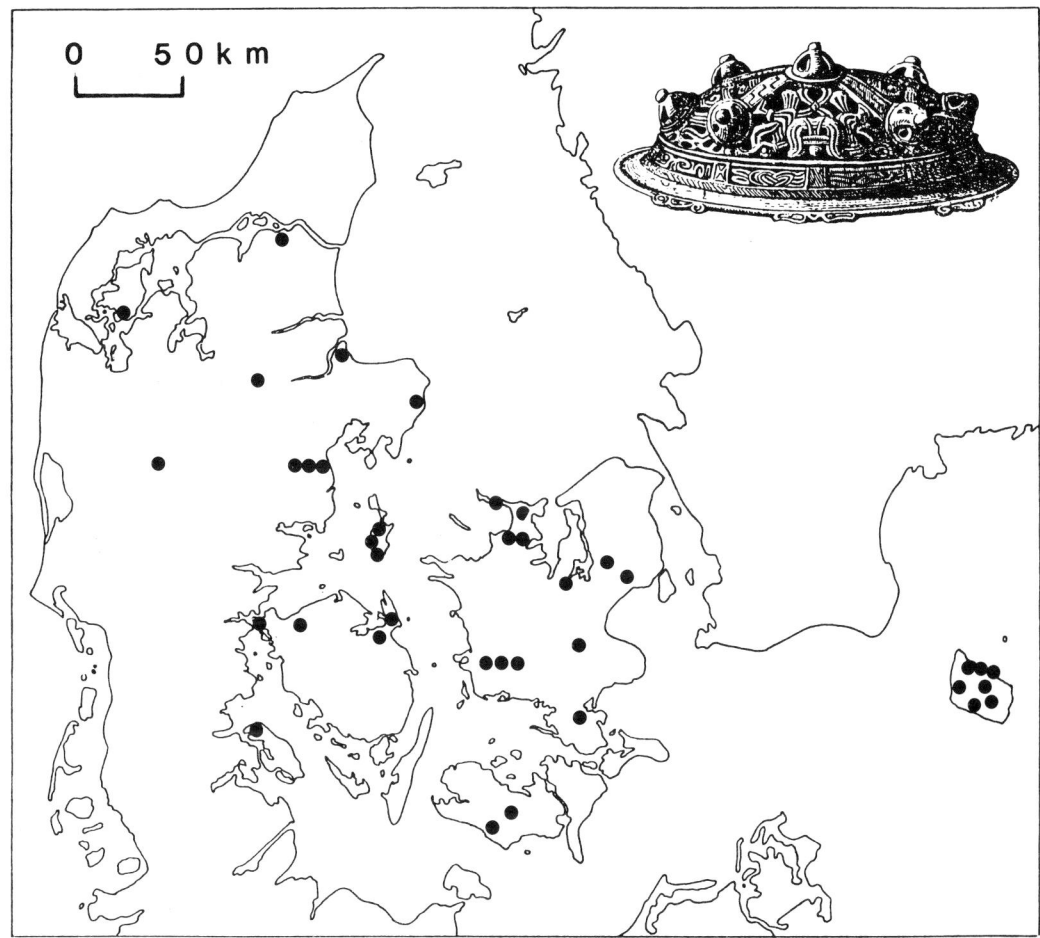

Fig. 12.2 10th-century tortoise brooches in Denmark

It would be reasonable to postulate a connection between this obvious predominance of tortoise brooches in eastern Denmark and the even stronger tradition of the two-brooch dress in East Scandinavia. Particularly in Birka in Sweden many tortoise brooches have been found with remains of textiles preserved on the reverse, and this has resulted in detailed analysis of textiles and of dress, with consequent interpretations of Viking period women's dress.[2] The Birka dress consists of the following articles: a shift, often of linen, a tunic, a shoulder-strapped dress and a kaftan or cape normally of wool.[3]

A Danish example of this costume comes from Køstrup on Funen, where a woman was buried with tortoise brooches in the 10th century. The textile impressions in the Køstrup brooches resemble closely those of the rich Swedish women's graves from Birka. In general we can say of the women's dress with tortoise brooches that it is of decidedly local, by which I mean Scandinavian, origin, although it has acquired oriental features, such as the kaftan jacket.

Dress fashion in the 'broochless' areas of Denmark

The dress fashion in south-western Denmark is more difficult to determine: hardly any tortoise brooches are found here from the 10th century. There is, however, evidence of contact with western Europe, partly in the written sources and partly in the presence of numerous imported objects. Of particular significance here is Frankish influence. In the 700's Charlemagne came to power in the Frankish kingdom and expanded his realm to its greatest extent, from north-east Spain to the south, as far as the Elbe to the east and the Eider to the north. Throughout this expansion there was lively trade and exchange across the frontiers. Frankish women's dress is best illustrated through pictures and written sources, as well as by very rich burials. It consisted of a peplos of Classical Greek origin, a tunic and a kaftan.[4] The costume thus received its inspiration from the Greek and Near Eastern regions.

The dress ornamentation most often consists of a disc-brooch, circular, adorned with sacred symbols including the cross, and enamelled. It is worn by both men and women. In the course of the Frankish expansion some of these brooches reached Scandinavia in the 9th century. Some researchers claim that the expansion of the Frankish women's costume is connected with the expansion of Christianity.[5] This cannot be shown to be true of Denmark, as no detailed archaeological analysis has been made of dress ornaments and textiles from south-west Denmark in the 10th century. Still, it does look as though a change of fashion takes place in precisely this area in the 10th century, since practically no tortoise brooches are found; and there is a change of religion from paganism to Christianity. So it would be natural to investigate more closely whether the introduction of Christianity involved a change of dress.

Social differences in dress fashion in Denmark

In addition to regional differences, social differences in dress fashion can be seen in Denmark. One can, for example, see in a catalogue of finds from Danish burials in the Viking period[6] that the undoubted women's graves that do not contain tortoise brooches are all either very poor or very rich. An example of the former is a grave from Karby on Mors, which contained a pottery vessel of typical Viking-period form and a hand-spindle. The person buried here was surely a poor woman, who either did not own a set of brooches or, perhaps more probably, one whose family could not afford to let her take them with her to the grave.

It is more significant, however, that tortoise brooches are absent in very rich graves. Two examples from Jutland can be given, the first from Hvilehøj near Randers. Here in 1880 a very rich grave was found in a low tumulus, dating to the 10th century.[7] The wealthy grave furnishings included 16 gold-in-glass beads and remains of the costume, comprising a silk material with woven and embroidered decoration in gold thread, fragments of a brown wool material with cross-shaped embroidery, together with a very fine brown fur and compressed down and feathers.[8] Both the burial furnishings and the textiles suggest that the grave was that of a lady of distinction. Silk, for example, is found in only a very few Viking-period graves in Denmark and must have been imported. There were no shoulder brooches, and the lady's costume had been Frankish-inspired, with a peplos-like garment of silk and, above it, a tunic and a cape, both of wool.

A similar situation is found in a chamber-tomb at Hørning, also dated to the 10th century.[9] While a thorough treatment of the contents is not yet available, the grave is interpreted as that of a woman, admittedly only on the evidence of beads. In the grave were found remains of enough clothing to give the impression of a costume of distinction, including in places edgings in silver thread. These very thin threads had completely dissolved, but some of the resultant silver compounds had had a conserving effect, preserving fragments of the material, and even of the pattern, which consisted of diamonds and rhomboids. There was a broad ribbon from the border of the cloak or wrap, of the same type as that shown worn by women on the 9th-century Oseberg tapestry.[10] It is thought that this garment is also identifiable in the 10th century, at Hvilehøj among other places. In the Hørning grave, similarly, no shoulder-brooches or other costume ornaments were found.

All this would suggest that at least some rich graves in 10th-century Jutland reflect a western influence upon Danish fashions, while the earlier fashion was strongly entrenched in eastern Scandinavia, as evidenced by the tortoise-brooched costume.

Summary

A dress with shoulder-straps and tortoise brooches can be shown to have been in use in Scandinavia from the 8th century and up to the first half of the 10th century, after which tortoise brooches rapidly disappear from the graves. As they are rare after the year 950 it is reasonable to assume that a change in women's dress occurred at that date. Although there are only a few Danish graves where the absence of tortoise brooches is accompanied by evidence of this change in fashion, there is in fact a large percentage of graves without tortoise brooches - in contrast to Birka, where the tortoise brooches are found in practically every rich woman's grave, highlighting the contrast between Denmark and the rest of Scandinavia.

Thus, all the evidence suggests that there was no identical costume over the whole of Scandinavia in the Viking period, but that there were local variations. Although there is other evidence for the Danish costume at this time, the relatively small number of tortoise brooches (characteristic of the shoulder-strapped dress), is paralleled by a scarcity of textiles, since corrosion of the tortoise brooch tends to preserve textile fragments. This paper, however, is meant to show that the strapped dress with its two tortoise brooches was much more common in Sweden and Norway than in Denmark, where a more varied range of fashion was found, with inspiration particularly from the area of the Franks in the 10th century.

Translated into English by Geoffrey Bibby, Moesgaard.

References

1. I. Jansson, *Ovala Spännbucklor. En studie av vikingatida standardsmycken med udgångspunkt från Björkö-fynden, Aun 7*, Uppsala, 1985, 12

2. I. Hägg, *Kvinnodräkten i Birka. Livplaggens rekonstruktion på grundval av det arkeologiska materialet, Aun 2*, Uppsala, 1974, 6

3. F. Bau, 'Seler og slæb i vikingetiden. Birkas kvindedragt i nyt lys', *KUML* 1981, 1982, 14

4. G. R. Owen-Crocker, *Dress in Anglo-Saxon England,* Manchester, 1986, 97

5. H. Vierck, 'Mittel- und westeuropäische Einwirkungen auf die Sachkultur von Haithabu/Schleswig', *Archäologische und naturwissenschaftliche Untersuchungen an Siedlungen im deutschen Küstengebiet*, 2: *Handelsplätze des frühen und hohen Mittelalters*, Weinheim, 1984, 405

6. J. Brønsted, 'Danish Inhumation Graves of the Viking Age. A Survey', *Acta Archaeologica 7*, 1936. 87-101

7. *Ibid*

8. M. Hald, *Ancient Danish Textiles from Bogs and Burials* (*Publications of the National Museum. Archaeological Historical Series*, 21), Copenhagen, 1980, 111; E. Munksgaard, *Oldtidsdragter*, Copenhagen, 1974, 175; L. Bender Jørgensen, *Forhistoriske Textiler i Skandinavien (Nordiske Fortidsminder*, serie B) 1986, 227

9. K. Krogh, O. Voss, 'Fra Hedenskab til Kristendom i Hørning', *Nationalmuseets Arbejdsmark*, 1961, 51ff; Munksgaard (1974), 175; Bender Jørgensen (1986), 227

10. B. Hougen, 'Osebergfunnets Billedvev', *Viking* 1940, 85-124

13. Herstellungsmethoden der in Gräberfeldern des 3.-13. Jh. im Gebiet Lettlands gefundenen Gewebe

Anna Zariņa

Rīgā

Die Untersuchungen von Kleidung der Bewohnern Lettlands sind in der archäologischen Literatur bisher hauptsächlich der Erforschung einzelner Kleidungteile und ihrer Verzierung gewidmet; nur vereinzelte Veröffentlichungen befassen sich mit Herstellungsmethoden der Gewebe für einzelne Kleidungsteile.[1] Etwas mehr Material ist über die Gräberfelder der Latgallen aus dem 7.-13.Jh. und der Liven aus dem 10.-13.Jh. anzuführen.[2]

Hier stellen wir eine gedrängte Übersicht der bisher eingehender untersuchten Gewebefunde aus Gräberfeldern des 3.-13.Jh. vor. Sie sind in vier Gruppen eingeteilt: 3.-4.Jh., 5.-9.Jh. und Stoffgruppen von zwei verschiedenen Gebieten aus dem 10.-13.Jh. (Abb. 13.1).

Aus dem 3.-4.Jh. sind sieben Fragmente von Wollgeweben erhalten, die sowohl im östlichen (Selen-Boķi, Razbuki), wie auch im westlichen (Kuren-Mazkatuži) Teil Lettlands gefunden wurden (Abb. 13.1.1). Bei einem Gewebe mit Tuchbindung (1/1) sind Ketten- und Schußfäden in Z-Richtung gesponnen, S-gezwirnt; die Fadendichte beträgt 6-8 Kettenfäden und 3 Schußfäden je 1cm. Die übrigen Gewebe sind gewöhnliche vierbindige Köpergewebe (2/2); bei den Selen bestehen sie aus in Z-Richtung gesponnenen Ketten- und Schußfäden (Z/Z), während bei Geweben der Kuren sowohl die Z/Z wie auch Z/S-Spinnrichtung angetroffen wird. Die Gewebedichte entspricht gemäß Nahliks Qualitätsgruppen der IV. Gruppe,[3] so daß sie als einheimische Gewebe zu bewerten sind.

Die ältesten Flachsfäden wurden in einer Bronzespirale aus einem Grab des 4.Jh. (Boķi) festgestellt.

Aus dem 5.-9.Jh. sind 42 Leinwandstücke (wahrscheinlich aus Flachs) und 60 Wollgewebe- stücke untersucht worden, sowohl aus dem Osten Lettlands (Selen, Latgallen-Kivti, Lejasbiteni, Aizkalne, Boķi u.a.), wie auch aus dem Westen (Kuren, Semgallen-Geistauti, Plavniekkalns, Simteni); außerdem noch 8 Wollgewebefragmente vom kurischen Tiras-Sumpf (Tiras purvs) im Südwesten Lettlands (Abb. 13.1.2).

Die Leinwandgewebe (1/1) sind aus Fäden mit Z/Z-Spinnrichtung in Tuchbindung gewebt. Sie sind ripsartig, entsprechen meistens der I. und II. Qualitätsgruppe (meistens 16-32 x 6-12); die Dichte der Kettenfäden ist zwei bis dreimal größer als die der Schußfäden. Bei den wenigen Geweben der III. und IV. Gruppe ist dieses Verhältnis viel niedriger. Vier der Wollgewebe haben Tuchbindung (1/1), 56 davon sind vierbindige Köper (2/2); sie gehören hauptsächlich zur IV. Qualitätsgruppe. Bei den Fragmenten aus Ostlettland wird nur die Spinnrichtung Z/Z angetroffen. In zwei Fällen sind Gewebeanfangskanten in Flechttechnik erhalten (Abb. 13.2.1); in einem ist eine Gewebeanfangskante mit geschlossenen Schlingen (Abb. 13.2.2) erhalten. Sonderlich ist ein vierbindiger Diamantköper (Musterrapport 20/18) mit Gewebeanfangskante in Brettchentechnik (aus Ludvigova); seine Ketten- und Schußfäden sind in Z/Z-Richtung gesponnen, in S/S-Richtung gezwirnt (8 x 6-7). Bei den Fragmenten aus dem Westen Lettlands überwiegt die Z/S-Spinnrichtung.

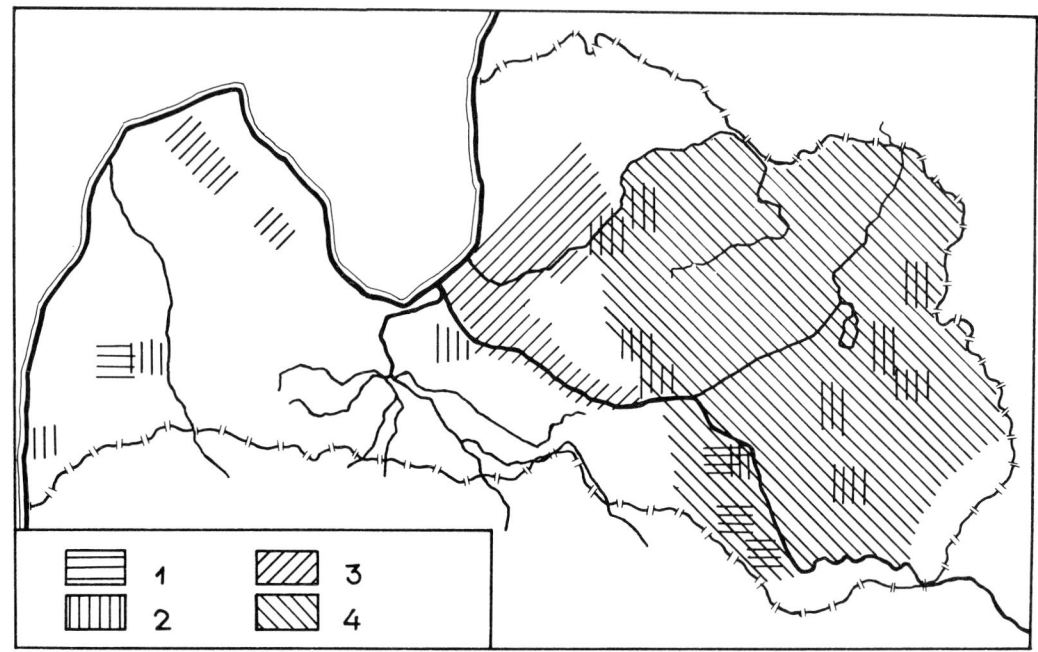

Abb. 13.1 Fundorten der archäologischen Textilien: 1. 3.-4.Jh., 2. 5.-9.Jh., 3., 4. 10.-13.Jh.

Im Depotfund des Tiras-Sumpfs aus dem 9.Jh., wo zusammen mit verschiedenen Gegenständen 8 verschiedene Wollgewebefragmente von Bekleidung gefunden wurden,[4] sind 2 Gewebe in Tuchbindung und 6 in vierbindigem Köper nachgewiesen. Unter den letztgenannten fällt ein Manteltuch auf, das man aus in Z-Richtung gesponnen, in S-Richtung gezwirnten Kettenfäden und abwechselnd je 4 Fäden eingewebten in Z- und S-Richtung gesponnen Schußfäden (16 x 10-12) gewebt hat, so daß ein Streifenmuster entsteht. Es sind auch in Brettchen gewebte Gewebeanfangs- und Abschlußkanten erhalten (Abb. 13.2.3). Aufmerksamkeit erwecken auch zwei vierbindige Fischgrätköper der I. und II Qualitätsgruppe aus Z/Z Fäden, bei denen nach je 10 Kettenfäden die Richtung des Einziehen der Litzen umgekehrt wird, wobei asymmetrische Trennstellen entstehen. Bemerkenswert sind auch die für hiesige Gewebe ungewöhliche, zur IV. Qualitätsgruppe gehörende karierte, aus hellen und dunklen Wollfäden hergestellte 1/1 und 2/2 Gewebe mit eingewebten Wollbüscheln und Vogelfedern.

Im Vergleich zu dem vorigen Zeitabschnitt kann man feststellen, daß im Ostteil Lettlands nur Gewebe mit Z/Z-, während im Westteil ohnedies noch auch diejenigen mit Z/S-Spinnrichtung, vorkommen.

Während beider Zeitabschnitte kommen im ganzen Lettland auch Gewebe aus gezwirnten Fäden vor, aus welchen besonders der 2/2 Diamantköper (8.Jh.) aus Ludvigova, wie auch das Manteltuchgewebe (9.Jh.) aus dem Tiras-Sumpf, als Einfuhrgüter anzusehen sind.

Reicheres Material stammt aus dem 10.-13.Jh. Die in den Gräberfeldern der Latgallen und Selen (Nukši, Kivti, Aizkalne, Lejasdopeles, Priednieki u.a.) im Ostteil Lettlands, 65 gefundene Leinwandgewebe (Abb. 13.1.4) haben sämtliche Z/Z-Spinnrichtung. Von ihnen haben 57 Tuchbindung (1/1); meistens gehören sie zur III. Qualitätsgruppe bei etwa proportionalem Ketten- und Schußfädenverhältnis (meistens 12-14 x 8-10). Nur bei wenigen Gewebefragmenten der I. und II. Gruppe ist die Kettenfädendichte 2 - 3 mal höher als die Dichte der Schußfäden, in manchen Fällen sind die Schußfäden doppelt. Unter den 8 Geweben aus dem 12.Jh. mit dreibindigem (2/1) und vierbindigem (2/2) Köper sind 6 Funde der I. und II. Qualitätsgruppe in Rhomb- und Diamantköper bemerkenswert. Ihre Musterrapporte variieren manchmal in der Fadenzahl.

108

Die Woll- und Halbwollgewebe wurden in Tuchbindung (1/1), vierbindigem (2/2) und dreibindigem (2/1) Köper, sowie auch kariert und gemustert, gewebt (Abb. 13.3.2).

Vierzehn Wollgewebe in Tuchbindung, überwiegend der III. Qualitätsgruppe, haben Z/Z-Spinnrichtung. Es dominieren Gewebe mit vierbindigem Köper (185), meistens der IV. Qualitätsgruppe (meistens 8-10 x 6-8). Gewebe der III. Qualitätsgruppe sind öfter unter Funden aus dem 12. und 13.Jh. anzutreffen. Fragmente der I. und II. Gruppe kommen nur vereinzelt vor. Die gewöhnliche Spinnrichtung ist Z/Z, nur bei einem Männerrockgewebe der I. Gruppe ist die Richtung Z/S bezeugt. Bei einem Gewebe der II. Gruppe sind die Kettenfäden gezwirnt, die Schußfäden Z-gesponnen. Auch bei einigen Halbwollgeweben der III. und IV. Gruppe sind die leinenen Kettenfäden S-gezwirnt. Anders als die üblichen einheimischen Gewebe ist ein Fischgrätköper der II. Gruppe aus dem 11.Jh. so wie ein Dickstoffgewebe der I. Gruppe aus dem 13. Jh.

Zwölf Gewebe mit dreibindigem Köper des 12.-13.Jh. sind vorhanden. Überwiegend ist Z/Z; es kommt auch die Z/S Spinnrichtung vor. Die Qualitätsgruppen sind verschieden, hauptsächlich III., auch I. und IV. Gruppe. Es sind übrigens Anzeichen von Walkung auszumachen. Mit dreibindigem Köper sind auch 19 karierte Gewebe mit dunkelblauen Wollfäden und gebleichten Leinfäden in der Kette sowie in dem Schuß (die Leinfäden sind meistens zerfallen) und symmetrischen Karos in verschiedenen Varianten hergestellt. Sie gehören zur IV. Qualitätsgruppe, Spinnrichtung Z/Z.[5]

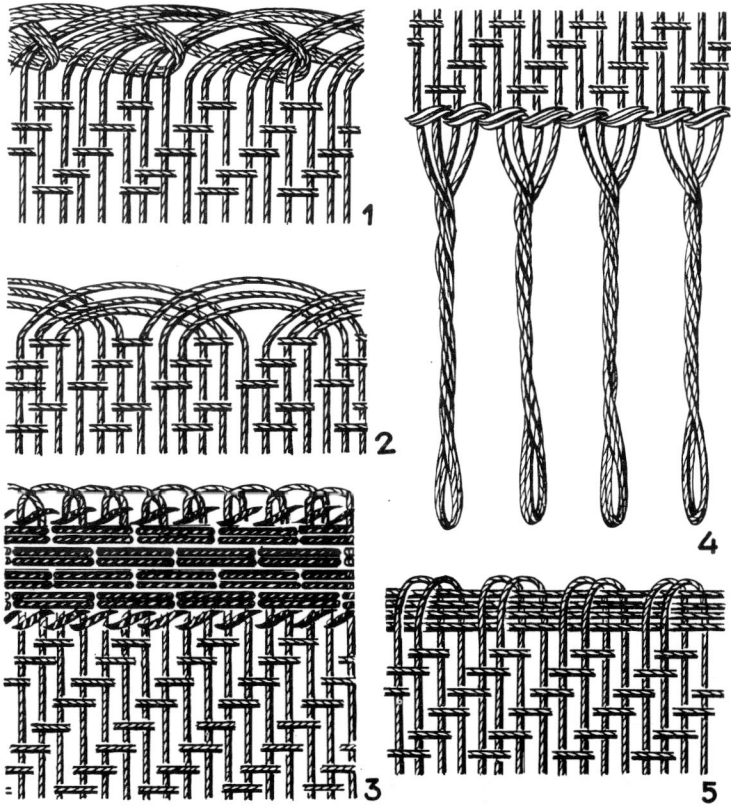

Abb. 13.2 Gewebeanfangskanten: 1. Geflochtene (Upmaļi), 2. mit geschlossenen Schlingen (Boķi), 3. Brettchengewebte (Tīras purvs), 4. halb gewebte, halb geflochtene (Ainava), 5. um Fadenbündel umgewickelte (Laukskola).

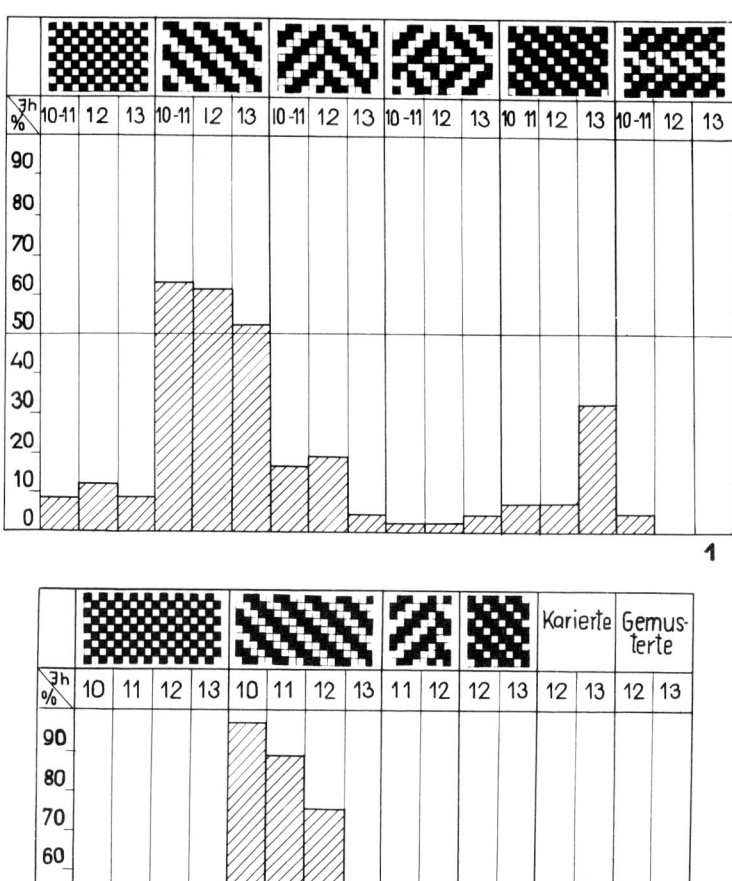

Abb. 13.3 1. Wollgewebearten der Liven aus dem 10.-13.Jh., 2. Wollgewebearten der Latgallen und Selen aus dem 10.-13.Jh.

Aus dem 12.-13.Jh. sind auch 8 gemusterte Gewebe mit dreibindigem Köper erhalten. Seltener sind Leinwandgrundgewebe, die der Dichte nach zur II. und III. Gruppe gehören. Die Musterfäden aus Wolle kann man in das Grundgewebe durch Auflesen des entsprechenden Teils des Musters, bzw. mit Spleißen, einweben. Die Muster sind zwei- bis vierteilig: Rhomben oder Vierecke. Die Grundeinheit hat je 2 Kettenfäden, 2 Schußfäden, 2 Musterfäden. Solche karierte und gemusterte Gewebe aus dem 12.-13.Jh. haben eine lokale Verbreitung genau im Territorium der Latgallen und Selen.[6]

Von den Gewebeanfangskanten, die von vierbindigen Köpergeweben erhalten sind, haben die meisten halb gewebte, halb geflochtene (oder mit zwei Brettchen gewebte) Gewebeanfangskanten

(Abb. 13.2.4). Solche Flechtwerke sind an den Rändern sämtlicher Umlegetücher anzutreffen; bei manchen sind 5-10cm lange Kettenfädenschlingen erhalten. Außerdem bei 4 einheimischen 2/2 Geweben aus dem 12.-13.Jh. wurden um Garnbündel umgewickelten Gewebeanfangskanten festgestellt; bei einem gemusterten Gewebe aus dem 13.Jh. besteht die Anfangskante aus einem Brettchenband.

Die 55 livischen Leinwandgewebe aus dem 10.-13.Jh. (Abb.13.1.3) sind Tuchbindungsgewebe sehr verschiedener Dichte, vorwiegend der III. Qualitätsgruppe, mit verhältnismäßig gleichem Verhältnis zwischen Ketten- und Schußfadenzahl. Die Fäden sind Z/Z gesponnen, mit Ausnahme eines Fragments, bei dem die Schußfäden abwechselnd 4 in Z- und 4 in S-Richtung gesponnen wurden (Zariņi).

In Wollgeweben sind Tuchbindung, dreibindige und vierbindige Köper und ihre Abarten vorgefunden (Abb.13.3.1). Die 29 Gewebe in Tuchbindung entsprechen meistens der IV. Qualitätsgruppe mit fast gleichem Verhältnis von Ketten und Schußfäden und Z/Z Spinnrichtung, mit Ausnahme einigen Geweben der III. Qualitätsgruppe, die in S-Richtung locker gesponnene Schußfäden haben. Schon im 11.Jh. sind hier karierte Gewebe aus Lein- und Wollfäden, die später bei Latgallen und Selen erkannt wurden, anzutreffen. Von den 160 Geweben in vierbindigem Köper überwiegen die III. und IV. Qualitätsgruppen, fast sämtlich mit Z/Z Spinnrichtung. Nur vereinzelt wird Z/S-Richtung angetroffen, bei manchen sind die Kettenfäden S-gezwirnt. Es sind auch in Schußfäden- oder Kettenfädenrichtung zweifarbig feingestreifte Gewebe vorhanden.

Als Abwandlungen der vierbindigen Köpergewebe aus dem 11. und 12.Jh. sind 42 Fischgratköper und 5 Diamantköper anzutreffen. Die ersten sind durch feine, in Z/S-Richtung gesponnene Fäden gekennzeichnet, die hauptsächlich der II. Qualitätsgruppe angehören: ihre Dichte beträgt meistens 14-16 x 12-14 je 1cm. Das Litzeneinziehen wird je nach 6 Kettenfäden gewechselt. Ein Teil der Fischgratköpergeweben sind bandartig (Haarbänder und Beinumbindungen). Die Diamantköper sind aus ähnlichen, aber in Z/Z-Richtung gesponnenen Fäden gewebt. Der Musterrapport konnte bei drei Fragmenten rekonstruiert werden, in jedem Fall mit einer verschiedener Fadenzahl je Musterrapport (20/18, 18/20, 26/26). Nach Qualität, Standardisierung der Stoffe und Webmethoden zu beurteilen, sind die Fischgratköper- und Diamantköper-Gewebe eingeführt.

Dreibindige Köper sind in Gräberfeldern der Liven aus dem 11.-13.Jh. (21 Beispiele) anzutreffen im Laufe der Zeit werden sie immer häufiger. Die Mehrzahl der Fragmente gehören zur III. Qualitätsgruppe. Ihre Spinnrichtung ist gewöhnlich Z/S; in den Schußfäden gibt es gröbere Garne. Manche Gewebe sind gewalkt.

Die 5 Fragmente von Rippenköper (1/2 und 2/1) (Laukskola, Zariņi, Cēsis) bestehen aus in Z/Z-Richtung drall gesponnenen feinen Fäden; der Dichte nach gehören sie zur I. Qualitätsgruppe und sind als eingeführt anzusehen.

Anfangskanten sind an 4 Fragmenten erhalten. Bei einem einheimischen Gewebe mit vierbindigem Köper ist sie um einen Garnbündel umgewickelt (Abb. 13.2.5). Zwei Gewebe mit Fischgratköper und ein Rippenköpergewebe haben mit Brettchen gewebte Anfangskanten.

Ein Vergleich von Geweben aus dem 10.-13.Jh. der Latgallen, Selen und Liven zeigt, daß ihre Herstellung als eine Hausindustrie auf etwa gleicher Entwicklungsstufe war. Doch ist zu bemerken, daß bei den Liven schon früher, schon im 11.Jh., Erzeugnisse spezialisierter Handwerker (z.B. dreibindige Köpergewebe) auftreten. Hier ist auch die Qualität der vierbindigen Köpergewebe besser. Dank der besseren geograpischen Situation und Handelsaktivitäten sind auch mehrere eingeführte Gewebe bezeugt (Fischgrat-, Diamant- und Rippenköpergewebe), die ähnlich wie einige Gewebe vom 8.-9. Jh., aus Westeuropa eingeführt sind, wo sich ihre Produktionszentren befanden.[7] Die eingeführten Gewebe sind selten (Abb. 13.3.1): sie werden in den Gräbern von Angehörigen der reicheren Oberschicht angetroffen.

Im 10.-13.Jh. im Gebiet Lettlands ebenso wie in der vorigen Periode überwiegen noch immer die 2/2 Gewebe. Gewebe in Tuchbindung bewahren ihre vorige Stelle. Im 11.Jh. fängt die Verbreitung dreibindiger 2/1 Köpergewebe an (Abb. 13.3.1,2).

Unter Leingeweben, bei denen im 7.-9.Jh. die ripsartigen Gewebe überwiegen, im 10.-13.Jh. dominieren die 1/1 Gewebe mit fast gleichem Ketten- und Schußfädenanzahlverhältnis.

Im 3.-13.Jh. sind in Lettland die zu dieser Zeit in Nordeuropa verbreiteten Grundarten von Geweben und ihre Herstellungsmethoden üblich; es sind Einflüsse von aussen zu beobachten, aber auch lokaler Sonderheiten (karierte und gemusterte Gewebe) sind bemerkbar.

Zur Frage der Webstuhltypen in dieser Periode können verhältnismäßig sichere Hinweise aus den Gewebeanfangskanten gewonnen werden. Geflochtene (Abb. 13.2.1), mit geschlossenen Schlingen (Abb. 13.2.2), sowie halb gewebte, halb geflochtene (Abb. 13.2.4) Gewebeanfangskanten kommen im 7.-13.Jh. bei einheimischen Erzeugnissen mit charakteristischer lokaler Verzierung vor. Sie sind für senkrechte Webstühle mit 2 Walzen kennzeichend,[8] welche in diesem Zeitabschnitt im Ostteil Lettlands dominierten. Im 11.-13.Jh. kommen bei Latgallen und Liven auch um Garnbündel umgewickelte Gewebeanfangskanten (Abb. 13.2.5) vor, welche für Gewichtswebstühle mehr geeignet sind. Hinweise auf die letzteren geben auch die in kleiner Anzahl in Siedlungen des 10.-12.Jh. gefundenen Gewichte. Nach den als Brettchenbändern gewebten Gewebeanfangskanten ist im Zusammenhang mit Gewichtswebstühlen auch das lokale gemusterte Gewebe aus dem 13.Jh. zu setzen. Alle früher vorkommenden Gewebe mit ähnlichen Anfangskanten, die man als Kennzeichen für Gewichtswebstühle ansehen kann, sind als Einfuhrwaren zu betrachten.[9]

Die 2/2 Gewebe mit schlauchförmigen Seitenkanten, welche im 3.-13.Jh. auf senkrechten Webstühlen hergestellt wurden (der Tradition nach bei der Benutzung einseitigen Litzen), wurden noch im 19.-20.Jh. bei der Herstellung von 2/2 Umlegetüchern an Trittwebestühlen gewebt.

Auf das Einführen der fortgeschrittenen Trittwebestühle weisen in Schichten des 12.-13.Jh. der Städte Riga und Koknese vorgefundene Teile von Webstühlen hin,[10] wie auch der Umstand, daß um diese Zeit einheimische Gewebe mit dreibindigem Köper besserer Qualität auftauchen.

Literatur

1. З.Д. Шноре, А.З. Зариня, У.Б. Даига, *Нукшинский Могилъник* (Gräberfeld Nukschi), *Материалы и исследования по археологии Патвияской* ССРI, Рига, 1957, 31-38; V. Urtāns, *Tiras purva depozits*(Depotfund von Tiras-Sumpf),*LSPR Vēstures muzeja raksti Arheologija*Rīgā, 1962, 83-93

2. A. Zariņa, *Seno latgaļu apgērbs*(Die Latgallischen Trachten), Rīgā, 1970, 216 A. Zariņa*Libiešu apgērbs 10.-13.gs.* (Livische Trachten 10.-13.Jh.), Rīgā, 1988

3. A. Nahlik, *Ткани Новгорода*, (Gewebe Nowgorods), *Материалы и исследования по археэ ологии СССР, И23*, Москва, 1963, 229; IV. Gruppe bis zu 10 Kettfäden x 8 Schußfäden; III. Gruppe 15 x 12; II. Gruppe 22 x 15; I. Gruppe über 22 x 15 je 1 cm.

4. Urtāns (1962), 90-92

5. Zariņa (1970), 99-106

6. Zariņa (1970), 106-108

7. L.Bender Jørgensen,*Forhistoriske Textiler i Skandinavien (Nordiske Fortidsminde*B 9), 1986, 352, 354, 356, 360, 361

8. Нахлик (1963), 277-279; Bender Jørgensen (1986), 344, 345

9. Bender Jørgensen (1986), 345

10. A. Caune,*Rīgas arheoloģiskās ekspedīcijas darbs 1972.gadā*(Die Rigaer archäologische Expedition 1972), *Zinātniskās atskaites sesijas materiāli par arheologu, antropologu un etnogrāfu 1972. gada pētījumu rezultātiem* Rīgā, 1973.g., 24 Zariņa (1970), 19

14. Eine kurzgefasste Übersicht über die Textilforschung in Mähren (Tschechoslowakei)

Marie Kostelníková
Brno

In diesem Beitrag möchte ich in groben Zügen die Ergebnisse der Textilforschung in der Tschechoslowakei, besonders in Mähren, erwähnen, denn in Mähren (historischem Gebiet im Osten der Tschechischen sozialistischen Republik, zwischen Böhmen und der Slowakei) begann bereits in den fünfziger Jahren ein tieferes Interesse für die Textilfunde. Damals hatten zwei Professoren der Textilmittelschule in Brünn (Brno) für den Leiter der Ausgrabungen in Staré Město-Valy, Doz. Dr Vilém Hrubý, Analysen der Textilfunden aus dem 9.Jh. n. Chr. durchgeführt.[1] Später war die Textilforschung beschränkt und erst in den siebziger Jahren wurde eine systematische Forschung im Gebiet Mährens aus der Zeit der Alten Slawen wiederhergestellt. Die meisten Fragmente der Textilien stammen aus den grossen Gräberfeldern der grossmährischen Burgwälle in Mikulčice (Bez. Hodonín), Staré Město (Bez. Uh. Hradiště) und Břeclav-Pohansko (Bez. Břeclav).

Auch Spezialisten von andern vorgeschichtlichen Kulturen haben dann ihr Interesse den Textilfunden gewidmet.

In Mähren stammen die ältesten Textilfunde aus dem Neolithikum, aus der Zeit der Linearbandkeramik, her. In Mohelnice (Bez. Šumperk) sind in einem Brunnen auf der Siedlung Teile von doppelgezwirnten Seilen aus Flachs gefunden worden (Abb. 14.1). Auf einem Gefäß derselben Kultur in Luleč (Bez. Vyškov) ist ein Abdruck einer Leinwand erhalten, deren Spuren vermuten lassen, daß es sich hier um Zwirnfäden handelte.

Die Produktion der Textilien im Äneolithikum ist durch eine Menge von Spinnwirteln, tönernen Gewichten und Spulen aus der Siedlung in Hlinsko (Bez. Přerov) belegt.[2] Aus dem 12.Jh. v. Chr. haben wir den Fund eines Wollstoffs aus Staré Město (Bez. Uh. Hradiště), der dicht eingestellt ist (22-20 Fäden auf 1cm). Im Schuß wechseln regelmässig einfache Fäden mit dreifachgezwirnten Fäden im Verhältnis 1:1.[3]

Im reichen hallstattzeitlichen Begräbnis in Býčí Skála Höhle (Bez. Blansko) waren Bruchstücke von Wollfilz gefunden worden. Für uns sehr interessant ist der Fund eines Textilfragmentes aus Pustiměř (Bez. Vyškov). Es handelt sich um die Reste eines 2/2 Köpers, in dem 2-3 Fäden mit scharfer Z-Drehung mit ähnlichen Gruppen von Fäden mit schwacher S-Drehung wechseln. Diese Art findet man in beiden Fadensystemen. Es handelt sich offenbar um ein den im Salzgebiet Österreichs gefundenen Textilien ähnliches Stück.[4]

Die Untersuchungen der latènezeitlichen Textilien sind bis jetzt auch nur gering. Es kommen hier Leinwand und Köper vor. In mehreren Fällen wurden grobe, mehr als 1mm dicke Fäden benützt. Bekannt sind aber auch feine Leinstoffe; sie wurden als Füllung der hohlen Armbänder benützt (Abb. 14.2). Auf einem Fragment ist der Ripsrand erhalten.

Die meisten Kenntnisse haben wir im Bereich der Forschung von slawischen Textilien des 9.-10. Jh. in Mähren.[5] Bis heute wurden 311 Textilreste von 37 Lokalitäten der Analyse unterworfen. Die grösste Zahl stammt aus Südmähren, wo sich die bedeutenden grossmährischen Burgwälle aus dem 8.-

Abb. 14.1 Ein Stück des Seiles aus Mohelnice, Linearbandkeramikzeit

Abb. 14.2 Die Gewebefüllung eines Armbandes aus Miroslav, Latènezeit

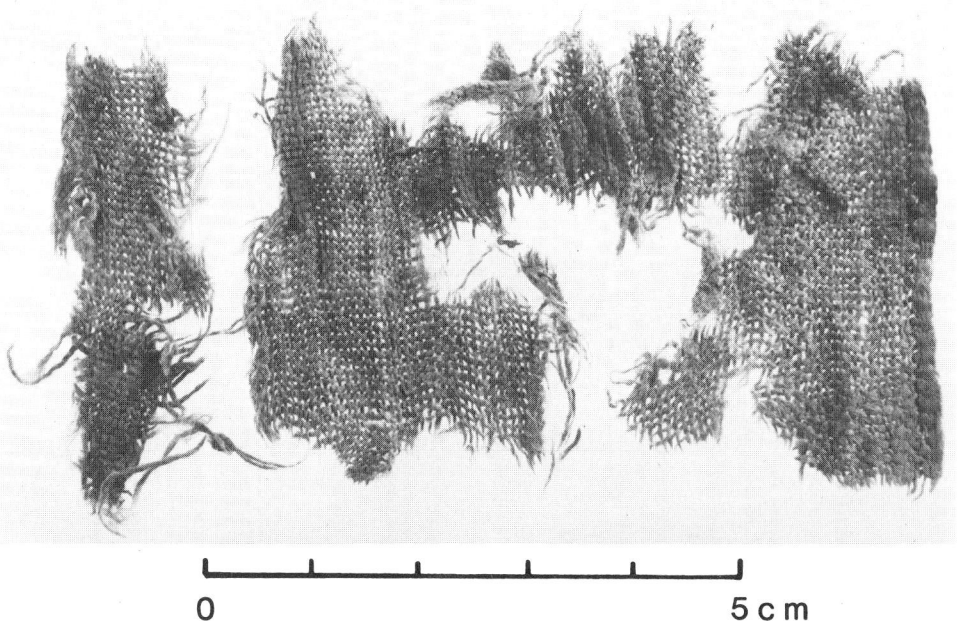

0   5 cm

11.Jh., aus der Zeit der Anfänge des Staates und des Christentums, mit den ersten gemauerten Kirchenbauten, befinden (Abb. 14.3). Staré Město liegt auf dem mittleren Flußlauf der March (Morava), Mikulčice auf ihrem unteren Lauf, Břeclav-Pohansko am Fluß Thaya (Dyje) und Rajhrad (Bez. Brno) auf der Svratka, südlich von Brno. Es waren offensichtlich reiche und bedeutungsvolle Zentren. Auf ihren Gräberfeldern sind manche Bewohner mit goldenem, silbernem oder vergoldetem Schmuck bestattet worden. Die bronzenen und eisernen Beigaben in den Gräbern haben die meisten Textilfragmente konserviert.

Die grösste Anzahl der Textilfunde ist bisher aus Mikulčice, 95 Fragmente, festgestellt. In 46 Gräbern fand man 64 messbare Fragmente von Leinwandgeweben, 10 Köpergewebe 3/2 und 2/1, ein Köper 2/2, ein Tuch und 10 Zweischußgewebe aus Flachs und Seide. Die zweitgrösste Anzahl Textilien stammt aus Staré Město mit 40 Fragmenten aus 24 Gräbern. Dort hat man auch broschierte und lancierte Fragmente gefunden. Es folgen Rajhrad-Rajhradice mit 36 Geweben in 13 Gräbern und Břeclav-Pohansko mit 25 Textilien in 16 Gräbern. Gewebe stammen auch von anderen Gräberfeldern. Das grösste war in Nechvalín, wo man 35 Stücke in 23 Gräbern fand. Die Bodenverhältnisse sind grösstenteils für die Erhaltung der Textilien ungeeignet. In Mikulčice, wo zur Zeit der Analyse ungefähr 900 Gräber aufgedeckt wurden, beträgt die Zahl der Gräber mit Textilfunden zirka 5%.

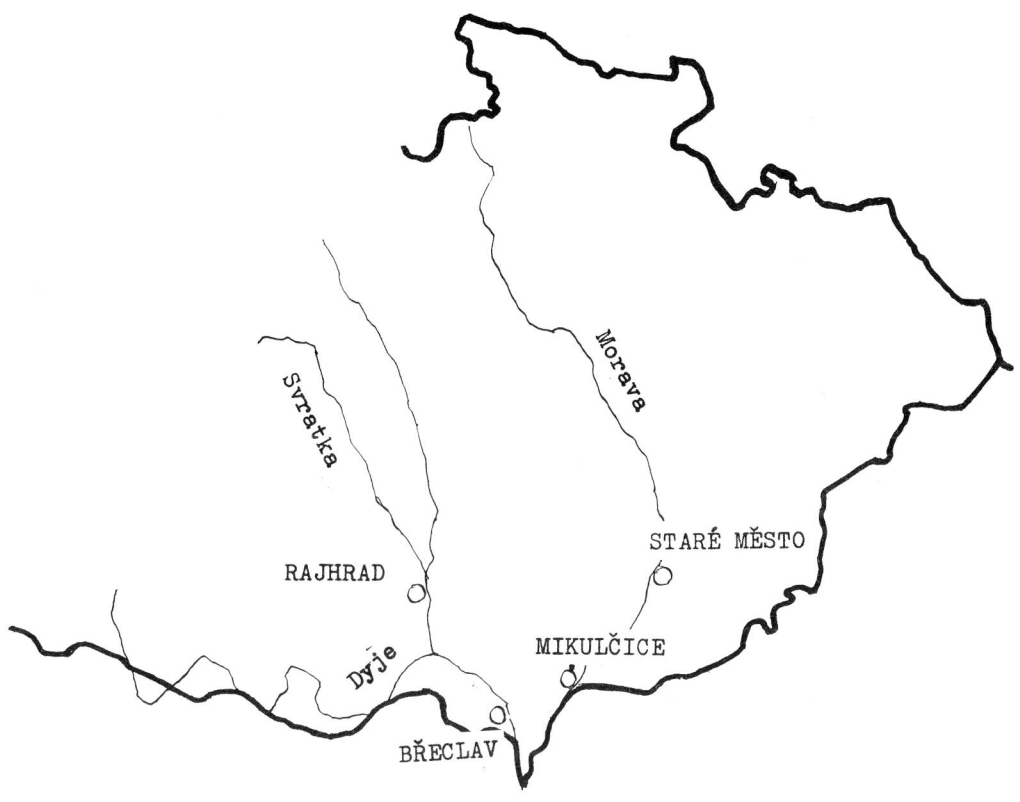

Abb. 14.3 Die bekannten grossmährischen Burgwälle in Mähren

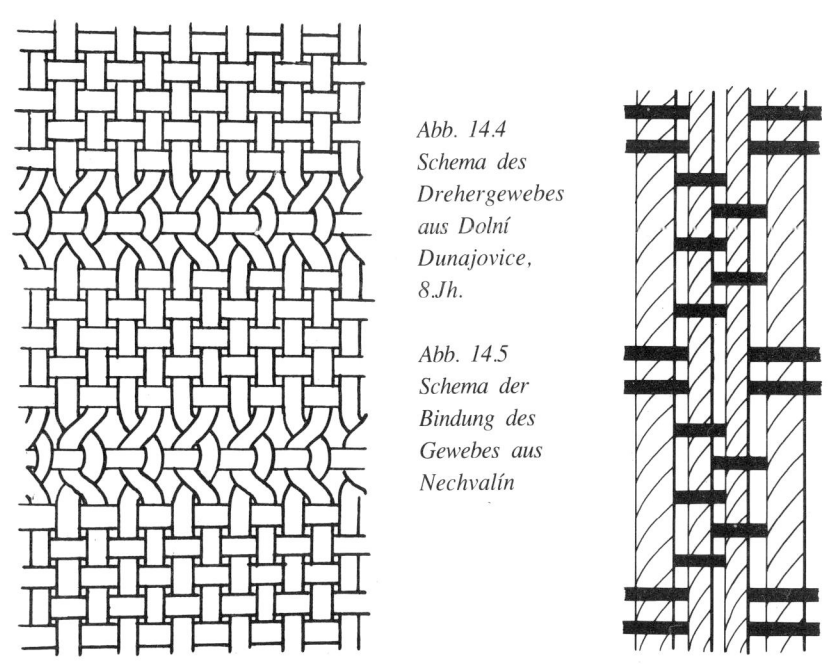

Abb. 14.4
Schema des
Drehergewebes
aus Dolní
Dunajovice,
8.Jh.

Abb. 14.5
Schema der
Bindung des
Gewebes aus
Nechvalín

Insgesamt sind die meisten der gefundenen Gewebe in Leinwandbindung, 227 mal; Köper kommen nur 32 mal vor, und gemusterte Köper sind noch nicht bekannt. Auf einer Riemenzunge aus Dolní Dunajovice (Bez. Břeclav) ist ein Drehergewebe erhalten (Abb. 14.4). Das Gewebe auf einem Schwert in Nechvalín (Bez. Hodonín) ist unter den Funden aus Mähren bisher eine Ausnahme. Es wechseln hier dicke Fäden mit 2 oder 3 dünnen Fäden abgebunden durch dünne Fäden in Leinwand- und Ripsbindung (Abb. 14.5). Auf keinem der Fragmente ist der Rand erhalten; die Fadenrichtungen sind deshalb unsicher.

Die Fäden der Leinwandgewebe haben in beiden Richtungen Z-Drehung, nur in einem Fall ist S-Drehung in dem einen und Z-Drehung in dem anderen Fadensystem bezeugt. Die Köper hatten im Gegenteil meistens diese S/Z Drehung.

Der Rohstoff wurde an ein Paar Fragmenten festgestellt. In 10 Fällen liegt Wolle vor, besonders in Staré Město. Hier fand man auch Angorawolle. Der Flachs kommt öfter vor - in 20 Fällen. Die zweischußigen Gewebe mit Füllkette waren höchstwahrscheinlich importiert (Abb. 14.6). Bisher sind sie nur in den vier grossen Burgwällen gefunden worden. Außer Seide ist manchmal auch Flachs gebraucht. In einem Fall, in Rajhrad, ist ein Fragment mit seidener Kette und einem seidenen Schuß: Der zweite, atlasartig gewebte Schuß ist aus Wolle. In diesem Fall handelt es sich um Vogts Bindung Nr 4 mit dünnen Doppelfäden in der Füllkette.[6] Ein farbiges Muster wurde nicht festgestellt, manchmal aber ändern sich die Fäden in der Abtönung.

In der Zeit des Grossmährischen Reiches hatte Mähren enge Beziehungen zu Byzanz. Der grossmährische Fürst Rostislav bat den byzantinischen Kaiser Michael III, ihm nach Mähren christliche Priester, die die slawische Sprache beherrschten, zu senden. Mähren hatte aber damals auch Beziehungen zu dem adriatischen Gebiet und zu dem Donauraum, zu Passau und Regensburg. Über die grossmährischen Burgwälle verliefen die Handelswege, aber woher die Seidenwaren im 9. Jh. gekommen waren, das wissen wir noch nicht.

Unsere Interesse richtet sich außer den Textilfunden auch den Textilwerkzeugen. Auf einem Textilfragment aus Staré Město wurde ein kleines gewebtes Löchlein festgestellt (Abb. 14.7). Einige Kettenfäden wurden losgemacht und in Richtung des Schußes umgedreht.

Wir schliessen daraus, dass man im 9.-10Jh. den vertikalen Webstuhl verwendet hatte. Es gibt keine Belege für den horizontalen Webstuhl. In Staré Město sind 3 Brettchen aus Knochen gefunden worden (Abb. 14.8), aber kein Erzeugnis davon, deshalb wissen wir nicht, ob mit ihnen verzierte

Abb. 14.6 Das Zweischußgewebe mit Füllkette

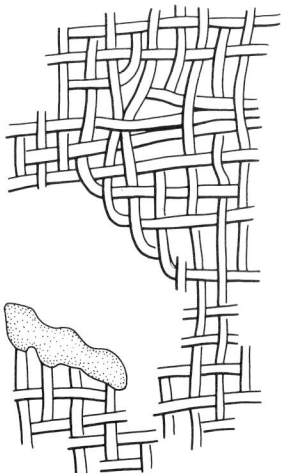

Abb. 14.7 Ein kleines Loch auf einem Stück Gewebe aus Staré Město

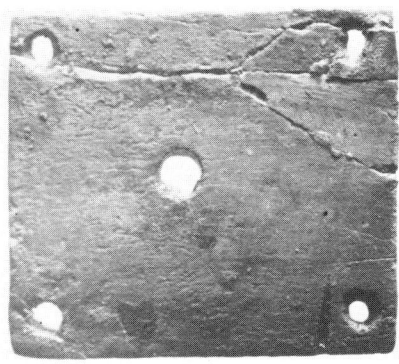

Abb. 14.8 Ein Knochenbrettchen aus Staré Město

Abb. 14.9 Die Netznadeln aus Mikulčice

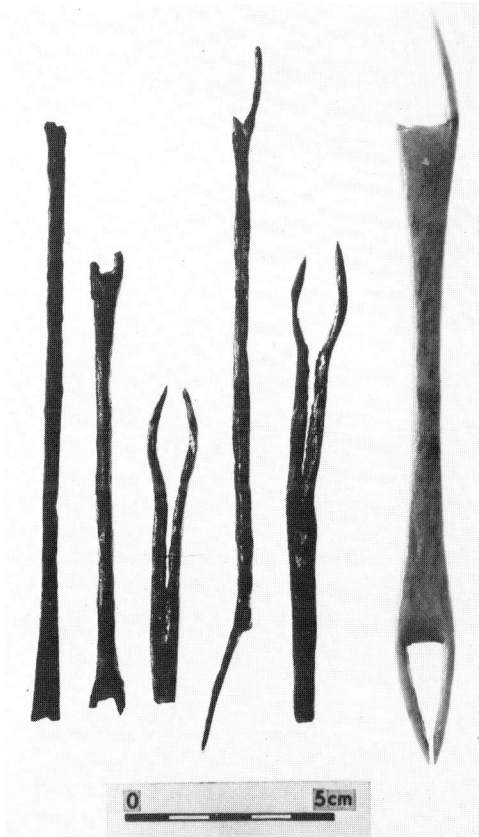

Ränder oder Gürtel gewebt wurden. Wir fanden auch keine Netze, die mit den Mikulčicer Netznadeln verfertigt wären (Abb. 14.9).

Bei der geologischen Untersuchung der Spinnwirtel aus Mikulčice ist festgestellt worden, daß nur ein geringer Teil tönerne Wirtel sind. Diese Kügelchen hatten aber so enge Öffnungen, daß es sich vielleicht nicht um Wirtel handelt. Die Tonwirtel waren immer aus Scherben hergestellt. Fast alle Wirtel sind hier aus weichen Gesteinen erzeugt (auch die, die als tönerne beschrieben wurden).

Unsere Aufmerksamkeit wird auch dem Zweck, dem die Textilien dienten, gewidmet. Wir wagen nicht aus den kleinen Textilfragmenten die Tracht der Bevölkerung des Grossmährischen Reiches zu rekonstruieren: Wir können nur schliessen, daß die Verstorbenen in mehreren Gewändern beigesetzt wurden, z. B. in Kleidung aus zwei Arten Leinen und aus Köpergeweben. Irgendein Teil der Kleidung wurde unter dem Kinn mit Hilfe von zwei Knöpfen und Schlaufen zugeknöpft. Die Männer trugen vielleicht lange Mäntel: Gewebe fand man auch an den Sporen. Reiche Frauen hatten irgendeine goldene Strickerei auf den Kleidern und goldene oder silberne gewebte Diademe. Die Kleidung wurde mit Textil- oder Ledergürteln zusammengezogen. Die Reiter trugen Lederschuhe und die Füsse schützten sie darin mit einem Stück Leinstoff, wie bei einem Fund aus Mikulčice beobachtet wurde. Dort war auf der Innenseite eines Sporns Leder, dann Gewebe und der Abdruck von menschlicher Haut. Das Gewebe lag also zwischen dem Schuh und dem Fuß.

Die Textilien wurden auch anders benutzt: als Schutz der scharfen oder wertvollen Gegenstände, als Decken, als Dichtungen der Achse einer Töpferscheibe. Das beweisen mehrere Abdrücke auf dem Boden der Töpfe in Mikulčice und Olomouc (Abb. 14.10).

Die Ausgrabungen setzen sich fort, und fortgesetzt wird auch die Textilforschung. In den letzten Jahren bearbeiten auch in Böhmen und in der Slowakei die Wissenschaftler systematisch die Textilfunde. Wir hoffen, daß wir der Textilforschung in Mitteleuropa auch weiterhin einen Beitrag leisten können.

Abb. 14.10 Abdruck eines Gewebes am Boden eines Topfes aus Mikulčice

Literatur

1. V. Hrubý, *Staré Město - velkomoravské pohřebiště na Valách*, Praha, 1955

2. J. Pavelčik, 'Drobné terrakoty z Hlinska u Lipníka (Okr. Přerov) II, *Památky archeologické* 74, 1983, 295-315

3. V. Hrubý, 'Nález tkaniny z mladší doby bronzové ve Starém Městě', *Časopis moravského muzea* 53/4, 1968-69, 51-58

4. H.J. Hundt, 'Vorgeschichtliche Gewebe aus dem Hallstätter Salzberg', *Jahrbuch des römisch-germanischen Zentralmuseums Mainz* 7, 1960, 126-150

5. M. Kostelníková, *Velkomoravský textil v archeologických nálezech na Moravě, Studie AŬ ČSAV Brno*, Praha, 1972

6. E. Vogt, 'Frühmittelalterliche Stoffe aus der Abtei St. Maurice', *Zeitschrift für schweizerische Archäologie und Kunstgeschichte* 18, 1958, 123

15. Medieval English and Flemish textiles found in Gdańsk

Jerzy Maik
Łódź

One of the most significant issues in the study of textile history is the problem of textile trade. The possibilities of such a trade in ancient times were discussed in Bergen in 1984.[1] A lot of data related to textile trade in the Middle Ages is supported by written sources. At the same time numerous finds of Medieval textiles in Poland coming mostly from excavations in towns give us a chance to recognise items of foreign origin among the archaeological material.

The present paper, reviewing the collection of Medieval textiles from Gdańsk (the largest in Poland), attempts to distinguish only those textiles which were imported from western Europe. Textile import from the East is a vast issue and requires to be discussed separately.

A fishing settlement of urban type mentioned in *The Life of Saint Adalbert* in 997 as *urbs Gyddanyzc* was established on the island in the Vistula river delta in the second half of the 10th century.[2] At the end of that century Gdańsk was already among the bigger towns of the Polish State and its further development proceeded in the 11th and 12th centuries. This development was, to a large extent, based on sea and land trade, but also on the local craftsmen's production and sea fishing. At the beginning of the 13th century the island appeared to be too small and the settlement moved to the mainland near the existing market. In 1308 Gdańsk and East Pomerania were occupied by Teutonic Knights; the town itself was burned and its fortifications were destroyed. In the second half of the 14th century the Teutonic Order built a castle which replaced the previous old ducal wooden castle. Some of the local Slav people living there were moved to the new settlement called Osiek; but some of them remained in the old settlement founded in the 13th century. Gdańsk was returned to Poland in 1466 as a result of the Thirteen Years' War with the Teutonic Order. From the 15th to the 18th century Gdańsk was one of the biggest and richest towns in Poland.[3]

In 1945 at the end of the Second World War Gdańsk was totally destroyed. That made it possible to carry out excavations on an immense scale, and they are still being continued. The brick and wooden structures of Medieval Gdańsk have been reconstructed to the original plan and its Medieval harbour has been discovered as well. Excavations also revealed very interesting data on people's jobs - handicrafts, fishing, trade both near and far. Ground conditions were favourable to the preservation of finds, not only inorganic, but organic as well, such as wood, leather and textiles.

Most of the 678 textiles were discovered on the oldest settlement site (no 1) in layers dating from about 980 to 1308. A smaller number of textiles (58) came from the 13th-14th century settlement sites (no 2 and 4), and eight from the 14th-15th century settlement of Osiek.[4]

Among those finds there are above all local products. This is attested by the remains of tools used in the textile industry, found in excavations together with the remains of the horizontal loom, which may be related to professional weaving.[5] It is possible, however, that some part of the textiles found in Gdańsk are of foreign origin and were brought to the town as a result of trade and exchange.[6]

Cloth played an important role in the Baltic Sea trade during the Middle Ages.[7] It was brought to the countries on the Baltic from western Europe initially by Frisian merchants, later by Gotland and finally by German Hanseatic traders, who from the 13th century monopolised the Baltic trade.[8] In the 13th and the 14th centuries it was mostly Flemish cloth.

The woollen industry in Flanders was already of a high standard in the 12th century, but it acquired international importance in the 13th century. Its production was organised by great merchants who imported wool from England and sold the finished products all over Europe. Apart from the merchants there were also retail tradesmen, especially in smaller towns. Cloth produced in the 13th century in Flanders was of the highest quality in North-West Europe and was meant primarily for export, being bought by the richer social classes. The woollen industry was called 'The Great Woollen Industry'.[9] It was most highly developed in cities such as Ypres, Ghent, Bruges and Brussels.

Thanks to Hanseatic merchants, Flemish cloth reached not only Novgorod Velikiy in Russia, but also eastern Pomerania, which in the 14th century and in the first half of the 15th century was ruled by the Teutonic Order.[10] In the Order's accounts cloth in stock in Gdańsk, Elbląg and Toruń was often listed.[11] Some of that cloth was used by the Order itself, but quite a large part was sold to Poland, where it reached the royal court.[12]

In the 14th century the Flemish woollen industry lost its leading position. This was mainly caused by the reduction in wool imports from England, which used wool as the tool of political pressure on Flanders. At the same time, the woollen industry developed considerably in England.[13] Flemish weavers were forced to look for new sources of wool and they found them in Spain, where Merino sheep with very good wool - sheep which were the descendants of Roman sheep - were bred.[14] Initially, however, Merino wool was accepted with reluctance in Flanders, since the use of the new material brought about a drop in the quality of Flemish products. In the 13th century Merino wool was already used in Bruges, where it was combined with English wool. During the 14th and 15th centuries Spanish wool became indispensable for the whole Flemish woollen industry.[15] Apart from the problem of getting raw materials, some problems in sales occurred which were caused by a drop in the income of the ruling classes for whom the luxurious cloth was meant.[16] The Flemish woollen industry used traditional and very complicated methods of production and was not able to simplify them to get cheaper products which could have been bought by poorer customers. It began to decline therefore in the big cities of Flanders. The woollen industry in smaller towns, however, the so-called 'New Woollen Industry', using simplified methods of production, became more and more significant.[17] The English woollen industry was still the most important in Northern Europe in the second half of the 14th century and the first half of the 15th century. English cloth was simpler and cheaper than Flemish, but very good. That is why it enjoyed a great popularity on the European markets.[18]

This decline in the Flemish woollen industry and the rise of the English is reflected in the accounts of Gdańsk merchants at the beginning of the 15th century. Principally English, occasionally Flemish and very occasionally Dutch, cloth was listed here.[19] It is worth mentioning that at the beginning of the 15th century cloth made up nearly 40% of all goods imported into Gdańsk. That level of import decreased in 1440, when cloth accounted for only 10% of all imports. In the second half of the 15th century the quantity of cloth imported into Gdańsk increased to up to 80%, but at that time it was mostly Dutch cloth that was brought in.[20]

It should be added here that in the 15th century products of the German woollen industry were imported into Pomerania. They were made like the Dutch textiles of local wool similar to that from Pomeranian sheep.[21]

In a given textile-producing area recognition of foreign raw materials and foreign technology helps to distinguish imported textiles from the local ones. Traces of many technological operations from western Europe were found in Gdańsk textiles which were certainly of local wool.[22] That criterion therefore may not be applicable in this case. The Merino wool used in the West European woollen industry or the wool of fine-fleeced English sheep have much thinner fibres than the wool of sheep bred in Pomerania - the primitive local sheep and sheep of marsh type.[23] Written sources tell us neither about the import of raw wool from the West to Pomerania nor about the import of Spanish or English sheep in the Middle Ages. It is well-known that Frisian sheep (Vagas) and Franco-Belgian sheep (Texel) appeared in Pomerania in the 12th and the 13th centuries. Their wool, however, like the wool of German sheep, resembles Pomeranian wool of marsh type and it is impossible to distinguish it in archaeological material only on the basis of textile measurements.[24] Merino sheep were only brought to Poland in the 18th century.[25] Its seems therefore that textiles of the 13th-15th centuries in which the wool of English fine-fleeced sheep or of Spanish Merino can be found, may be regarded as of Flemish or English provenance.

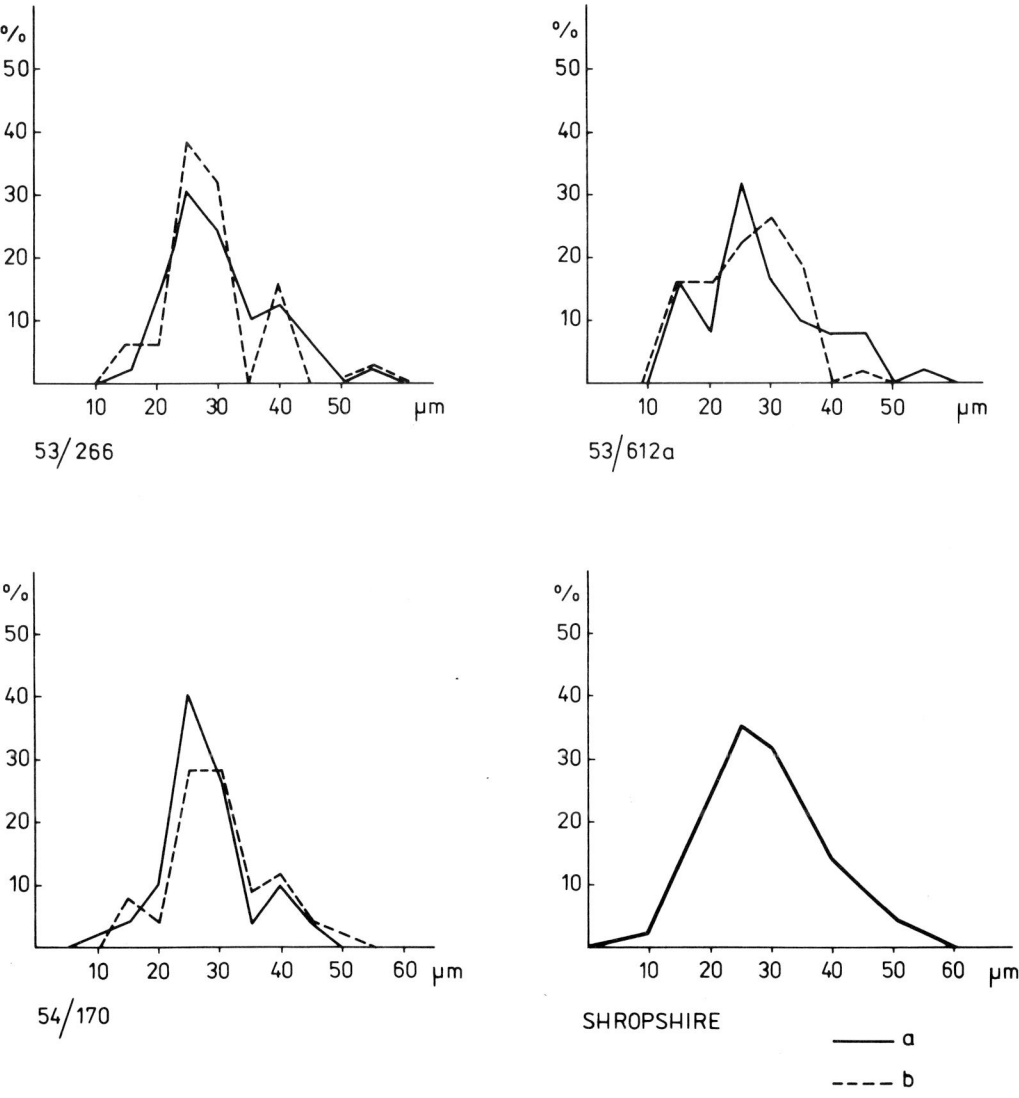

Fig. 15.1 Diagrams of fibre thickness of the Medieval merino wool found in Gdańsk and of the present-day Spanish merino wool : a. warp, b. weft

In order to distinguish wool of English and Merino sheep it would be most convenient to compare wool of textiles found in Gdańsk with wool of Medieval textiles found in western Europe - England, Belgium and Holland. Unfortunately, I have no access to such material. A. Nahlik while examining textiles from Novgorod Velikiy 25 years ago did not have access either. Yet he managed to compare the thickness of wool fibres from Novgorod with the mean thickness of the fine wool fibres of present-day English shortwool sheep of Shropshire and Hampshire types, and also with the mean thickness of wool fibres of the present Spanish Merino sheep.[26] This method seems to be very effective in detecting imported wool, even if we accept that Spanish and English sheep were subjected to various treatments to improve their fleece. I have tried to use this method while studying Pomeranian wool. But I did not look for wool of English longwool sheep, since it seems to be close to the wool of marsh-type sheep bred in the Middle Ages on the southern coast of the Northern Sea and the Baltic.[27] I am afraid that the possibility of making a mistake would be too high in this case.

According to Nahlik's calculations the wool of Medieval Merinos would have a mean fibre diameter of about 18-25μm and a coefficient of variation of 20-38% (fig. 15.1), and the wool of Medieval English shortwool sheep a mean fibre diameter of 25-29μm and a coeffiecient of variation of 20-38% (fig. 15.2).[28]

Only those Gdańsk textiles which were found at sites no 2 and 4 and at Osiek were examined and had their wool diameters measured. The coefficient of variation in a given sample was recorded and a check was made on whether samples contained hair and kemp.[29] In this way it could be stated that 14 fragments of textiles contained English wool while eight fragments contained Merino wool. All those textiles date to the 13th-15th centuries.

English wool was identified in seven woollen cloth fragments from the 13th-15th centuries. Traces of red dye were observed in two fragments and one fragment was clearly grey. Six fragments of the cloth were made in 2/1 twill and one fragment in tabby. English wool was also found in seven fragments of non-fulled textiles from the 13th-14th centuries: three of them are in tabby, two in 2/2 twill and one in 2/1 twill.

Spanish Merino wool was found in three fragments of red woollen cloth from the 13th-15th centuries. All those fragments were woven in tabby. Merino wool was discovered in five fragments of non-fulled textiles from the 13th-15th centuries as well. One of those fragments was in 2/1 twill, three of them in 2/2 twill. The last weave, 3/2 twill, is completely unknown in Poland. I do not know any analogous textile from other areas.

Two of the non-fulled textiles in 2/2 twill made of Merino wool deserve to be described in detail and considered separately in further studies. They can be distinguished from others because of an unusual thread-count. One of them dating back to the first half of the 14th century, from site no 2, was woven from worsted yarn in ZZ spin direction and has 115-120 warp-threads and 16 weft threads per cm (Fig. 15.3). The other, dating back to the 14th-15th centuries from Osiek, also of worsted yarn in ZS spin direction, has 72 warp-threads and 14 weft-threads per 1cm (fig. 15.4). In the weft of the latter a little thicker wool was used and it could be English fine wool.

In Poland in Medieval written sources woollen textiles were called in Latin *pannus* or in German *Laken* or *Tuch*.[30] These terms are translated into Polish as *sukno* (woollen cloth) which nowadays means fulled woollen textiles. However, it seems correct to identify them with archaeological examples of Medieval woollen fulled and non-fulled textiles. The Medieval cloth-weaver made woollen textiles, some of which were fulled. A weaver did the fulling himself in his own workshop or mechanical fulling mill. The latter were already in use in the second half of the 10th century in Italy. In western Europe they became popular in the 11th-13th centuries; in Poland they appeared probably in the 12th century.[31] The analysis of archaeological material indicates that initially only a small number of textiles were fulled, but their proportion systematically increased.[32] Textiles made of woollen yarn were being fulled, but some, both cheap simple textiles and expensive worsted textiles, were left without fulling.[33] In Poland, the term *sukno (Pannus, Laken, Tuch)* must have meant in the beginning all kinds of woollen textiles. It is thus understood by the authors of the *Old Polish Dictionary*.[34] The equation of *sukno* and fulled woollen textiles - woollen cloth - must be put later.

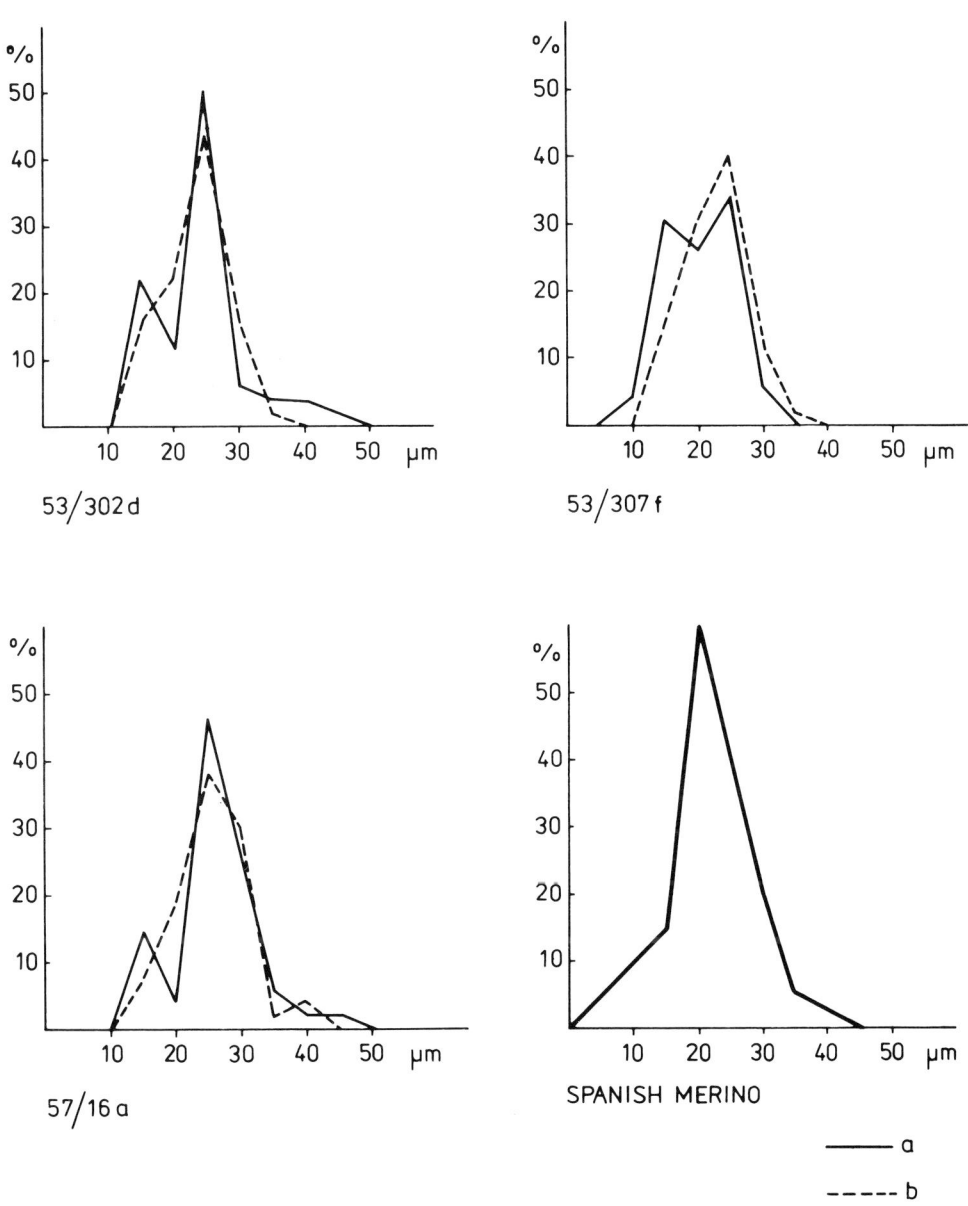

Fig. 15.2 Diagrams of fibre thickness of the Medieval English wool found in Gdańsk and of the present-day wool of English Shropshire sheep: a. warp, b. weft

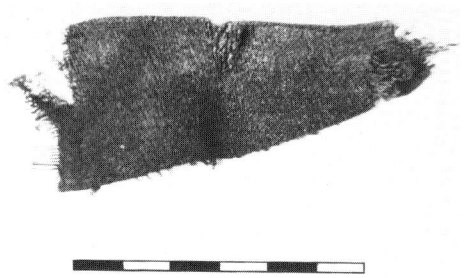

Fig. 15.3 Textile of Birka type (14th century)

Fig. 15.4 Textile of Birka type (14th-15th century)

Fig. 15.5 Flemish woollen cloth in tabby (13th century)

Fig. 15.6 Flemish non-fulled textile in tabby (13th century)

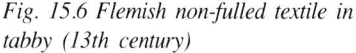

I will attempt to answer the question as to which of the textiles named by me as West European came from Flanders and which from England. Firstly, Flemish cloth of the first class made initially of English wool, and later of Merino wool, was exported at the beginning of the 13th century. During the 14th century its export decreased and the cloth which reached European markets was of lower quality. Secondly, English cloth, less complicated than the Flemish, and made of English wool, began to be sold in Pomerania at the end of the 14th century. Thus textiles which contain Merino wool (which was not used in England) and those made of English wool which are older than the latter half of the 14th century should be considered as Flemish products. To be regarded as English, cloth must be produced of English wool, be relatively simple and be dated to the end of the 14th century, or at least to its second half or to the 15th century. It is likely that the written sources known to us did not note the beginnings of import of English textiles into Pomerania.

On such criteria most textiles which I have examined came from Flanders. Among products from the 13th century there are four woollen cloth fragments in 2/1 twill of English wool and one woollen cloth fragment in tabby (fig. 15.5) as well as two fragments in tabby (fig. 15.6), one fragment in 2/1 twill (fig. 15.7) and two fragments in 2/2 twill non-fulled and all made of English wool, together with one fragment in 3/2 twill of Merino wool (fig. 15.8).

Among textiles from the first half of the 14th century there are two woollen cloth fragments in 2/1 twill of English wool (fig. 15.9) and one fragment of non-fulled textile in tabby, also made of English wool, which may have been produced in Flanders. However, two woollen cloth fragments in tabby and one fragment of non-fulled textile also made in tabby are probably dated to the 14th century. The Merino wool in those textiles indicates their Flemish origin. A relatively simple and fairly thick woollen cloth on tabby, found in Gdańsk and dated to the 14th-15th centuries could be imported from England (fig. 15.10). It is likely that a fragment of non-fulled textile in 2/2 twill from the second half of the 14th century may be an English product, but its relatively high thread-count would suggest rather a Flemish origin (fig. 15.11).

To set eighteen or nineteen Flemish textiles against one or two English textiles does not of course reflect accurately the sources of the West European cloth imported into Gdańsk during the 13th to 15th centuries; for the majority of textiles found in Gdańsk are dated to the 11th-14th centuries, that is, to a period when English cloth was seldom brought to Gdańsk.

The problem of the origin of two worsted textiles with extremely high thread-counts still remains to be considered (Fig. 15.3, 15.4). The closest parallels geographically and chronologically are textiles with similar thread-counts from Birka dating to the 9th-10th centuries[35] and from Novgorod Velikiy dating to the 10th-14th centuries.[36] Other textiles with similar thread-counts were found in numerous graves dating to the 7th-10th centuries in Norway, Sweden and Denmark[37] and are also found in smaller numbers in eastern Friesland.[38] Three textiles from Palmyra in Syria (2nd century) and one later textile from Antinoë in Egypt, which has up to 160 warp threads and 26 weft threads per cm should be mentioned.[39]

The discussion of the origin of those textiles was begun in 1938. Its participants are as follows: A. Geijer, M. Hald, M. Hoffmann, E. Carus-Wilson, A.S. Ingstad and L. Bender Jørgensen.[40] The debate was presented in detail in an article by A.S. Ingstad in 1979 and in the work of L. Bender Jørgensen. It is known, I presume, to all NESAT members and therefore I do not feel obliged to quote it once again. Let me only mention that the following suggestions on the origin of the textiles in question have been put forward: Friesland, Britain, Syria and West Norway.

Fig. 15.7 Flemish non-fulled textile in 2/1 twill (13th century)

Fig. 15.8 Flemish non-fulled textile in 3/2 twill (13th century)

Fig. 15.10 English woollen cloth in tabby (14th-15th century)

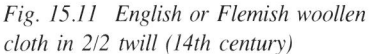

Fig. 15.9 Flemish woollen cloth in 2/1 twill (14th century)

Fig. 15.11 English or Flemish woollen cloth in 2/2 twill (14th century)

In fact, the discussions disregarded the materials from Novgorod Velikiy which have been mentioned above. These textiles, of which 61 fragments were found, date from the end of the 10th or the beginning of the 13th century, and a few later ones occur as late as the mid-14th century. All of them are woven in 2/1 twill and five fragments have a diamond pattern. Thirteen textiles are made of ZZ yarn, and 48 textiles of ZS yarn. The thread-count of the warp is 27-75 threads and of the weft 6-20 threads per 1cm. One of the textiles from the beginning of the 12th century has loops, which may show that it was produced on a tubular loom. The wool these textiles were made of is similar to the present-day wool of English sheep of Lincoln type and it was called by A. Nahlik 'English long-thick-fleece-wool'. On the basis of his analysis of the wool and production technology A. Nahlik considered those textiles to have been imported from England. He called them 'special' ones and identified them with 'worsted' textiles which had been exported from England to Germany and Slav countries in the Middle Ages.[41] Nahlik's hypothesis is supported by the studies of historians dealing with the English woollen industry. According to them English textiles of the 'worsted' type were produced from longwools, in contrast to fulled woollens made of shorter-fibred wool.[42]

The hypotheses presented by A. Geijer, M. Hald, M. Hoffmann, E. Carus-Wilson, A.S. Ingstad and L. Bender Jørgensen have not been based on any raw material analyses. Thus one of the criteria which could be useful in establishing the region of production of those textiles was ignored. A. Nahlik did perform the analyses of the wool, but to name it as English longwool fleece does not solve the problem. It is well-known that until the mid-14th century English export of wool exceeded cloth export.

I would like here, so far as I am able, to evaluate the ideas on the origin of the textiles which for the purpose of convenience I will call with L. Bender Jørgensen the 'Birka type'.[43] However, I would be inclined to include in this type all wool textiles made of worsted yarn with over 30 threads per cm, independently of the spin direction of the yarn and the weave, since it seems that this extraordinary thread-count should be of decisive significance while defining textiles of this type.

One hypothesis, which on the basis of the present data seems to be unlikely, is that of a Near Eastern origin for the type discussed. It is based on the textile finds in Palmyra and Antinoë. Their yarn and weave are definitely different from the majority of textiles from the South and East of the Roman Empire. But they are characteristic for the northern provinces and also for the barbarians who lived in neighbouring areas.[44] In my opinion, those textiles could be regarded as imported from the North. They could have been brought to the Near East by Roman legionaries whose units had been quartered earlier in the northern Roman provinces. For instance, Legio I Minervia was moved from the Rhineland to the Near East in the 2nd century AD and it took part in the Parthian Wars.[45] Despite Syrian production of textiles of high quality in antiquity and the Middle Ages, therefore, textiles of Birka type are quite likely to have been imported from the northern provinces of the Roman Empire.

The hypothesis of an English origin for the textiles of Birka type was put forward independently of each other by A. Nahlik and E. Carus-Wilson. A. Geijer, too, did not exclude this possibility. I have already spoken about my doubts relating to the raw material of the 'special' textiles of Novgorod. On the other hand, since I am not a linguist, it is hard to evaluate Carus-Wilson's hypothesis, as well as the hypothesis of A. Geijer on the origin of Birka textiles in Friesland or the hypothesis of L. Bender Jørgensen about the origin of those textiles in West Norway. Since it has been impossible for me to analyse the raw material of textiles from Western Europe I will try to establish hypothetically the production region for the Birka textiles.

It seems to be right to assume that it must have been one centre - a region, rather than one place - producing different kinds of textile which would have in common a high standard of craftsmanship and extremely high thread-count. That centre could have produced other textiles as well. It would have functioned at least from the 2nd to the 14th century. It should have been located in North-West Europe, either in Friesland or Flanders or in England or Norway. Since the textiles dating to the 2nd and 3rd century were found in Syria this could suggest that such a centre should have been located in territories occupied in antiquity by the Roman Empire or at least influenced by it. The hypothesis of an English origin for the Birka textiles should be treated very seriously, but as we recognise a lack of similar textiles in the vast textile material from Vindolanda,[46] I would rather support the hypothesis according to which the production of textiles of Birka type is placed on the Continent, perhaps in Friesland, or more probably in later Flanders, ie in Roman Gallia Belgica. Unfortunately, I do not know of any finds which could confirm or perhaps destroy this hypothesis. Let me add, however, that in antiquity Gallia Belgica was well known for good sheep and the production of famous Gallic *saga*.[47] Some authors derive *pallia fresonica* from there.[48] It should be stressed that Birka-type textiles found in Novgorod are made of English wool and those found in Gdańsk of Merino wool and perhaps of English wool as well (used in Flanders from the 12th or 13th century). It seems that A. Geijer, who initially related the textiles of Birka type to *pallia fresonica* may be right. That term might have come from Frisian merchants selling the textiles in northern Europe. Those textiles would reach England and west Norway, which are not very far by sea from Friesland, and they could also have come to Birka. The textiles would be delivered to Novgorod by Gotland merchants and later by German Hanseatic ones. The latter would bring them to Gdańsk as well.

Undoubtedly this hypothesis is not complete. We do not know anything about the wool which was used in Flanders before the 12th century, whether it had already been imported from England. Moreover, we do not know the character of the wool in Birka-type textiles found in western Europe. I assume, therefore, that the final conclusions as to the origins of those textiles may depend on results of studies on the wool of west European textiles. As long as such studies are not undertaken we should restrain ourselves from putting forward this or that hypothesis.

While writing the present article I had to confine myself to forming hypotheses, for my research is incomplete. The analyses, for example, which were performed on pollens of plants taken from the famous Shroud of Turin are the kind of experiment which I was not able to conduct on any textiles from excavations.[49]

Medieval written sources tell us about relatively early and well developed importation of textiles into Poland. According to historians, that was one of the reasons which hampered the growth of professional weaving in Poland.[50] This point of view, put forward by historians, seems to be confirmed by my recognition that nearly 35% of Gdańsk textiles from sites no 2 and 4 and Osiek are imported ones. It should be remembered, however, that there was a harbour in Gdańsk through which a considerable quantity of cloth imported into Prussia by the Teutonic Knights and into Poland had been passing. The archaeological material revealed by excavations of districts inhabited by craftsmen in other towns of Pomerania, Great Poland or Silesia indicates that only a small percentage of all textiles were imported ones.[51] Thus the cloth import, confirmed by written sources, must have been meant first of all for the richer classes of society. The case of Gdańsk is not a typical example and it should not be treated as such.

Translated by Elżbieta Lubińska

References

1. J.P. Wild, L. Bender Jørgensen, 'Clothes from the Roman Empire, Barbarians and Romans' in L. Bender Jørgensen, B. Magnus, E. Munksgaard, *Archaeological Textiles: Report from the 2nd NESAT Symposium 1.-4.V. 1984, Arkaeologiske Skrifter* 2, 1988 65-98

2. J. Karwasińska, *Świętego Wojciecha i męczennika żywot pierwszy* (Pomniki dziejowe Polski), series III, vol. IV, part 1, Warszawa, 1962, 40, §XXVII

3. K. Jażdżewski, 'La genèse de la ville de Gdańsk developpement et son artisanat au Haut Moyen-Age', *Ergon III: L'artisanat et la vie urbaine en Pologne médiévale, Kwartalnik Historii Kultury Materialnej* no 1/2, 1962, 410-417; A. Zbierski, 'The Early Medieval Gdańsk in the Light of Recent Researches', *ibid* 418-434; K. Jażdżewski, J. Kamińska, R. Gupieńcowa, 'Le Gdańsk des Xᵉ-XIIIᵉ siècles', *Archaeologia Urbium: Pologne*, fasc. 1, 1966, 1-30

4. J. Kamińska, A. Nahlik, 'Textiles from site no 1', *Włókiennictwo gdańskie w X-XIII w.*, Łódź, 1958; textiles from other sites worked on by J. Maik, not published, see also: J. Kamińska, A. Nahlik, 'Études sur l'industrie textile du Haut Moyen-Âge en Pologne', *Archaeologia Polona* 3, 1962, 89-119

5. Kamińska, Nahlik (1958), 198-206; A. Nahlik, *Tkaniny wsi wschodnioeuropejskiej X-XIII w.*, Łódź, 1965, 76-84; J. Maik, *Wyroby włókiennicze na Pomorzu z okresu rzymskiego i ze średniowiecza*, Wrocaw-Warszawa-Kraków-Gdańsk- Łódź, 1988, 148, 160-163

6. Kamińska, Nahlik (1958), 231-240; J. Maik (1988), 171-176

7. H. Samsonowicz, *Późne średniowiecze miast nadbałtyckich, (Studia nad dziejami Hanzy nad Bałtykiem w XIV-XV w.)*, Warszawa, 1968, 123, tabl. 14; H. Samsonowicz, 'Struktura handlu gdańskiego w pierwszej połowie XV w.', *Przegląd Historyczny* 53, 1962, ex. 4, 707-708, tabl. V

8. M. Małowist, *Wschód a Zachód Europy w XIII-XVI w.*, Warszawa, 1973, 62

9. G. de Poerck, *La draperie médiévale en Flandre et en Artois, Technique et Terminologie*, Brugge, 1951, 75-76; M. Małowist, *Studia z dziejów rzemiosła w okresie kryzysu feudalizmu w zachodniej Europie w XIV i XV w.*, Warszawa, 1954, 38-44

10. A. Nahlik, *Tkaniny wełniane importowane i miejscowe Nowogrodu Wielkiego X-XV w.*, Wrocław-Warszawa-Kraków, 1964, 106-110

11. M. Małowist (1954), 92-94; M. Małowist (1973), 69; A. Mączak, *Sukiennictwo wielkopolskie XIV-XVII w.*, Warszawa, 1955, 228

12. Mączak (1955), 229; Małowist (1954), 38, 216

13. Małowist (1954), 38, 216

14. H. Gryncewicz, O. Sztaniszkis, *Wełna*, Warszawa, 1959, 135-136; A. Lipson, *A Short History of Wool and its Manufacture*, Melbourne-London-Toronto, 1953, 28

15. Małowist (1954), 69

16. Małowist (1954), 112

17. Małowist (1954), 78

18. Małowist (1973), 82

19. Małowist (1954), 94, 98; Małowist (1973), 70

20. Samsonowicz (1962), 707-708, tabl. V; Małowist (1973), 82-84

21. Samsonowicz, 'Handel zagraniczny Gdańska w drugiej połowie XV w. (rejonizacja handlu na podstawie ksiąg cła palowego)', *Przegląd Historyczny* 47, 1956, ex.2, 329-332; K. Tidow, 'Untersuchungen an Wollgeweben aus einem Brunnen auf dem Schrangen in Lübeck', *Lübecker Schriften zur Archäologie und Kulturgeschichte* 6, 1982, 270

22. Kamińska, Nahlik (1958), 200-202; Maik (1988), 153

23. Maik (1988), 110-115

24. Kamińska, Nahlik (1958), 149, 232-233, 236; A. Niesiołowska-Wędzka, 'Wyniki badań nad tkaninami z najstarszych warstw grodu w Santoku', *Archeologia Polski* 10, 1965, ex.1, 320; Tidow (1982), 270

25. K. Myczkowski, 'Mikroskopowe badania szczątków owłosienia zwierząt, przędzy, tkanin, pilśni i sznurków z XIII-XIV-wiecznych warstw stanowiska 1 w Międzyrzeczu Wielkopolskim' in A. Urbańska, K. Myczkowski, M. Klichowska, *Wytwórczość włókiennicza średniowiecznego Międzyrzecza,* Poznań, 1964, 90

26. Nahlik (1964), 72-74

27. Maik (1988), 110-115

28. Nahlik (1964), 75-76

29. Maik (1988), 51-53: method of research described in J. Maik, 'Das Vorkommen des sogenannten römischen Schafes in Pommern', *Fasciculi Archaeologiae Historicae* 1, 1986, 63-64

30. Numerous examples of these notions can be found in: *Rationes curiae Vladislai Iagiellonis et Hedvigis regum Poloniae* (ed. F. Piekosiński), *Monumenta Medii Aevi Historica* 15, Kraków, 1896 and in *Das Marienburger Tresslerbuch der Jahre 1399-1409* (ed. Joachim), Königsburg, 1896: see also T. Hirsch, *Danzigs Handels- und Gewerbgeschichte unter der Herrschaft des Deutschen Ordens*, Leipzig, 1858

31. P. Malanima, 'The First European Textile Machine', *Textile History* 17, 1986, 119-120, fig. 3

32. Maik (1988), 155-156

33. K. G. Ponting, *The Woollen Industry of South-West England*, London, 1971, 7; F. Pipponier, *Costume et la vie sociale, la cour d'Anjou XIVe-XVe siècle*, Paris, 1970, 108-112

34. *Słownik staropolski* VIII, Wrocław-Warszawa-Kraków-Gdańsk, 1972-1981, 504

35. A. Geijer, *Die Textilfunde aus den Gräbern, Birka* III, Uppsala, 1938, 22-34

36. Nahlik (1964), 37-46

37. A.S. Ingstad, ' "Frisisk klede?" En diskusjon omkring noen fine textiler fra yngre jernalder', *Viking* XLIII, 1979, 81-95; L. Bender Jørgensen, *Prehistoric Scandinavian Textiles,* København, 1986, 312-324, 358-360

38. See footnote no 37 and K. Tidow, P. Schmid, 'Frühmittelalterliche Textilfunde aus der Wurt Hessens (Stadt Wilhelmshaven) und dem Gräberfeld von Dunum (Kreis Friesland) und ihre archäologische Bedeutung', *Probleme der Küstenforschung im Südlichen Nordseegebiet* 13, 1979, 134

39. R. Pfister, *Nouveaux textiles de Palmyre*, Paris, 1937, 24-25; R. Pfister, 'Le rôle d'Iran dans les textiles d'Antinoë', *Ars Islamica* XIII, 48; M. Hoffmann, *The Warp-Weighted Loom*, Oslo, 1964, 251

40. A. Geijer (1938), 40-47; M. Hald, *Olddanske tekstiler*, København, 1950, 202-203; M. Hoffmann (1964) 229-257; E. Carus-Wilson, 'Haberget: A Medieval Textile Conundrum', *Medieval Archaeology* XIII, 1967, 148-166; Ingstad (1979), 81-95; Bender Jørgensen (1986), 358-360

41. Nahlik (1964), 37-46, 74, 98-103; Małowist (1954), 232

42. Ponting (1971), 7

43. L. Bender Jørgensen, 'North European Textile Production and Trade in the 1st millennium AD - A Research Project', *Journal of Danish Archaeology* 3, 1984, 131; Bender Jørgensen (1986), 357

44. Wild, Bender Jørgensen (1988)

45. E. Stein, *Die kaiserlichen Beamten und Truppenkörper im römischen Deutschland unter dem Prinzipat*, Wien, 1932, 112-113

46. J.P. Wild, *The Textiles from Vindolanda 1973-1975*, *Vindolanda III*, Hexham, 1977, 5-26

47. Strabo, *Geographica* IV, 3, 3, 196 (ed A. Meinecke, 1866)

48. H. Pirenne, *Histoire Economique et Sociale du Moyen-Âge*, Paris, 1963, 30 H. Pirenne 'Draps de Frise ou draps de Flandre', *Vierteljahrschrift für Sozial- und Wirtschaftsgeschichte*, 1909, 308

49. The Shroud studies suggest that among the pollen there was some which came from plants growing only in Palestine. If that is so, the shroud of Turin must have been there once: I. Wilson, Całun Turyński Warszawa, 1983, 89-93

50. J. Wyrozumski, 'Tkactwo w Polsce w X-XIII w.', *Kqaratalnik Historii Kultury Materialnej* 13, 1965, 518

51. Maik (1988), 179, A. Urbańska, 'Włokiennictwo międżyrzeckie w 2 połowie XIII i l połowie XIV w.' in A. Urbańska, K. Myczkowski, M. Klickowska, *Wytworczocs włokiennicza sredniowiecznego Miedzyrzecza*, Poznan, 1964, 5-54; W. Hołubowicz, *Opole w wiekach X-XII*, Katowice, 1956, 189-216

16. Die Gewebe aus dem Gräberfeld des 12.-16.Jh. in Stary Brześć, Wojewodschaft Włocławek

Jacek Moszczyński
Łódź

Das antike Textilkunde betreffende Material, mit dem wir uns hier beschäftigen werden, stammt aus einer mittelalterlichen Begräbnisstätte in Stary Brześć, Wojewodschaft Włocławek (Fundstelle 4).[1] Die Ausgrabungsarbeiten sind in dieser Fundstelle in den Jahren 1955-1958 von Wissenschaftlern der Lehranstalt für Anthropologie der Lodzener Universität und von dem Museum für Archäologie in Łódź durchgeführt worden.[2] Diese Begräbnisstätte datiert in die letzten Jahre des frühen Mittelalters und in die ganze Periode des späten Mittelalters, dh. von der Mitte des 12.Jh. bis zur Mitte des 16.Jh.[3] Unter den Altertümern, die uns hier interessieren, können wir Gewebe und die zur Textilproduktion benutzten Werkzeuge (Spinnwirtel, Federscheren, Nadeln) nennen.

Die Gewebe weisen große Mannigfaltigkeit auf. Wir verfügen über Gewebe mit sowohl einfachen als auch komplizierten Bindungen. Es gibt ein Posamentenstück, ein Geflecht (und vielleicht Gewebe?), weiter die Fragmente einer Verzierung (Strickerei?) aus wollenen Fäden mit Metallgeflecht.

Bei der Besprechung fange ich mit den Geweben an. Die mit einer gemeinsamen Katalognummer IV-1957/209 und Inventarnummer IV-1957/164 bezeichneten Gewebe sind im Grab 564 gefunden worden. Es sind die Fragmente von zwei Geweben (Abb. 16.1-6) und ein Posamentenstück (Abb. 16.7-10). Die Fragmente der Gewebe sind so aneinandergenäht, wie es auf den Abbildungen gezeigt worden ist. Zuerst werde ich versuchen, das einfachere Gewebe (Abb. 16.1) zu analysieren.

Es ist dunkelbraun und aus Wolle. Man hat kernlose Fasern und Fasern mit Kern ohne Schalen (Hülsen) festgestellt. Die Fasern sind von 15μm bis 27μm dick; im Einschuss sind auch etwa 9μm dicke Anflugfäden zu bemerken. Das Gewebe besitzt eine Fadenzahl in der Kette von 60 Fäden pro Zentimeter und im Einschuss von 30 Fäden pro Zentimeter. In der Kette haben wir mit einem nicht besonders stark in Z-Richtung gesponnenen Garn zu tun. Der Einschuss ist viel dicker; es ist leider nicht gelungen, die Spinnrichtung festzustellen. Die Dicke der im Gewebe auftretenden Fäden ist differenziert. Das ist besonders im Einschuss sichtbar (von 0,3 bis 0,5 mm). Die Fäden in der Kette sind etwa 0,15mm dick. Bei diesem Gewebe hat man die Ripsbindung angewandt. Diese Bindung entsteht dadurch, daß man einen Faden des Einschusses über die Kette schlägt. Das Gewebe wurde mit einem Webstuhl fertiggestellt, an dem man zwei Schäfte und zwei Trittstufen benutzt. Die technische Zeichnung der Bindung und die Art und Weise des Durchwebens der Fäden der Kette und des Einschusses sind auf Abb. 16.2 wiedergegeben.

Samitum(?)

Die Struktur des nächsten Gewebes (Abb. 16.3) ist komplizierter, als sie im oben besprochenen Fall war. Das Gewebe ist aus Wolle gefertigt und besteht aus einer Kette und zwei Einschüssen. Die Dichtheit des Stoffes ist 60 Fäden der Kette und 60 Fäden des Einschusses I und II auf einem Zentimeter. Die Fäden der Kette sind relativ stark gedreht; man hat dabei die Z-Spinnrichtung

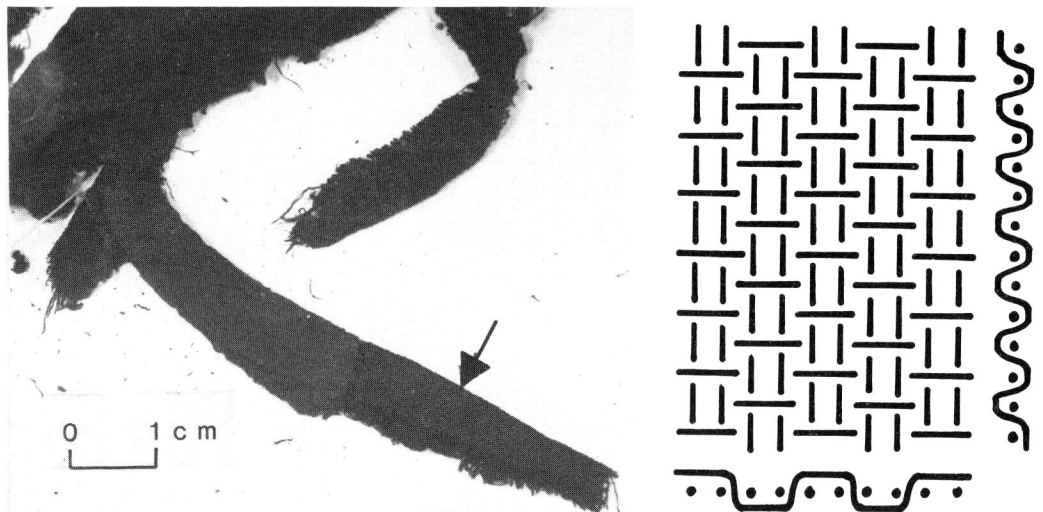

Abb. 16.1 Halbpanamagewebe aus Grab 564   *Abb. 16.2 Patrone des Halbpanamageswebes aus Grab 564*

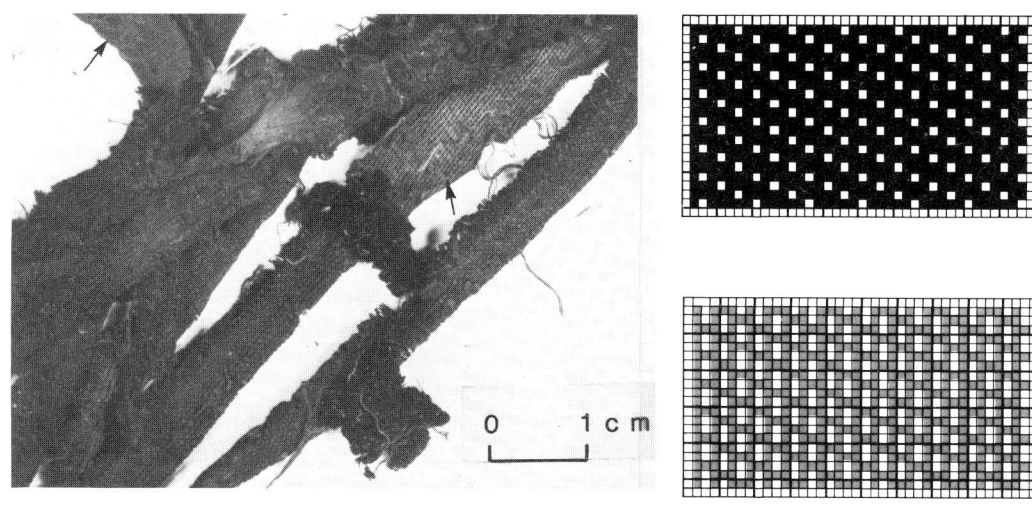

Abb. 16.3 (Mitte, links)   Das Samitum aus
Grab 564

Abb. 16.4 (Mitte, oben rechts) Das Samitum
aus Grab 564: Einschuss I auf der rechten
Seite des Gewebes (schwarz eingetragen)

Abb. 16.5 (Mitte, unten rechts)   Das Samitum
aus Grab 564: Einschuss II auf der linken Seite
des Gewebes (grau eingetragen)

Abb. 16.6 (rechts) Das Samitum aus Grab 564:
Einschuss I auf der rechten Seite des Gewebes
(schwarz) und Einschuss II (graue Kreuze)

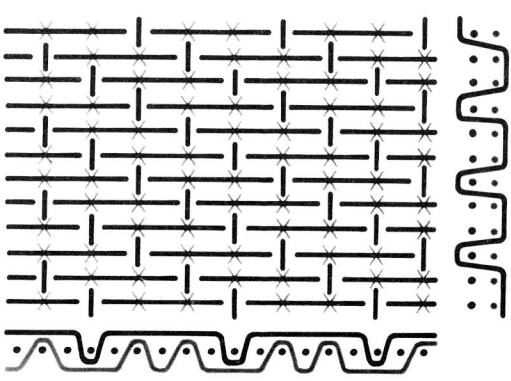

132

angewandt. Die Fäden sind etwa 0,15mm dick. Zur Kette hat man eine Mischwolle gebraucht (die Fasern bis 25µm dick); es gibt auch eine kleine Menge Anflugfäden, die etwa 10µm dick sind. Beide Einschüsse sind relativ schwach gedreht. Es ist schwer, die Spinnrichtung festzustellen. Die Dicke des Einschusses I beträgt etwa 0,15-0,2mm; die Dicke des Einschusses II etwa 0,2mm. Zum ganzen Einschuss hat man die gleichartige Wolle gebraucht (die Dicke der Fasern ist etwa 17µm). Die rechte Seite des Gewebes unterscheidet sich erheblich von der linken Seite. Zwei Einschüsse sind mit der Kette auf solche Weise gebunden, dass der Einschuss I nur auf der rechten Seite des Gewebes (Abb. 16.4 und 6, schwarze Fäden) und der Einschuss II nur auf der linken Seiten (Abb. 16.5 und 6 rote Fäden) sichtbar sind. Die rechte Seite des Gewebes entsteht dadurch, daß man den Einschuss I über fünf Fäden der Kette und dann unter einen Kettfaden schießt. Es entsteht dabei eine glatte und glänzende Oberfläche. Die linke Seite des Gewebes entsteht dadurch, daß man den Einschuss II unter drei Fäden, über einen Faden und unter einen Faden der Kette schlägt. Sowohl diese Bindung als auch die Art und Weise des Durchflechtens der Einschüsse zeigt Abb.16.6.

Das Posamentenstück

Das nächste Gewebefragment, das mit derselben Katalog- und Inventarnummer bezeichnet ist wie die zwei obengenannten Gewebe, gehört zu den interessantesten Funden. Es ist ein Posamentenstück mit einem eingewebten geometrischen Muster. Dieses Stück ist 13mm breit. In der Kette (also in der ganzen Breite des Bandes) befinden sich 58 Zwirne. Jeder Zwirn der Kette besteht aus zwei dünneren Fäden. Es tritt hier eine relativ starke S-Spinnrichtung auf. Die Fäden in der Kette sind etwa 0,3 bis 0,35mm dick: sie sind dunkelbraun.

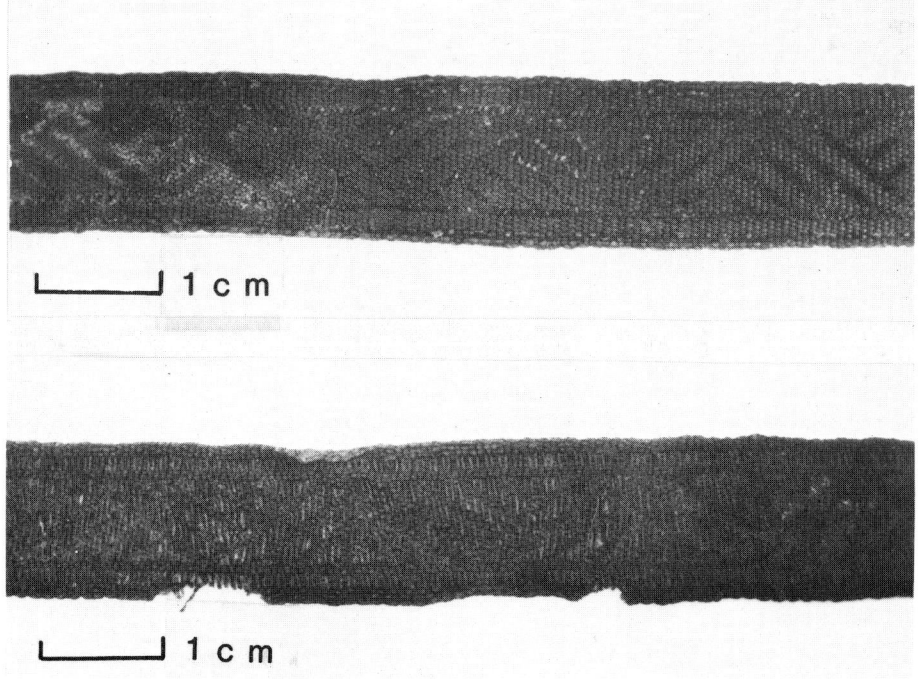

Abb. 16.7 (oben) Das Posamentenstück: Ruckseite   Abb. 16.8 (unten) Das Posamentenstück: Schauseite

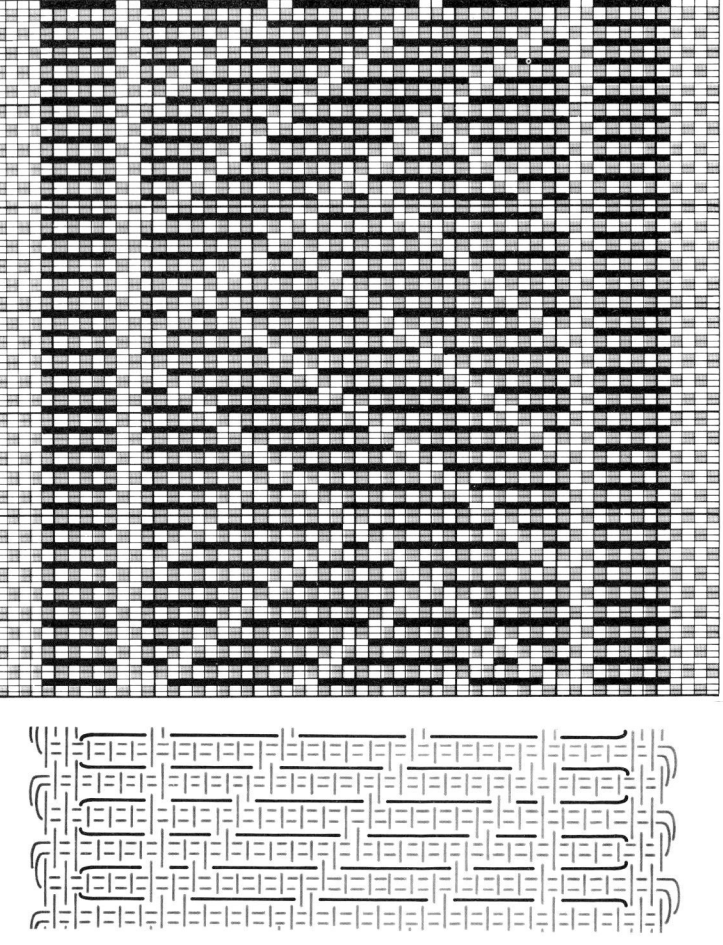

Abb. 16.9 Aufbau des Posamentenstücks: grau- Einschuss I, schwarz - Einschuss II
Abb. 16.10 Struktur des Posamentenstücks: Einschuss I (zwei Fäden) ist in grauer Farbe, Einschuss II in schwarzer Farbe angegeben.

Im Einschuss des Posamentenstückes sind drei Fäden angewandt. Zuerst sind es die zwei Fäden des Grundeinschußes I (graue Farbe auf Abb. 16.10), dann ein Faden des Einschusses II (schwarze Farbe auf Abb. 16.10). Der Einschuss I verbindet sich mit der Kette in Ripsbindung: der Einschuss II bildet dagegen auf der oberen Seite des Posamentenstücks das Muster. Die Fäden des Einschusses I haben dieselbe Farbe wie die Kette. Sie liegen im Fach nebeneinander. Jeder von ihnen zeigt eine schwache Z-Spinnrichtung und ist etwa 0,25mm dick. Der das Muster auf dem Posamentenstück bildende Einschuss II ist ein Faden mit Metallgeflecht. Die Farbe des Kernfadens ist heller als die braune bis goldene Farbe des Grundeinschusses I. Im etwa 0,3mm dicken Einschuss II haben wir mit einer schwachen S-Spinnrichtung zu tun. Um den Kern ist ein Metallbändchen umgewickelt worden; es ist schlecht erhalten und in mehreren Stellen sind von ihm nur die abgedruckten Spuren erhalten geblieben. Das Metallbändchen war etwa 0,4mm breit und umwickelte den Kern in S-Richtung, also in linker Drehrichtung.

Das Posamentenstück ist mit einer Broschiertechnik hergestellt worden. Der Ripsbindung aufweisende Grundeinschuss I band sich mit den Fäden der Kette auf der ganzen Breite des Posamentenstücks, also auf 58 Kettfäden. Nach einem Schuss der paarweise verlaufenden Einschussfäden I lief der musterbildende Einschuss II. Das Muster bildeten die 50 mittleren Fäden der Kette (Abb. 16.9, 16.10).

Man hat hier Wolle gebraucht, die Fasern mit bzw. ohne Mark aufwies; die Fasern in der Kette sind von 20μm bis 30μm dick; die durchschnittliche Dicke der Fasern des Einschusses beträgt etwa 25μm.

Die dem beschriebenen Posamentenstück ähnliche Textilreste sind auch in einigen anderen Ausgrabungsstätten entdeckt worden, u.a. in Gdańsk[4], Tum/Łęczyca[5]. Sie unterscheiden sich von dem oben beschriebenen Stück sowohl in der Dichtheit, als auch in der Bindung und in dem dafür gebrauchten Rohstoff. Nur das Posamentenstück aus Gdańsk hat dieselbe Breite. Was die Herstellung des Posamentenstücks aus Stary Brześć betrifft, da kann ich mich wohl der Suggestion von A. Nahlik bedienen, die die Herstellung des seidenen Posamentenstücks aus Gdańsk angeht.[6] In beiden Fragmenten (aus Stary Brześć und aus Gdańsk) sind zwei Einschüsse aufgetreten; ein Grundeinschuss und ein Ziereinschuss. Der Grundeinschuss bindet sich mit der Kette in Tuchbindung (Gdańsk). Die Ziereinschüsse bilden in beiden Fällen das Muster. Der Ziereinschuss in Gdańsk weist auch Spuren von dem Metall, mit dem er umwickelt war, auf. Das Stück aus Stary Brześć konnte auch, wie jener aus Gdańsk, mittels Brettchen mit einem Stammschussfach und mit einem bewegten Schussfach für die Versetzung des Grundeinschusses I gewebt werden. Die Anwendung eines Stäbchens für die Fertigstellung des Musters (die Bildung des Schussfachs für den das Muster bildenden Einschuss) wäre denkbar.

Die Verzierungen der Bekleidung

Die nächsten mit der Katalognummer IV-1958/12 und Inventarnummer IV-1958/12 bezeichneten Textilreste sind kleine Fragmente, die wahrscheinlich zur Verzierung der Bekleidung gedient haben (Abb. 16.11,12). Sie sind im Grab 646 gefunden worden. Es sind dicht nebeneinander gelegte Fadenfragmente erhalten, die wahrscheinlich ursprünglich um etwas steifes umwickelt waren. Es handelt sich um wollene Zwirnarten. Die Analyse der Zwirne weist die Zugabe von Hautwolle auf; die Fasern mit Kern sind etwa 30μm dick, die ohne Kern bis 12μm dick. Zur Zeit sind sie dunkelbraun. Jeder Zwirn besteht aus zwei dünneren Fäden: wir haben hier mit einer relativ starken S-Spinnrichtung zu tun. Der so gedrehter Zwirn ist etwa 0,2mm dick. Auf diese dicht nebeneinander gelegten Zwirne ist ein Faden mit Metallgeflecht genäht. Der Kern dieses Fadens ist aus Wolle und sehr gut erhalten. Er ist weiss, wobei man auch den grünen aus der Zersetzung des ihn umwickelnden Metallbandes

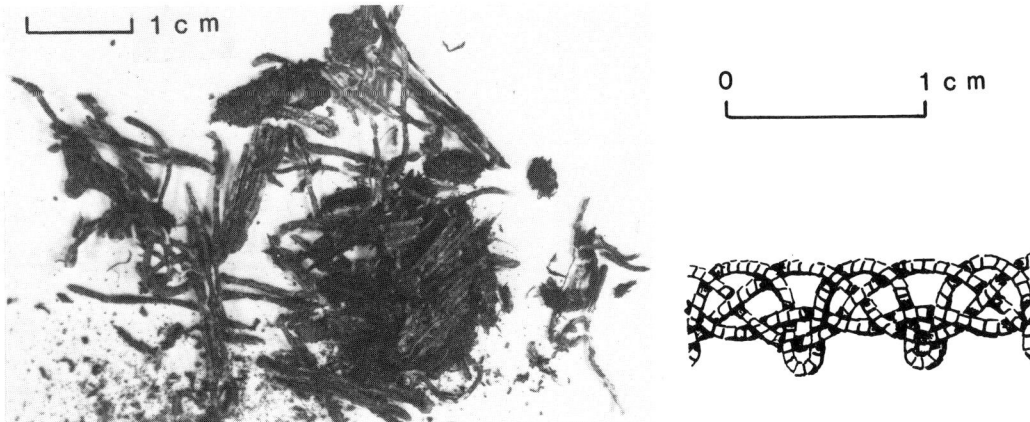

Abb. 16.11 Kleiderverzierung aus Grab 646

Abb. 16.12 Struktur der Kleiderverzierung aus Grab 646

135

stammenden Farbton bemerken kann. Der Kern besteht aus zwei stark in S-Richtung miteinander gedrehten Fäden und ist etwa 0,5mm dick. Um den Kern ist ein Metallband gewickelt, das etwa 0,8 bis 0,9mm breit ist. Hier haben wir auch mit der S-Spinnrichtung zu tun. Dieses Metallband ist stark verwüstet. Der hier beschriebene Zwirn war ein Zierfaden, der entsprechend gebogen und nebeneinandergelegt bestimmte Ornamente gebildet hat. Es ist sehr schwer die Form der Ornamente und die Art und Weise der Verzierung festzustellen, weil wir nur über kleine und verwüstete Fragmente verfügen. Abb. 16.12 zeigt die Konstruktion dieser Verzierung bzw. Geflechtes.

Das Gürtelchen

Ein Gürtelchen ist im Grab 101 (Katalognummer IV-1955/102, Inventarnummer IV-1955/71) in der Hüftengegend des Toten gefunden worden. Das erhaltene Stück ist etwa 23cm lang und an der breitesten Stelle etwa 1cm breit (wenn man die angehängten Plättchen nicht berücksichtigt). Das Gürtelchen bilden zwei wollene Zwirnarten: ihre Fasern sind von 18μm bis 27μm dick.

Der Zwirn I ist 0,3 bis 0,4mm dick. Mit diesem Zwirn hat man eine Schnur (Abb. 16.16b) an das Gewebe (Abb. 16.16c) genäht. Der Zwirn I besteht aus zwei dünnen Einzelfäden, die in S-Richtung gedreht sind (Abb. 16.16a). Beide sind aus den sehr schwach mit Z-Spinnrichtung gedrehten Fasern erzeugt. Sie sind etwa 0,2mm dick.

Der Zwirn II (mit Metallgeflecht) ist etwa 0,7 bis 0,9mm dick. Der Kern bildet ein S-gesponnener Wollfaden. Um den Kern ist ein Metallband in S-Richtung gewickelt. Das Metallband ist sehr gut erhalten; es ist etwa 0,5 bis 0,7mm breit, mit dem dunklen Beschlag bedeckt. In den Stellen, die nicht so sehr auf die Wirkung äusserlicher Faktoren (das Anlegen des Bandgeflechtes) gesetzt worden sind, glänzt das Bändchen auffallend goldfarbig.

Das Gürtelchen besteht aus einer aus Zwirn I und II gedrehten Schnur und aus einem auf sie mit dem Zwirn I angenähten schmalen Ziergeflecht.

Die Schnur (Abb. 16.16b) besteht aus den oben besprochenen Zwirnarten I und II. Sie ist etwa 2,5mm dick. Ihre Bestandteile sind also zwei miteinander in S-Richtung gebundene Fadengruppen.

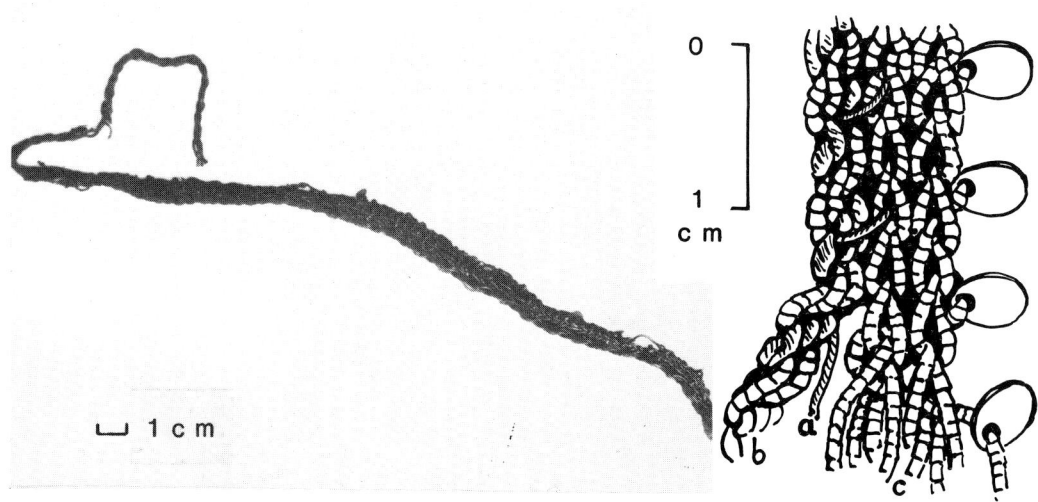

Abb. 16.13 Aufnahme des Gürtelchen aus Grab 101   *Abb. 16.14 Struktur des Gürtelchen aus Grab 101*

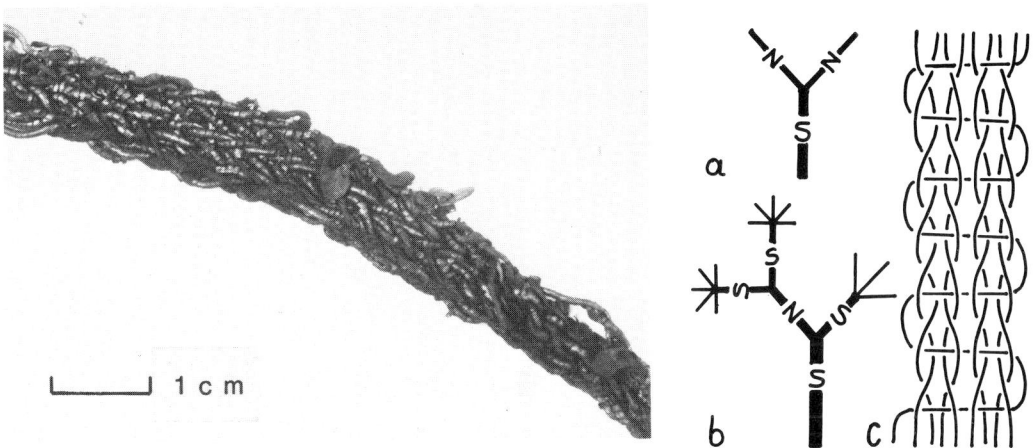

Abb. 16.15 *Vergrösserte Ansicht des Gürtelchen aus Grab 101*
Abb. 16.16 *Gürtelchen aus Grab 101: a. Zwirn I, b. Schnurzusammensetzung, c. Aufbau des Gürtelchen*

Die erste Fadengruppe bilden drei Zwirne II mit Metallgeflecht, die miteinander schwach in S-Richtung gedreht sind. Die zweite Gruppe bilden die wollenen in Z-Richtung gedrehten Fäden. Diese Gruppe besteht aus zwei Untergruppen, wobei wir in jeder Untergruppe mit S-Drehrichtung zu tun haben. Jede Untergruppe bilden 5 der früher besprochenen Zwirne I. Es ist genau auf der Zeichnung Abb. 16.16b gezeigt.

Auf die Schnur ist mit einem anderen Zwirn (I) ein 0,7mm breites Ziergeflecht angenäht. Das Geflecht ist aus den Zwirnen mit Metallgeflecht hergestellt (Zwirn II). Die Kette besteht aus acht, der Einschuss aus einem Faden (Abb. 16.16c). Die hier angewandte Technik ist etwas besonders, weil sie das Durchflechten und das Weben verbindet. Die Fäden der Kette arbeiten zu zweit. Während der erste von ihnen auf einem Faden des Einschusses liegt, befindet sich der zweite unter dem Faden des Einschusses. In dem Raum zwischen den Einschüssen sind die Kettfäden in der Richtung Z oder S gedreht und beim nächsten Einschussfaden ist jener, der früher unten war, oben und der zweite umgekehrt. Eine sehr wichtige Sache ist hier die Fadeneinkreuzung, die im Schussfach entsteht. Sie ist immer S für das eine Fadenpaar und Z für das andere Fadenpaar. Im hier besprochenen Gewebe (Geflecht) wurden diese Fadeneinkreuzungen abwechselnd für jedes Fadenpaar angewandt (also Z,S,Z,S). Das ist auch der Grund für das Entstehen eines Strickmacheneffekts auf der oberen Seite. Diese Technik ist jedoch eine Webetechnik, weil zwischen den Fäden, die ein gedrehtes Paar bilden, ein Schussfach für den Faden des Einschusses entsteht. Der Einschuss läuft jedesmal unter 4 Fäden der Kette und gleichzeitig über 4 Fäden der Kette und dann kehrt nach der Umdrehung der Fäden der Kette auf diesselbe Weise zurück. In diesem Gewebe ist ein Rand zusätzlich mit den sich auf dem Einschussfaden befindenden Plättchen verziert (Abb. 16.14) Die Plättchen befinden sich auf jedem Bogen des Einschusses, der bei der Umdrehung entsteht. Die Plättchen sind oval und besitzen jedes ein Loch. Durch dieses Loch läuft der Einschussfaden. Zur Zeit fehlt die Mehrheit der Plättchen. Diese Verzierung ist vermutlich auf dem Ort, wo sie gefunden wurde, von einem Amateur und nicht von einem Handwerker hergestellt. Das Gewebe ist aus Fäden gemacht worden, die früher schon fertig vorbereitet worden sind. Den Anfang bilden vier in der Hälfte gebogene Fäden (die in der Kette Paare bilden), die miteinander mit Hilfe eines zusätzlichen Fadens gebunden worden sind. Letzten Endes bilden sie eine Gruppe von neun Fäden. Bei der Anfertigung bilden vier Fadenpaare die Kette und der angebundene Faden wird zum Einschuss. Das Ende des Gewebes schaffen alle neun Fäden, die gesammelt, umwickelt und stark gebunden sind, was das Aufknüpfen vorbeugen sollte.

137

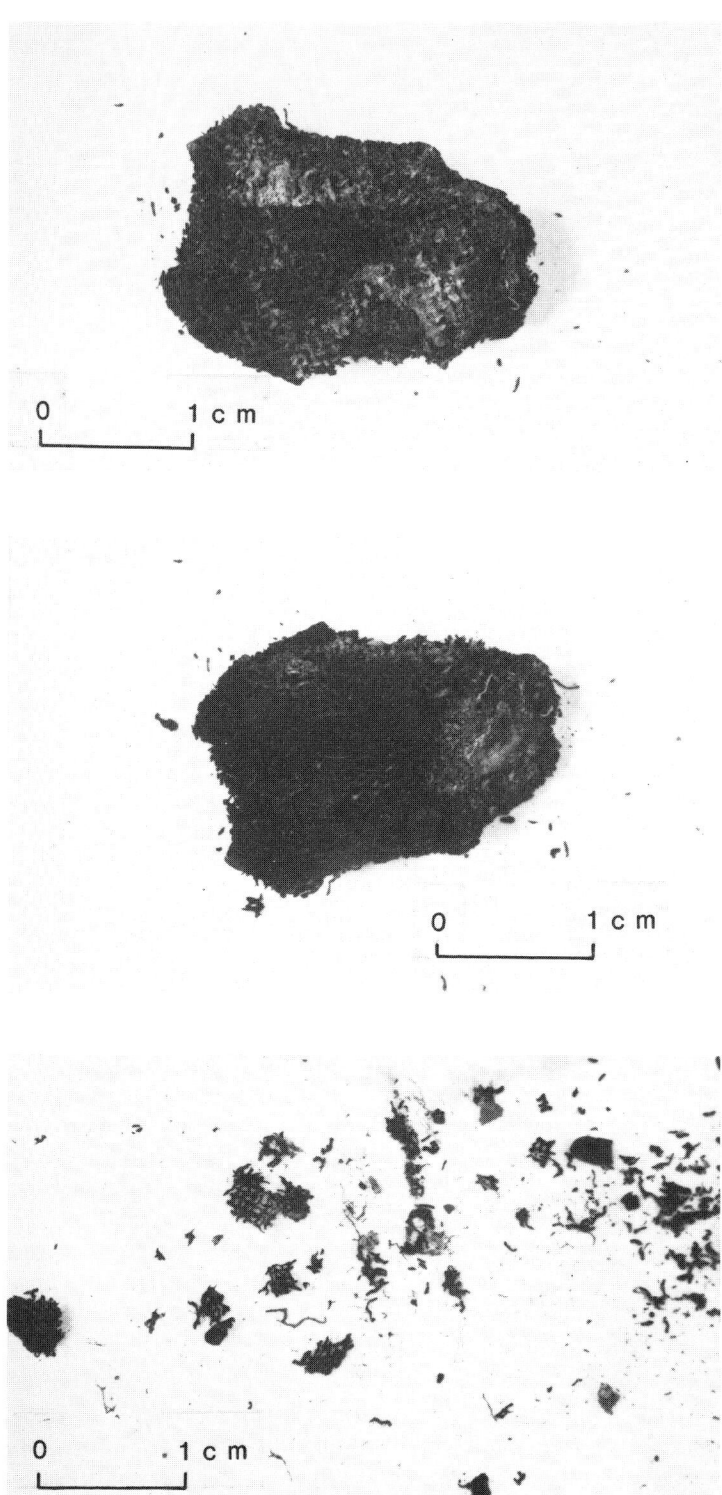

Abb. 16.17-19 Gewebe in Tuchbindung aus Grab 330

Die Art und Weise der Anfertigung weist auf die mit Brettchen hergestellten Gewebe. Unser Gewebe konnte auch auf einem derartigen Webstuhl gemacht werden. Ich habe schon oben bemerkt, dass dieses Gewebe wahrscheinlich von einem Amateur und nicht von einem Handwerker gemacht worden war, sonst würde es in grösserer Menge hergestellt. Höchstwahrscheinlich wäre es ein längeres, später geschnittenes, appretiertes Gewebeband. Es würde dann das Umbiegen der Fäden am Anfang fehlen. Als Bestätigung der These, dass dieses Gewebe von einem Amateur hergestellt worden ist, kann hier die Art und Weise der Anfertigung der Schnur dienen. Sie ist unregelmässig gedreht. Bei der richtigen Umdrehung treten die Spinnrichtungen bei den Fäden abwechslungsweise auf. Die Fäden mit Z-Richtung werden miteinander mit S-Richtung gedreht. Hier kommen diese Spinnrichtungen nicht auf diese Weise vor. In der Schnur hat man, um eine ähnliche Dicke der Gruppe der wollenen Fäden (I) und der Gruppe der Fäden mit dem Geflecht (II) zu erreichen, die Zahl der wollenen Fäden (I) vervielfacht. Es wäre einfacher, die dickeren wollenen Fäden anzuwenden. Es ist das einzige mir bekannte Beispiel diese Typs. Aber die Technik der Anfertigung des Gewebes ist der Technik, in der ein Gewebe-Fragment aus Feddersen Wierde[7] hergestellt worden ist, ähnlich.

Die Gewebe mit Tuchbindung

Der nächste Textilrest ist ein Gewebe von einem Band, das aus Bronzeplättchen besteht. Es stammt aus dem Grab 330 (Katalognummer IV-1957/133, Inventarnummer IV-1957/112) und ist auf den Fotos Abb. 16.17-19 gezeigt. Das Gewebe ist in Tuchbindung gefertigt. Es ist los gewebt, so dass relativ grosse freie Räume zwischen Fäden entstehen. Das hier erhaltene Stück besteht aus zahlreichen, aufeinandergelegten und sehr kompakten Schichten. Auf beiden Seiten sind grüne Fragmente sichtbar; die Farbe stammt von Bronzeplättchen aus dem Band. Die Tatsache, dass sich das Gewebe zwischen den Plättchen befand, war für die Erhaltung ausschlagebend.

Der schlechte Zustand macht es schwer, den Rohstoff, der zur Fertigstellung des Gewebes diente, festzustellen. Die Dichtheit des Gewebes in der Kette beträgt etwa 20 Fäden pro cm, im Einschluss etwa 13 Fäden pro cm. Die Dicke der Fäden im Einschuss und in der Kette ist ähnlich. Die Kettfäden sind von 0,25 bis 0,4mm dick. In der Kette tritt die Z-Spinnrichtung auf, im Einschuss dagegen ist die Spinnrichtung nicht festzustellen.

Wir verfügen auch über einige Fragmente des mineralisierten Gewebes, das sich auf einem eisernen Vorlegeschloss erhalten hat. Dieser Metallgegenstand (das eiserne Vorlegeschloss hat Katalognummer IV-1958/63 und Inventarnummer IV-1958/47) hat die Erhaltung des Gewebes ermöglicht. Das Gewebe hat seinen elastischen Charakter verloren und infolgedessen kann man es vom Vorgeschloss nicht trennen. Deswegen war es notwendig, die Untersuchung nur auf eine oberflachliche Beobachtung zu beschränken.

Auf den Bildern Abb. 16.20-23 sind vier Fragmente des Gewebes gezeigt. Alle vier sind in Tuchbindung hergestellt. Im ersten Fragment (Abb. 16.20) ist die Dichtheit der Fäden in der Kette etwa 15 pro cm, im Einschuss etwa 11 pro cm. Die Fäden sind 0,5 bis 0,6mm dick. Es ist leider nicht gelungen, die Spinnrichtung zu ermitteln. Im zweiten Fragment (Abb. 16.21) ist die Dichtheit der Fäden in der Kette 10 pro cm, im Einschuss etwa 7 pro cm. Die Fäden sind von 0,6 bis 0,7 mm dick. Es ist gelungen, Z-Spinnrichtung in der Kette festzustellen; was aber den Einschuss betrifft, da sind wir nicht imstande, die Spinnrichtung zu bezeichnen. Im dritten Fragment (Abb. 16.22) ist die Dichtheit der Fäden dem zweiten Fragment ähnlich, also Fäden von 0,5 bis 0,7mm dick. In der Kette und im Einschuss haben wir mit einer Z-Spinnrichtung zu tun. Im vierten Fragment (Abb. 16.23) ist die Dichtheit der Fäden in der Kette 12 pro cm, im Einschuss 9 pro cm. Die Einschussfäden sind von 0,8 bis 1mm dick, die Kettfäden etwa 0,7mm dick. In der Kette und im Einschuss haben wir mit Z-Spinnrichtung zu tun. Es ist nicht möglich, den Rohstoff, aus dem man das Gewebe gemacht hat, zu bestimmen.

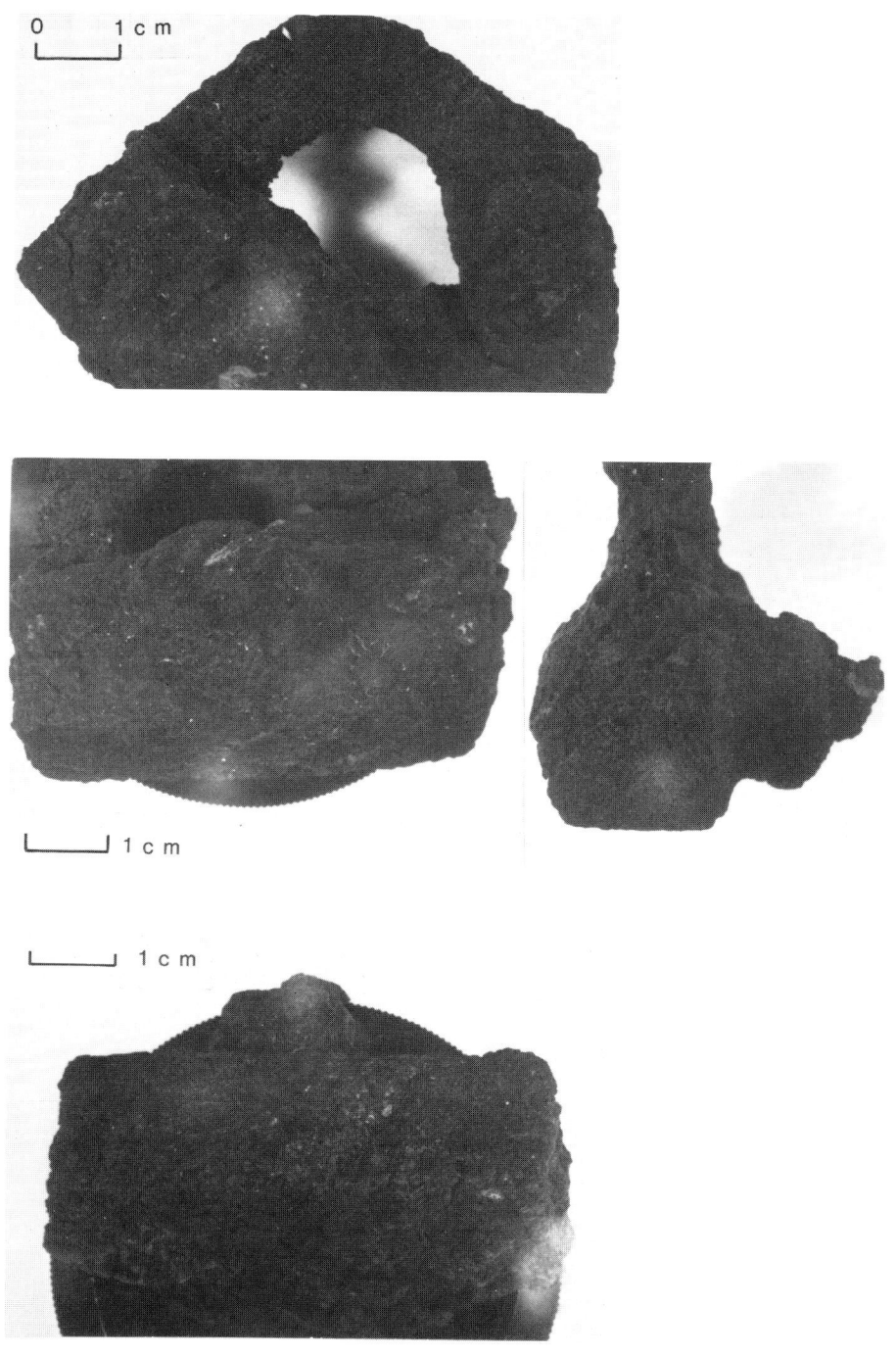

Abb. 16.20-23   An einem eisernen Vorlegeschloss anhaftende Textilreste

Ich bin der Meinung, dass die Fragmente wahrscheinlich von einem einzigen Gewebe stammen. Die Unterschiede in der Dicke oder in der Dichtheit sind die Folge des Verderbens und der Verzerrung des Gewebes.

Die oben beschriebenen Gewebe von dem Vorlegeschloss und von dem Band gehören zu den einfachsten, die man in Stary Brześć gefunden hat.

Andere Funde

In der Ausgrabungsstätte in Stary Brześć hat man auch einige Funde entdeckt, die in naher Verbindung mit der Textilkunde stehen. Darunter ist ein Exemplar einer eisernen Federschere (Katalognummer IV-1957/92, Inventarnummer IV-1957/173) (Abb.16.28). Die Schere ist 13cm lang. Man hat sie mit der Technik des Schmiedens hergestellt. Die Schere dieser Art ist seit der Latenezeit bekannt[8] und ist in fast unveränderter Form bis heute hergestellt worden. Obwohl bestimmte Unterschiede sichtbar sind in der Form des Bügels, der Form der Schneiden, es bestehe auch Möglichkeit, dass wir im Fall des Vergleichens einer grösseren Anzahl Schereexemplare auch Unterschiede im Grössenverhältnis der einzelnen Schereteile beobachten würden. Die hier beschriebene Schere unterscheidet sich von den Scheren aus z.B. Gdańsk[9] sowohl in der Grösse (in Gdańsk von 13 bis 22cm) als auch in der Form des Bügels (in Gdańsk ist er rund, in Stary Brześć oval).

Solche Scheren sind auch dank den ethnografischen Arbeit bekannt. Zum Beispiel die Scheren aus Polesie, die von K. Moszyński beschrieben worden sind,[10] sind ähnlicher jenen aus der Latenezeit als diese aus dem Mittelalter und sind manchmal noch heute in den Dörfern zu treffen. Es ist selbtverständlich, das die Scheren diese Typs ein universales Werkzeug sowohl zur Schafsschur, als auch im Schneidehandwerk waren und sind. Man hat sich der Scheren beim Ausschneiden der Zierwaren aus buntem Papier bedient und man benutzt sie bis heute dazu.

In den Gräbern 768, 396 und neben dem Grabloch 768 (Abb. 16.25-27) hat man drei Spinnwirtel gefunden. Alle sind aus Ton gefertigt und haben eine doppelkonische Form. Ihre Ausmässe sind ähnlich, nämlich etwa 31mm im Durchmesser mit einer Lochweite von etwa 9-12mm, und einer Dicke von 11-12mm. Ihre Rolle bestand darin, die Spindel während des Spinnens zu beschweren. Die Stärke der Spinnrichtung berücksichtigend, hat man die schweren (beim Weben der stark gedrehten besonders zur Kette gebrauchten Fäden) oder die leichteren (beim Weben der los gedrehten, zum Einschuss gebrauchten Fäden) Spinnwirtel benutzt.

Die letzten Funde, die unserem Thema gehören, sind Bronzenadeln (Abb. 16.28). Sie stammen aus den Gräbern 653 und 75 und aus dem Erdloch 22. Nach W. Hensel können die in den Gräbern gefundenen Nadeln das Vorhandensein von Schneiderhandwerkern bezeugen. Es waren die Werkzeuge, die nicht nur von den Fachleuten, sondern allgemein benutzt worden sind. In der römischen Periode traten oft Nadeln in weiblichen Gräbern auf.[11]

Der Abschluss

Das oben beschriebene Textilkunde betreffende archäologische Material ist nicht besonders reich, wenn man von der Zahl ausgeht und wenn man es mit vielen anderen Ausgrabungsstätten vergleicht, z.B. in Gdańsk,[12] Wolin,[13] Opole.[14] Es ist aber sehr interessant, weil die Funde verschiedenartig sind. Das Samitum ist hier besonders beachtenswert.

Die Aussergewöhnlichkeit des Exemplars aus Stary Brześć besteht darin, dass es aus Wolle hergestellt worden ist. Alle Samitgewebe, die mir bekannt sind, sind aus Seide.

Ist das Samitum aus Wolle aus Stary Brześć eine Einfuhrware? Es scheint mir, dass es kein Weg besteht, es festzustellen. Obwohl man sagen muss, es wäre unmöglich ohne jeden Zweifel die Meinung zu vertreten, es sei ein lokales Erzeugnis, trotzdem bin ich der Meinung, es sei möglich, dass dieses Gewebe doch ein lokales Erzeugnis ist. Das kann aber nur eine Vermutung mit hohem Grad der Wahrscheinlichkeit sein. Ich glaube, dass wenn schon das Samitum eine Einfuhrware wäre, dann wäre

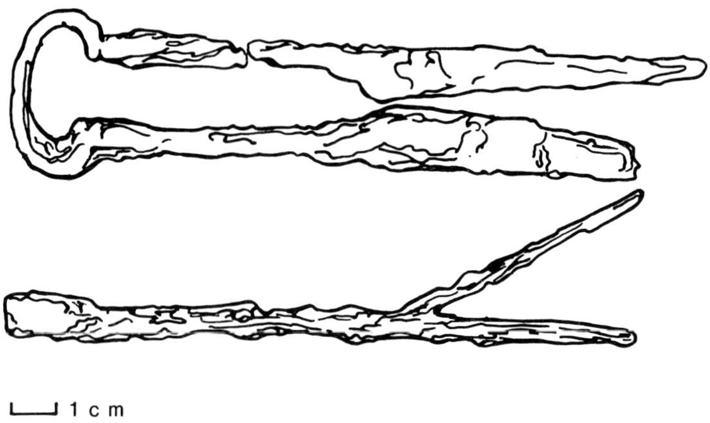

Abb. 16.24 Eiserne Schere

es aus einem wertvollen (also aus Seide und nicht aus Wolle) Rohstoff sein. Vielleicht haben die Weber aus diesem Gebiet, die haüfiger mit Wolle zu tun gehabt haben, die Bindung nachgeahmt, die sie in Seidengwebe beobachtet haben. Die Anfertigung des Gewebes aus Wolle in einer für Samitum charakteristischen Bindung verursachte den interessanten Effekt der glatten, glänzenden rechten Gewebeseite. Es hat sowohl den ästhetischen Wert erhöht als auch ein derartiges Gewebe wertvoller gemacht. Wenn meine Bemerkung richtig wäre, wäre es ein Beweis für die hohe Fachkenntnis der lokalen Weber, die sich bemüht hatten, eine neue Webtechnik ihren Bedürfnissen sehr gut und schnell anzueignen.

Eine wesentliche Sache ist hier auch die Qualität der Wolle, die zur Anfertigung des Samitum gebraucht worden ist. Die sowohl für die Kette als auch für den Einschuss gebrauchte Wolle ist sehr genau vorbereitet (das bezeugt die sorgfältige Sortierung der Fasern) und sehr gut gewebt. Es ist schwer, an dieser Stelle, aufgrund der geführten Analyse und bei der Berücksichtigung der Tatsache, dass es das erste Gewebe solcher Art ist, die Vermutungen anzustellen, ob die Wolle aus diesem oder aus einem anderen Gebiet stammte. Ich bin mich jedoch bewusst, dass es für die oben geführte Analyse ausschlaggebend wäre.

Auch das Posamentenstück ist in der Anfertigungtechnik den schon bekannten Posamentenstücken, z.B. aus Gdańsk,[15] ähnlich. Aber im Gegensatz zu dem Posamentenstück aus Gdańsk, ist es nicht aus Seide sondern aus Wolle gemacht worden. In diesem Zustand der Untersuchung stelle ich keine seine Herkunft betreffende Vermutungen an. Die vorgeführten Vermutungen, die die Herkunft des Samitum betrafen, könnte man auch in dem Fall vom Posamentenstück gebrauchen. Man muss aber hier unterstreichen, dass diese Vermutungen sehr problematisch sind.

Das originelle 'Bändchen', das aus einer Schnur aus wollenen Fasern mit Metallgeflecht und aus einem Gewebe aus denselben Fasern besteht, hat keine Entsprechung in den mir bekannten Ausgrabungsstätten in Polen. Es ist klar, dass es eine Zierfunktion zu erfüllen hatte. Wie ich es schon früher betont habe, könnte dieses Gewebe mit Brettchen gemacht werden. Aber es ist, meiner Meinung nach, auch möglich, dass es handgewebt sein könnte. Bei einer solchen Anfertigungstechnik wäre es also kein Gewebe sondern ein Geflecht. Das ist natürlich meine erste Vermutung. Damit verzichte ich nicht auf die oben angeführte Meinung, dass es eine Webetechnik ist. Es können doch kleinere Fragmente des Gewebes in einer Webetechnik handgewebt werden. Ein Problem könnte dann auftreten, wenn man ein grösseres Stück handweben möchte. Eine solche Art der Anfertigung wäre zeitraubend und kostspielig und oft nicht durchzuführen. In diesem Fall erlauben uns die geringe

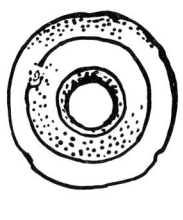 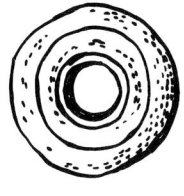

└─┘ 1 c m   └─┘ 1 c m

Abb. 16.25 Spinnwirtel aus Ton aus Grab 768

Abb. 16.27 Spinnwirtel aus Ton von der Nähe des Grablochs 768

Abb. 16.26 Spinnwirtel aus Ton aus Grab 396

Abb. 16.28 Bronzenadeln aus Gräbern 653, 75 und Erdloch 22

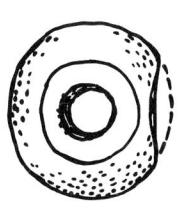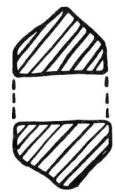   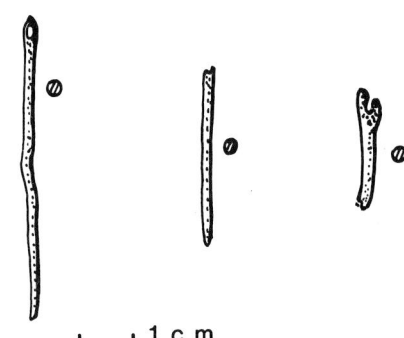

└─┘ 1 c m   └─┘ 1 c m

Menge der Fasern, ihre Dicke und überhaupt der kleine Ausmass des Bändchens zu vermuten, es hätte handgemacht werden können.

Schade, das die erhaltenen Fragmente der Kleiderverzierung und das Geflecht so klein sind. Es ist heute schwer, ihre Funktion (u.a. Zierfunktion) und die Form des Ornaments eindeutig zu erklären. Ich möchte noch bemerken, dass die Gewebe aus Stary Brześć eine hohe Fachkenntnis und die Anwendung der Fäden mit Metallgeflecht (die beim Weben, beim Durchflechten der verschiedenartigen Verzierungen, bei der Strickerei gebraucht worden sind) bezeugen. Die Gewebesammlung ist nur fragmentarisch (man hat einige hundert Gräber untersucht und die Gewebefragmente sind nur in einigen Gräber gefunden) und bestimmt entspricht sie der Menge der im Mittelalter gebrauchten Gewebe verschiedener Art nicht. Sie kann auch keineswegs den Anteil der einzelnen Gewebearten, die in Gebrauch waren, wiederspiegeln. Das Gewebe mit Ripsbindung, das mit dem Samitum gefunden worden ist, gehört in Hinsicht auf die Dichtheit der Fäden der Kette und des Einschusses zu den Geweben von höher Qualität. Dieses Gewebe und das Samitum besitzen diesselbe Dichtheit der Kettfäden. Die Gewebe mit Tuchbindung sind leider in sehr schlechtem Zustand. Bei der Analyse hat man sich nur auf die oberflächliche Beobachtung beschränkt. Es ist unmöglich mehr zu sagen, als das, was schon von ihnen oben gesagt worden ist. Die sonstigen Funde (Schere, Spinnwirtel, Nadeln) können eventuell bei der Bearbeitung ähnlicher Funde aus einem grösseren Gebiet genutzt werden, wenn die grössere Zahl der Beispiele Verallgemeinerungen ermöglicht.·

Literatur

1. Die Funde befinden sich in dem Museum für Archäologie in Łódź.

2. E. Byrska-Kaszewska, 'Cmentarzyska średniowieczne w Starym Brześciu pow. Włocławek (stan.4)', *Prace i Materiały Muzeum Archeologicznego i Etnograficznego w Łodzi*, S.A. 2, 85-124

3. *Ibid*, 95

4. J. Kamińska, A. Nahlik, *Włókiennictwo gdańskie w X-XIIIw.*, Łódź, 1958, 110-111

5. A. Nahlik, 'Tkaniny z XVI-wiecznych grobów z kolegiaty w Tumie, pow. Łęczyca', *Acta Archaeologica Universitatis Lodziensis* 4, 107

6. J. Kamińska, A. Nahlik (1958), 110-111

7. R. Ullemeyer, K. Tidow, 'Die Textil- und Lederfunde der Grabung Feddersen Wierde', *Probleme der Küstenforschung im Südlichen Nordseegebiet* 10, 1973, 80

8. K. Jażdżewski, *Urgeschichte Mitteleuropas*, Warszawa, 1984, 333, Abb.156,17

9. J. Kamińska, A. Nahlik (1958), 32

10.. K. Moszyński, *Kultura ludowa Słowian* I, Kraków, 1929, 298 Zeich. 265

11. W. Hensel, *Słowiańszczyzna wczesnośredniowieczna*, Warszawa, 1965, 252-254

12. J. Kamińska (1958)

13. A. Nahlik, 'Tkaniny wykopaliskowe z wczesnośredniowiecznego Wolina', *Materiały Zach-Pomorskie* 5, 1959, 257-276

14. W. Hołubowicz, *Opole w wiekach X-XIII*, Katowice, 1956

15. J. Kamińska, A. Nahlik (1958), 110-111

17. Eine mittelalterliche Abtsmitra aus Braunschweig: Bergung, Konservierung und Rekonstruktion/Nachbildung

Anneliese Streiter
Nürnberg

Es handelt sich um eine Abtsmitra, die bei Grabungen in der Kirche des ehemaligen Benediktinerklosters St Aegidien in Braunschweig, zusammen mit weiteren Textilfragmenten und Grabbeigaben, zutage gefördert wurde.[1]

Das Kloster wurde im Jahre 1115 von Markgräfin Gertrud, der letzten Brunonin, gestiftet. Sie war die Schwiegermutter Lothars von Süpplingenburg, des späteren Kaisers Lothar III, Großvater Heinrichs des Löwen. 1179 erließ Papst Alexander III ein umfangreiches Schutzprivileg für das Kloster. In dieser Urkunde, so vermutet man, wurden dem damaligen Abt von St Aegidien, Rengerus, die Rechte eines infulierten Abtes zugesprochen. (Die Infulierung entspricht der rangmäßigen Gleichstellung eines Abtes mit einem Bischof).

Die nach einem um 1750 erstellten Grabplattenplan hinlänglich lokalisierte mittelalterliche Grablege der Äbte des Benediktinerklosters war durch den Bau eines axialen Heizungskanals (1977/78), dessen Verlauf nicht geändert werden konnte, von der Zerstörung bedroht. Eine Rettungsgrabung wurde kurzfristig angesetzt und interdisziplinar durchgeführt. Dabei wurden in fünf höhendifferenzierten Bestattungshorizonten sieben Gräber freigelegt. Darunter befanden sich nach Sargtyp, Beigaben und Befunden drei mittelalterliche Abtsbestattungen. Größte Bedeutung kam den Grab Nr 5 zu, dem auch eine ausführliche Untersuchung galt, da der Verstorbene mit den Insignien eines infulierten Abtes, wie Abtstab, Mitra und Cingulum, beigesetzt worden war. Außerdem fanden sich Reste des Ornats, nämlich von Albe, Kasel, Stola und Kutte (?), sowie Teile eines Lederschuhes. Der zweite, sowie Reste von Beinkleidern, konnten nicht aufgefunden werden, da eine jüngere, stark gestörte Bestattung (Grab Nr 6) den unteren Teil des Grabes Nr 5 überdeckte.

Letzte Forschungen haben ergeben, daß der Abt in Grab Nr 5 wahrscheinlich mit älteren Insignien und Gewändern bestattet worden war. So ist der hölzerne Krummstab in die Mitte bis zwei Hälfte des 12. Jahrhunderts zu datieren.[2] Die Mitra, auf die im folgenden näher eingegangen wird, entstand gegen Ende des 12. Jahrhunderts. Die Stola, ein Gewebe mit Seiden- und Leinenkette, sowie mit Seiden- und Metallschuß, eine sog. Halbseide, gehört wohl eher in die erste Hälfte des 13. Jahrhunderts.[3] Endgültige Aussagen über das Alter von Kasel und Cingulum stehen noch aus, sodaß eine gesicherte Identifizierung unseres Abtes zur Zeit noch nicht möglich ist. Jedoch steht fest, daß die Bestattung vor der städtischen Brandkatastrophe im Jahre 1278 vorgenommen worden sein muß, denn St Aegidien wurde durch das Feuer weitgehend zerstört, und während der langen Wiederaufbauphase wurde hier über einen längeren Zeitraum nicht bestattet. Es ist nicht gesichert, ob die Infulierung für einen bestimmten Abt, eventuell Rengerus, galt, oder aber ganz allgemein für alle nachfolgenden Äbte des Klosters, wie es für St Michael in Hildesheim belegt ist. Papst Innocenz III verlieh erst im Jahre 1200 allen Äbten das Recht "an den Festtagen sich des Ringes und der Mitra zu bedienen".[4]

Abb. 17.1 Situation vor der Bergung der Mitrenfragmente. Pfeil weist auf Fragment 3

Zur Bergung der Mitrenfragmente

In Anbetracht der Bedeutung, die nach ersten Feststellungen dem Grab 5 beigemessen wurde - Pedum und Mitra waren ohne archäologisches Herauspräparieren erkennbar - beschloß man, nach Herstellung von photogrammetrischen Aufnahmen, dieses Grab in situ zu bergen, um die Bearbeitung des Komplexes später ohne Zeitdruck vornehmen zu kommen (Abb. 17.1).[5]

Die gesamte Bestattung war auf eine Höhe von etwa 5cm zusammengedrückt. Die im Schädel- und Halsbereich liegenden Textilfragmente gehörten eindeutig zur Mitra. Sie waren zum Teil hart, spröde, verformt, braun verfärbt und durch anhaftenden Schmutz verkrustet. Die an der Sargwand hinter den Halswirbeln eingeklemmten Textilteile (es handelte sich hierbei um die Fanones, die Bänder der Mitra) waren zum Teil mit Erde verklumpt. Die Fundstellen der einzelnen Fragmente innerhalb des Grabes wurden jeweils mit Bezeichnung der Fund-Nummer in die Lageskizze eingezeichnet.[6]

Nach dem Fotographieren und Beschreiben des Zustandes der Bestattung begann man mit dem Suchen nach weiteren Textilteilen in Bereichen, wo sie sich vermuten ließen. Dies geschah mittels einer feinen Insektennadel. Beim vorsichtigen Durchstechen der erdigen Mulchschicht spürte man beim Auftreffen auf textiles Material einen charakteristischen Widerstand. So konnten außer den Mitrenfragmenten noch Teile der Stola, sowie das Cingulum geortet werden. Den über dem Textil liegenden Sand entfernte man mit einem Ministaubsauger, die zusammengepreßte Erde konnte in Teilen nach und nach mit einer federnden, flachen Pinzette abgenommen werden, wobei sich der Feuchtigkeitsgehalt des Materials positiv auswirkte. Durch wiederholtes Sprühen einer 5%igen Lösung (dest. Wasser plus Netzmittel) aus einer Höhe von etwa 20cm über dem Skelett, konnte die Feuchtigkeit konstant gehalten werden. Ein Austrocken hätte Erde und Textilfragmente aufbrechen lassen. So wurde auch während der Nacht die Bestattung mit Folie gut abgedeckt, unter Zufügung von Schälchen mit Paradichlorbenzolkristallen, als Präventivmaßnahme gegen Schimmelbildung.

Die nach dem Herauspräparieren freiliegenden Textilteile wurden durch Unterschieben von abgerundeten säurefreien Kartontäfelchen vorsichtig herausgehoben. Von Vorteil erwies sich dabei die Eigenschaft des säurefreien Kartons, die Erdfeuchtigkeit schnell aufzunehmen, wodurch er flexibel wurde und sich der Form des zu bergenden Materials anpaßte. In der Aufbewahrungsschachtel besprühte man die Fragmente jeweils leicht mit einer 10%igen Äthanol-Glycerin-Lösung, um die Austrocung zu verhindern. So konnten sie, mit Folie abgedeckt, bis zur weiteren Bearbeitung im Restaurierungsatelier aufbewahrt werden.

Zur Konservierung der Mitra

Fünf Teile der Mitra haben sich erhalten (Abb. 17.2-17.5):

1. Die beiden Hörner (Tituli) - Borte A
2. Ein Teil des Stirnbandes (Circulus) - Borte A
3. Zweites Teil des Stirnbandes mit einem angenähten, rückwärtigen Band (Infula) - Borten A,B,C
4. Zweites rückwärtiges Band (Infula) - Borten B,C

Im Restaurierungsatelier wurden nach Zustandaufnahmen die konservatorischen Maßnahmen eingeleitet. Die Vorgehensweise und alle während der Behandlung zutage tretenden Informationen hielt man in der Dokumentation fest.[7]

Unter Zuhilfenahme eines Stereomikroskopes entfernte man in einer ersten, mechanischen Reinigung den aufliegenden Schmutz. Die darauf folgende Naßreinigung wurde ebenfalls unter dem Mikroskop durchgeführt. Dabei wurden die Fragmente einzeln in entmineraliertem Wasser, mit einem Zusatz (10%ig) eines neutralen Netzmittels bei einer Temperatur von 21°C behandelt, unter

Benutzung eines weichen Pinsels bzw. winziger Schwämmchen, die man in der Form den Anforderungen gemäß zuschnitt.

Nach dreimaligem Spülen in entmineralisiertem Wasser, wobei die Fragmente nicht bewegt wurden, transferierte man sie mit Hilfe einer Netzfolie auf eine Glasplatte, nahm die überschüssige Nässe durch Tupfen mit Schwämmchen ab und überdeckte die Teile mit einer zweiten Netzfolie. Dies geschah, um ein Hochbiegen der Kanten während des Trocknungsprozesses auszuschließen.

Bei Fragment 3, Circulus mit Band, lagen mehrere Schichten verkrustet übereinander (Abb. 17.3). Durch eine Röntgenaufnahme konnte die Anordnung der Schichten und damit die weitere Verfahrensweise bestimmt werden. Um das Teil gefahrlos entfalten zu können, mußte es durch Zufügen von Feuchtigkeit flexibel gemacht werden. Dies geschah unter einer Plexiglashaube, in einer Art Feuchtkammer. Die darauf folgende Naßreinigung geschah in der vorher beschriebenen Weise.

Form und Höhe der Mitra lassen sich aus den Maßen der Borten bestimmen: aus der Breite des Circulus, 10,7cm, und der Höhe der Hörner, 13,6cm, ergibt sich eine Höhe von 24,3cm. Der Kopfumfang, 53cm, ist aus der Länge der beiden Teile des Circulus zu errechnen. Die Endkanten des

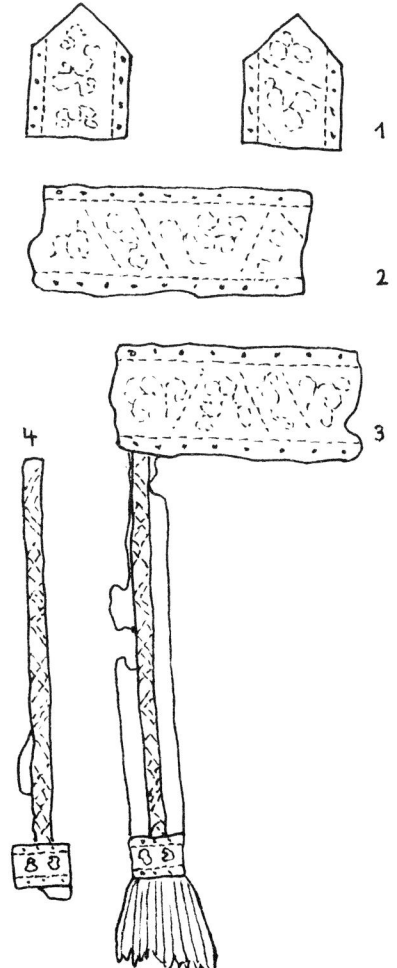

Abb. 17.2
Erhaltene Mitrenfragmente:
1. Zwei Hörner;
2. Ein Teil des Stirnbandes;
3. Ein zweites Teil des Stirnbandes mit einem rückwärtigen Band;
4. Ein rückwärtiges Band

Abb. 17.3 Teil des Stirnbandes mit rückwärtigen Band vor der Konservierung, Fragment 3

Circulus schließen in der hinteren Mitte durch eine Längsnaht mit Überwendlingsstichen. An der unteren Kante des Circulus finden sich stellenweise Reste von zwei übereinanderliegenden Einfassungen. Die untere, ein leinwandbindiges Seidengewebe, ist verstürzt um den ca 0,3cm breiten Randstreifen genäht und auf der Innenseite mit Überwendlingsstichen, entlang der Begrenzungslinie zwischen Mittelfeld und Randstreifen, befestigt. Ein Flechtbörtchen ist als wulstartige Verstärkung für die Kante mit eingefügt. Darüber liegt ein dichteres Seidengewebe als zweite Einfassung, die untere überdeckend. Es ist ebenfalls verstürzt mit groben Stichen angenäht. Innen ist es, in variierender Breite (1,4-4cm), in grober Nähweise, die sich auf der Vorderseite im Mittelfeld des Stirnbandes abzeichnet, befestigt. Es scheint sich hier um eine spätere Veränderung zu handeln, die möglicherweise vorgenommen wurde, um den Umfang der Mitra zu verkleinern. Diese zweite Einfassung endet innen auslaufend, an der Naht des Circulus, dort, wo die Infulae ansetzen. Die ca 6cm breiten Infulae sind aus einem doppelt liegenden Halbseidengewebe gearbeitet. Die Verbindungsnaht auf der Vorderseite ist durch eine 2cm breite Borte (C) abgedeckt.

Abb. 17.4 Erhaltene Mitrenfragmente liegend in ursprünglicher Anordnung

Die Längsseiten der Infulae sind ebenfalls zweimal eingefaßt, wobei die zuunterst liegende, ca 0,6cm breite Einfassung identisch ist mit der unteren des Circulus. Sie ist wie diese überdeckt von einem leinwandbindigen Seidengewebe.

Den Abschluß der Infulae bilden 4,75cm breite Borten, die, jeweils doppelt genommen, an der inneren Seitenkante zusammengenäht sind. Lange Seidenfransen waren an den unteren Rändern befestigt. Sie sind jedoch nur noch teilweise an einem Band erhalten. Die Länge der Bänder (Infulae) beträgt, incl. Fransen 52,5cm; die Höhe der Mitra, wie eingangs erwähnt, 24,3cm. Somit kommen wir auf eine Gesamthöhe von 76,5cm.[8]

Zur Technik und historischen Einordnung der Borten

Wir haben es hier mit einer Gruppe von Goldborten zu tun, die im hohen Mittelalter als kostbare Besätze überliefert sind, wie z.B. an den Kaisergewändern in der Weltlichen Schatzkammer, Wien. Auf sie läßt sich wohl auch die Bezeichnung 'Palermitaner Borte' zurückführen, die bis heute in der kunsthistorischen Literatur aufsche.[9]

Noch immer schwanken die Meinungen in Fachkreisen über die Herstellungstechnik. Wir meinen, daß es sich um Brettchengewebe handelt, wie auch Peter Collingwood, der in seinem Buch *The Technique of Tablet Weaving* ähnliche Borten aus Augsburg und Cleveland als Brettchengewebe vorstellt.[10]

Die drei Borten (A,B,C) unserer Mitra sind technisch gleich, wenn sie auch in den Maßen und der Musterung voneinander abweichen. Während die Borte A eine reiche Ornamentik mit vegetabilen Motiven und phantastischen Tieren aufweist, ist die Borte B einfacher, die Borte C dagegen flächig geometrisch gemustert.[11]

Die Mitra aus St Aegidien gehört, zusammen mit einer fast identischen aus Mainz,[12] zu einer Gruppe bedeutender Mitren des 12.Jahrhunderts, die sich in Halberstadt,[13] Brixen, Salzburg, Lausanne und Basel erhalten haben. Leonie von Wilckens vergleicht die abwechslungsreiche Borte unserer Mitra mit der im 18.Jahrhundert von Daniele graphisch vereinfachten Darstellung der Borte der Grabkrone Heinrich VI (gest.1197) und datiert sie, auch auf Grund der Höhe von 24,5cm, in das Ende des 12.Jahrhunderts. Ein weiteres Indiz für die Datierung ist die dreieckige Form der Mitra, die erst nach der Mitte des 12.Jahrhunderts üblich wurde.[14]

Wie Quellen und erhaltene Beispiele bezeugen, waren die Mitren des hohen Mittelalters weiß. Von welcher Art der Grundstoff unserer Mitra war, läßt sich leider nicht mit letzter Sicherheit bestimmen. Vermuten läßt sich eine ungemusterte Halbseide, eventuell identisch mit dem Grundstoff der Bänder. Winzige Reste an den Hörnern unterstützen diese Annahme.

Zur Aufbewahrung und Präsentation

Ursprünglich war geplant, die gereinigten Fragmente auf eine Mitrenform zu montieren, um der ursprünglichen Anordnung moglichst nahe zu kommen. Es erwies sich jedoch, daß sie durch den langen Verbleib im Grab an Flexibilität eingebüßt hatten, sodaß die Spannung im Falle der Anpassung an die Form zu groß gewesen wäre. Deshalb entschloß man sich, die Teile zur Präsentation in der entsprechenden Anordnung, flach auf eine bezogene Platte in Schräglage zu bringen. Sie wurden hier mit langen, kaum sichtbaren Überfangfäden festgelegt. Die Fransen sicherte man zusätzlich durch Überfangen mit Seidentüll. Eine Plexiglashaube im Abstand von 12cm dient als Abdeckung (Abb. 17.6).

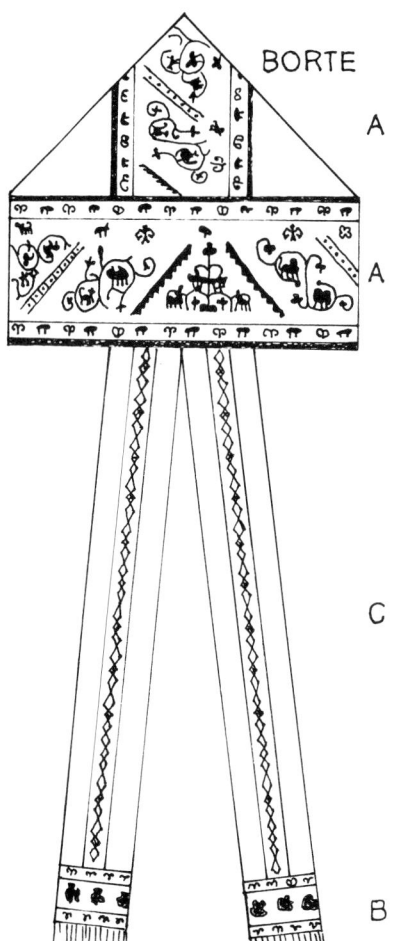

BORTE

A

A

C

B

Abb. 17.5
Rekonstruktionszeichnung mit den
Borten A B C: A = 10,70cm Breite;
B = 4,75cm Breite;
C = 2,00cm Breite

Abb.17.6 Aufliegende Fragmente
unter der Plexiglasabdeckung

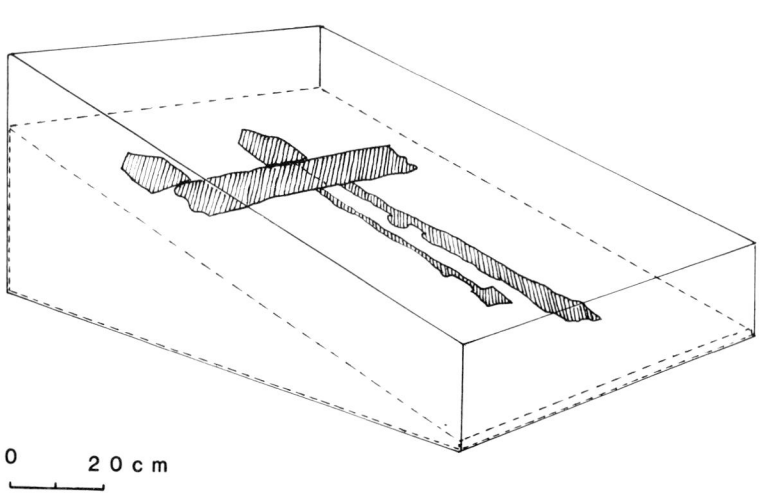

0   20 cm

Zur Nachbildung

Da die Herstellung von originalgetreuen Kopien der Borten auf Grund der technischen Schwierigkeiten von vornherein ausschied, entschloß man sich, durch übertragen des Musters mittels Farbstiften auf geeignetes Material, die ursprüngliche Form der Mitra nachzubilden. Nach den gegebenen Maßen fertigte man die Grundform aus einem weißen Seidengewebe an.[15] Für die Borten wählte man einen roten köperbindigen Seidenstoff, auf den goldene Dekastoffarbe in Schußrichtung aufgetragen wurde. Dabei achtete man darauf, daß die Vertiefungen zwischen den Köpergraten ur:berührt blieben, wodurch eine weitgehende Annäherung an die ursprüngliche Oberflächenstruktur möglich wurde. Das Muster wurde dann mit Wachsstiften auf den 'Goldgrund' gelegt und durch Reiben mit einem Falzbein fixiert. In der Wahl der Farben orientierte man sich an Beispielen gut erhaltener Goldborten des gleichen Typs.

Wir meinen, daß Nachbildungen wie diese geeignet, ja in vielen Fällen sogar notwendig sind, um die ursprüngliche Wirkung, Aussage und Funktion der im Boden meist stark reduzierten Überreste einst bedeutender Zeugnisse der Geschichte nachvollziehbar darzustellen.

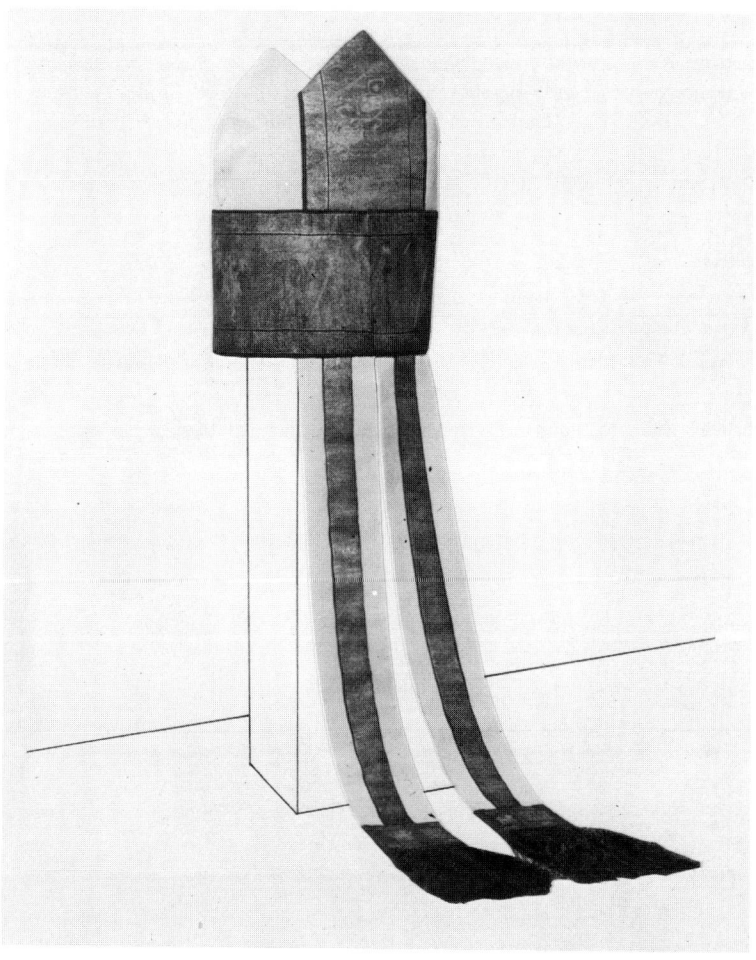

Abb. 17.7 Nachbildung der Mitra

Anmerkungen

1. Angaben zur Lokalgeschichte, sowie zur Grabung sind folgenden Publikationen entnommen: a) U. Römer-Johannsen und Ch. Römer, *800 Jahre St Aegidien (Veröffentlichungen des Braunschweigischen Landesmuseums 22)*, Braunschweig, 1979; b) Herausgeber U. Römer-Johannsen, *St Aegidien zu Braunschweig 1115-1979* (Festschrift), Hildesheim, 1979; c) H. Rötting, *Stadtarchäologie in Braunschweig (Forschungen der Denkmalpflege in Niedersachsen* 3), Hameln, 1985; d) *Stadt im Wandel, Landesausstellung Niedersachsen*, Band 1, Braunschweigisches Landesmuseum, 1985

2. Hartmut Rötting, '*Der Abtsstab von St Aegidien*' in Römer-Johannsen (1979), 40-44

3. Leonie von Wilckens, 'Seidengewebe in Zusammenhang mit der Heiligen Elisabeth' in *Sankt Elisabeth: Fürstin - Dienerin - Heilige*, Sigmaringen, 1981, 285-302

4. Römer-Johannsen (1979), 33 Anm.10

5. Ebda 16, 17, 25

6. Anneliese Streiter, Sibylle Ruß, 'Zum Arbeitsstand der Textilkonservierung von Grab 5, St Aegidien' in Rötting (1985), 299-305

7. Anneliese Streiter, Leonie von Wilckens, 'Die "Mitra aus St Aegidien zu Braunschweig" und weitere Textilfunde aus Grab 5' in Römer-Johannsen (1979), 34-39

8. Vgl. Anm. 6

9. Ruth Grönwoldt, 'Kaisergewänder und Paramente' in *Die Zeit der Staufer, Geschichte - Kunst - Kultur*, Ausstellung Württembergisches Landesmuseum, Stuttgart, 1977, 607 - 644; Agnes Geijer, *A History of Textile Art*, London, 1979, 218f; Saskia Durian-Ress, *Meisterwerke mittelalterlicher Textilkunst*, München/Zürich, 1986, 96 - 101

10. Peter Collingwood, *The Techniques of Tablet Weaving*, London, 1982, 282, 346

11. Vgl. Anm. 6

12. Unveröffentlicht

13. Friederike Happach, 'Die Textilfunde' in Gerhard Leopold, Ernst Schubert, *Der Dom zu Halberstadt*, Berlin, 1984, 94-97; Friedrich Bellman, 'Zur kunstgeschichtlichen Bestimmung der Textilfunde', ebda 98-103

14. Leonie von Wilckens, 'Textilkundliche Anmerkungen zur Datierung von Grab 5, St Aegidien' in Rötting (1985), 295-297

15. Bei der Erstellung der Nachbildung waren Ursula Hofmann und Magdalena Verenkotte der Verfasserin behilflich.

18. Patterned cloths from 14th-century London

Frances Pritchard

London

Highly finished woollens dyed a single hue are often considered to epitomise cloth produced in the later Middle Ages, but one only has to glance at 14th-century manuscript illuminations to notice that patterned cloths were used with great exuberance and virtuosity. As the late Dame Joan Evans observed in her seminal work on dress in Medieval France, a *robe* (or suit of clothing) was usually made of the same, or similar, coloured cloth, in the 13th century,[1] whereas by the second quarter of the 14th century garments were co-ordinated to dazzle the eye, and this was achieved not only by wearing clothes of contrasting colour but by teaming patterned fabrics with plain ones.

This paper is concerned with examining the range of patterned cloths that are preserved from 14th-century deposits in the City of London. Wool and silk fabrics are discussed, but, as usual, linen and union cloths, such as fustian, have left little imprint on the archaeological record, thereby introducing a misleading bias towards cloths woven from animal protein fibres. Horizontal stripes were the favourite form of patterning on cloths woven from wool, whereas patterns on silk fabrics range from geometric ornament to the fantastical; but underlying the obvious differences is the stimulus that patterned silks gave to the wool industry, along with a greater inclination to experiment with different bindings on the horizontal loom and a burgeoning sense of fashion.

Several sites in London with 14th-century deposits have produced textiles, but the largest assemblage was recovered from a public watergate beside the Thames, close to a Medieval property known from the 1450's as Baynard's Castle. Two large dumps of material were excavated there in 1972, one dating to *c.* 1330-1340 and the other to the last quarter of the 14th century. They afford, in consequence, a rare opportunity to compare the jettisoned textiles of one generation with those of another later in the same century and enable differences to be charted among the patterned fabrics. These will be discussed in detail elsewhere;[2] the intention here is to single out a few examples.

Turning first of all to woollen cloths with a tabby binding (which is a type of fabric that was often dyed in the piece), a cuff of a gown or tunic can be recognised as having been cut from a checked cloth: this is made up of alternate groups of red and white threads, outlined with two threads of a darker colour in both the warp and the weft (fig. 18.1). These yarns, therefore, would have been dyed in the fleece or the hank. The close-fitting character of the sleeve, which fastened below the elbow with twelve small cloth buttons, and the silk facing and edging, show that it was originally a stylish garment. This modishness is also reflected in the choice of a checked cloth, perhaps a conscious attempt to imitate patterned velvet, which in the Great Wardrobe Accounts of the 1340's is often described as being checkered.[3]

While checked patterns on wool cloths appear to have gained a fresh impetus from velvet-weaving in the early 14th century, they were not a new departure and among the many cloths in the old-fashioned three-shed twill binding from the 1330's deposit at Baynard's Castle is a small number of checked fabrics. They include, for example, a piece patterned with alternate red and white checks composed of groups of six red and six white ends interlaced with four white and four red picks. The character of this type of twill, warp-faced on the front and weft-faced on the reverse, gives a very different appearance to a checked pattern; for on the front the coloured threads of the warp show up in the form of vertical stripes, whereas on the reverse the coloured threads of the weft predominate.

Some 14th-century wills and inventories refer to cushions and coverlets being made from checked cloths[4] and this was a purpose for which worsteds, with their smooth shiny surface, are better suited than woollens, which are prone to pill. A worsted cloth woven in tabby binding with a bold plaid-like pattern in two colours (fig. 18.2) was recovered among the late 14th-century textiles from London, and from its appearance it is tempting to interpret it as a furnishing fabric.

Another simple type of colour effect with a long history of use was produced by warp and weft yarns of contrasting colour. Where this form of patterning was adopted for tabby-woven cloths, a mottled appearance was usually the result. Variations, however, were sometimes created. One cloth from the first half of the 14th century in London has a tabby binding with white warp yarn and two weft yarns, alternately red and white. I would again venture to suggest that a new stimulus to the production of these mottled fabrics was provided by the popularity of shot silks, the subtlety of which is emphasised by the names by which they were then known, 'changeable sarcenet', and 'changeable taffeta'. A fragment of a shot silk tabby is indeed present among the textiles recovered from late 14th-century London. It appears to be a weft-faced fabric with the lighter coloured picks covering the dark ends in a ratio of 2:1, and none of the yarn is twisted, so that the light-reflecting properties of the silk were exploited to good effect.

A few four-shed twills woven from Z-spun worsted yarn are similarly patterned with warp and weft yarns of contrasting colours and these fabrics often appear to have been used to line fashionable

Fig. 18.1 Sleeve of a garment made from a woollen cloth patterned with small red and white checks outlined in a third colour. From a deposit of c. 1330-40. Width of wrist edge 167mm. Photograph: Edwin Baker, copyright Museum of London

garments. Less common from 14th-century London are 2/2 twills with mixed spinning. A group of these twills is made from hairy yarns spun from the fleece of double-coated sheep and they frequently exploit the different natural brown and grey shades of pigmented wool to form a variety of narrow stripes and open checks. Since dyed yarn was not required for cloths coloured in this manner they would have fallen into the lower end of the market and it has been argued that they were a type of material known as *wadmal*.[5]

None of the colour effects described above was in any sense innovative. There are, however, a group of cloths which combine weave effects with that of colour patterning in ways not attempted before in northern Europe. The finest example from 14th-century London is a six-shed twill woven from worsted yarn (fig. 18.3). The two fragments of the cloth show areas of a waved, weft chevron twill with a point repeat, woven with a red warp yarn and a white weft yarn. Through the waved twill runs a band, 4mm wide, of 20 throws, in a similar patterned weave but with a red weft yarn matching that of the warp. The band is edged on each side with six throws of pale purple yarn followed by six throws of white yarn, woven in extended tabby, the weft passing alternately over and under three ends. The wool used for this cloth has a very high lustre and the pattern imitates those found on certain 13th-century silk fabrics which were probably produced in Hispano-Moresque workshops, and which include examples from the tomb of the Infante don Felipe (died 1252) and his wife, at Villalcázar de Sirga, Palencia, in northern Spain,[6] and others from the tomb of Leonor, Queen of Aragon (died 1244), in the convent of Las Huelgos, Burgos.[7]

Fig. 18.2 Cloth woven from worsted yarn with a two-tone plaid pattern. Surviving height 110mm. From a deposit of the late 14th century. Photograph: Edwin Baker, copyright Museum of London

157

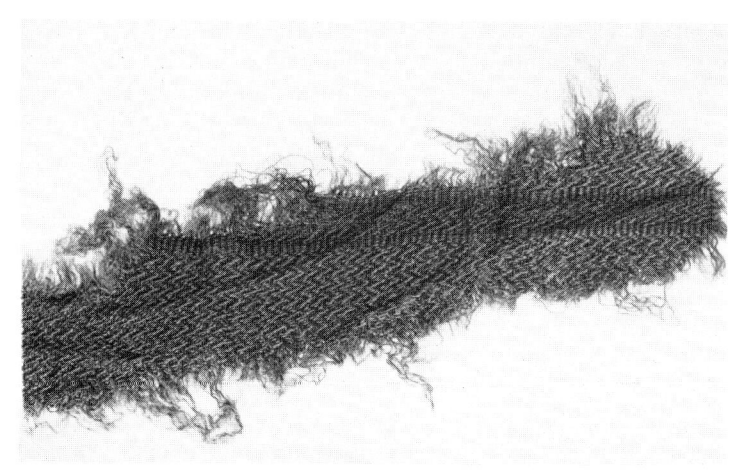

Fig. 18.3 (right) Worsted six-shed twill with colour and weave effects. Width of contrasting band 8mm. From a deposit of c. 1330-40. Photograph: Jon Bailey, copyright Museum of London

Fig. 18.4 (below left) Armhole of a 'supertunic' made from a wool cloth patterned with narrow bands of plied silk thread spaced 90mm apart. From a deposit of c. 1330-40. Photograph: Edwin Baker, copyright Museum of London

Fig. 18.5 Wool cloth patterned with a weft-faced band, 31mm wide, woven in three colours, light brown, purple and red. From a deposit of the late 14th century. Photograph: Edwin Baker, copyright Museum of London

Most bands woven on textiles from 14th-century London are less elaborate and no others are in six-shed twill. Nevertheless, they do make play with the order in which the shafts were lifted on the loom and the degree to which the weft was beaten in, in order to accentuate the pattern. In the early 14th century the bands remained relatively narrow and only one or two colours tended to be used.

Additional patterning sometimes took the form of a mottled, two-tone main weave between the bands. Occasionally natural brown wool was used to provide colour at a lower cost, but most of the yarn was dyed in shades of red, purple, yellow, tawny, green and blue.

Another feature of cloths from early 14th-century London was the use of silk thread woven into wool cloth, which is a type of patterning that has also been recorded on cloths excavated from deposits dating to the first quarter of the 14th century in Amsterdam.[8] Two-ply, undyed silk thread was invariably used and only in very small amounts, but the effect could still be eye-catching. Considerable care was taken as to the way such cloth was cut for clothing, as can be seen on an armhole from a sleeveless 'supertunic' (fig. 18.4).

By the second half of the 14th century striped fabrics of this type included a greater number of colours in each band, which accordingly increased in width, extending to 65mm on one example. The colours were arranged in contrasting dark and light tones, or were subtly shaded, and the effect was sometime enhanced with shots of silk thread, by introducing bands of four-shaft twill, and by using weft yarns of contrasting spin and thickness (fig. 18.5-18.9). There can be little doubt that these cloths, with their bewildering variety of patterns, correspond to those called 'rays' in late Medieval documents.[9]

Bands of different colours and texture were similarly employed on silk fabrics in the 14th century. A lightweight silk cloth with this type of patterning is preserved from the late 14th-century deposit at Baynard's Castle, London. The main weave is a pinkish-mauve tint and running across it is a weft-faced band, 23mm wide (fig. 18.10). This includes three white stripes in 1/3 twill with two stripes in between, woven with a weft yarn which has disintegrated. The missing yarn could have been made from a cellulosic plant fibre, or a coloured silk - perhaps green - dyed with an iron mordant, or it may have been metallic. Whatever it was it would have further enlivened the pattern of the cloth.

A few even lighter silk fabrics, which were presumably intended for use as veils since they are transparent, are characterised by a series of self-coloured bands woven at each end in thicker yarn (fig. 18.11). These veils come from the late 14th-century deposit at Baynard's Castle.

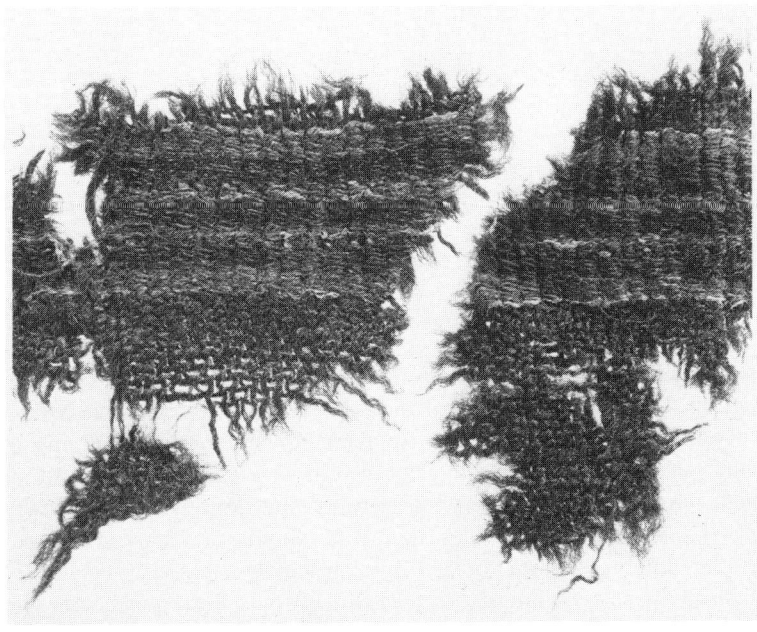

Fig. 18.6 Dark reddish-purple wool cloth patterned with a weft-faced band, 14mm wide, woven in undyed silk thread, 'light brown' wool and darkish purple-black wool. From a deposit of the late 14th century. Photograph: Edwin Baker, copyright Museum of London

Fig. 18.7 Wool cloth patterned with a weft-faced band, 35mm wide, of four colours. The band is edged with two throws of dark purple yarn woven in tabby and the rest of the band is woven in extended tabby, except for the stripes on either side of the red centre which are bound in 2/2 twill and use a fine, worsted Z-spun yarn. From a deposit of the late 14th century. Photograph: Edwin Baker, copyright Museum of London

Fig. 18.8 Wool cloth patterned with a weft-faced band, 32mm wide, woven in three colours, purple, 'light brown', and red. The centre of the band is woven in 2/2 weft chevron twill with a single point repeat while the other fourteen stripes are woven in extended tabby. From a deposit of the late 14th century. Photograph: Edwin Baker, copyright Museum of London

Striped silken cloths were relatively cheap in comparison with highly decorated fabrics since it took much less time to set up a striped pattern on a loom than it did to mount a figured one. More costly, heavy fabrics were able to withstand a longer period of wear and tended to be recycled. Thus among the silk textiles from mid 14th-century London are a few pieces which were undoubtedly woven in earlier centuries. Perhaps more surprising is that amongst the city's rubbish of this period are two fragments of a Chinese twill damask patterned with peonies (fig. 18.12). Similar cloths began to flood into western Europe in the late 13th century in the wake of the reopening of trade routes to the Far East.[10] The appearance, however, of Chinese textiles in England may be associated, at least in part, with the

Fig. 18.9 Dark reddish-purple wool cloth patterned with a weft-faced band, 30mm wide, woven in three differently coloured wool yarns (dark purple, reddish-purple and brown) and undyed silk thread. The four silk stripes within the band are woven in 2/2 twill, with the diagonal reversing in alternate stripes, and the band is edged with two throws of dark purple yarn woven in tabby. From a deposit of the late 14th century. Photograph: Edwin Baker, copyright Museum of London

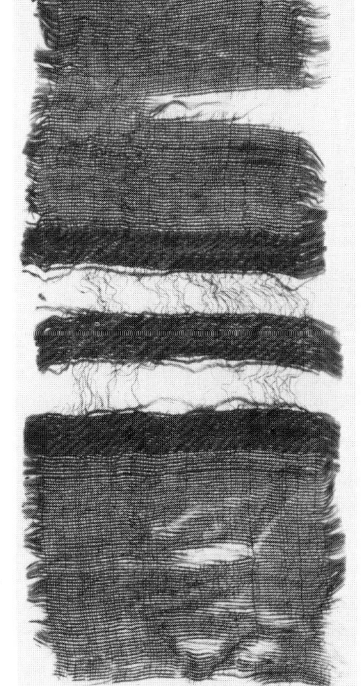

Fig. 18.10 Silk cloth patterned with a contrasting weft-faced band, 23mm wide, bound in 1/3 twill. One of the two patterned wefts has disintegrated. From a deposit of the late 14th century. Photograph: Edwin Baker, copyright Museum of London

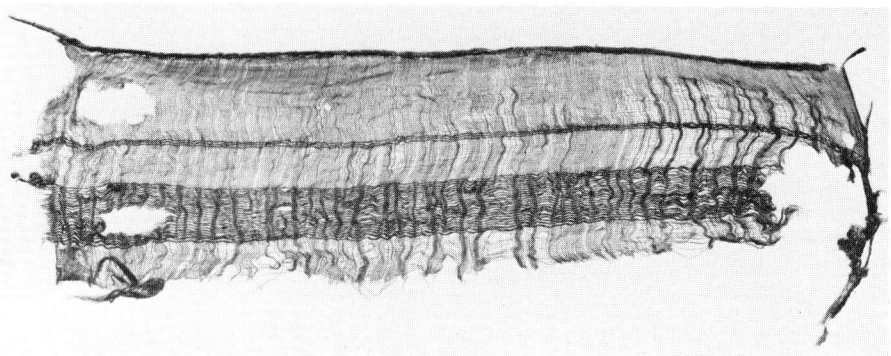

Fig. 18.11 One end of a silk veil, patterned with two horizontal bands woven from thicker yarn. Surviving height 26mm. From a deposit of the late 14th century. Photograph: Edwin Baker, copyright Museum of London

Fig. 18.12 Silk twill damask with a pattern of peonies. From a deposit of c. 1330-40. Photograph: Edwin Baker, copyright Museum of London

sending of three diplomatic missions by the Tartar princes ruling in the western dominions of the Mongol empire to the courts of Edward I and Edward II in 1300, 1303 and 1307.[11] This was done with the aim of gaining English support for a bid by the Mongols to drive the Mamluks out of Palestine. Silk cloths and porcelain, one would imagine, were included among the gifts exchanged, just as on the better known occasion in 1323, when Mongolian ambassadors presented the Sultan of Egypt with 700 oriental cloths.[12] Fine Chinese textiles and oriental dress impressed themselves on the popular imagination and at a tournament held in Cheapside, London, in 1331, Edward III and his courtiers dressed up in the apparel of Tartars.[13] Cloth design was also strongly influenced by these eastern imports and this is apparent in textiles produced in weaving centres all around the Mediterranean.[14]

Numbered among the patterned silk cloths of European origin from the late 14th-century rubbish dump at Baynard's Castle are fragments of eight lampas-woven cloths, whereas none is represented in the earlier 14th-century deposit. Three are woven with a pattern bound in tabby on a tabby ground and five have patterns bound in tabby on a 2/1 twill ground. All have a warp proportion of three main ends (usually paired) to one binding end. Most are narrow strips but stitches and stitching holes indicate that they were not thrown away unused. A rectangular piece was made into a small pouch finished with a tablet-woven edging and a handle made from a fingerloop braid. The pattern of this cloth, woven in white on a pinkish-purple ground, consists of rows of hexagons containing birds and sprays of flowers which are repeated in reverse in alternate hexagons. Between each hexagon is a vertical panel containing two pseudo-heraldic devices, one with lozenges and the other with waved

162

chevrons. The width of the pattern repeat on this cloth is 88mm but the complete height of the repeat is not preserved. Heraldic motifs were popular as patterns on many different types of cloth, both woven and embroidered, in the 13th and early 14th centuries, and indeed they became common on all sorts of artefacts ranging from leather sheaths and enamelled caskets to earthenware tiles and jugs.

Lampas-woven silk fabrics, with the pattern bound in tabby on a twill ground, include more exotic patterns amongst those excavated from London, which, like the warp-faced twill of the ground, were copied from Chinese cloths. The outlines of fantastic birds, beasts and peacock feathers can be distinguished on some fragments (fig. 18.13), apparently woven in two or possibly three colours, and clearly none fell into the most expensive range of cloths interwoven with 'gold' thread. One cloth from London is particularly interesting because its pattern is small compared to the expanse of its pinkish-red background. The pattern appears to show a scroll of lettering unfurled behind a spray of three flowers (fig. 18.14). The small area of this pattern offers a contrast to those usually associated with the 14th century, which have every inch of available space taken up with patterning. The relative cheapness of the cloth is further emphasised by the fact that a lichen purple dyestuff,[15] probably orchil, was used to dye the silk yarn of the main warp and this would have quickly faded on exposure to the light. This London piece, therefore, provides a useful corrective to many luxuriant silk cloths preserved in ecclesiastical treasuries and art collections.

Fig. 18.13 Strip of a silk lampas cloth with a tabby pattern on a 2/1 twill ground. The large-scale pattern is incomplete, but part of a bird, a knotted cord and two peacock feathers can be distinguished. Height of strip 202mm. From a deposit of the late 14th century. Photograph: Edwin Baker, copyright Museum of London

Fig. 18.14 Strip of silk lampas cloth with a tabby pattern on a 2/1 twill ground. More than half of the scroll and flower pattern can be seen in the centre of the photograph and part of two repeats in the foreground. Height of strip 233mm. From a deposit of the late 14th century. Photograph: Edwin Baker, copyright Museum of London

The number of patterned textiles from 14th-century London is small compared with the quantity of plain cloths. Their importance, however, should not be underestimated; for they reveal that a new range of fabrics woven from wool, particularly worsted yarn, was developed in the late 13th to 14th centuries, influenced, at least to some extent, by silk, half-silk, and mixed cotton and linen cloths. Silk yarn was also being used on a growing scale by weavers in northern Europe. The patterned cloths recovered from London, therefore, provide a new perspective on the consumption of textiles in England's capital city and are an invaluable source for reconstructing the period's sartorial brilliance.

Acknowledgements

I owe an enormous debt of gratitude to Elisabeth Crowfoot, who undertook the initial cataloguing of the textiles discussed here, in allowing me to publish this article. I should also like to thank my colleagues at the Museum of London, especially Jon Bailey and Edwin Baker for the photography and Tony Dyson, Kay Staniland, Ian Ridler and Alan Vince for their help and advice in preparing this paper.

References

1. J. Evans, *Dress in Medieval France*, Oxford, 1952, 20

2. E. Crowfoot, F. Pritchard, K. Staniland, *Textiles and Clothing, Medieval Finds from London* 4, forthcoming

3. L. Monnas, 'Developments in figured velvet weaving in Italy during the 14th century', *Bulletin de Liaison du C.I.E.T.A.*, 63/64, 1986, 65

4. For example the Wills of William de Derby, 1361, and Agnes Pikerell, 1373, in R.R. Sharpe (ed), *Calendar of Wills, Court of Husting, London*, Part 2, London, 1890, 31 and 155. *Worthstede skackata* is mentioned four times in D.A. Watkin (ed), *Inventory of Church Goods temp Edward III*, Part 1, Norwich Record Society, 4, 7, 60 and 61

5. E. Crowfoot, 'Textiles', in H. Clarke and A. Carter, *Excavations in King's Lynn 1963-1970 (Soc. Medieval Archaeol. Monograph Ser. 7)* 374-6

6. I. Errera, *Catalogue d'Étoffes Anciennes et Modernes*, 3rd edn, Brussels, 1927, 39 No 17

7. D.G. Shepherd, 'The textiles from Las Huelgas de Burgos', *The Bulletin of the Needle and Bobbin Club* 35, 1951 Nos 1-2, 10-13

8. S.Y. Vons-Comis, 'Medieval textile finds from the Netherlands', in L. Bender-Jørgensen, K. Tidow (edd), *Textilsymposium Neumünster: Archäologische Textilfunde*, Neumünster, 1982, 156

9. Some examples imported from Flanders and Brabant are mentioned in L.J. Buyse, *The Market for Flemish and Brabantine cloth in England from the XIIth to the XIVth century*, MA thesis, London University, 1956, 184-90, and in V.A. Harding, 'Some documentary sources for the import and distribution of foreign textiles in later medieval England ', *Textile History* 18/2, 1987, 211. They were also produced in England, where their width was regulated by statute: A.R. Bridbury, *Medieval English Clothmaking: an Economic Survey*, London, 1982, 108-9

10. R.S. Lopez, 'European merchants in the Medieval Indies: the evidence of commercial documents', *Journal of Economic History* 3, 1943, No 2, 164

11. L.H. Hornstein, 'The historical background of the King of Tars', *Speculum* 16, 1941, 413-4

12. A.F. Kendrick, *Catalogue of Muhammadan Textiles of the Medieval Period*, London, 1924, 39

13. E.W. Safford, 'An account of the expenses of Eleanor, sister of Edward III, on the occasion of her marriage to Reynald, Count of Guelders', *Archaeologia* 77, 1928, 112

14. O. von Falke, *Kunstgeschichte der Seidenweberei*, vol. 2, Berlin, 1913, 67,69-74

15. The dyestuff was identified by Penelope Walton, using solvent extraction followed by absorption spectrometry.

19. Spätmittelalterliche und frühneuzeitliche Textilfunde aus Lübeck und ihre früheren Verwendungen

Klaus Tidow
Neumünster

Bis in die Mitte der 70er Jahre war in Deutschland die wissenschaftliche Bearbeitung von Textilfunden aus dem Spätmittelalter und der Frühneuzeit aus Ausgrabungen ein wenig beachtetes Gebiet der Textilforschung. Auch im Textilmuseum Neumünster hatte der erste Direktor, Karl Schlabow, vorwiegend bronze- und eisenzeitliche Gewebe untersucht. Nur 1955-56 befaßte er sich eine zeitlang intensiver mit spätmittelalterlichen Textilfunden aus Lübeck. Die Resultate dieser Untersuchungen wurden jedoch bereits 1956 veröffentlicht. Sein Nachfolger im Textilmuseum Neumünster, Rudolf Ullemeyer, hat im Rahmen seiner Bearbeitungen von spätmittelaltlichen Lederfunden aus Lübeck auch einige wenige Gewebefragmente analysiert, die aber erst 1978 veröffentlicht wurden. 1976 begann der Verfasser mit der systematischen Erfassung aller in Lübeck und anderen norddeutschen Städten bei Ausgrabungen geborgenen Gewebe, Gestricke und Filze. Im Mittlepunkt der bisherigen Untersuchungen standen die textiltechnischen Analysen, die im letzten Jahr zunächst einmal abgeschlossen wurden.[1]

Nunmehr soll eine zusammenfassende Bewertung aller Lübecker Textilfunden erfolgen, ehe mit der Bearbeitung der seit 1986 in Lübeck ausgegrabenen Textilien begonnen werden kann. Parallel zu den textiltechnischen Untersuchungen läuft ein Projekt, das sich mit der Beurteilung und Einordnung der Lübecker Textilien hinsichtlich ihrer früheren Verwendungen befaßt. Diese sich über einen längeren Zeitraum erstreckenden Bearbeitungen werden vom Verfasser in Zusammenarbeit mit Gisela Jaacks durchgeführt, die sich in den letzten Jahren u. a. ausführlich mit der städtischen Kleidung des Mittelalters befaßt hat.[2] Altfunde, die unter der Leitung von Werner Neugebauer vom Amt für Vor- und Frühgeschichte (Bodendenkmalpflege) der Hansestadt Lübeck in den Jahren nach dem zweiten Weltkrieg ausgegraben bzw. bei Notgrabungen geborgen wurden, und Neufunde, die von Neugebauers Nachfolger Günter P. Fehring und seinen Mitarbeitern besonders in den Jahren 1974 bis 1983 im Rahmen eines Sonderforschungsprogrammes ausgegraben wurden. Viele dieser Neufunde sind gut datiert und deshalb für die Erforschung alter Textiltechniken von großer Bedeutung.

Nür wenige der Lübecker Textilfunde sind so gut erhalten, daß sie eine eindeutige Aussage hinsichtlich ihrer früheren Verwendung zulassen. Karl Schlabow stellte im Rahmen seiner bereits erwähnten Publikation zwei Wollmützen vor, die in das 15.Jh. datiert sind. Die eine Mütze wurde aus einem Wollgewebe mittelfeiner Qualität (Tuchbindung T 1/1) geschneidert, die andere Mütze aus Wollgarnen gestrickt.[3] Zu den herausragenden Textilfunden aus Lubeck gehört zweifellos der 265cm lange und 3cm breite Gürtel aus Seidenzwirnen in Köperbindung (K 3/1) aus dem frühen 15. Jh., der vom Verfasser erstmals 1978 vorgestellt wurde.[4] Unveröffentlicht sind dagegen ein Stoffball und ein Teerquast, die noch nicht datiert sind, aber aufgrund der Gewebekonstruktionen wohl im späten Mittelalter oder in der frühen Neuzeit entstanden sind. Der Stoffball (Fundstelle: An der Untertrave 78, 027, Fd. -Nr. 7-1) hat einen Durchmesser von 10cm und besteht aus zwei verschiedenen Wollgeweben grober Qualität (T 1/1 und K 2/1). Für den Teerquast (Fundstelle: Sandestraße 8-12,

0186, Fd. -Nr. 51-1) hat man mehrere mittelfeine Wollgewebe in Tuchbindung verwendet. Teerquaste sind auch in anderen Städten ausgegraben worden, so hat z. B. Sandra Vons-Comis die aus Amsterdam bereits 1979 vorgestellt.[5]

Außer den genannten Textilien gibt es unter den Lübecker Geweben, Gestricken und Filzen noch zahlreiche Fragmente mit Bearbeitungsspuren, wie z. B. Schnittkanten, Nähten und Säumen. Sie geben manchmal Hinweise auf ihren früheren Verwendungszweck. Von diesen haben wir zunächst solche ausgewählt, die vielfältige Bearbeitungsspuren aufweisen. Zwei solcher Funde sollen hier als Beispiele ausführlicher besprochen werden. Dazu kommt eine Seidenhaube, die zwar schon einmal untersucht worden ist, aber bisher nicht veröffentlicht wurde. Die ersten Zeichnungen dieser drei Funde während der Bearbeitung und die Analyse der Nähte besorgte Johanna Banck, die im Winter 1986 im Auftrage des Amtes für Vor- und Frühgeschichte (Bodendenkmalpflege) der Hansestadt im Textilmuseum gearbeitet hat. Die endgültigen Gewandschnittzeichnungen werden nach Abschluß der trachtenkundlichen Untersuchungen angefertigt.

Eine Haube aus Seidendamast

Die Haube (Fundstelle: Holstenstraße 24, 0111, Fd. -Nr. 36) (Abb. 19.1) besteht aus einem Seiden-damast (Grundbindung: Atlas A 1/7) und wurde aus 0,1 bis 0,3mm feinen Garnen gewebt. Auf je 2cm kommen ca.160 Kett- und ca.65 Schußfäden. Die Kettfäden sind leicht gedreht. Die Motive der großrapportigen Musterung deuten darauf hin, daß die Haube im 16. oder 17.Jh. entstanden ist.

Bereits 1956 hatte Karl Schlabow diese Haube einmal untersucht. In seinem unveröffentlichen Bericht hat er geschrieben, daß die Haube das Kopfhaar von der Stirn bis zum Nacken und die beiden Ohrseiten bedeckt. Die Haube ist aus sechs Teilen zusammengenäht und besteht aus einem Vorder- und einem Hinterteil. Das Vorderteil ist ein langgezogenes Rechteck, an dessen kürzeren Seiten jeweils ein kleines, dreieckiges Teilstück angesetzt ist. An das Vorderteil schließt sich das halbel-lipsenförmige Hinterteil an. Die von Schlabow geäußerte Vermutung, daß es sich bei dieser Haube um eine aus Reststücken gefertigte Kopfbedeckung handelt, wird bei dem Hinterteil besonders deutlich, da die linke Seite aus zwei kleinen Stücken zusammengenäht ist, während die rechte Seite nur aus einem Stück besteht. Von der Stirn bis in den Nackenbereich ist die Haube etwa 28cm lang, während sie von der rechten zur linken Seitenhälfte ca.40cm mißt. Die Hauptnaht, die Vorder- und Hinterteil verbindet, ist eine Überwendlichnaht, wofür vorher die Geweberänder umgelegt worden sind. Die kleineren Teilstücke des Vorderteils sind hingegen nur durch einfache Heftstiche an das größere Stück genäht. Eines der dreieckigen kleinen Teilstücke ist im Wangenbereich am Rand noch mit einem Rollsaum versehen. Die umgelegten Ränder der 3 Stücke des Hinterteils der Haube sind sehr sorgfältig mit einer doppelten Vorstichnaht aneinander genäht.

Ein am hinteren Rand im Nackenbereich der Haube angebrachtes, 2cm breites Band in Taftbindung diente zur Verstärkung. Die verwebten Garne des Besatzbandes sind etwa 0,2 bis 0,5mm fein. Auf jeweils 2cm kommen rund 44 Kett- und 44 Schußfäden, wobei die Kettfäden als ungezwirnte Doppelfäden eingewebt worden sind.

Reste eines Wamses aus Leder und Seidentaft

Bei dem aus einem Lederstück und zwei Seidengeweben zusammengenähten Fragment (Fundstelle: Alfstraße 31/Gerade Querstraße 6-8, 023, Fd. -Nr. 6) handelt es sich ebenfalls um den Rest eines Kleidungsstückes (Abb. 19.2). Das Fragment mißt heute etwa 32 mal 24cm. Die Seidengewebe sind in Taftbindung gewebt und auf jeweils 2cm kommen etwa 68 Kett- und 54 Schußfäden. Die Garne sind 0,1 bis 0,3mm fein und leicht gedreht. Außerdem sind die Seidengewebe noch mit steck-nadelgroßen Löchern durchsetzt.

Abb. 19.1 Seidenhaube (Lübeck-Holstenstraße, 0111, Fd. -Nr. 36) M 2:3

Die Schichtenfolge des Lederstückes und der beiden Seidengewebe ist deutlich im Bereich der Knopflochleiste zu erkennen, da die Knopflöcher durch die drei Schichten geschnitten sind und mit einem 1mm dicken Seidenzwirn in S-Drehung sorgfältig umnäht sind. Zwischen den vollständigen Knopflöchern und einem nur noch teilweise vorhandenen Knopfloch lag lediglich ein Abstand von ca.1cm, so daß die Knopflochleiste dicht mit stabilen Seidenzwirnen umnähten Knopflöchern versehen ist, die den Gewandrest als ein robustes Kleidungsstück ausweist. Die Kante der Knopflochleiste ist durch einen umgelegten Lederstreifen verstärkt. Der Lederteil und die Gewebestücke sind jedoch mehr oder weniger stark zerschlissen. Trotzdem kann aus diesen Fragmenten geschlossen werden, daß sie ein Reststück eines Wamses sind, wie er im 16. und 17.Jh. getragen wurde (Diesen Hinweis verdankt der Verfasser den Mitarbeiterinnen der Textilrestaurierwerkstatt des Germanischen Nationalmuseums in Nürnberg Anneliese Streiter, Erika Weiland und Katharina Knefelkamp anläßlich eines Besuches in Nürnberg im November 1986).[6] Vom Körper aus gesehen handelt es sich bei diesem Fragment um die linke Knopflochleiste des Wamses. Bei diesem Gewandrest können außer den umnähten Knopflöchern noch verschiedene Reste von Nähten festgestellt werden, von denen hauptsächlich nur noch die umgelegten Geweberänder, jedoch selten der genaue Verlauf der Nähgarne, ausgemacht werden können.

Abb. 19.2 Reste eines Wamses (Lübeck-Alfstraße 31/Gerade Querstraße 6-8, 023, Fd. -Nr. 6) M c. 1:2

Reste einer Wolljacke?

Bei diesem bisher undatierten Geweberest (Fundstelle: Wahmstraße 1-11/ Breite Straße 95 - 99, 0214, Fd. -Nr. 91) von einer Größe von etwa 42 mal 29cm, handelt es sich um ein Wollgewebe in Tuchbindung mit Ripsstreifen (Abb. 19.3). Auf jeweils 2cm kommen 27 Kett- bzw. 22 Schußfäden im Bereich der Tuchbindung, während die Ripsstreifen etwas enger eingestellt sind. Die Garne in einem Fadensystem (wohl der Kette) sind in z-Drehung, die im anderen (wohl der Schuß) in s-Drehung gesponnen. Als Besonderheit in diesem Gewebe sind die 1,2cm breiten Streifen aus einer Kombination von Rips- und Tuchbindung, die in Abständen von 4,5cm eingewebt sind, zu erwähnen. Die Ripsstreifen werden an jeder Seite von einem schwarzbraunen Wollfaden in Tuchbindung begrenzt, von dem ebenfalls zwei in der Mitte des Streifens eingewebt sind. Zwischen den Rändern und der Mitte des Streifens befindet sich jeweils ein Streifen in Ripsbindung, der durch zwei gelbbraune Seidenfäden in zwei gleiche Hälften unterteilt ist. Der Seidenfaden hat eine Stärke von 0,3mm. Sieben solcher Streifen sind noch erhalten geblieben. Die Garne der Tuchbindung sind etwa 0,5mm stark und heute von dunkelbrauner Farbe.

Unsere Vermutung, daß es sich bei diesem verhältnismäßig großem Gewebefragment um den Rest eines Kleidungsstückes (einer Jacke?) handelt, wird durch drei umgelegte Geweberänder, an denen sich aber keine Nähgarne erhalten haben, bestätigt. An einem dieser umgelegten Ränder befindet sich noch ein Stoffknopf (Wollgewebe in T 1/1 ?) mit einem Durchmesser von 1,2cm. Er ist mit einem Seidenzwirn in S-Drehung angenäht. (In diesem umgelegten Geweberand befindet sich etwa 1cm vom Knopf noch ein winziger Rest eines Seidenzwirns, der möglicherweise das Nähgarn eines zweiten Knopfes war.) Der etwa 3cm lange umgelegte Geweberand läuft in die Mitte des Gewebes senkrecht hinein, dürfte aber nicht länger als 9cm gewesen sein, da danach das Gewebe nicht mehr von einem umgelegten Rand unterbrochen wird. Ob dem Knopf (bzw. Knöpfen) Knopflöcher gegenüber lagen, ist nicht mehr auszumachen, da der Erhaltungszustand in diesem Bereich sehr schlecht ist. Die umgelegten Geweberänder an den äußeren Seiten verlaufen parallel zu dem eben beschriebenen Rand. Während der eine von einer Länge von ca.4cm keine Besonderheiten aufweist, laufen von dem anderen, noch 12cm langen, sechs parallel zueinander gerichtete Schlitze von maximal 3cm Länge waagerecht in das Gewebe. Ob es sich bei diesen Schlitzen um Knopflöcher handelt, ist unwahrscheinlich, da sie nicht umnäht sind.

Wollgewebe mit Schnittkanten, Nähten und Säumen

Konnten wir für die bisher vorgestellten Lübecker Gewebefunde den früheren Verwendungszweck mehr oder weniger eindeutig nachweisen, so wird das sicherlich für viele der mit Bearbeitungsspuren versehenen Gewebe, Gestricke und Filze nicht in jedem Fall möglich sein.

Im vorigen Jahr haben wir damit begonnen, zunächst die Wollgewebe von drei der wichtigsten Lübecker Fundstellen hinsichtlich ihrer früheren Verwendungen zu untersuchen. Es sind dies die Wollgewebe aus einem Abfallschacht vom Grundstück der ehemaligen Ratsapotheke in der Dr-Julius-Leber-Straße 3-5,[7] aus der Kloake (Brunnen) auf dem Schrangen, die zur Lübecker Fronerei gehörte,[8] und von mehreren Grundstücken in der Hundestraße 9-17 im früheren Handwerkviertel.[9] Die Funde aus den Abfallgruben und Kloaken sind in das 15. und 16.Jh. datiert, die Funde aus den Siedlungsschichten in der Hundestraße in das 13.Jh. Die dort in Kloaken geborgenen Textilien stammen überwiegend auch aus dem 15. bzw. 16.Jh.

Abb. 19.3 Reste einer Wolljacke ? (Lübeck-Wahmstraße 1-11/Breite Straße 95-99, 0214, Fd. -Nr. 91) M 1:4

Recht zahlreich sind unter den Textilfragmenten dieser Fundstellen Wollgewebe mit Schnittkanten. Die meisten Stücke sind sehr klein und kaum größer als eine Handfläche. Überwiegend haben wir es mit gleichmäßigen Formen wie Rechtecken, Dreiecken, Trapezen und schmalen Streifen von 1 bis 5cm Breite und bis zu 30cm Länge zu tun. Bei diesen Geweberesten dürfte es sich wohl um Abfälle handeln, die beim Zuschneiden bzw. Ausbessern von Kleidungsstücken anfallen, wie sie auch von Penelope Walton unter den Textilfunden aus Newcastle aus dem 15. und 16.Jh. nachgewiesen werden konnten.[10] Hinzuweisen ist außerdem auf einige Sonderformen, die allerdings auch in anderen europäischen Städten bei Ausgrabungen gefunden worden sind.[11] Aus Lübeck liegen zwei schmale Streifen von etwa 4cm Breite mit ausgestanzten Rundungen vor (Fundstelle: Schrangen, HL 2, Fd. -Nr. 433-1/1 und 345-1/25), die in die Zeit um 1500 datiert sind. Aus dem frühen 16.Jh. (1520/30) stammt ein drittes bemerkenswertes Fragment: Es ist ein Streifen von 5cm Breite, der in einem Abstand von jeweils 1cm etwa 4cm lang eingeschnitten ist (Fundstelle: Schrangen, HL2, Fd. -Nr. 202-3/6). Alle drei Gewebe sind in Tuchbindung gewebt, von mittelfeiner Qualität und außerdem mehr oder weniger stark gewalkt.

Unter den über 7000 Wollgeweben vom Schrangen befinden sich etwa 200 Gewebe, an denen Schnittkanten und Nähte vorhanden sind. Die Nähgarne sind jedoch fast immer vergangen. Nur dreimal konnten wir noch Seidenzwirne in S-Drehung nachweisen (HL 2 Fd. -Nr. 279-1/7, 202-3/1 und 200-2/40). Die Einstichlöcher und die Nahteindrücke in den anderen Geweben zeigen aber, daß in den meisten Fällen mit Vorstich- bzw. Überwendlichnähten gearbeitet worden ist. Auch unter den Wollgeweben aus der Hundestraße sind nur selten solche mit Nähgarnen erhalten geblieben. In einem Fall handelt es sich um einen Seidenzwirn an einem umnähten Rand eines mittelfeinen Tuchgewebes

Abb. 19.4
Wollgewebe (Lübeck-
Hundestraße 9-17, HL 1, Fd.
-Nr. 800/1) M 2:3

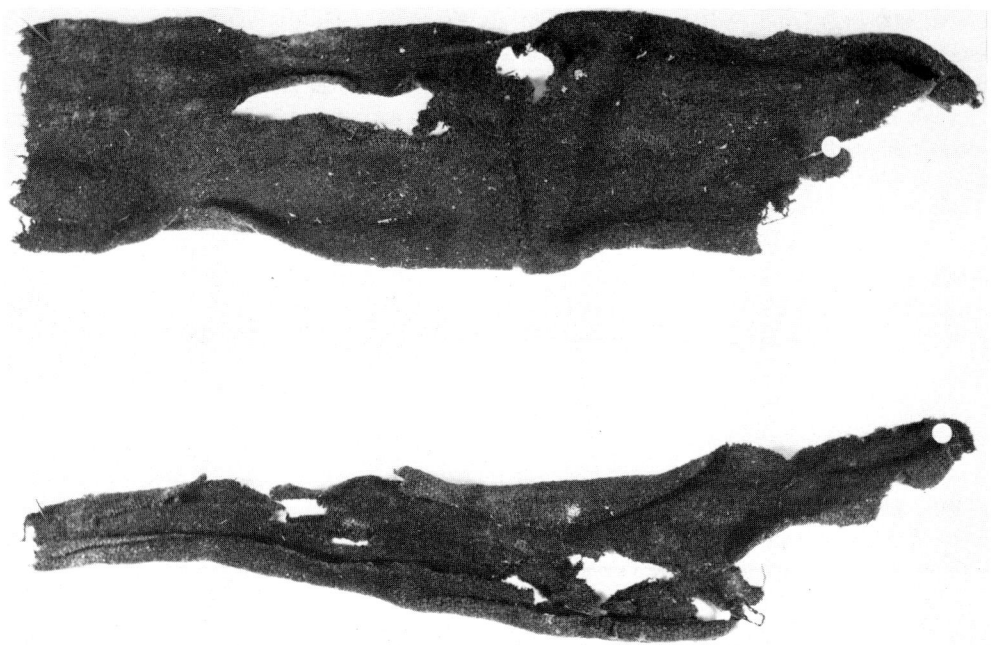

Abb. 19.5 Wollgewebe (Lübeck-Hundestraße 9-17, HL 1, Fd. -Nr. 915/1 u. 931/35) M c. 1:2

(HL 1, Fd. -Nr. 935/2) und in einem anderen Fall um ein Köpergewebe (K 2/1) von feiner Qualität mit einer Kappnaht, vermutlich genäht mit einem Leinenzwirn (z/S) (HL 1, Fd. -Nr. 1066/2). Beide Gewebe sind in das 13.Jh. datiert. Reste von Seidenzwirnen in S-Drehung konnten außerdem noch an drei anderen Wollgeweben bestimmt werden. Sie werden aufgrund ihrer anderen Besonderheiten weiter unten beschrieben.

Außer den Gewebefragmenten mit Bearbeitungsspuren von den drei bereits genannten Lübecker Fundstellen, gibt es von anderen Fundstellen nur ganz wenige, größere Stücke, die in diesem Zusammenhang von Bedeutung sind. Zu ihnen gehört ein Wollgewebe, das als Lesefund in der Lübecker Königstraße 59 (HL 3) gefunden wurde. Den Fundumständen nach stammt es aus dem 13. - 15.Jh., der Gewebeart nach kann es aber im 14.Jh. gewebt worden sein. Das Stück ist heute noch 25 x 17cm groß und fast rechteckig. Nur ein kleines Stück an einer Seite dürfte fehlen. Es dürfte also fast so erhalten sein, wie es früher einmal benutzt worden ist. An zwei sich gegenüberliegenden Seiten sind noch die umgelegten Geweberänder, die mit einer Überwendlichnaht umnäht worden waren, vorhanden. Die dritte Seite mit dem fehlenden Stück wird von einer Gewebeseitenkante begrenzt, während sich an der vierten Seite drei zungenartige, ausgeschnittene Formen befinden, an denen teilweise noch die Eindrücke der Überwendlichnaht erkennbar sind. Das Wollgewebe in Tuchbindung (T 1/1) ist mit einer Streifenmusterung von 14 mittelbraunen Schußfäden versehen, die viermal im Gewebe vorhanden sind. Die Garne des übrigen Gewebes sind heute von gelbbrauner Farbe. Auf jeweils 2cm kommen 16 Kett- und 14 Schußfäden, so daß es sich um ein großes bis mittelfeines Gewebe handelt, wie sie im Spätmittelalter nicht ungewöhnlich waren.[12]

Welche textil- und nähtechnischen Informationen auch die kleinsten Textilfragmente liefern können, soll hier an einigen Beispielen aus Lübeck ausführlicher dargestellt werden.

Zu den interessantesten Funden aus der Lübecker Hundestraße gehören die Reste von sehr feinen Wollgeweben in Tuchbindung, die in die Zeit um 1300 datiert sind. Für zwei dieser Gewebe (HL 1,

Fd. -Nr. 800/1+2) (Abb.19.4) hat man sowohl als Kette als auch als Schuß Garne in z-Drehung verwebt, während das dritte Gewebe (HL 1, Fd. -Nr. 800/7) in einem Fadensystem aus Garnen in z-Drehung und im anderen aus Garnen in s-Drehung besteht. Auf je 2cm kommen 40 Kett- und 30 Schußfäden. Das besondere an den beiden ersten Geweben ist ihre fast identische, beinahe dreieckige Form (Größe ca.13 mal 10cm bzw. 12 mal 9cm) und die Reste von Nähten, für die man sehr feine Seidenzwirne von gelber Farbe in S-Drehung verwendet hat. Die Nähte befinden sich jeweils an den Schnittkanten. Außerdem sind an beiden Stücken im Bereich der Nähte noch sehr feine Einstiche zu erkennen. Hervorzuheben ist auch die einseitige Verfilzung an einem Gewebe (HL 1, Fd. -Nr. 800/ 2). Da die Schnittkanten nur noch zum Teil vorhanden sind, kann davon ausgegangen werden, daß beide Gewebe früher größer waren. Vielleicht waren die Gewebe auch einmal übereinandergenäht. Zu welchem Kleidungsstück sie allerdings damals gehörten, müssen weitere Untersuchungen ergeben.

Zwei andere Wollgewebefragmente (Abb. 19.5), die sicherlich früher auch zu Kleidungsstücken gehört haben, stammen ebenfall aus der Lübecker Hundestraße, doch sind sie in das frühe 16.Jh. datiert. Es sind Wollgewebe in Tuchbindung von mittelfeiner Qualität, da auf je 2cm 24 Kett- und 24 Schußfäden bei einem Gewebe (Hl 1, Fd. -Nr. 915/1) und 24 Kett- und 28 Schußfäden bei dem anderen Gewebe (HL 1, Fd. -Nr. 931/35) gezählt wurden. Beide Gewebe sind verfilzt und demnach gewalkt. Nähtechnisch interessant sind beide Gewebe deshalb, weil sie an ihren Längsseiten mit umgelegten

Abb. 19.6
Wollgewebe (Lübeck-Schrangen, HL 2, Fd. -Nr. 200-2/37+38) M 2:3

Geweberändern von jeweils etwa 1cm Breite versehen sind. Das Nähgarn ist allerdings nicht mehr vorhanden, sehr feine Einstichlöcher sind jedoch noch zu erkennen. Mit umgelegtem Gewebeland haben beide Gewebe eine durchschnittliche Breite von 4cm. Auch unter den Funden vom Schrangen konnten wir ein Wollgewebe dieser Form nachweisen. Es ist ebenfals ein Gewebe in Tuchbindung von mittelfeiner Qualität, allerdings stärker gewalkt und etwa 5cm breit. Es lag in einer Fundschicht, die der Zeit zwischen 1500 und 1520 zugeordnet wird (HL 2, Fd. -Nr. 200-2/16).

Zu den Wollgeweben mit Bearbeitungsspuren gehören auch zwei kleine Fragmente vom Schrangen (Abb. 19.6). Die Gewebe dürften im frühen 16. Jh. (1500-1520) in die Kloake gelangt sein. Das eine Gewebe (HL 2, Fd. - Nr. 200-2/37) besteht in einem Fadensystem aus Garnen in z-Drehung und im anderen aus Garnen in s-Drehung. Auf jeweils 2cm kommen 20 Kett- bzw. 22 Schußfäden. Es ist also ein mittelfeines Gewebe. Das zweite Gewebe (HL 2, Fd. -Nr. 200-2/38) ist etwas gröber, da 16 bzw. 14 Fäden auf je 2cm gezählt wurden. Beide Gewebe sind stark gewalkt. Das kleinere Stück hat eine Dreiecksform mit einer Seitenkante von jeweils ca. 7cm. Deutlich sind noch die Eindrücke einer Überwendlichnaht zu erkennen. Diese Überwendlichnaht und auch die dreieckige Form können wir gut auf dem anderen Gewebe erkennen, so daß ziemlich sicher ist, daß das Dreieck einmal auf diesem Gewebe aufgenäht war. An dem zweiten Gewebe läßt sich außerdem noch ein umgelegter Rand nachweisen. Das Nähgarn fehlt allerdings auch hier. Wo und an welchem Kleidungsstück diese Applikation einmal gesessen hat, können wir noch nicht sagen.

Zusammenfassung

In diesem Beitrag wurden neue Untersuchungsergebnisse an Textilfunden aus Lübeck vorgestellt. Und zwar handelt es sich um solche Gewebe, die Bearbeitungsspuren aufweisen. Sie wurden hinsichtlich ihrer früheren Verwendungen begutachtet. Es sind eine guterhaltene Haube, die Reste eines Wamses und vermutlich der Teil einer Jacke sowie etwa 250 Fragmente von Wollgeweben mit Schnittkanten, Nähten und Säumen, die vermutlich alle früher zu Kleidungsstücken gehört haben. Eine abschließende Bewertung steht allerdings noch aus. Sie wird von Gisela Jaacks durchgeführt. Die Resultate dieser Bearbeitungen sollen in den Lübecker Schriften zur Archäologie und Kulturgeschichte veröffentlicht werden.

Anmerkung:

In der Textbeschreibung weist der kleine Buchstabe z bzw. s auf die z- bzw. s-Spinnrichtung hin, der grosse Buchstabe Z oder S auf die Z- bzw. S-Drehung im Zwirn.

Literatur

1. Der Verfasser dankt Johanna Banck und Svenja Tidow, die die hier vorgestellten Gewebefunde gezeichnet haben.

2. G. Jaacks, 'Städtische Kleidung im Mittelalter', *Aus dem Alltag der mittelalterlichen Stadt, Hefte des Fockemuseums* 62, 1982, 291-232

3. K. Schlabow, 'Spätmittelalterliche Textilfunde aus der Lübecker Innenstadt', *Zeitschrift des Vereins für Lübeckische Geschichte und Altertumskunde* 36, 1956, 133-153

4. K. Tidow, 'Textilfunde aus einem Brunnen auf dem Schrangen in Lübeck', *Lübecker Schriften zur Archäologie und Kulturgeschichte* 1, Frankfurt/Bern, 1978, 146

5. S. Y. Vons-Comis, '15de en 16de eeuwse textielvondsten uit Amsterdams stadskernonderzoek: Poetsdoeken en teerkwasten', *Textiele bodemvonsten*, Amsterdam, 1981, 18

6. J. Arnold, 'Two Early Seventeenth Century Fencing Doublets' *Waffen- und Kostümkunde* 21, 2, 1979, 107-120

7. Schlabow (1956)

8. K. Tidow, 'Untersuchungen an Wollgeweben aus einem Brunnen auf dem Schrangen in Lübeck', *Lübecker Schriften zur Archäologie und Kulturgeschichte* 6, Bonn, 1982, 251-286; 'Untersuchungen an Leinen- und Seidengeweben aus der Kloake des Fronen auf dem Schrangen in Lübeck', *Lübecker Schriften zur Archäologie und Kulturgeschichte* 12, Bonn, 1986, 173-182; 'Textiltechnische Untersuchungen an Gestricken und Filzen aus der Kloake des Fronen auf dem Schrangen in Lübeck', *Lübecker Schriften zur Archäologie und Kulturgeschichte* 12, Bonn, 1986, 183-189

9. K. Tidow, 'Spätmittelalterliche und frühneuzeitliche Textilfunde aus der Hundestraße in Lübeck', *Lübecker Schriften zur Archäologie und Kulturgeschichte* 8, Bonn, 1984, 33-40

10. P. Walton, 'The Textiles (from the Castle ditch, Newcastle upon Tyne 1974-76)', *Archaeologia Aeliana*, 5th series 9, 1981, 201-228

11. J. Maik, J. Gula, 'Zaopatrzenie Zamku W Rawie Mazowieckiej W Wyroby Włókiennisze W Kóńcu XIV i W XV Wieku', *Archeologia Polski*, 24, 2, 1980, 394; A. Kjellberg, 'Tekstilmaterialet fra "Oslogate 7"', *De Arkeologiske Utgravninger i Gamlebyen, Oslo 2*, Øvre Ervik, 1979, 91; J. Arnold, 'Decorative Features: pinking, snipping and slashing', *Costume* 9, 1975, 23

12. R. Ullemeyer, K. Tidow, 'Textil- und Lederfunde aus der Lübecker Innenstadt', *Lübecker Schriften zur Archäologie und Kulturgeschichte* 1, Frankfurt/Bern, 1978, 133-138

20. Seventeenth-century garments from grave 579, Zeeuwse Uitkijk, Spitsbergen

Sandra Vons-Comis
Diemen

Introduction

In the period spanning the years 1979 to 1981, a series of campaigns was undertaken by the excavation team of the Arctic Centre, under the direction of Dr L. Hacquebord (University of Groningen). The archaeologists investigated the material remains left by the 17th- and 18th-century whalers on Spitsbergen. Much attention was paid to the remains of the Dutch whaling station Smeerenburg on Amsterdam Island in the North West of Spitsbergen, where, during the summer months of AD 1614 to 1660, the harpooned whales were processed.[1]

The remains of several furnaces and buildings in the station were excavated. A considerable number of textiles was recovered from the domestic refuse in and behind the buildings. The total of well over 1000 scraps and large rags ultimately proved to belong to about 600 different, mostly woollen, textiles, predominantly work-clothing and bedding remains.[2]

Two members of the excavation team in 1980 investigated a cemetery on Zeeuwse Uitkijk or Ytre Norskøya, a small isle in the neighbourhood of Amsterdam Island, where dead whalers were buried from *c.* 1640 until the end of the 18th century. Fifty 17th- and 18th- century graves were opened for skeletal analysis by Dr G.J.R. Maat from the University of Leiden.[3]

It caused some surprise that garments were found in many of the graves in addition to the well-preserved bones. Since not all clothing had survived burial equally well, it was impossible to recover all the material, but in all 33 knitted caps, one leather cap trimmed with fur, 7 jackets, 3 knee breeches, 5 pairs of stockings and a beautiful embroidered piece of cloth were brought back to Holland for further study.

In contrast to the well-dated finds from the settlement, Smeerenburg, these garments have as yet only been cursorily treated, as research is still in progress.[4] In anticipation of the definitive publication of these exceptional cemetery finds we will begin to raise the curtain just a little by a thorough treatment of the textile assemblage from a single burial: no 579.

The textiles in grave 579

Grave 579 contained the skeleton of a man who had died aged about 66 (fig. 20.1). Skeletal analysis revealed that he had suffered from scurvy, though whether this was the actual cause of death could not be established. The man was 164cm tall.

On his death he was probably laid in his coffin fully clothed, though without his shoes, before being buried in the island cemetery. Thanks to the permafrost in this arctic area, much of the clothing has survived. When the excavators opened the intact coffin, they found the following garments on the skeleton: a knitted cap, a jacket and two knitted stockings, all of which were made of wool (fig. 20.2).

The absence of breeches, which are known from other graves, is remarkable. The explanation

Fig. 20.1 Grave 579 on Zeeuwse Uitkijk, Spitsbergen

is probably that the man had worn breeches made of linen, which perished in the soil. The numerous loose components of the jacket, for example, indicate that the linen sewing thread has perished: in other words, the conditions in the grave were only favourable for the preservation of wool, and not for linen or cotton. It has already been established that these vegetable fibres are very quickly affected in the soil in North West Europe, so that they are rarely, if ever, preserved. However, more detailed examination revealed that remains of vegetable fibres were still present in a sleeve of the jacket (see C below).

The textiles from this grave were cleaned by Mrs E. van Dienst, then working for the State Service for Archaeological Investigations in the Netherlands (Amersfoort), and I would at this point like to record my gratitude to her for this work.

Prior to tackling the dating of the garments, a detailed report on the individual pieces will be presented.

A. Knitted cap (nos. 579/1a & b)

The deceased wore a woollen cap on his head (fig. 20.3). This is a single thickness (red?) brown cap with a turned-up brim, with light brown (originally white?) and dark blue stripes. The cap is 26cm long including the 5cm turned-up brim. The circumference of the cap at the junction from crown to brim is 50cm, with the greatest circumference, 60cm, reached at the lower end of the brim.

Knitting probably began at the lower edge, by casting on stitches with (red?) brown wool and knitting one row in plain stitch. After this, two rows in purl stitch were knitted alternately light brown (white?) and dark blue. There are 1.5 stitches per cm, and 4 rows per cm (table 1). As the brim is felted it is not entirely certain whether the yarns are (Z-?) plied or not. The number of stitches is decreased regularly at two points in the cap which lie directly opposite one another.

After 5cm, one round was knitted in purl with (red?) brown, thinner wool. Then the cap was continued in the same colour using plain stitch, so that when the brim was turned up only plain stitch would be visible on the outside. Yarn composed of two S-twisted threads which were not plied, or hardly plied, was used for the crown. The count also differs: 1.6 - 1.8 stitches per cm and 3 rows per cm. The cap is slightly felted inside. Some damage seems to have occurred in the coffin as a result of either the effects of the decay of the corpse or soil conditions. No patches or darns were discovered.

B. Jacket (no. 579/2-33)

A blue woollen sleeved jacket was found in situ in the grave (fig. 20.4,5). The front parts are 65cm long and 34-44cm wide, with a triangular piece of identical material sewn to the lower edge of each part, just below the buttonholes. The other edges of the front parts are folded over to the back where they are sewn to the back part. Only the lower 8cm are not stitched. To prevent tearing, the top of these has been reinforced by a bar sewn woollen thread. The back is 30cm wide along its bottom edge, tapering to an extremely narrow waist (20cm). This creates a close-fitting jacket with a flaring lower edge. The circumference of the waist is 86cm.

The body of the jacket is lined. The sleeves are 55cm long and have a seam front and back. The front seams of both sleeves have a triangular strip of material inserted. Originally the sleeves were only half-attached to the body. Each sleeve was only sewn along the top of the shoulder, leaving the part under the armpit open. Thus the wearer of the jacket had ample room for movement in his work.

The jacket was closed by buttons down the front and at the wrists. At the front, some of the buttons were still in place in the buttonholes, indicating that the jacket had been closed when the man was buried. Numerous darns and patches are evidence of intensive wear over a long period of time.

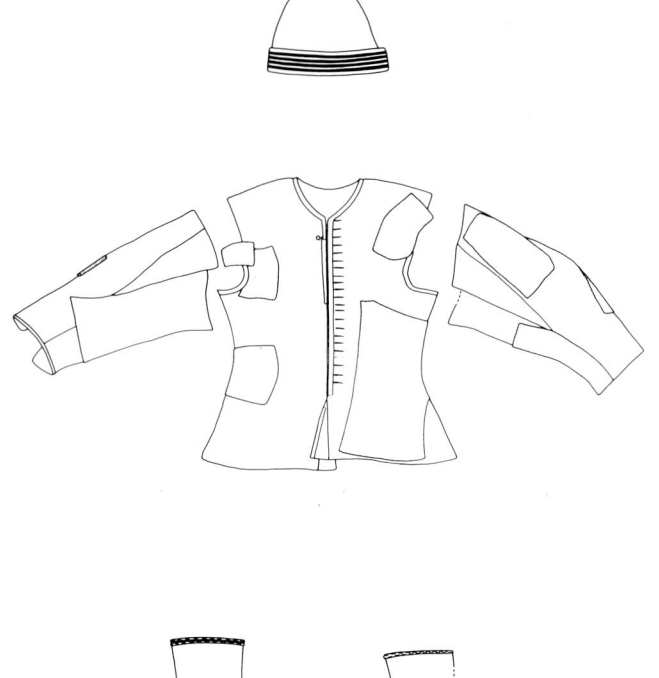

Fig. 20.2
Reconstruction of the
woollen garments
from grave 579:
a. fold/seam/hem; b.
reconstruction fold/
seam/hem; c.
damaged part; d.
edge with sewing
holes and thread
impressions; e. patch;
f. relief decoration

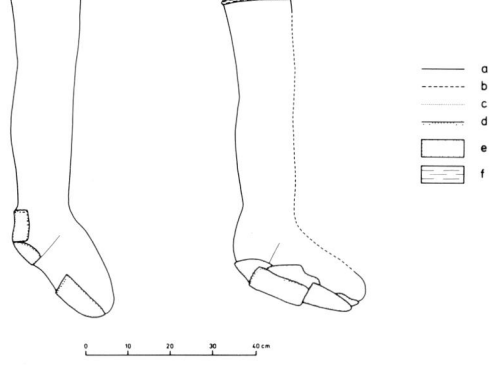

a
b
c
d
e
f

   The jacket is made of a medium-quality blue twill fabric (no. 579/2). The inside of the body is lined with a light brown, coarse woollen fabric in tabby (no. 579/3). An extra piece of lining-fabric was sewn in at the neck of the back. Additional pieces of material were inserted between the back part and the lining to serve as shoulder padding. Each pad consists of two layers of material: a blue fabric identical to the fabric of the jacket and a light brown fabric, cut from the same material as the lining. All the pieces are 12cm wide at the top, tapering to a mere 3cm at the bottom. These more or less triangular pads are each cut in three pieces. Thread impressions indicate that the pieces were laid on the inside of the back part of the jacket and were held in place by large zig-zag stitches. Later the lining was put on the pads and the jacket.

The sleeves are unlined, though dark blue reinforcement strips made of a somewhat finer quality twill (no 579/4) are sewn in along the bottom edge.

The jacket is trimmed at various points, as for example along both fronts along the line of the fastenings. A red-blue band in warp chevron twill was originally sewn along the left part (no. 579/5). The triangle attached at the bottom of this part is edged with a yellow (originally white?) and blue band, also in chevron twill (no. 579/7). Remains of this band also occur along the right front. With several interruptions, this band runs from the triangular piece at the bottom, right up to the neck opening. Subsequently, pieces of two other bands were sewn over the edging on the left front, either for repair or reinforcement. In the middle there is a blue tablet-woven band (no. 579/10) while at the top and around the neck opening a blue band in a variation of chevron twill was attached (no. 579/6).

The sleeves, too, are trimmed at the wrists with a woollen band, 2.4cm wide, woven with tablets each with two holes (no. 579/9). Where the sleeve was not attached to the body at the armpit, the lower edge of the arm-hole was edged with the same tablet-woven band as at the wrists. In some places on the left arm-hole, however, a fragment of a half-woollen (tablet-woven?) fabric is visible (no. 579/8).

It has already been mentioned that a different band was sewn over one of the trimmings. This was not the only repair to the jacket, which had been repeatedly patched up, beginning with darning the worn areas. All the seams at vulnerable points, such as the arm-hole and the back of the waist, had torn out at least once and had been crudely darned with thick woollen yarn. The lower edge of the left sleeve was almost entirely filled with two light brown Z-twisted yarns, plied in S-direction. On the other hand, larger tears and holes were patched with fabrics of various sizes.

In total 22 patches were retrieved, some still in place, while others had come adrift. On the outside of the jacket are ten dark blue patches in 2/2 twill, and five brown patches in tabby are sewn to the lining on the inside. Furthermore there are seven loose patches, the original positions of which can no longer be ascertained.

Fig. 20.3 (Red?) brown woollen knitted cap with striped brim from grave 579

Fig. 20.4 Front of the blue jacket

Only three patches possess a more or less similar thread-count to the blue material used for the jacket itself (nos. 579/16, 20 and 26). All the other blue patches, with two exceptions, are of finer quality. The patches on the inside of the jacket are, like the lining, brown in colour and woven in coarse tabby. The loose patches, five dark blue and two brown (nos. 579/26-32), were probably attached so as to match the colours of the outside and the inside respectively. In addition, there was also a fragment of a band with red, blue and white stripes lengthwise (no. 579/33).

The 22 buttonholes, each 2.5cm long, are set in the left front. The holes are spaced at approximately 2cm intervals. The edges are finished off with a light brown S-plied woollen thread formed of two single Z-twisted yarns in buttonhole stitch. Three similar buttonholes are present at the end of the sleeves, for fastening at the wrist. The space between these holes varies between 2.5 and 3.5cm.

Despite the number of buttonholes on the jacket, only 10 metal and 5 bone buttons were retrieved (fig. 20.6). Three buttons were still in place in the buttonholes, three more are in their original position, but the others have worked loose with the decay of the linen sewing thread. The metal (pewter?) buttons have a wire eye underneath; they are 1cm in diameter and 1.2cm high.[5] The bone buttons have a large head varying between 1.7 and 2.0cm in diameter, with a short, flat, perforated stalk underneath.

C. Shirt? (no. 579/34)

From historical and iconographic sources it is known that men wore a linen shirt underneath the jacket. As has already been mentioned, linen is only sporadically preserved on Spitsbergen: in the Smeer-enburg settlement for instance only 4% of the preserved textiles consist of fabrics made of vegetable fibres.[6] However, while cleaning the jacket, small, blackened fragments of linen (?) fabric were recovered from the inside of the sleeve. These fragments vary in size between 1.0 by 1.5cm and 3.0 by 3.0cm. The thread-count in both warp and weft direction is *c.* 15 per cm. The spin direction is unknown.

D. Stockings (nos. 579/35-43)

Two long stockings encased the leg bones above the knee (fig. 20.7). At present they are in poor condition as the knitting of both is ripped down the entire length of leg at the front. According to the excavators this was caused by the sharp front edge of the leg bones cutting through as the knitting became saturated and heavy in the grave.

Both stockings are round knitted using a light brown (originally white?) woollen yarn. They are knitted in plain stocking stitch with rows of purl at the top. Although both stockings are of equal length - 63cm from border to below the heel and a foot of 30cm - they do not form a pair.

Thus Stocking 1 displays a border consisting of two rows of purl, two rows of plain and two more rows of purl, with the rest of the stocking continuing in plain stitch. For this stocking a Z-plied yarn was used which is made of two or perhaps three S-twisted threads. The knitting is relatively coarse with 2.5 stitches per cm and 5 rows per cm.

The starting border of Stocking 2 differs from that of Stocking 1. Here the border consists of one row plain and one row purl. In addition, it was knitted with a single thread with a high twist in S-direction, so not with plied yarn. The number of stitches per cm more or less matches that of Stocking 1 (2.5 - 3 per cm), but, on measurement, it transpired that only 4.5 rows were knitted per cm.

This stocking has a false seam knitted in at the back, from edge to heel. The seam is marked by knitting a purl stitch at the same point in each round. Shaping for the calf was achieved by increasing the number of stitches at various points below the knee and taking in at the ankle. There are no forms of decoration at the ankle, though such gussets are known from other Smeerenburg stockings.[7]

How exactly the underside of the foot was finished off can no longer be discerned, as too little of the original knitwear remains intact here. Both stockings are extensively darned. In contrast to the repairs carried out on the jacket, patches were chosen at random, tabby or twill, in yarns varying from coarse to fine. Three patches were sewn under the foot of Stocking 1 (nos. 579/36-38) and five under Stocking 2 (nos. 579/40-43).

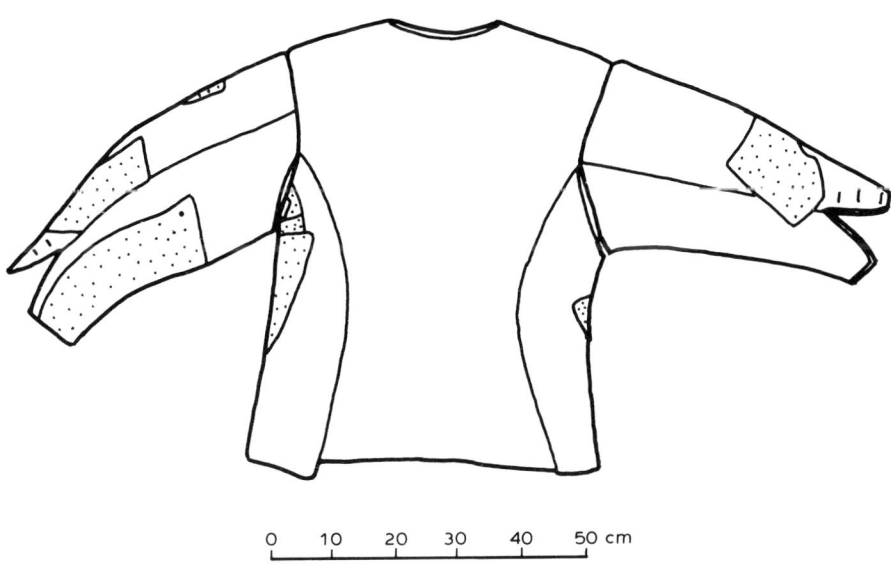

0   10   20   30   40   50 cm

Fig. 20.5 Drawing of the back of the blue jacket

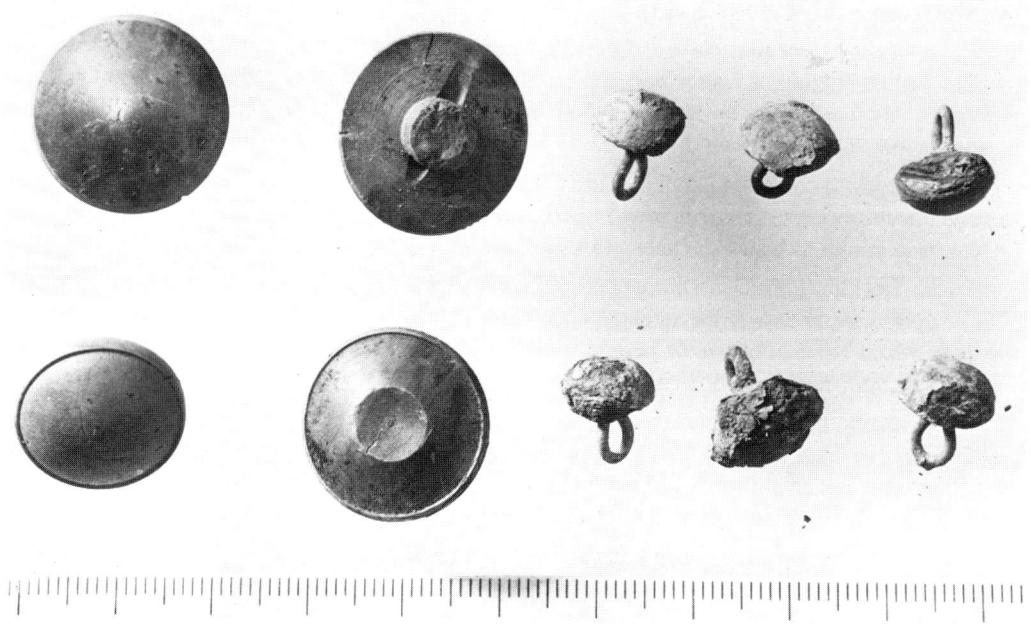

Fig. 20.6 Four bone and six metal buttons from the jacket

Results

From the description of the textiles given above and summarized in the table, it will be clear that there were no fewer than 43 different fabrics in grave 579. These can be divided into categories: knitting (3 pieces plus the distinctive knitting used for the cap brim), band-woven fabrics (4), tablet-woven bands (2), and woven fabrics (34). With the exception of a single linen fabric and three half-woollens, the textiles are all made of wool. As regards weaving patterns and quality, the textiles are closely comparable to other 17th-century finds, including those from Smeerenburg.

The entire context of the coffin may be regarded as a closed find assemblage. However, it should be remembered that these textiles are by no means representative of all the types of fabrics in use during that period. In a burial in particular, the find composition will be dominated by the garments, and in this case specifically by the number of patches. Great selectivity is evidenced in the choice of patching materials used for repairs. Patches of blue woollen twill were deliberately sewn to the outside of the jacket, and on the inside too; the type and quality of fabric used for patching was matched to that of the lining. Here, this results in a pronounced over-representation of the 2/2 twills in the find complex.

The evidence from grave 579 therefore cannot and should not be directly compared with the textiles from cess pits and refuse deposits. Certainly in the Netherlands cess pits contain only that part of textile waste originating from clothing and furnishings which was too far gone to be of any further use. From the 16th century at least we have evidence that woollens finished up as cleaning rags; the linen and cotton fabrics were bought up by the paper manufacturers. What remained, and what is recovered from these pits, is very often only the silk fabrics.[8]

The textiles on Smeerenburg were also deposited in atypical conditions. Here we are concerned primarily with discarded workmen's clothing and to a lesser degree with furnishings. Moreover, in the absence of the ragman, relatively large pieces of garments were discarded, though only after the useful pieces had been removed for use in patching up old clothes.

Dating and comparisons with other clothing

The absence of any artefacts other than the clothing in the grave means that dating depends entirely on the evidence of the garments and the buttons. There are few examples of 17th-century clothing in the Netherlands, and the garments which have been preserved in costume collections usually owe their survival to their great costliness. In contrast, grave 579 contains specifically workmen's clothing. Such garments will always be worn to the last stitch and are therefore unlikely to survive long enough even to enter a collection.

An additional difficulty is that working clothes, and in this case sailors' clothing, is hardly influenced by fashion, so that dating by means of stylistic characteristics is impossible. The dress of the whaler buried in grave 579 is very similar to the garments worn in the first half of the 17th century: knee breeches, a jacket, a broad brimmed felt hat or knitted cap, long stockings and low shoes. They are typical garments worn in winter in North-West Europe and known from Dutch paintings of ice-skating scenes.[9] Paintings from the later 17th century show that not only fishermen, but also whalers continued to wear these practical garments. Only the metal buttons in the grave give an indication of the dating: second half of the 17th century.

The only useful parallels are the garments from other graves in the cemetery on Zeeuwse Uitkijk, and clothing excavated on nearby Danskøya.[10] Unfortunately, these garments are equally poorly dated. Other late 17th- and 18th-century clothing is known from bog-bodies in Scotland and Ireland, but these do not resemble the finds from grave 579.[11]

Fig. 20.7 Two stockings: left: Stocking 1; right: Stocking 2

Acknowledgements

I would like to thank P. Vons for financing this study. Participation in the NESAT Symposium was made possible by a grant from the Netherlands Organization for the Advancement of Pure Research (Z.W.O). My thanks are likewise due to Mrs C. van Driel-Murray for translating the text, F. Gijbels (Albert Egges van Giffen Instituut voor Pre- en Protohistorie, Amsterdam) for the photographs and H. Waterbolk (Rijksuniversiteit van Groningen) for preparing the drawings.

Table: Fabrics from Zeeuwse Uitkijk, grave 579 (Spitsbergen)

Wa = warp; We = weft, all fabrics are woollens

No.	Fabric		Twist Wa We	Ply Wa We	Count Wa We	Colour/Remarks
A. Cap						
1a	knitting		S,S	Z	1.6-1.8st/cm & 3 rows/cm	red brown crown
1b	knitting		?	Z?	1.5 st/cm & 4 rows/cm	Brim of cap light brown and dark blue stripes
B. Jacket						
2	weave	2/2 twill	S S		11 11	dark blue
3	weave	tabby	S S		7 7	light brown lining
4	weave	2/2 twill	S S		13 13	dark blue
5	band	chevron twill	Z,Z Z,Z	S S	14 c.16	wa: red we: dark blue
6	band	variation chevron twill	Z,Z Z	S -	18 20	dark blue
7	band	chevron twill	Z,Z Z,Z	S S	14 16	wa: blue we: yellow light brown wa: wool we: vegetable fibres (now decayed)
8	weave	?	Z ?			
9	band	tablet-woven	S Z	S? -	15x2 12	woven with 18 tablets light brown
10	band	tablet-woven	Z,Z S	S -	8x2 12	woven with 17 tablets blue
Patches in situ on blue jacket:						
11	weave	2/2 twill	Z S		14 11/12	blue
12	weave	2/2 twill	Z S		16 12	blue, later darned with blue yarn
13	weave	2/2 twill	S S		12 10	blue
14	weave	2/2 twill	S S		10 8	dark blue
15	weave	2/2 twill	S S		14 12	dark blue
16	weave	2/2 twill	S S		11 10	dark blue
17	weave	2/2 twill	S S		17 16	dark blue
18	weave	2/2 twill	S S		12 12	dark blue
19	weave	2/2 twill	S S		12 9	dark blue

No.	technique	weave	spin			thread count		description
20	weave	2/2 twill	S	S		11	10	dark blue

Patches in situ on lining

No.	technique	weave	spin			thread count		description
21	weave	tabby	Z	?		12	?	brown wa: wool we: vegetable fibres (now decayed)
22	weave	tabby	S	S		7/8	7/8	light brown
23	weave	tabby	S	S		7	7	brown
24	weave	tabby	S	S		7	7	brown
25	weave	tabby	S	S		6	6	brown

Patches not in situ

No.	technique	weave	spin			thread count		description
26	weave	2/2 twill	S	S		11	10	dark blue
27	weave	2/2 twill	Z	S		14	14	dark blue
28	weave	2/2 twill	S	S		9	9	dark blue
29	weave	2/2 twill	S	S		16	14	dark blue
30	weave	2/2 twill	S	S		18	15	dark blue
31	weave	tabby	S	S		7/8	6	light brown
32	weave	tabby	S	S		8	7	light brown
33	band	tabby	Z, Z Z	S -		16	14	2 selvedges red, blue, yellow-brown wa: wool + vegetable fibres we: wool

C. Shirt

No.	technique	weave	spin			thread count		description
34	weave	?	?			c.15	c.15	black linen?

D. Stocking 1

No.	technique	weave	spin			thread count		description
35	knitting		S,S (S?)	Z		2.5 st/cm 5 rows/cm		light brown no false seam starting border: 2 rows purl, 2 rows plain, 2 rows purl

Patches on Stocking 1

No.	technique	weave	spin			thread count		description
36	weave	tabby	Z	S		13	13	dark brown
37	weave	tabby	Z	S		6	5	dark brown
38	weave	tabby	Z	S		13	11	dark brown

E. Stocking 2

No.	technique	weave	spin			thread count		description
39	knitting		S			2.5-3.0 st/cm 4.5 rows/cm		light brown false seam, starting border: 1 row plain, 1 row purl

Patches on Stocking 2

No.	technique	weave	spin			thread count		description
40a+b		weave	tabby	Z	S			14 14 brown
41	weave	2/2 twill	Z	S		12	10	brown
42	weave	?	?			?		dark brown, strongly felted
43	weave	tabby	S	S		7	4/5	dark brown with 1.5cm wide selvedge

References

1. L. Hacquebord, *Smeerenburg: het verblijf van Nederlandse walvisvaarders op de westkust van Spitsbergen in de zeventiende eeuw* (Ph.D.), Amsterdam, 1984; L. Hacquebord, 'A historical-archaeological investigation of a seventeenth- century whaling settlement on the west coast of Spitsbergen in 79° north latitude ', *Norsk Polarinstitutt Rapportserie* 38, 1987, 19-34

2. S.Y. Vons-Comis, 'Textielvondsten ' in L. Hacquebord, *Smeerenburg: het verblijf van Nederlandse walvisvaarders op de westkust van Spitsbergen in de zeventiende eeuw (*Ph. D), Amsterdam, 1984a, 203-214; S.Y. Vons-Comis, 'Zeventiende en achttiende eeuwse kledingresten van Spitsbergen ', *Kostuum* 1984b, 32-36; S.Y. Vons-Comis, 'Workman's clothing or burial garments? Seventeenth and eighteenth century clothing remains from Spitsbergen ', *Norsk Polarinstitutt Rapportserie* 38, 1987, 79-87

3. G.J.R. Maat, 'Osteology of human remains from Amsterdamøya and Ytre Norskøya ', *Norsk Polarinstitutt Rapportserie* 38, 1987, 35-54

4. Vons-Comis (1987)

5. J.M. Baart *et al.*, 'Knopen aan het Hollandse kostuum uit de zestiende en zeventiende eeuw ', *Antiek 9,* 1974, 17-50

6. Vons-Comis (1987), 80

7. Vons-Comis (1984b), afb.1

8. S.Y. Vons-Comis, 'Achttiende-eeuwse textiel opgegraven op het Waterlooplein te Amsterdam ', *Verslag van de Textieldag, 11 November 1983,* 's-Gravenhage, 1985, 5-18

9. E. van Straaten, *Koud tot op het bot,* 's-Gravenhage, 1977

10. I. Lütken, 'Textiles from Danskøya ', *Norsk Polarinstitutt Rapportserie* 38, 1987, 89-107

11. H. Bennett, 'A murder victim discovered: clothing and other finds from an early 18th-century grave on Armish Moor, Lewis ', *Proceedings of the Society of Antiquaries of Scotland* 106, 1974-1975, 172-182; A.S. Henshall, 'Clothing found at Huntsgarth, Harray, Orkney ', *Proceedings of the Society of Antiquaries of Scotland* 101, 1968-1969, 150-159

21. The coffins of two royal children in Roskilde Cathedral

Else Østergård
Copenhagen

Roskilde Cathedral, half-an-hour's journey from Copenhagen, has been the burial place of the Danish royal family ever since the beginning of the 15th century. Some years ago the coffins of two children from the crypt under Saint Birgitte Chapel were restored. The coffins contained the bodies of two children of Kirsten Munk, wife of Christian IV (King of Denmark 1588-1648). The outer coffins of wood were completely rotted and needed replacing. When the inner coffins, which in this case were of metal, are not sealed it is the practice to notify the National Museum so that details of the clothing on the bodies can be recorded, and thus it was on this occasion. All the investigations and photography were executed down in the crypt in the Cathedral.

Kirsten Munk (1598 - 1658) gave birth to ten children in the space of ten years during her marriage to the king. The last child, born in 1629, was disowned by the king. 'The rejected maid' was one of the nicknames he bestowed upon her. The best known of the children, however, is Leonora Christine, who, in her epic *Jammers Minde* (Recollections of Misery), wrote of the 22 years during which she was imprisoned in the Blue Tower in Copenhagen Castle.

Two of Kirsten Munk's children died young and it is the coffins of these two which were opened and it is the clothing therein which is described here. Frederik Christian died in 1627 at two years of age and Maria Cathrine in 1628, only three months old. To judge by the accessories in the coffins, which were made up as small beds in similar style, the children undoubtedly received a royal funeral.

Upon opening, the colours of some of the textiles had completely disappeared, whilst others had changed in hue and intensity, but the many gilded threads still reflected an extravagance, the beauty of which colour pictures can only hint at. Uppermost in the coffin of Frederik Christian (fig. 21.1) was dried lavender strewn on a striped silk sheet which enclosed the mummified body between quilts and pillow. The silk for the quilts had a gold effect with a pattern known as the 'Parrot and Rosebush'; in addition there was a signature in ink on the left-hand side of the length of fabric. This can possibly be traced to the imperial workshops in Isfahan in western Persia. The pillow was richly embroidered with many kinds of gilded thread, spirals and sequins. Both children were attired in headgear but of widely differing types. Frederik Christian was laid in his coffin with a pearl studded 'crown' made of a pair of richly decorated cuffs (fig. 21.2). Maria Cathrine wore a primitively made cap, fashioned from a rectangular piece of silk fabric seamed together at the ends. One long edge was closely gathered to form the cap's crown, and the other edge was turned under but not hemmed.

In the coffin of Maria Cathrine (fig. 21.3) there was a layer of dried lavender intermingled with some coriander seeds, uppermost in the coffin. Beneath this scented covering was a fragmentary coffin sheet (chiné). It passed from the head end to the foot end, where it turned under beneath the bedding, continuing up to the head end.

Maria Cathrine's quilts were made of a silk damask and the golden pillow was embroidered. The pillow consisted of two rectangular pieces of gold-brocade silk fabric, seamed together on all four

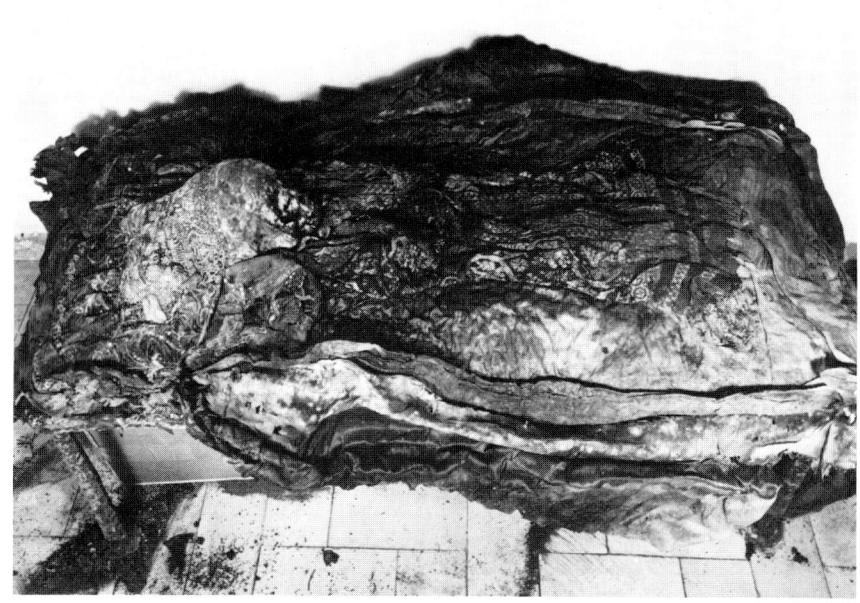

Fig. 21.1 Frederik Christian in his grave-bed. The coffin sheet, the over-quilt and two sashes have been removed and the child lies as if sleeping in a little bed.

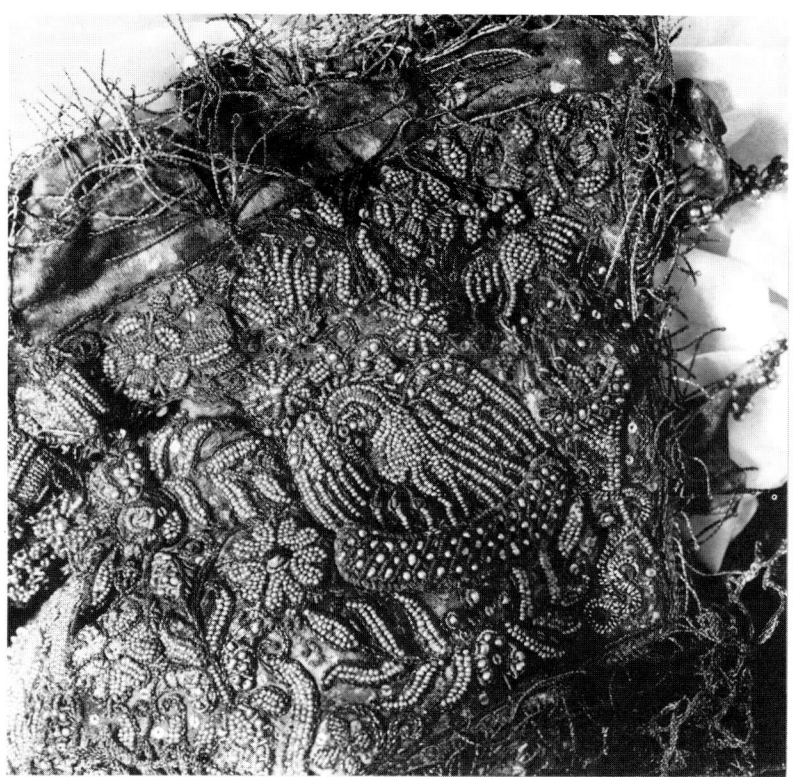

Fig. 21.2 Frederik Christian's pearl-embroidered grave-cap is like a crown. Glittering embroidery in gilded thread, with garnets and seed pearls, entirely cover the fabric beneath. The crown is trimmed with bobbin lace and fringes of gilded braid.

sides. The seams were hidden by a gold-brocaded band. In each corner was attached a tassel (fig. 21.4) made of loops of silk ribbon edged with lace, held together at one end in a little ball of silver and gilded thread.

The burial clothes

The children were dressed in knitted jackets of indigo silk embellished with gilded thread. Frederik Christian's jacket carried a design of pine-cones flanked by decorative leaves (fig. 21.5). Above the pine-cones are eight-leaved rosettes. Maria Cathrine's jacket features vases or urns from which flowers are growing. Between each vase is a double eagle with outspread wings. Both jackets were of the same size and kind. Along the lengths of the jackets' openings at the front and towards the bottom the main motifs were bordered by narrow trimmings. The same motifs are to be found on the sleeves with the corresponding narrow trimmings above and below. Each jacket consists of two front pieces and a back, each of which was knitted 'backwards and forwards' (fig. 21.6). Apart from the wristband with a slash, the sleeves were knitted round with increases along a prominent seam. The pieces were sewn together at the sides and shoulders and the sleeves were similarly attached. In addition, the edges down the front were sewn together to within about ten centimetres of the neck, the rest remaining open as a slash.

Fig. 21.3 (left) Maria Cathrine was revealed after the quilt was raised. She lay on a quilt in her grave-bed, her head resting on a golden pillow. Remains of the pearl circlet that lay on her cap can be seen.
Fig. 21.4 (right) Tassel from Maria Cathrine's pillow. In each corner was attached a tassel made of loops of silk ribbons edged with lace, held together at one end in a little ball of silver and gilded thread. The ball is 2cm in diameter.

Fig. 21.5 Detail of Frederik Christian's knitted silk jacket. The two front pieces are sewn together at the centre front of the jacket. Notice the scallops at the lower edge.

Fig. 21.6 Diagram of the jackets. The measurements are in centimetres. Drawn by Ian Rogers.

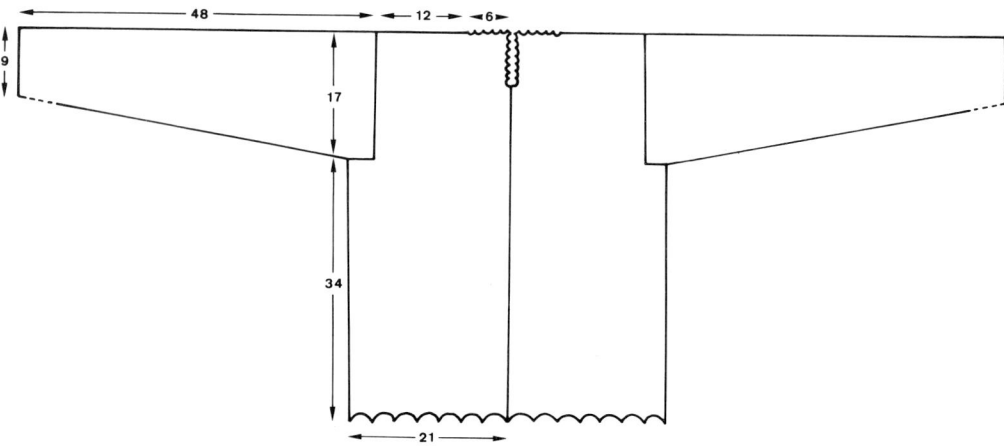

190

As an elegant finishing touch the lowest knitted border had scalloped edges. Corresponding edging is found at the neck and slash. These scallops must have been added when the knitting was finished, a procedure which would have had to be repeated after each wash. On the crests of the scallops it was still possible to see the marks from pins used to hold the knitting during drying. The jackets were not knitted for children, as the measurments indicate that they were obviously full-size. These over-large jackets, which served as the children's shrouds, covered their feet and the long sleeves were pushed back to the wrists in tight folds, tied in place there with a ribbon. The ends of the ribbon were trimmed with knotted red silk and white beading.

When the jackets were carefully folded back so that they could be examined on the inside, long stockings were revealed. And like the jackets, the children's stockings were far too big for them. The tops of the stockings were doubled back down the legs. Each child had both legs tied together at knee level with silk ribbon, finished with decorative knots.

Frederik Christian's knitted stockings were madder red with various patterns in gilded thread (fig. 21.7). The stockings were well preserved and had a 42cm long leg and an 18cm foot. They were in circular knitting with 200 stitches at the top. Along the length of the rear seam the number of stitches was evenly reduced, so that the width of the stocking became narrower towards the foot. A gusset between heel and instep, which was knitted in a pattern of curves, formed a clock on each side of the foot and at the same time contained an increase in stitching to the foot.

Fig. 21.7 Frederik Christian's stockings. There is 'a seam' up the back of the stocking where stitches are decreased. The stocking has different patterns on the stocking itself, on the gusset and beneath the foot. Red (madder) silk and gilded thread.

Fig. 21.8 Detail of the toe from Frederik Christian's stocking. The toe is beautifully joined together.

The toe (fig. 21.8) was beautifully finished with the last 17 stitches being knitted together to form a closure. On the soles of the feet was a checked pattern. The top of the stocking had scalloped edges - all in all a pair of stockings of remarkably intricate workmanship.

Maria Cathrine's silk stockings (fig. 21.9) were also knitted with stocking stitch in the round, but here the borders and clocks were purl knitted and on top of that embroidered with gilded thread. The stockings were now brownish. Along the back of the leg ran a zig-zag trimming where there were increases and decreases to the pronounced calves which were found on this pair of stockings. The heel was knitted straight down and finished under the foot.   Both stockings were poorly preserved, particularly at the toes, and consequently the length of the foot is uncertain; however, fragments from the foot indicate a length of about 16cm. This figure taken in conjunction with the stockings' leg size of 48cm would suggest that the stockings were made for a child of eight to ten years.

The embroidered clocks depict a peacock with an outspread tail above a five-petalled flower, the stalk of which continued down the foot of the stocking with leaves and flower buds. The embroidery was carried out in such a way that all the stitches were on the outside of the knitting, sewn around a single thread. Thus the metal threads on the stockings would not have irritated the wearer's feet. The stockings worn by the mummified three-month-old infant looked as though they fitted, but upon closer examination proved to be the stockings of an older child. The legs of both stockings were arranged in tight folds, and the toes of the stockings were folded under and held in place with pins.

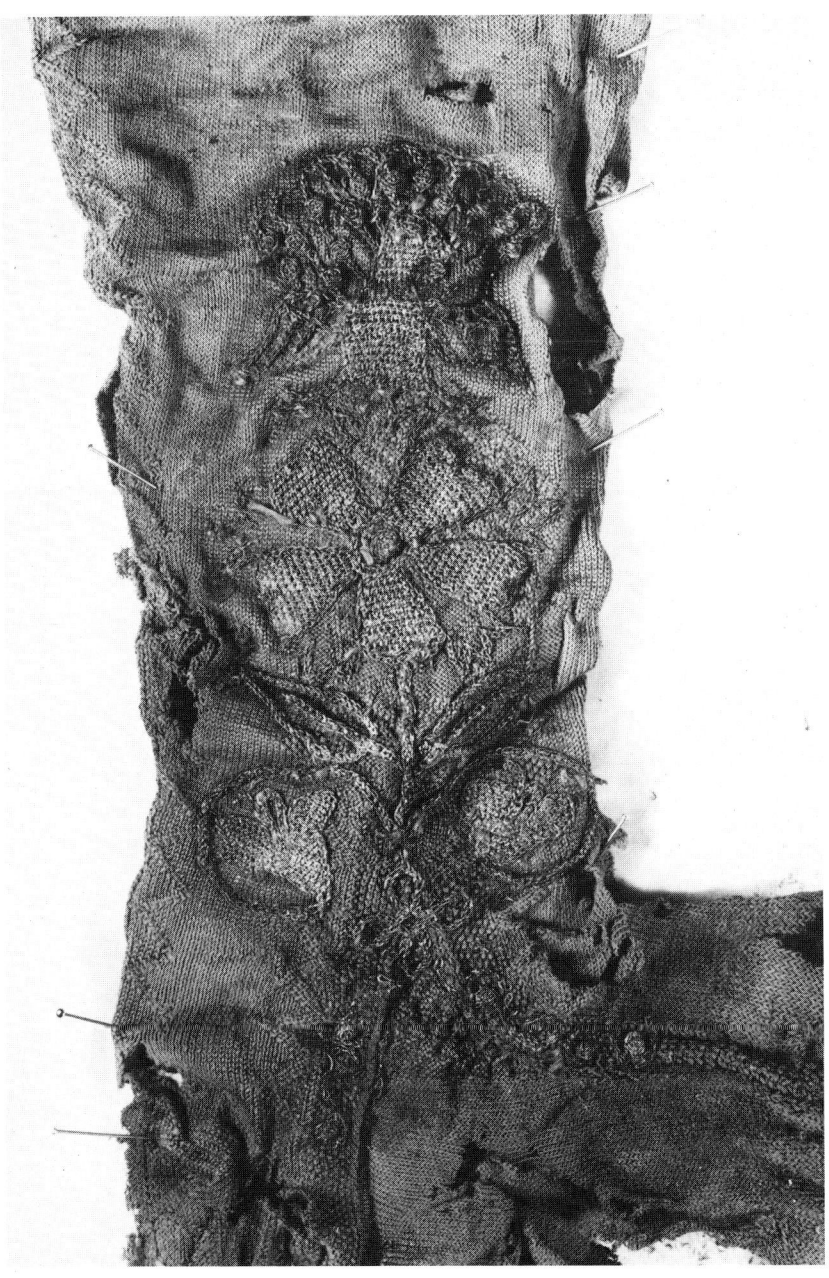

Fig. 21.9 Maria Cathrine's stocking. The embroidery is about 14cm from top to bottom, mostly executed in chain stitch and chain stitch with a gilded thread sewn on top.

Well-preserved textiles from the early 17th century in Denmark are extremely rare and so it was important for us to document both the preparation of the coffins and the burial clothes. As a result we were able considerably to extend our knowledge of the subject. In addition our understanding of funeral customs from a time when Catholic traditions were still in evidence is limited. The common people still maintained the Catholic custom of a quick funeral after death, while the nobility sought to extend the proceedings. According to Catholic traditions the deceased was like a sleeping infant and should be wrapped accordingly. The Protestant idea was quite different: the deceased was seen as living on into adulthood and should be dressed in all splendour for an honourable parting. The funeral was a kind of celebration which required time to prepare.

Reference

B. Bøggild Johannsen, A. Kruse, C. Paludan, L. Warburg, E. Østergård, *Fru Kirstens Børn: To Kongebørns Begravelser i Roskilde Domkirke*, Copenhagen, 1988 (extensive English summary)

22. The Svalbard textile conservation project

Elizabeth E. Peacock
Trondheim and Manchester

Introduction

The Svalbard Textile Conservation Project was a joint project between the Kulturvernet (Conservancy for Historic Remains and Ancient Monuments) for Svalbard and Jan Mayen, Tromsø Museum, and the University of Trondheim Museum, Norway. It addressed the conservation of all textile finds recovered from the Nordic archaeological expeditions to arctic Svalbard (1955 - 60), which were later deposited in the Tromsø Museum.

The project initiated investigations into the application of the technique of freeze-drying to archaeological textiles; and an investigation of various methods of mounting suitable for conserved textiles which were too fragile to be handled, but needed to be accessible for academic research and analyses. The project illustrated the need for research into materials and techniques employed in the conservation of archaeological textiles. In addition, it stressed the importance of collaboration between archaeologist, find specialist, and conservator at all stages of the research process.

Background

Joint Nordic archaeological expeditions to arctic Svalbard (fig. 22.1) began in 1955 to investigate and document evidence of: 1) an earlier Stone Age culture; 2) trafficking between mainland Norway and Svalbard and over-wintering during the Middle Ages; and 3) the activities and culture of the 17th- and 18th-century north Russian hunting stations, as represented by that at Russekeila on Isfjord.[1] Similar expeditions returned in 1958 and 1960. In 1958 investigations concentrated on Midterhuken in Bell Sund/Sound and in 1960 on Russekeila and Trygghamna in Isfjord all along the west coast of West Spitsbergen (fig. 22.2).

Upon excavation, the terrestrially-wet textile material was packed into brown paper bags and later moved about from one temporary store to another in northern Norway. None of the storage facilities had a controlled climate; but the material was probably never subjected to tropical conditions. The finds were packed and placed neither safely nor systematically and had neither chemically nor physically stable packaging.

The textile collection consists of over 350 fragments and larger pieces of clothing, footwear and bedding, constructed of woven, knitted, braided, felted and *nålebundet* wool. There was little vegetable fibre. The collection represents the mid 18th-century Russian fur-hunting settlements and associated burial areas along the west coast of West Spitsbergen. Also represented are the English, Dutch and Danish-Norwegian whaling stations at Midterhuken, Amsterdamøya, and Danskøya. The finds from the latter two islands are isolated and have no detailed provenance (fig. 22.2).

The history of this collection following excavation and up to 1982 is poorly documented, if at all. It was collected by different teams of archaeologists at different times, under varying conditions

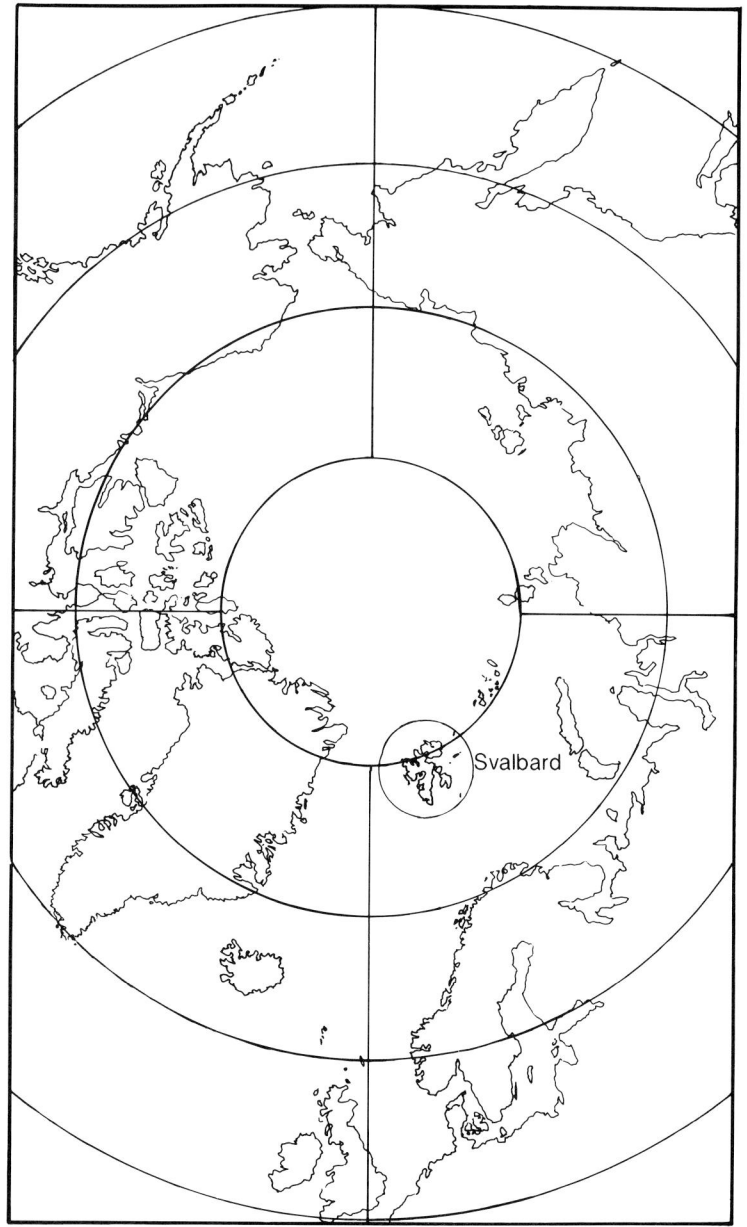

Fig. 22.1 The northern hemisphere and Svalbard viewed from the North Pole (drawing L.V. Jensen)

and with varying criteria for collecting - finally being stored in the Tromsø Museum, Norway. The categories of condition of this material in 1982 were: 1) no previous treatment; 2) immersion in an oily substance; and 3) incomplete previous conservation.

The international nature of archaeological expeditions to Svalbard has resulted in the scattering of recovered finds over Northern Europe and Russia. Consequently, it is difficult for archaeologists, textile specialists and conservators to become familiar with the material, or to learn where it is, and whether and how it has been conserved. Since excavation the textile finds deposited in Tromsø have not been examined by either archaeologists or textile specialists. Much of this material has never been accessioned.

Prompted by inquiries from abroad concerning the nature of the textiles stored in Tromsø, the Svalbard Textile Conservation Project was begun in 1982 and was completed in 1986. The scope of the project was to rescue the material from the then storage conditions, and, by pursuing a policy of minimal intervention, prepare it for academic research, analysis and stable storage. The conservation work was carried out at the University of Trondheim Museum Conservation Laboratory in Trondheim, Norway.

Fig. 22.2 Archaeological expeditions to Svalbard (1955-60) (drawing E.E. Peacock)

Description

The textiles which had not been previously treated were characteristically stiff, wadded together, and retained the adhering soil matrix (fig. 22.3). There was also evidence of substantial insect infestation during storage.

The second group of textiles appeared to have been impregnated with an oily substance either during use or after excavation (fig. 22.4). These textiles, fortunately a minority, were soft, but the pieces crumbled to the touch. The fibres were severely degraded, having 'rotted' from interaction with the impregnating agent. These pieces also exhibited insect infestation and mould attack during storage.

The last category was a selection of footwear and clothing treated in 1978. The footwear had been placed in water to soften the component materials. The softened leather and textiles were separated, soaked in 5% ethylene diamine tetra-acetic acid (EDTA) (type not specified) for one day, rinsed and the process repeated. The textile pieces were immersed in a 2.5% aqueous solution of Lissapol (non-ionic surfactant) for one day, rinsed, and immersed in a Modocoll (ethyl hydroxyethyl cellulose) - polyethylene glycol (PEG) 600 solution.

Neither the details of this impregnating solution nor the duration of the impregnation was documented. Impregnated pieces were placed directly in a domestic chest freezer at -20°C. Some time later it was discovered that the freezer had been out of order for at least a month. All the material had thawed out and was partially or completely covered with a variety of species of fungi. The textiles were disinfected in ethanol and returned to the cleaned and repaired freezer in 1978.

When collected in 1982, the affected textiles were characterised by a green hue and terrible odour. They were covered in mould and crystals of the impregnating agent, and dessicated, having undergone natural, uncontrolled freeze-drying. The pieces were hard, brittle and collapsed (fig. 22.5).

Fig. 22.3 A typical selection of textile pieces as received

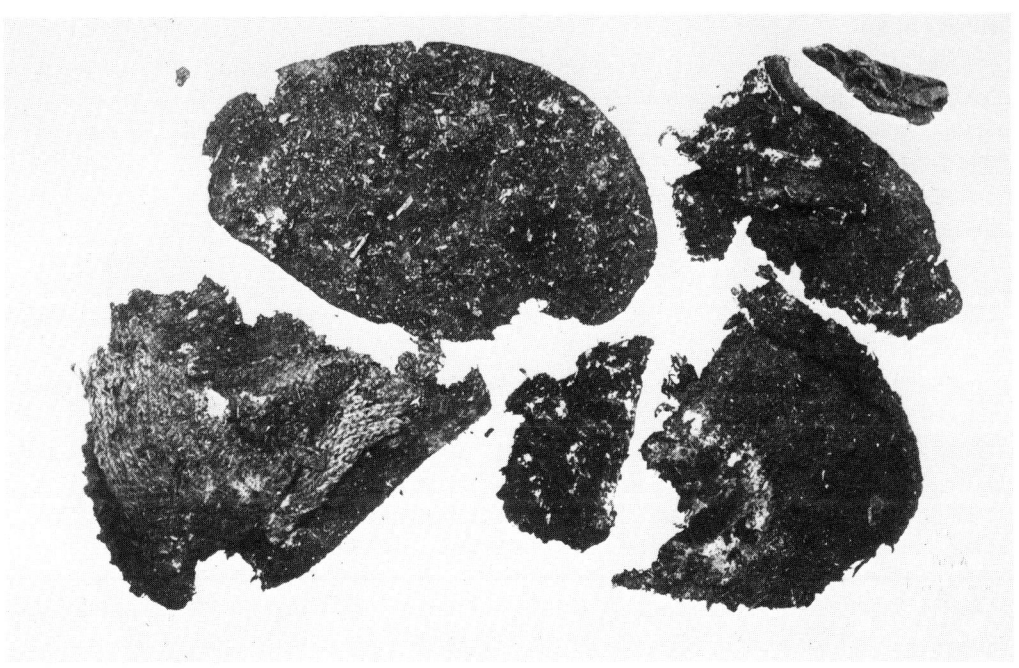

Fig. 22.4 'Oily' and insect-damaged fragments

Fig. 22.5 Previously treated textiles

Conservation

The extent of conservation work to be undertaken needed careful consideration. Any conservation intervention by its nature destroys some of the information unique to each textile. The Svalbard textiles are a study collection. In their state at that time, study was not possible. Neither the excavator nor a textile specialist was available for consultation during the conservation project.

Based upon the criteria established for the Svalbard textile collection, three categories of conservation were identified:

No conservation - this entailed suitable packaging for stable storage.

Minimal conservation - minimal mechanical cleaning, x-radiography and suitable packaging for storage.

Partial conservation - mechanical and wet cleaning, plasticising, pre-freezing, freeze-drying and packaging or mounting.

These categories of conservation omit phases of treatment traditionally identified with the conservation of ancient textiles. None of the textiles received either complete conservation or exhibition standard conservation: that is, neither reconstruction and replacement of missing parts nor cosmetic treatment for display was undertaken. Complete and display standard conservation were beyond the scope of the project. In addition such techniques were judged too hazardous to many of the objects, possibly destructive of information sought by a textile specialist or requiring subjective interpretation. All the textiles, regardless of the selected degree of conservation, were extensively documented before and after treatment, including x-radiography of wads and collapsed footwear.

Objects which received no conservation consisted of a group of brittle wads of loosely woven vegetable fibre. The threads were charred, thus irreversibly 'frozen' into position. These textiles were packed so that they were physically supported and cushioned for stable storage.

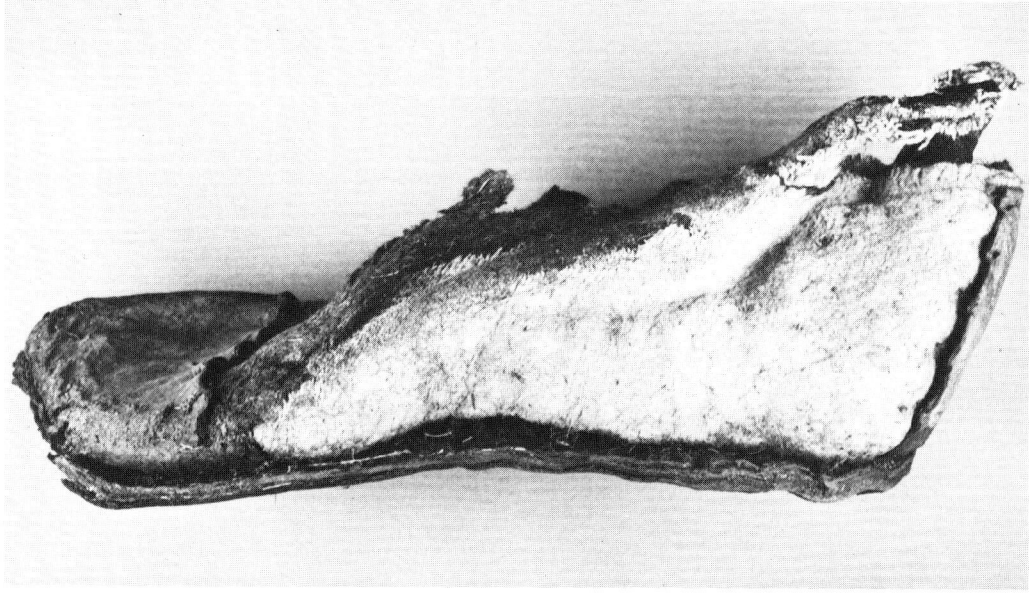

Fig. 22.6 Leather and textile composite shoe

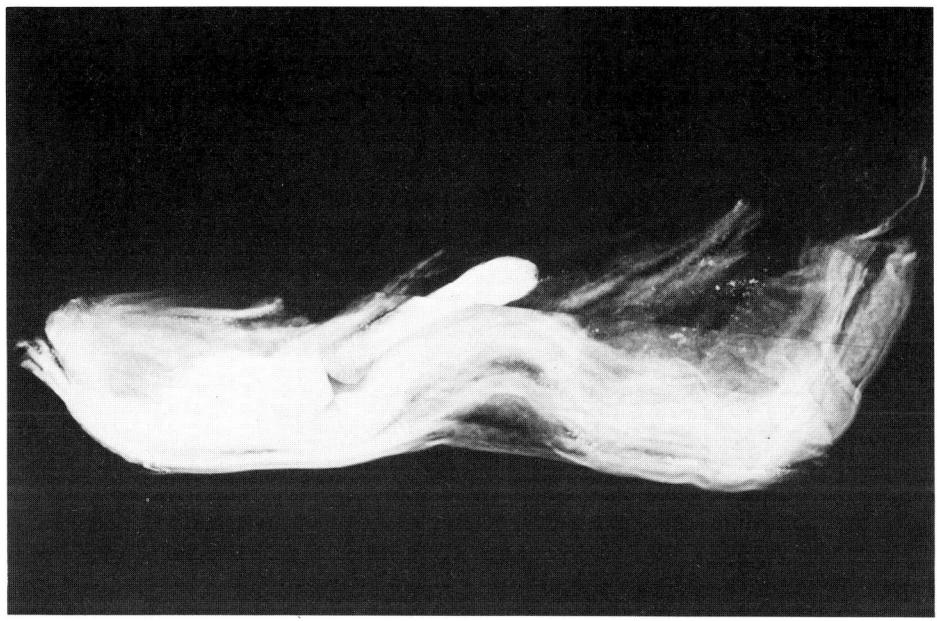

Fig. 22.7 X-radiograph of composite shoe in fig. 22.6. In-situ bones and shoe construction are revealed

Figure 22.6 is an example of an object which received minimal conservation. It is a collapsed shoe from a burial at Russekeila and is constructed of leather and multiple layers of woven and felted wool. The shoe is inflexible, the leather is hard, and the textiles are dehydrated and stiff, although not brittle. The shoe was firmly intact and none of the component layers showed signs of exfoliation.

X-radiography revealed the presence of some of the bones of one foot of the last owner. It also provided detailed information concerning the construction of the shoe (fig. 22.7). Even the weave of some of the textile layers is visible. This object was surface cleaned and packaged for storage.

Packaging for these two categories of conservation and the three-dimensional objects such as footwear consists of transparent polystyrene boxes of various sizes in which the object is suported by crumpled acid-free tissue. The transparent plastic enables the object to be identified and studied without disturbing the textile. The textile can be removed from the box for closer examination.

Figure 22.3 is one example of a find which received partial conservation. It is representative of the majority of the textiles. The dehydrated fragments were received wadded together in a brown paper bag. First the fragments were surface-cleaned with the aid of a binocular microscope, to remove as much of the adhering soil and sand as possible. These textiles were characterised by very thin rootlets from arctic vegetation, which had worked their way in and around individual yarns of the weave, thus effectively 'sewing' the textile together. These rootlets had to be removed carefully with tweezers.

The fragments were rehydrated and gently cleaned and relaxed. The rewetting and relaxing process took an average of two weeks per textile. Neither detergents nor chemicals were used to assist the cleaning process as the amount of rinsing required to remove these agents safely was considered possibly damaging.

Fig. 22.8
Freeze-dried
textiles

Drying investigations

The Svalbard Conservation Project is an example of a conservation project which requires alternative methods to meet the project's goal. Two conservation problems arose. The first was drying the textiles after wet-cleaning. Results of initial trials employing controlled air-drying were unacceptable, as were similar trials of controlled air-drying, following plasticising in low concentrations of humectants. The nature of the wool textile fibres was such that they were nearly or completely collapsed and no longer possessed the ability to regulate moisture. Re-hydrating the textile regained much of what was the original shape and body; but during the process of controlled air-drying the surface tension and drying stresses (capillary action of the evaporating water) returned the textile to its initial, inflexible, collapsed condition.

It was concluded that the textiles required an alternative method to controlled air-drying. The technique of freeze-drying was investigated. It is a technique which is not common in textile conservation, but is routine in the conservation of wet archaeological wood and leather. With this method drying stresses are reduced. The aqueously cleaned textile is frozen and then the ice is sublimed under vacuum. The water in its solid phase as ice is converted directly to the gaseous phase thus by-passing the liquid phase and the associated stresses present with the evaporation of water.

The freeze-drying technique was tried both with and without pretreatment with a plasticising medium. Pretreatment with either a bulking or plasticising medium is common when freeze-drying wet wood and leather. For the textiles the added material needed to perform three functions: 1) provide internal structural support to the degraded fibres; 2) lubricate the fibres; and 3) assist in maintaining an acceptable moisture content in the fibres.

Freeze-drying from solutions of plasticising media yielded consistently acceptable results for textiles plasticised in aqueous solutions of 10 - 15% polyethylene glycol (PEG) 400 or 4 - 8% glycerol (fig. 22.8).

Mounting

The Svalbard Project prompted an investigation of various storage systems suitable for two-dimensional textiles which are too fragile to be handled, but must be accessible for study and analysis. The textiles required a system which is: 1) chemically stable, non-reactive and provides physical support to the textile; 2) leaves as much of the textile to view as possible; and 3) protects the textile from possible mechanical damage and chemical contamination from handling during the research process.

The mounting system adapted for the flat textiles is based upon those introduced separately by McLean and Pritchard,[2] both of which have subsequently been adapted by many conservators. The basic system consists of a double-window mount (fig. 22.9). Two identical mats are cut out of acid-free museum-quality mat-board. The mats are lined with either a sheer fabric such as crêpeline (silk or polyester) or Stabiltex (polyester multi-filament or clear polyester film. For thicker textiles the space between the two lined window mats is built up with layers of unlined window mats. The textile is placed between the two prepared mats and the edges joined. The entire mount is placed in an envelope constructed of clear polyester resin film.

Prototype mounts were constructed and evaluated. Both fabric-lined and polyester-lined mats provide successful double-window mounts. The different qualities of these materials, as well as alternatives for joining the system together, must be considered when selecting the appropriate

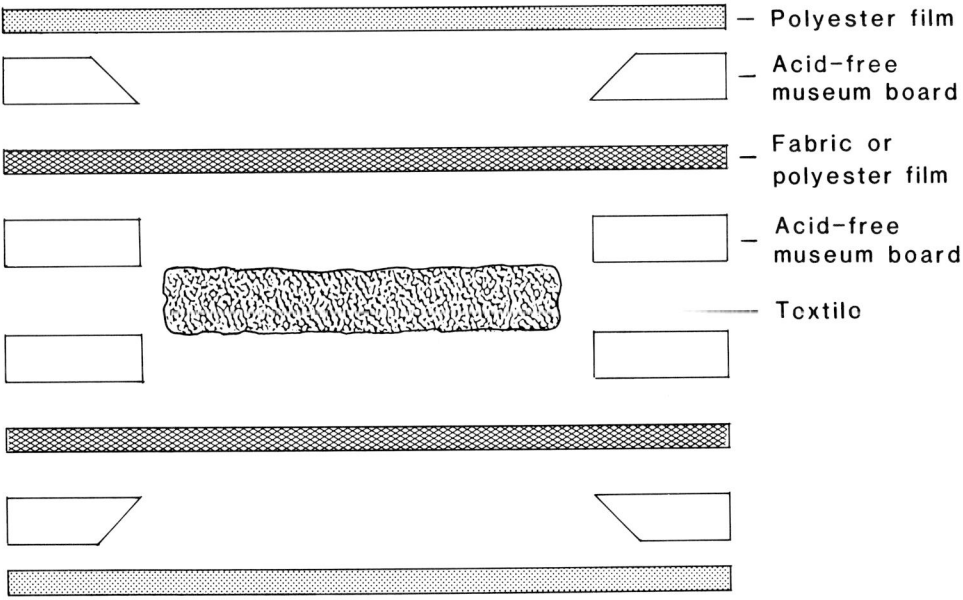

— Polyester film

_ Acid-free museum board

_ Fabric or polyester film

_ Acid-free museum board

Textile

MOUNTING SYSTEM

Fig. 22.9 Mounting system (drawing E.E. Peacock)

Fig. 22.10 A selection of mounted textile pieces

mounting solution for the mounting project at hand. Silk crêpeline was employed for the Svalbard textiles; but dyed varieties of Stabiltex in muted earth tones were found better to complement archaeological textiles.[3]

Conclusion

The conservation problems associated with the Svalbard textiles were the result of inappropriate care, both when the textiles were excavated and later under transport and storage. The project illustrated that the conservation of archaeological textiles is not routine and of secondary importance. Often new or alternative materials and methods must be investigated and employed. As conservation strives, physically and chemically, to stabilise an archaeological find for study and analysis, employing minimal intervention, it is important that conservation be an intimate part of the archaeological textile research process.

All photographs and x-radiographs by E.E. Peacock

References

1. P. Simonsen, 'Fra den forste arkeologiske Svalbardekspedisjons arbeid', *Polarboken* 1957, 76-84

2. C. C. McLean, 'Mounting small fragile textiles to be viewed from both sides', *Art Conservation Training Programs Conference 1980*, National Technical Information Service, Commerce (Virginia), 1980, 77-83; F. Pritchard, The Museum of London, personal communication, 1984

3. E. E. Peacock, 'Anthropological textiles; a mounting solution', *ICOM Committee for Conservation, 8th Triennial Meeting, Sydney Preprints*, Getty Conservation Institute, Marina del Rey, 1987, 407-411

23. The benefit of meeting with a Kurdish immigrant woman weaver, from the point of view of a research worker in the field of prehistoric looms

Karen-Hanne Stærmose Nielsen
Rungsted

Lately I have had a few experiences in the field of primitive loom studies that may be of some interest to this assembly. The experiences were of a literary as well as of a practical nature.

In 1921, when passing through Cairo, Grace M. Crowfoot was lucky enough to see the famous model of an Egyptian weaving workshop, then newly excavated by H.E. Winlock and H. Burton from the tomb of Mehenkwetre at Thebes, dated to 1900 BC, the Middle Kingdom (Metropolitan Museum Egyptian Expeditions) (fig. 23.1 top). Crowfoot noticed that the two model looms were of the same kind as those studied by herself in Sudan, but, to quote Crowfoot, 'one very essential part of the Sudani loom is missing in the model loom: the fixed heddle-rod supports, which are various in kind, stones, baked clay pillars, Y-shaped sticks etc'.[1] What, in the opinion of Crowfoot, might tentatively be interpreted as heddle-rod supports for the model looms were some strange wooden pegs of a shape as shown. As they were lying on the floor, however, not far from the heddle-rod but in a haphazard way, Crowfoot was not quite sure of the function of these pegs.

In the following year, 1922, Winlock wrote[2] that he, independently of Crowfoot, had come to the conclusion that the wooden pegs were actually heddle-rod supports, the so-called heddle-jacks, and he believed he had found 'ample confirmation of the correctness of this solution' on the monuments and in the original heddle-jacks at University College and in another original in the Cairo museum (fig. 23.1). To quote Winlock, the original heddle-jacks are 'wooden cylinders, about a foot high with a round spoon-like head and a notch in one side'. Further on Winlock writes 'in all cases the heddle-rod is lowered to form the counter shed, but to form the shed some appliance must be provided for raising the heddle-rod and the alternate warp-threads leashed to it'.[3] For this purpose the heddle-jacks themselves are designed to simplify the process as much as possible. The spoon-shaped top is expressly formed to slip under the ends of the heddle-rod when it is close to the floor. The rod-end then slides into the notch, a quick jerk is given and the jack stands upright, firmly held on its broad base by the tension of the warp-threads. To lower the heddle-rod a smart blow on either jack brings down the whole affair'.

Recently one of the Danish ethnographers in the process of establishing the great new National Museum of Bahrain, showed me some photos and raised some questions about mat-weaving. The mat loom of an old Bahrain weaver has been purchased by the museum and will soon be on display. Seeing the photographs of this modern mat weaver I at once remembered a notable 1933 article by Crowfoot entitled 'The mat weaver from the tomb of Khety', describing an illustration which, like the model loom workshop, is dated to the Egyptian Middle Kingdom (1900 BC). Crowfoot presents different drawings made after the one which the excavator himself made (fig. 23.2b); we are told that tthe excavator's sketch of the Khety mat loom has been copied many times and with scanty knowledge of working looms, with

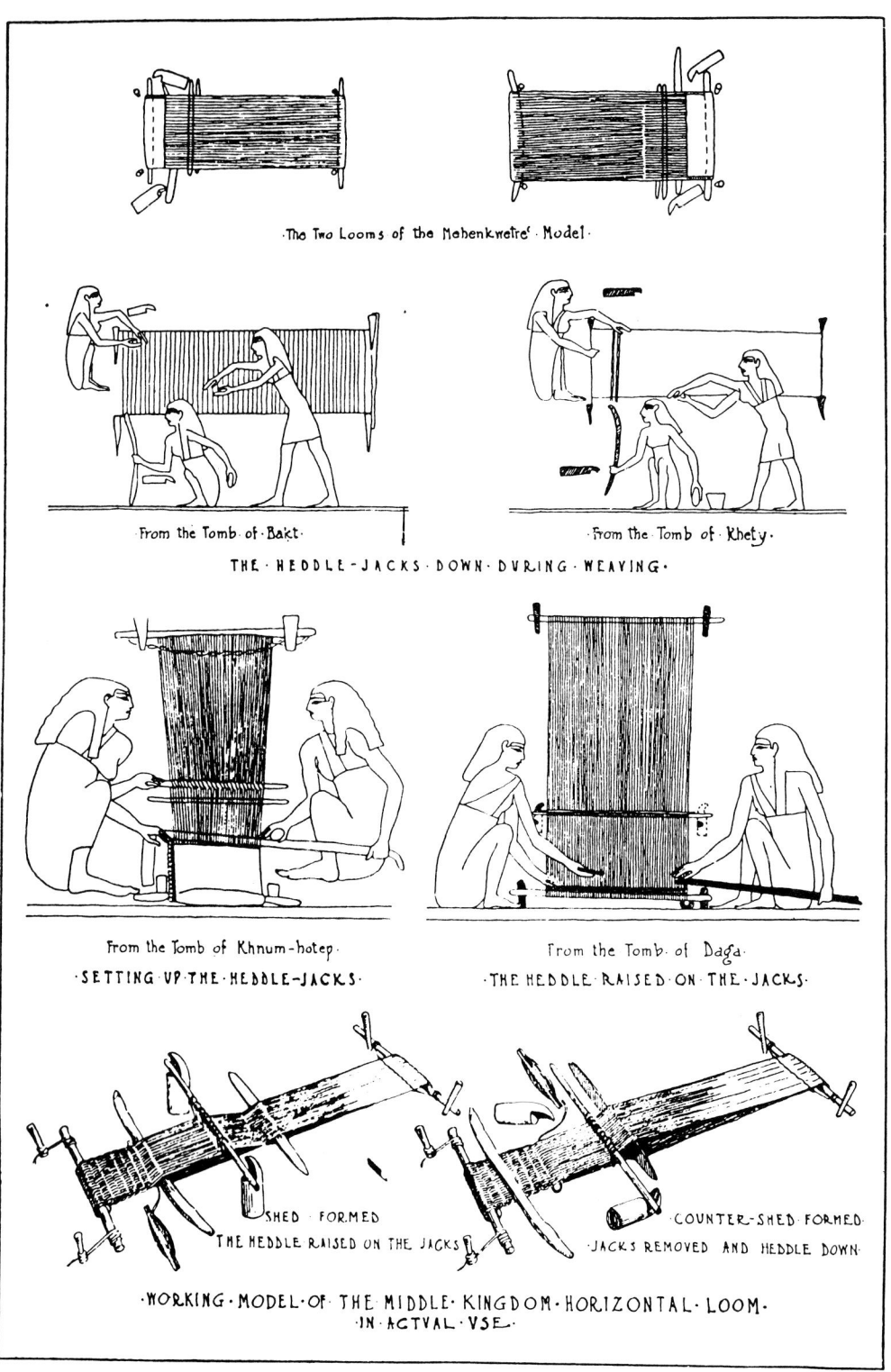

Fig. 23.1 Egyptian looms with heddle-jacks (after H.E. Winlock, Ancient Egypt *1922, III, 73, fig. 2*)

the result that all interpretations are of the same nature[4] (only two examples are shown in fig. 23.2a,c). Most interpreters are in big trouble when explaining the lines going crosswise over the unwoven warp. Crowfoot had seen this kind of work, still done in Sudan and Egypt, and therefore knew that the problematic cross-lines were simply strands of reed lying ready for the mat weaver to use as weft. This is exactly as the Bahrain weaver has his reeds lying beside him on top of a wooden board.

As may be seen from the Khety sketch (fig. 23.2b) as well as from the Bahrain photograph, the mat loom does not operate with a shed. The warp-threads are threaded through the row of holes of the wooden bar and do not change level or position in relation to each other, except that every other warp-thread is pressed a bit downwards by a finger as the stiff weft reed proceeds across the width of the mat between odd and even warp-threads. The perforated bar also acts as an effective beater-in. Thought-provoking! A procedure unchanged for over 4000 years. In ten years, however, you may not find the handicraft any more, anywhere, for, as the old mat weaver told the Danes, neither his own sons, nor the sons of his few colleagues, wanted to succeed their fathers in this craft.

Many years ago M. Hald stated that wide loom fabrics of prehistoric Denmark and of pre-Columbian South America indicate that more than one weaver was working in front of the loom at one time. When reconstructing the famous Danish Huldremose woman's dress, of a loom width of 1.85m, the weavers of the Archaeological-Historical Research Centre at Lejre had to work occasionally four people at a time in order to produce three weft-crosses of each weft-pick in the original Iron-Age textile. A photograph of this experiment clearly shows that four adult weavers had little space and difficulty in moving their arms freely. One day, however, during a school visit to the Lejre centre, a Turkish girl told our weavers that she had seen a similar situation in her homeland, although of the four weavers the two in the middle were children. This arrangement favoured a process of learning for the young ones while the more time-consuming selvedges were taken care of by the more skilled grown-ups.

I enjoyed the latest experience a year ago, during 'field studies' done without leaving my own country, by hunting up people from far-away countries now living in Denmark. The Kurdish immigrant woman, Zultan Yilmas, sits on the floor in her family flat in a suburb of Copenhagen, weaving in the nomad manner on her upside-down coffee table (fig. 23.4); she uses the four legs of this table as pegs for the two beams around which, with the aid of her daughter, she winds the heavy warp-threads in one continuous movement and she does not make the so-called figure-of-8-cross.

The warp is in the shape of a cylinder and, as such, is designed to revolve around the beams when required. Zultan knots the two outermost warp-threads together in a special way in order to allow the free revolving of the warp. Next, the heddle-rod-to-be, fixed with a heavy cord, is ready to be placed high on top of a somewhat provisional-looking heddle support. The heddles are then made from a ball of yarn, by passing the heddle yarn from the heddle-rod and around every other warp-thread. Next, the warp-threads not caught up by the heddle loops are cleverly lifted up on a thin rod, so that the figure-of-8 warp-cross and the heddles are made in one step. The thin rod is replaced by a heavier one, the shed rod, which is then pushed backwards, as seen in fig. 23.4. As the counter-shed in function here is very narrow, Zultan inserts the weaving-sword in the flat position. When fully inserted the sword is raised to widen the shed for the passage of the weft.

We have now got to know two different principles of shedding. Principle one is to be found in the Egyptian model loom with movable heddle-rod and heddle-jacks, and shed-rod in fixed position (fig. 23.3 upper three diagrams). Principle two was seen in those looms encountered by Crowfoot in 1921 in Sudan and modern Egypt: these have heddle-rods on fixed jacks (or heddle-rod supports) and a movable shed-rod. The loom of Zultan follows the latter principle with its fixed heddle-rod and movable shed-rod. As to the principle of warping, however, the loom of Zultan is quite unlike the ones mentioned above - but this is a question of a different nature.

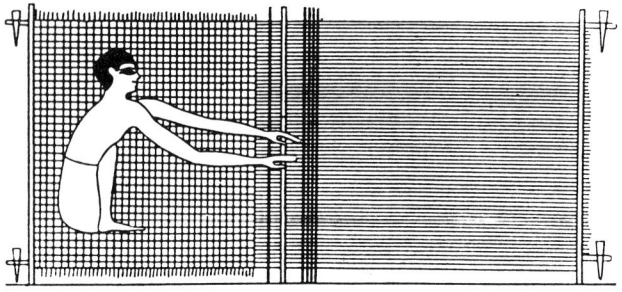

FIG. 1.

FIG. 2.

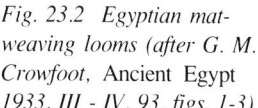

Fig. 23.2 Egyptian mat-
weaving looms (after G. M.
Crowfoot, Ancient Egypt
1933, III - IV, 93, figs. 1-3)

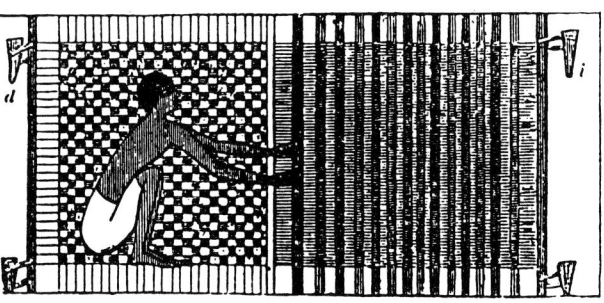

FIG. 3.

Zultan sits all the time on the floor in front of the loom. This she can do very well, because, as I mentioned previously, the warp revolves freely around the two beams, so that a new area of unwoven warp may be brought to the weaver when wanted. Consequently she does not need to weave in an uncomfortable position. On the other hand she has to take up an uncomfortable attitude when pulling the distant shed-rod towards herself, in order to make the natural shed.

In order to avoid too difficult a position when working every other shed, the weavers using this principle mount the heddle-rod on top of the supports or heddle-jacks, at a level which is high enough to allow space for the arms of the weaver under the heddle-rod. I have to confess a little something. When I first visited and made my notes at Zultan's place, I was wondering why it was so important for her to create that high scaffold-like stacking of pots and blocks of wood as supports for the heddle-rod. Not until much later, when studying the photos at home, did I understand the significance and importance of the high heddle-jacks of this special loom. A Lebanese rug weaver would sit on top of the woven cloth and move along as the work progresses at the same time as the heddle-rod and jacks are moved backwards. Zultan remained in the same position as she worked which is quite different from a Lebanese woman, who takes up varying attitudes, according to what is to be done. Thus we learn that weavers at all times and everywhere have been experts in using and finding solutions from their surroundings.

I have not yet mentioned that the product of Zultan's loom is a very small rug, the surface of which is an all-over hand-knotted pile. The pile yarn, which is wool and variously coloured, is cut into small measured pieces, before being knotted around two warp-threads each. The pile is made with the Turkish or Ghiordes knot. A few years ago Zultan made this small rug for her son as her first task after having been in Denmark for about eight years. In this time she had not practised the craft, which she had been taught by an aunt at the age of six or eight (in Kurdistan, as she still calls her native country, now part of eastern Turkey).

I should point out that this rug was woven before my visit. The fact is that at my first meeting with Zultan I showed her a book of mine about Turkish rug weaving and designs. She begged urgently to borrow the book - and on my next visit she proudly showed me the result of her inspiration from this book. It is up to you to judge whether or not I should have given her the book. Zultan made room in her new rug for the name of her home in Denmark, Avedøre Stationsby, and the year 1986. Most interesting, however, is the sign in the uppermost right corner of the rug. This sign is a replica of the logo of the local housing-association of the family.

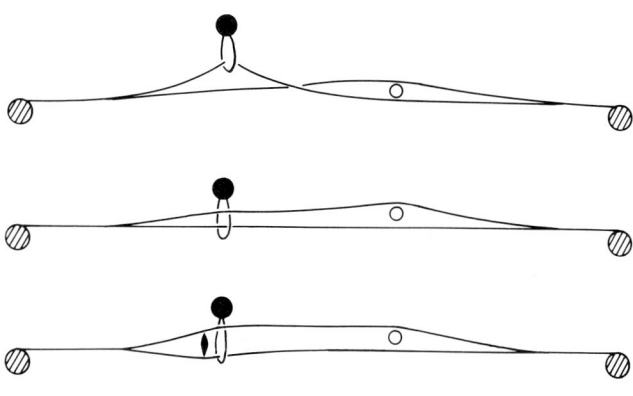

Fig. 23.3 Methods of opening the shed on two-beam ground-looms

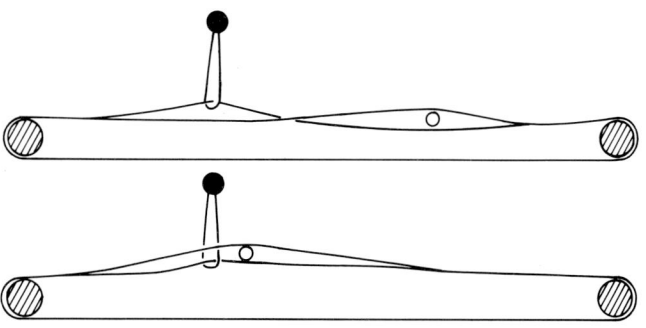

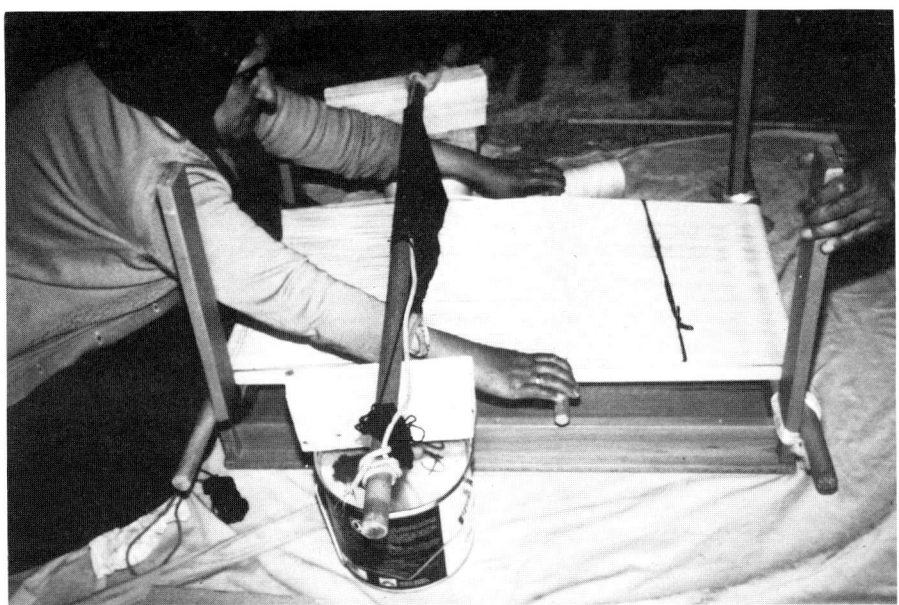

Fig. 23.4 Mrs Zultan Yilmas weaving on her 'ground-loom' in the Kurdish manner

My intention in presenting miscellaneous phenomena, apparently unrelated, has a double nature. First, I wish to support Marta Hoffmann in her pioneering among archaeologists for a more extensive usage of the 'living tradition', even when solving problems of a character seemingly purely theoretical. The mat weavers of modern Egypt, Sudan and Bahrain, and Zultan's very high heddle-jacks, are good examples of this, not to forget the story about the two adult weavers from Turkey having their small girls sitting in the middle - a nice sort of weaving school, incidentally.

Next, notice the manner in which Zultan handled the designs in her small rugs. The practice of Zultan once more illustrates the travelling and toughness of patterns. The corner application of the logo of the housing-association is much more typical for a craftsman than usually accepted, I believe. The artisan, modern as well as prehistoric, takes up motifs and patterns from widely different objects and areas and often unscrupulously includes a new element among the traditional ones.

It was important and useful for me to get to know the loom of Zultan, because it clearly shows which parts and functions of a loom can be easily changed according to circumstances, and which parts, on the other hand are so fundamental to the whole process that they remain unchanged. Finally I am pleased to be able to use a bit of the great treasure of ability and resources which the ethnic peoples living in our country possess. Living, as most of them do, on the lowest step of society's ladder, I find it valuable for both them and us each time a chance arises of letting these people from far away sense that they possess - among other things - skill and dexterity that we care for, realizing that long ago we have forgotten and lost those abilities.

References

1. G. M. Crowfoot, H. Ling Roth, 'Models of Egyptian Looms', *Ancient Egypt* 1921, Part IV, 97-101

2. H. E. Winlock, 'Heddle-jacks of Middle Kingdom Looms', *Ancient Egypt* 1922, Part III, 71 - 74

3. There is some confusion as to Winlock's definition of what is shed and countershed.

4. G.M. Crowfoot, 'The Mat Weaver from the Tomb of Khety', *Ancient Egypt* 1933, Parts III - IV, 93 - 99

24. A tandem accelerator dating

Elisabeth   Munksgaard
Copenhagen

When NESAT met at Neumünster in 1981, Karen-Hanne Nielsen and I introduced you to a Gallic coat from Rønbjerg of supposed Iron Age date (fig 24.1). I regret to say that the finding place is not Rønbjerg bog in Jutland, but a cardboard box in the Medieval Department, where the coat was stored together with a Medieval man's coat of the same pattern as those from the Norse cemetery at Herjolfsnes in South-West Greenland. The Gallic coat has no museum number and its provenance is unknown.

When we worked with this coat in 1981 in collaboration with the textile conservation department, there was not enough material for a C^{14} dating. Later, however, the tandem accelerator dating system was established, not in Copenhagen, but in Uppsala, Oxford and Utrecht. An accelerator dating has the great advantage that it requires only 50mg of material.

In August 1986 Else Østergård and I collected the required amount of milligrams and sent it to the laboratory in Uppsala. The result was staggering: 510 before present, ie late 15th century (put that in your pipe and smoke it!).

The problem is that pollution alone cannot account for such a difference. The Uppsala laboratory has discussed the discrepancy and states that the extremely fine quality of the fibres excludes a pollution which would push the dating from the Roman Iron Age to the 15th century. This would mean 72% of modern pollution - and that was considered impossible. The conclusion is that the coat cannot be as old as we expected.

The other problem is that, if we accept the 15th century dating, there are no Medieval parallels, either in actual finds or in pictures of this costume. The weaving technique is warp repp made of Z-spun, S-twisted yarn in both warp and weft, and this is a most unusual feature in Scandinavian Prehistoric textiles. The thread count is 14 warp and 4-5 weft threads per cm.

Dr Ryder analysed the wool in 1981 and stated that the fibres were typical of the Roman Iron Age, but that one of the weft plies had a more symmetrical fibre distribution approaching that of modern shortwool type - which has not previously been observed earlier than Roman times. He also stated that "the fibres were originally light grey - a typical Iron-Age feature. There was an unusually high percentage (mean 70%) of medullated fibres (ie having a core) for wools with few hairs and this was brought about by the presence of a medulla in fine fibres. This extremely unusual feature has been observed in at least one Bronze-Age wool sample".

Having received these shocking results Else Østergård and I have also played with the mad thought that this garment might be of South American origin, handed down perhaps from the Royal Curio Cabinet (the 'Kunstkammer') - although it is not mentioned in any of the Kunstkammer inventories from the 18th century. The weaving technique, with extra warp threads added to broaden the shoulder width, is known also from Inca ponchos. In a way, however, I should consider it highly improbable that such a modest garment as this - not to say repulsive rag - would ever interest those persons who collected rarities for the Royal collection. After all, the coat has a decided dark brown

Fig. 24.1 The tunic photographed during conservation in the textile department of the National Museum

peat bog patination, so it may derive from a raised bog somewhere in Jutland; and the very hard twist of the threads points in both Prehistoric and Medieval directions, although the two-ply yarn does not.

The tandem accelerator dating is as yet so new that it may not be quite reliable. If only our Prehistoric Department could scrape together the 5,000 Danish kroner which is the cost of dating in Oxford I should like to send another 50mg there, and then another 50mg to Utrecht where there is no charge because they want to acquire experience. Then we may compare three different dates and be worse off than before.

Postscript

It was very difficult to place the coat in a Scandinavian Medieval context, as there were no parallels whatsoever. The technique is also unknown in Danish Iron-Age or later material: the yarn is Z-spun and S-twisted in both warp and weft, with a very hard twist.

As the findspot is unknown there is only one way to proceed: to start at the beginning and look for similar clothes elsewhere in the world. Where do we find a coat or tunic in warp repp, with extra width across the shoulders obtained by adding extra warp threads (fig. 24.2)? The answer is, in Peru. Our tunic is sewn together at the sides like the Peruvian tunics, not open like the poncho. The tunic was worn with a belt and our tunic has signs of wear around the waist, and the slit for the neck is woven, not cut, as is the case with ponchos.[1]

The material was in 1981 determined by M.L. Ryder as a primitive sheep's wool,[2] but the Museum of Natural History in Aarhus has determined the wool as that of llama or alpaca! To be quite certain another sample was sent to York to be examined by Penelope Walton who reports as follows: "The cross-sectional shapes and the scale patterns are compatible with fibres from llama-type animals. There are, however, none of the coarse fibres with bipartite or multipartite medulla which are the most distinctive feature of llama-type fibres. Nor is there evidence for a thick cuticle, another diagnostic feature." The conclusion is "that it is not possible to give a definite identification beyond non-wool animal coat fibres - although llama and alpaca are certainly likely candidates." Another sample was sent to Penelope Walton in June 1988, and this time the results were promising as both bipartite and quadripartite medullas were found. And such fleeces have no relatives in the Old World.[3]

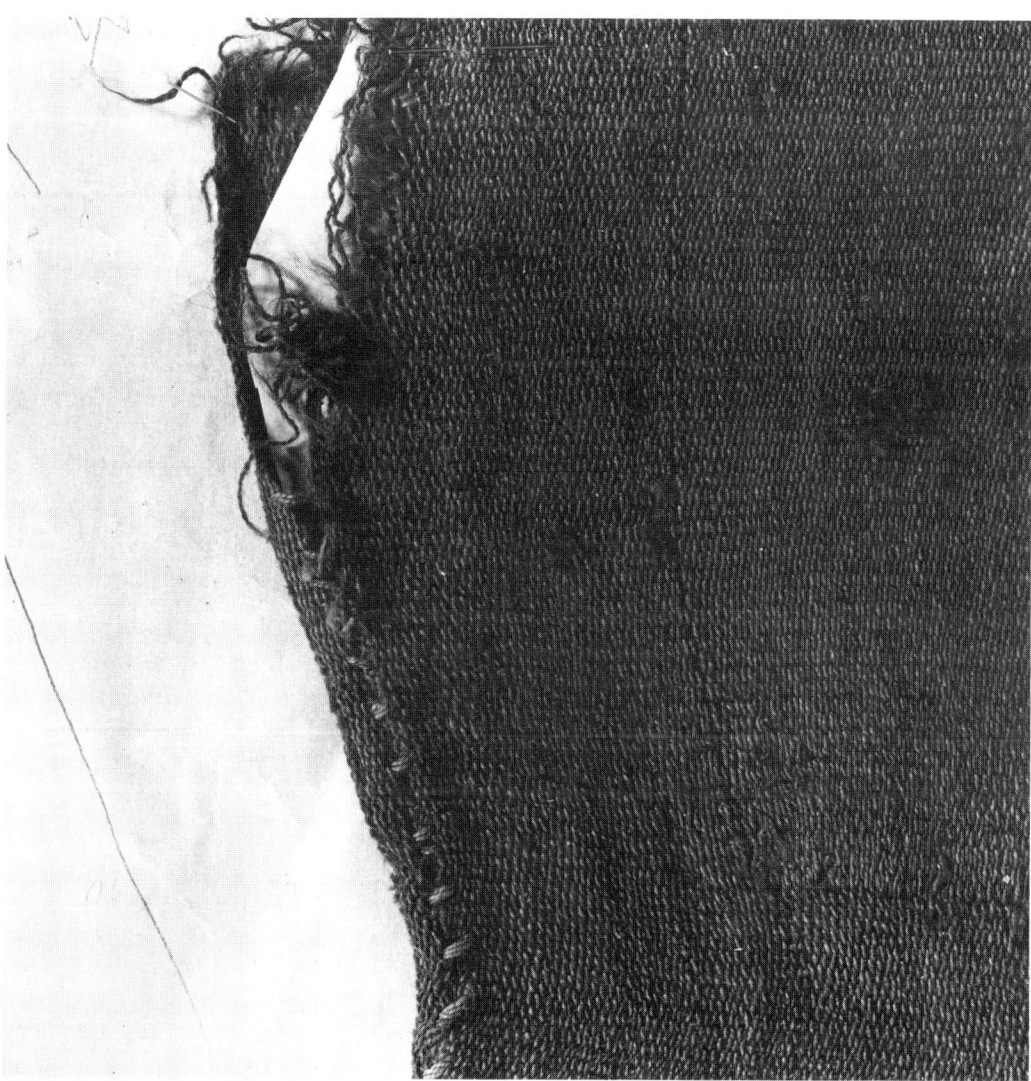

Fig. 24.2. Close-up of the tunic showing the extra warp-threads which shape the extra width across the shoulders (just under 1:1)

As to dyes we had the problem that a Danish dye analysis from 1981 gave *Alnus glutinosa*[4] - alder bark. But alder bark dye is made up of tannins, the main component being ellagic acid, with traces of gallic acid and, perhaps, catechine. Ellagic acid was the main component in our samples, and these tannins are widely available in nature, especially in nuts and barks, "so the identification of alder bark in the sample must be only one of several possibilities".[5] Of the two different yarns of which the tunic is made, dark brown and reddish brown, the dark brown is naturally pigmented; the reddish brown was the yarn in which artificial dye was found.

It has, unfortunately, not been possible to trace the tunic's way from Peru to the cardboard box in the National Museum. It is not mentioned in any of our Kunstkammer inventories from 1737, 1775, 1807 or 1827. It is not mentioned either in any of the published lists in *Antikvarisk Tidsskrift*[6] containing all the gifts to the Museum brought home by the Danish frigates Bellona and Galathea which sailed around the world in 1840-41 and 1845-47. These gifts were the beginning of the so-called 'American Cabinet' of the Old Norse Museum,[7] later the Department of Ethnography.

But even if we cannot trace the tunic's way to Denmark, the dating to 510 B.P. $\pm$ 100 (B. P. = before 1950) thus makes it one of the oldest South American garments in a European Museum.

References

1. Raoul d'Harcourt, *Textiles of Ancient Peru and their Techniques*, London, 1974, 5 ff; Julian H. Steward (ed), *Handbook of South American Indians 2, The Andean Civilizations*, Washington, 1946, 240 ff.

2. Unpublished letter to the Prehistoric Department, October 1980; see also K-H. Nielsen, 'The Rønbjerg Garment', *Textilsymposium Neumünster*, Neumünster, 1982, 50.

3. A.B. Wildman, *The Microscopy of Animal Textile Fibres*, Leeds, 1954, reference kindly supplied by Penelope Walton in report to the Prehistoric Department, July 1988.

4. Nielsen (1982), 58

5. Report by Penelope Walton, see note 3

6. For the years 1840-41, 1846-48, and 1852-54

7. From 1892, the National Museum

25. The evidence of wear and damage in ancient textiles

Bill Cooke and Brenda Lomas

Manchester

The development of the Cambridge Stereoscan Scanning Electron Microscope (SEM) in the 1960's introduced a new phase in the study of the morphologies of fibre fracture and breakdown. The very much greater depth of focus and resolution, as compared with even the best optical microscopes, allowed the fine structure of fibres to be examined and recorded for the first time. The Department of Textiles at UMIST (University of Manchester Institute of Science and Technology) was fortunate to obtain one of the very first commercial Stereoscans in 1968. This enabled Hearle to establish a continuing programme of research, which has resulted in an understanding of the many mechanisms of fibre damage and an extensive range of archive photomicrographs. Most of this work has concentrated on fibres used by the modern textile industry. In 1974 a programme of research was started by Lomas into the fibre damage asssociated with the use of woven articles such as shirts and sheets, and in 1978 Cooke initiated a similar project involving the study of knitted goods. The results of this research have found a ready application in the textile industry in many sectors ranging from aerospace to rope-making; with the development of contacts between the Departments of Archaeology and Textiles in the University of Manchester, this knowledge has started to be applied to ancient textiles. The use of these methods in the study of archaeological and museum textiles depends on a wider access to the results of the research. This paper will therefore present the main elements of a basic fracture atlas and consider the results of a number of studies in ancient fabrics.

The significance of fibre fracture morphology

The nature of the damage which develops at the fibre level when a fabric is worn, or subjected to other mechanical treatments such as washing, is dependent on two main factors. The fracture morphology is dependent on the fibre micro-structure and is significantly different for each of the main classes of natural fibres used since the earliest times. Fracture analyisis can therefore be used as a means of fibre identification where other means are inapplicable, eg if the fibre surface is badly eroded, or where fibre ends protrude from the matrix, in carbonised or metal-replaced textiles. The different mechanisms of damage or wear also produce distinct and often easily recognisable patterns of damage, both on the fibre and on the fabric surface. These patterns are clearly visible and can be identified with the aid of an SEM.

Fibre fracture morphology and wear/damage identification

Despite the complex nature of the process of wear, the individual fibres within the yarns which make up the textile can only be subjected to a limited number of mechanically induced deformations, viz axial strain, torsional strain, bending strain and shear. Each of these deformations produces a distinct form of fracture morphology. Tensile failure resulting from the tearing or bursting of a fabric, the snapping of a cord, or the penetration of a projectile through a textile, produces the types of damage illustrated in figs. 25.1 - 25.4, on wool, cotton, linen, silk.

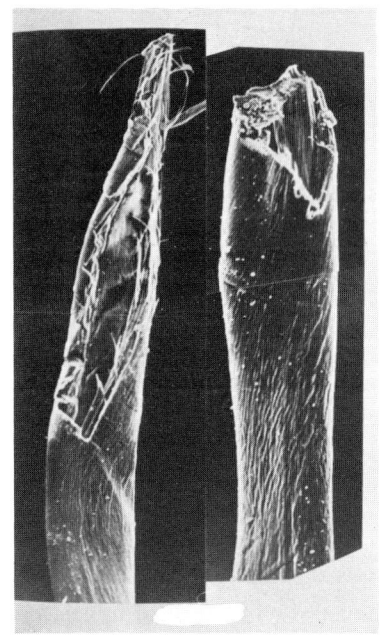

Fig. 25.1 (above) Wool: tensile break (x2000)

Fig. 25.2 (right) Cotton: tensile break (x2500)

Fig. 25.3 (below left) Flax: tensile break (x3500)

Fig. 25.4 (below right) Silk: tensile break (x3000)

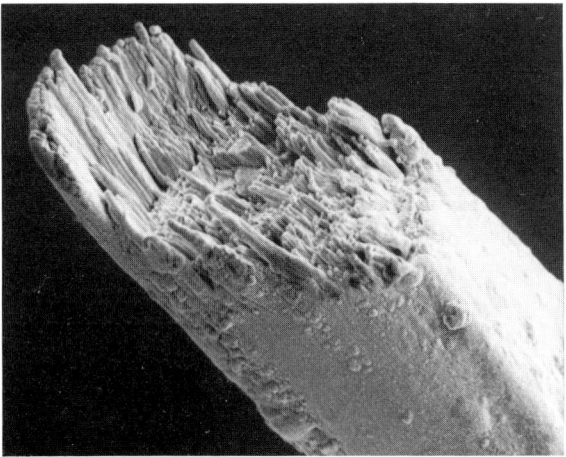

The process of wear generates a combination of axial, torsional and bending strain in the fibres resulting in a characteristic progressive fatigue damage. This breaks the fibres down into their structural units, macrofibrils or fibrils. With all the natural organic fibres such damage results in a brush-like fracture, which only occurs after extensive flexing (figs. 25.5 - 25.8, wool, cotton, linen, silk).

216

Fig. 25.5 Wool: fatigue break in leg bandage from Vindolanda (x1200)

Fig. 25.6 Cotton: wear damage (x800)

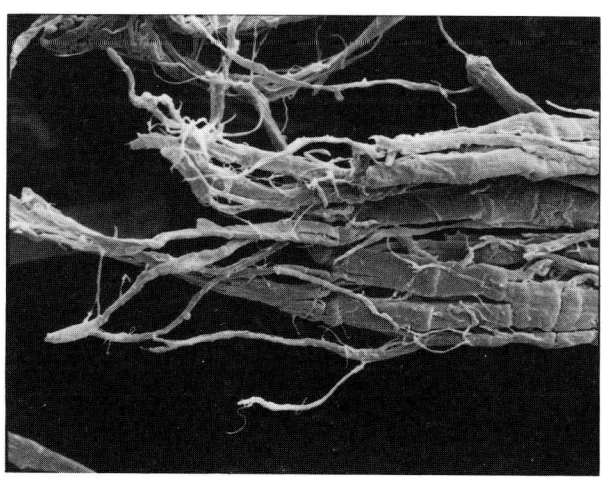

Fig. 25.7 Flax: fatigue break (x3500)

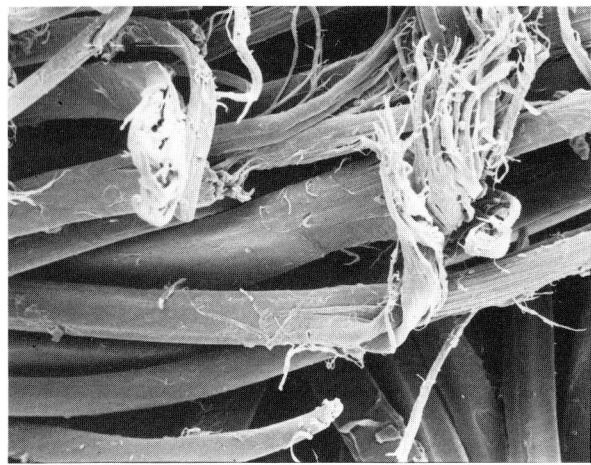

Fig. 25.8   Silk: fatigue damage (x1200)

In contrast the process of ageing due to oxidation, hydrolysis, light, chemical, fungal or bacterial attack, results in fragmentation of the long chain molecules from which the fibres are formed. As a consequence the strength of the fibrils is reduced to the point where crack propagation can take place across the fibre axis, with the formation of brittle breaks. This type of brittle failure can only occur after the tendering process, ie after burial or prolonged exposure to light or heat (figs. 25.9 - 25.10, linen, silk).

Shear damage results from the specific action of cutting a fabric or cord with a sharp instrument and it is possible to distinguish between the damage caused by a razor, scissors, or a knife (figs. 25.11 - 25.14).

The washing of textiles subjects them to a combined mechanical and chemical attack. The mechanical action is mainly one of rubbing which is combined with the alkaline action of the soaps or soda ash used as cleaning agents. This alkaline attack destroys the intermolecular links in cotton, linen and other cellulosic fibres and results in a generalised fibrillation. These fibrils are then entangled and smeared on the surface of the textile by the rubbing action of the washing process (fig. 25.15).

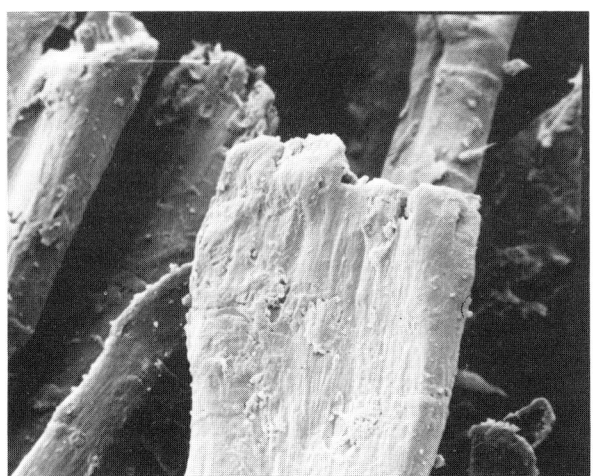

Fig. 25.9   Flax: brittle break (x2000)

Fig. 25.10 (top right) Silk: brittle break (x2000)

Fig. 25.11 (centre left) Wool: razor cut (x3000)

Fig. 25.12 (centre right) Wool: scissor cut (x3000)

Fig. 25.13 (bottom left) Cotton: scissor cut (x4500)

Fig. 25.14 (bottom right) Cotton: knife cut (x4000)

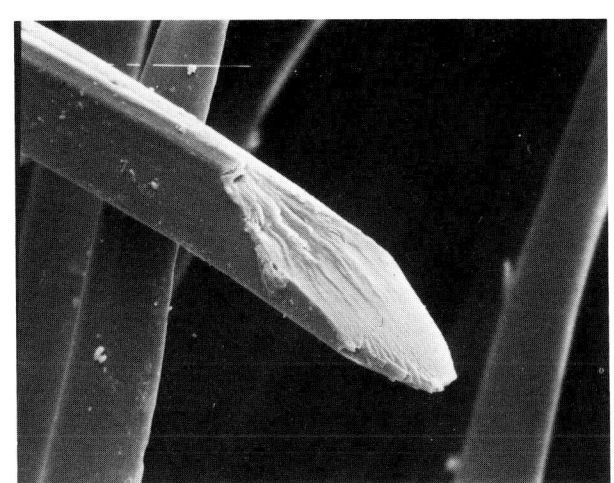

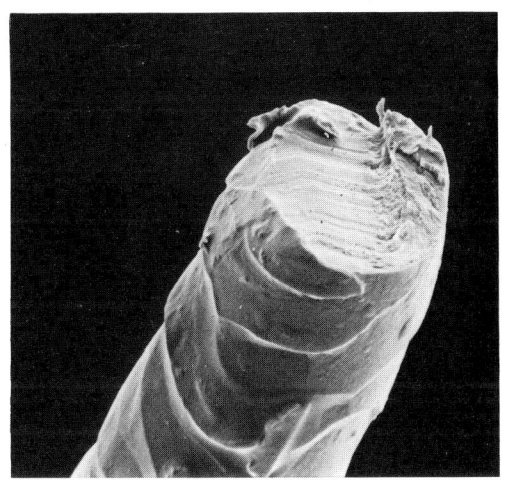

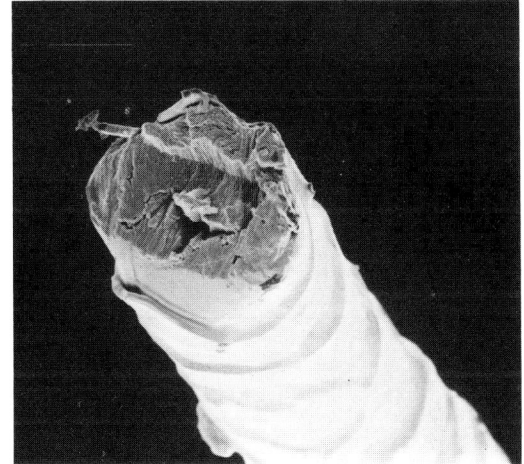

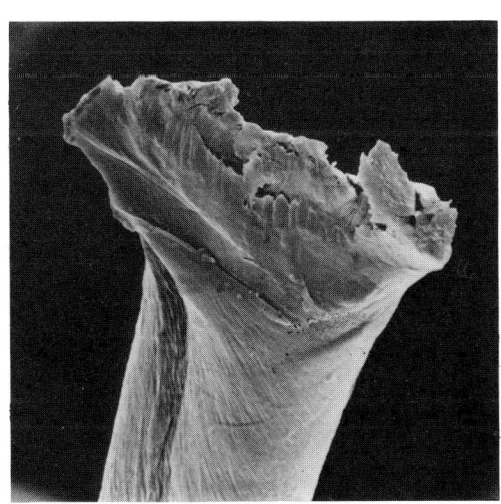

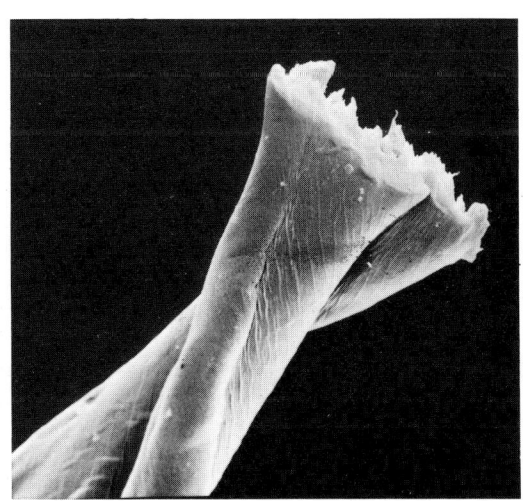

Fabric surface damage

A sequence of changes occurs in the surface layers of a fabric due to the normal process of abrasive wear. At each intersection, the uppermost thread tends to project above the general level of the surface. This projection which is called a weft or warp 'crown' is usually the first portion of the fabric to show the effects of wear. The first signs are usually light rubbing of the surface fibres, followed by surface fibrillation, which eventually leads to fibre breakage with the characteristic 'brush-like' broken ends. Continued abrasion will lead finally to a break in the yarn structure. The brush-like projections are also subject to further wear, and the fibrils break off leaving a rounded end in the interstices of the weave. This sequence of changes is illustrated in figs. 25.15 - 25.19. If the yarns are softly spun or hairy, or if the fabric is knitted, a different process occurs at least initially, or possibly throughout the wear process. This is known as pilling and results in the formation of small balls of fibre, or pills, over the worn area. Pills are generated by the entanglement of surface fibres which are then progressively pulled out of the yarn structure and rolled up by the rubbing action. They are usually sufficiently big

Fig. 25.15 (left)
Fibrillated cotton (x1000)

Fig. 25.16 Damaged crowns (x100)

220

Fig. 25.17 Silk: damaged crowns (x130)

Fig. 25.18 Fibrillation and fatigue in crown damage (x340)

Fig. 25.19 Fatigue breaks in weave interstices (x460)

221

to be seen with the naked eye, but the process of wear eventually causes them to break off, at which time they leave a characteristic type of damage at the surface of the fabric: this takes the form of a ring or group of 'brush-like' broken ends at the point where the anchors fracture. In addition the anchors often show a series of cases of fatigue damage which occur along their length as they are pulled out of the yarn structure. This evidence is easily recognised with the SEM.

If the textile is repeatedly rubbed against a hard smooth surface, for example a clerk's bench (fig. 25.22) or a linen rubber, or suffers excessive ironing, a typical smoothed surface results. Alternatively, abrasion against a hard rough surface, for example the knees of a miner's overalls against rock, creates a very different result (fig. 25.23).

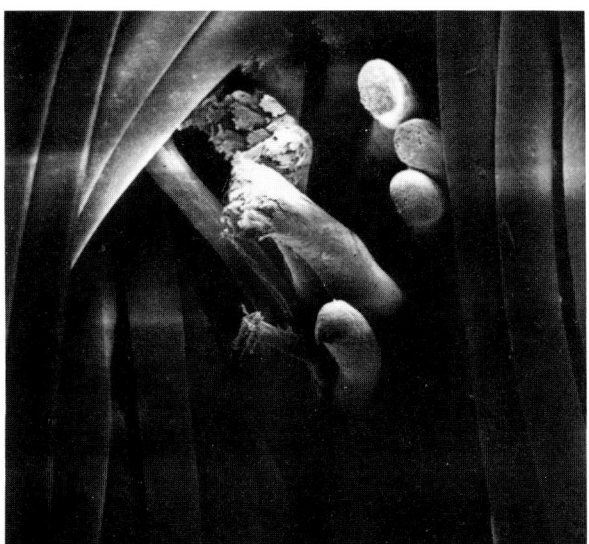

Fig. 25.20 Rounded ends in weave interstices (x800)

Other forms of historical evidence

In addition to revealing the detailed fibre structure, the SEM can detect other evidence of interest to the archaeologist, historian, or conservator. Fabrics may retain evidence of the occupation of the wearer, for example metal splashes from smelting, slate fragments from slate splitting, wood dust or metal swarf from wood or metal working, or even grass pollen from hay-making. If this evidence is to be detected it is obvious that the object must not be washed prior to examination. Equally, if any significant conclusions are to be drawn from such evidence the exact details of the context of the find must be available. Furthermore the SEM examination must be carried out in conjunction with a careful survey of the whole of the object using a good stereoscopic optical microscope, as details of colour and distribution play an important role in identification and determination of the source of the inclusion. One problem associated with the use of the SEM is the need to coat the specimen with gold prior to examination. From a museum view-point the specimen is therefore destroyed. Set against this disadvantage, however, is the fact that considerable information can be gleaned from a small fragment, such as 2 - 3mm of yarn, provided that an optical examination has shown that the small sample is representative.

Fig. 25.21 Yarn breakdown (x120)

Fig. 25.22 Surface smoothing and smearing (x1000)

Fig. 25.23 Abrasive wear in miners' overalls (x2000)

The study of a number of ancient textiles

In order for the above techniques to be considered to have an essential role to play in the study of ancient textiles, it is important to demonstrate that the evidence of wear survives burial. An initial project has been carried out on two samples of Roman wool fabric, recovered from the compacted floor of a building in the *vicus* of the fort at Vindolanda. Sample number TT/85/91, 40cm long and 4cm wide, with selvedges, was considered to be a section of a leg bandage and sample TT/85/15, 16.5 cm long and 7cm wide, was shaped to the form of a child's shoe insole. The leg bandage showed signs of use as it was ragged with several holes, whilst the insole appeared to be unworn.

The authors were asked to establish whether the damaged condition of the bandage was due to extensive wear or to degradation during burial. The method of examination involved three stages. Firstly, fibre debris and dust were collected from the plastic bag in which the sample had been stored. This material was placed on a glass slide, covered with a coverslip and mounted with distilled water. The examination of the slide involved the use of an Olympus BH polarising microscope, using magnifications up to x500. Many of the broken fibres had 'brush-like' features, and thus it was clear

Fig. 25.24 Wear in Vindolanda leg bandage (x24)

Fig. 25.25 Broken fibres in Vindolanda leg bandage (x60)

224

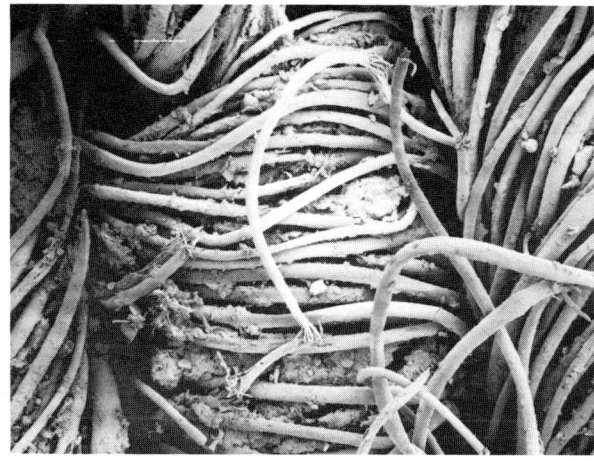

*Fig. 25.26 Multiple fatigue in
Vindolanda leg bandage (x100)*

that the bandage had seen use. There was also evidence of fibres with brittle fracture, indicating tendering, probably during burial.

In the second stage of the investigation the fabric was subjected to an intensive examination with an Olympus stereozoom microscope. Particular attention was given to the edges of the textile and to the edges of the holes. The magnifications used were from x5 to x45. This examination confirmed that the bandage had suffered considerable use. There was evidence of crown flattening, fibre fibrillation on the crowns, with yarn thinning, and 'brush-like' fractures in the interstices of the weave. The broken fibres around the hole did not have 'brush-like' features and there were many brittle fractures, so that it is probable that the holes were formed by decay. Finally a small fragment was removed from a representative area of the bandage, gold sputter-coated and examined with an ISI 100A SEM, with an accelerating voltage of 10Kv. The SEM study confirmed the above findings, provided a photographic record, and the high resolution of the instrument showed the presence of groups of fibres with instances of multiple fatigue damage, indicating that the bandage had pilled during use (figs. 25.24 - 25.28).

*Fig. 25.27 Multiple fatigue in
Vindolanda leg bandage (x100)*

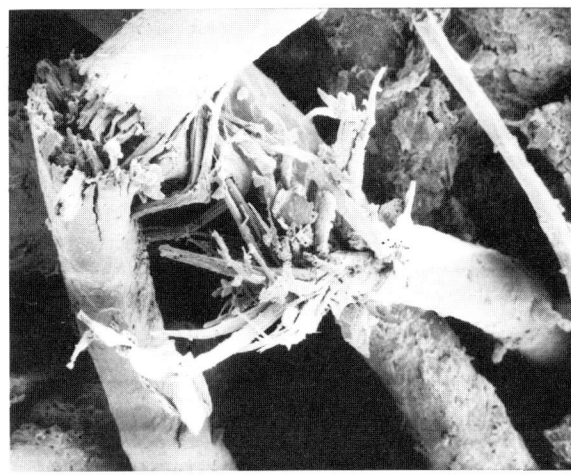

Fig. 25.28 Fatigue in Vindolanda leg bandage (x1000)

The same examination techniques were used for sample number TT/85/15, except that the beautifully intact condition of the object precluded the removal of a sample for SEM study. Again, the first step was the collection of dust and debris from the bag and again a large proportion of the fibre ends had 'brush-like' features. This indicated that the fabric had been worn, either as an insole or as a garment prior to cutting. The second stage of examination with the stereozoom microscope showed that the fabric had a raised nap of irregular height. There was evidence of considerable use in the surface fibres, but no trace of specific positional wear typical of foot contact, ie toes and heel. Furthermore the fibres around the periphery were cleanly cut, without traces of the 'brush-like' fracture which should have been present if the insole had been worn within a shoe. It would appear that this insole had been cut from a heavy cloth that had already given considerable service, possibly as a cloak, and then for some reason was discarded. As a result of this initial study it is clear that evidence of wear can survive almost 2000 years of burial, if the textile is preserved under favourable conditions. It will now be necessary to extend the scope of the work to demonstrate the viability of the techniques when applied to finds from other contexts.

Conclusions

The extensive experience in the examination of fibre and fabric wear and degradation which has been built up at UMIST through painstaking research makes it possible to draw conclusions regarding the type and extent of use of ancient textiles. It is important that samples should be retained without any cleaning treatment, if the maximum potential for SEM study is to be preserved. In many respects the use of the SEM holds the key to the success of this type of investigation. It is possible, however, to learn much about an object by the judicious use of optical microscopy, provided the researcher has in mind the main features to look for. The fracture atlas presented in this paper is the first attempt to provide the necessary visual data-base for such investigations to be carried out successfully. It is to be hoped that a continuing programme of work at UMIST will establish the importance of this type of examination with a wide range of samples from contexts with many differing types of preservation.

List of Participants

Carmen ALFARO, Gobernador Viejo 34, 3º, E 46003 VALENCIA

Lise BENDER JØRGENSEN, Bryggerivej 8 ⁴ᵗᵛ· DK 2500 VALBY

Mildred BUDNY, Corpus Christi College, CAMBRIDGE CB2 1RH

Bill COOKE, Dept of Textile Technology, University of Manchester, Institute of Science and Technology, MANCHESTER M60 1QD

Elisabeth CROWFOOT, Riverview, Big Row, Geldeston, BECCLES NR34 0LY

Lis DOKKEDAL, Historisk-Arkaeologisk Forsøgscenter, Slange Allé 2, DK 4320 LEJRE

Glynis FORD, Ancient Monuments Lab., Fortress House, 23 Savile Row, LONDON W1X 2HE

Hero GRANGER-TAYLOR, 22 Park Village East, LONDON NW1 7PZ

Su GRIERSON, Newmiln Farm, Tibbermore, PERTH PH1 1QN

Elsa GUÐJONSSON, National Museum of Iceland, Þjóðminjasafn Islands, Box 1489, I 121 REYKJAVIK

Thor GUÐJONSSON

Egon HANSEN, Skovmøllevej 43, DK 8270 HØJBJERG

Elizabeth HECKETT, Dept of Archaeology, University College, CORK, Eire

Anne Stine INGSTAD, Vettaliveien 24, N 0389 OSLO 3

Anne KJELLBERG, Norsk Folkemuseum, N 0287 OSLO 2

Udelgard KÖRBER-GROHNE, Institut für Botanik, Universität Hohenheim, D 7000 STUTTGART 70

Anne Hedeager MADSEN, Institut for Forh. Arkaeologi, Moesgaard, DK 8270 HØJBJERG

Jerzy MAIK, Zakład Archeologii IHKM PAN, PL 90-364 ŁODŹ, Tylna 1

Anita MALMIUS, Riddarvägen 27A, S 181 32 LIDINGÖ

Elisabeth MUNKSGAARD, Nationalmuseet, Afd. 1, Frederiksholms Kanal 12,
DK 1220 KØBENHAVN

Karen-Hanne NIELSEN, Gl. Hovedgade 8', DK 2970 HØRSHOLM

Anna NØRGAARD, Historisk-Arkaeologisk Forsøgscenter, Slange Allé 2, DK 4320 LEJRE

Gertrud Grenander NYBERG, Fyrverkarbacken 21, S 11260 STOCKHOLM

Elizabeth PEACOCK, Archaeology Dept., University of Trondheim Museum, Erling Skakkesgt. 47b
N 7000 TRONDHEIM

Frances PRITCHARD, Dept. of Urban Archaeology, Museum of London, London Wall,
LONDON EC2Y 5HN

Ellen SCHJØLBERG, Allégaten 38, N 5000 BERGEN

Anneliese STREITER, Germanisches Nationalmuseum, Kartäusergasse 1, D 8500 NÜRNBERG

George TAYLOR, 46 Harlow Moor Drive, HARROGATE, N. Yorks

Birgitte Krag THOMSEN, NM Bevaringssektionen, Brede, DK 2800 LYNGBY

Klaus TIDOW, Textilmuseum Neumünster, Parkstr. 17, D 2350 NEUMÜNSTER

Dominic TWEDDLE, York Archaeological Trust, 1 Pavement, YORK YO1 2NA

Sandra VONS-COMIS, Griend 87, NL 1112 KZ DIEMEN

Penelope WALTON, Textile Research, 12 Bootham Terrace, YORK YO3 7DH

Erika WEILAND, Germanisches Nationalmuseum, Kartäusergasse 1, D 8500 NÜRNBERG

John-Peter WILD, Manchester Ancient Textile Unit, Dept of Archaeology, The University,
MANCHESTER M13 9PL

Else ØSTERGÅRD, NM Bevaringssektionen, Brede, DK 2800 LYNGBY

Bibliography

Note: only literature cited in abbreviated form by author and year is listed in this bibliography

Bender Jørgensen, Tidow (1982)	L.Bender Jørgensen, K.Tidow (edd), *Textilsymposium Neumünster: Archäologische Textilfunde: 6.5 - 8.5.1981*, Neumünster, 1982 (= *NESAT* I)
Bender Jørgensen (1986)	L. Bender Jørgensen, *Forhistoriske Textiler i Skandinavien: Prehistoric Scandinavian Textiles (Nordiske Fortidsminder* B9), København, 1986
Bender Jørgensen, Magnus, Munksgaard (1988)	L. Bender Jørgensen, B. Magnus, E. Munksgaard (edd), *Archaeological Textiles: Report from the 2nd NESAT Symposium 1.-4.V.1984 (Arkaeologiske Skrifter* 2), København, 1988 (= *NESAT* II)
Crowfoot (1936-37)	G.M. Crowfoot, 'Of the Warp-Weighted Loom', *Annual of the British School at Athens* 37, 1936-1937, 36-47
Crowfoot (1973)	E. Crowfoot, 'Textile Fragments from Polhill' in B.J. Philp, *Excavations in West Kent 1960-1970*, Dover, 1973, 202-203
Grieg (1928)	S. Grieg, Kongsgaarden, *Osebergfundet* 2, Oslo, 1928
Grierson (1986)	S. Grierson, *The Colour Cauldron*, Perth, 1986
Guðjónsson (1985)	E.E. Guðjónsson, 'Nogle bemaerkninger om den islandske vaegtvaev, *vefstaðir*', *By og Bygd. Festskrift til Marta Hoffmann, Norsk Folkemuseums Arbok* 30, 1983-1984, 116-128
Hald (1950)	M. Hald, *Olddanske Textiler (Nordiske Fortidsminder* 5), København, 1950
Hald (1980)	M. Hald, *Ancient Danish Textiles from Bogs and Burials*, Copenhagen, 1980
Hoffmann (1964)	M. Hoffmann, *The Warp-Weighted Loom*, Oslo, 1964
Hundt (1981)	H.-J. Hundt, *Die Textil- und Schnurreste aus der frühgeschichtlichen Wurt Elisenhof, Elisenhof* 4, Frankfurt a.M., 1981
Jirlow (1931)	R. Jirlow, 'Sländspinning i Sverige' in S.Erixon, S. Wallin (edd), *Svenska Kulturbilder* 5/9, Stockholm, 1931
Jørgensen (1986)	see Bender Jørgensen (1986)
Kamińska, Nahlik (1958)	J. Kamińska, A. Nahlik, Włokiennictwo gdańskie w X-XIII w., Łódź, 1958
Kok (1966)	A. Kok, 'A Short History of the Orchil Dyes', *The Lichenologist* 3, 1966, 248-272
MacGregor (1982)	A. MacGregor, Anglo-Scandinavian finds from Lloyds Bank, Pavement, and other sites, *The Archaeology of York* 17/3, London, 1982
Mączak (1955)	A. Mączak, *Sukiennictwo wielkopolskie XIV-XVII w.*, Warszawa, 1955

Maik (1988) J. Maik, *Wyroby włókiennicze na Pomorzu z okresu rzymskiego i ze średniowiecza*, Wrocław-Warszawa-Gdańsk-Łódź, 1988

Małowist (1954) M. Małowist, *Studie z dziejów rzemiosła w okresie kryzysu feudalizmu w zachodniej Europie w XIV i XV w.*, Warszawa, 1954

Małowist (1973) M. Małowist, *Wschód a Zachód Europy w XIII-XVI w.*, Warszawa, 1973

Matthews (1962) C.L. Matthews, 'The Anglo-Saxon Cemetery at Marina Drive, Dunstable', *Bedfordshire Archaeological Journal* 1/2, 1962, 25-47

Meaney (1981) A. Meaney, *Amulets and Curing-Stones (British Archaeological Reports* 96), Oxford 1981

Munksgaard (1974) E. Munksgaard, *Oldtidsdragter*, København, 1974

Nahlik (1964) A. Nahlik, *Tkaniny wełniane importawane i miejscowe Nowogrodu Wielkiego X-XV w.*, Wrocław, 1964

Nielsen (1982) K.-H. Nielsen, 'The Rønbjerg Garment in Tunic-Form' in L. Bender Jørgensen, K. Tidow (edd), *Textilsymposium Neumünster: Archäologische Textilfunde: 6.5-8.5.1981*, Neumünster, 1982, 44-62

Owen-Crocker (1986) G.R. Owen-Crocker, *Dress in Anglo-Saxon England*, Manchester, 1986

Ponting (1971) K.G. Ponting, *The Woollen Industry of South-West England*, London, 1971

Pritchard (1984) F. Pritchard, 'Late Saxon Textiles from the City of London', *Medieval Archaeology* 28, 1984, 46-76

Roach Smith (1856) C. Roach Smith, *Inventorium Sepulchrale*, London, 1856

Römer-Johannsen (1979) U. Römer-Johannsen, *St. Aegidien zu Braunschweig 1115-1979*, Hildesheim, 1979

Rötting (1985) H. Rötting, *Stadt im Wandel, Landesausstellung Niedersachen* 1, Braunschweigisches Landesmuseum, 1985

Samsonowicz (1962) H. Samsonowicz, 'Struktura handlu gdańskiego w pierwszej połowie XV w.', *Przeglad Historyczny* 53, 1962, ex.4, 707-708

Schlabow (1956) K. Schlabow, 'Spätmittelalterliche Textilfunde aus der Lübecker Innenstadt', *Zeitschrift des Vereins für Lübeckische Geschichte und Altertumskunde* 36, 1956, 133-153

Schlabow (1982) K. Schlabow, *Der Thorsberger Prachtmantel. Der Schlüssel zum altgermanischen Webstuhl*, 2te Auflage, Neumünster, 1982

Sherratt (1983) A. Sherratt, 'The secondary exploitation of animals in the Old World', *World Archaeology* 15/1, 1983, 90-104

von Stokar (1938) W. von Stokar, *Spinnen und Weben bei den Germanen (Mannus-Bücherei* 59), Leipzig, 1938

Thomson (1957) R.H. Thomson, *Naturally-Occurring Quinones*, London, 1957

Urtāns (1962) V. Urtāns, Tiras purva depožits (Depotfund vom Tiras-Sumpf), LSPR Vestures muzeja raksti: Arheologija, Rīgā, 1962

Vallinheimo (1956) V. Vallinheimo, *Das Spinnen in Finnland unter besonderer Berücksichtigung schwedischer Tradition (Kansatieteellinen Arkisto* 11), Helsinki, 1956

Vons-Comis (1984b) S.Y. Vons-Comis, 'Zeventiende en achtiende eeuwse kledingresten van Spitsbergen', *Kostum* 1984, 32-36

Vons-Comis (1987)　　　　　S.Y. Vons-Comis, 'Workmens' clothing or burial garments? Seventeenth and eighteenth century clothing remains from Spitsbergen', *Norsk Polarinstitutt Rapportserie* 38, 1987, 79-87

Wallace (1985)　　　　　　　P.F. Wallace, 'The Archaeology of Viking Dublin' in H.B. Clarke, A. Simms (edd), *The Comparative History of Urban Origins in Non-Roman Europe (British Archaeological Reports International Series* 255), Oxford, 1985, 103-145

Wild (1970)　　　　　　　　J.P. Wild, *Textile Manufacture in the Northern Roman Provinces,* Cambridge, 1970

Wild, Bender Jørgensen (1988) J.P. Wild, L. Bender Jørgensen, 'Clothes from the Roman Empire. Barbarians and Romans' in L. Bender Jørgensen, B. Magnus, E. Munksgaard (edd), *Archaeological Textiles: Report from the 2nd NESAT Symposium* 1.-4.V.1988 (*Arkaeologiske Skrifter* 2), København, 1988, 65-98

Zariņa (1970)　　　　　　　A. Zariņa, *Seno latgaļu apgerbs (Die Latgallischen Trachten)*, Rīgā, 1970